CONTENTS

Red Wine Pork Shanks 254
Tuscan Pork and Cauliflower Rice 254
Indian Pork Masala 255
Sausages in a Cheese and Onion Sauce 255
Hot Jalapeño Pork Meatballs 255
Greek-Style Pork 255
Bacon-Wrapped Cheesy Pork 256
Spicy Satay Pork 256
Pork and Turnip Pie 256
Hoisin Pork 256
Meatballs in Tomato Sauce 257
Pork and Cauliflower Pie 257
Pork Lo Mein 257
Sambal Pork Noodles 257
Pulled Pork Pasta Bake 258

Lime Chimichurri Tenderloin 258
Green Bean Pork Fettuccine 258
Pork and Cauliflower Goulash 259
Prosciutto and Basil Pizza 259
Bell Pepper Noodles and Avocado Pork 259
Caribbean Jerk 259
Pork and Pesto Pasta 259
Barbecue Pork 260
Spiralized Kohlrabi and Sausage 260
Chorizo Pizza 260
Chessy Sausage Pizza with Bell Peppers 260
Sweet Pork and Spaghetti Squash 261
Spicy Spareribs 261
Asian Pork and Celeriac Noodles 261

What is a Ketogenic Diet?

The keto diet is a simple, low-carb diet that is increasingly well-known. It causes the body to produce ketones in the liver, which will then become energy. There are lots of different names for this diet, including the ketogenic diet, low-carb high-fat (LCHF), and low-carb diet, but all have different standards. We'll be discussing the standards of keto.

High-carb foods cause your body to produce insulin and glucose. Glucose is a molecule that your body finds easiest to convert and use as energy, meaning it will be chosen over other energy sources. Insulin processes the glucose in your bloodstream, and moves it around the body.

On a normal, high-carb diet, the body will use glucose as the primary form of energy. This means that your fats are not being used as an energy source. Since they're not needed, they're stored in your body.

If you lower your intake of carbs, your body is induced into a state known as ketosis.

What is Ketosis?

No matter what you eat, ketosis happens in your body all the time, as your body processes the different types of nutrients to create the energy it requires.

Proteins, fats, and carbs can all be processed for use, but the things you eat will alter the speed at which this is done. Eating a low-carb, high-fat diet will increase this process in a safe, normal chemical reaction.

When you eat carbohydrates or lots of protein, your body will break this down into glucose in order to create ATP (an energy molecule). This fuels daily activities and the maintenance required inside our bodies.

Your body needs a lot of calories, as you'll know if you've ever calculated your required intake. For your body to maintain itself, it needs nutrients, and that's not even factoring in your daily activities. If you eat enough food to meet this calorific requirement, however, there will likely be more glucose than your body needs.

So what happens to the glucose your body doesn't need?

- **Glycogenesis.** It is converted into glycogen and stored in your liver and muscles. Approximately fifty per cent of your daily energy can be stored as glycogen.
- **Lipogenesis.** Once there's enough glycogen, your body will convert it into fats, and store it.

Ketosis is what happens when your body has no more glucose or glycogen. When there's no food for your body, such as when you sleep, fat is burned and your body creates molecules called ketones. This is the aim of a ketogenic diet—to reduce the glucose in your body, leaving it to burn fat for energy instead.

When the body breaks down fat, ketones (acetoacetate) are made, thus creating fatty acids which are burned off in the liver. This process is called betaoxidation, and the end result is the creation of two different ketones (BHB and acetone). These are used to fuel the brain and muscles.

Although glucose is the main source of fuel, the brain uses these two ketones—BHB and acetone—when the body is lacking food—or in particular, carbohydrates. In other words, when you don't have any more glucose or glycogen, ketosis is kick-started, and your body will start to use your fat as energy instead.

Let's be honest, ketosis is awesome but do you know what? It gets better! According to the latest studies, the brain and body actually prefer using ketones, as they can run 70% more efficiently than glucose. How cool is that?

11

How Does It Work?

Fatty acid and glycerol are released the moment when fat is broken down by the liver. Fatty acid is further broken down in this process called ketogenesis, and acetoacetate—a ketone body—is produced.

The two other types of ketone bodies that are created are:

- **Beta-hydroxybutyrate (BHB)** – Once your body has got used to the keto diet, your muscles will convert the acetoacetate into BHB. This ketone body is the preferred fuel of the brain.
- **Acetone** – These can be metabolized into glucose occasionally, but it's mostly excreted as waste. As a result, most ketogenic dieters experience a distinct, smelly breath.

As your body gets used to the diet, it will release fewer ketone bodies. This may lead you to think that ketosis is slowing down.

It's not. All that's happening is that your brain is burning the BHB as fuel, and your body provides your brain with as much efficient energy as it can.

What Should You Eat?

If you want to go on a keto diet, you have to plan ahead. It's recommended to eat between 20g and 30g of net carbs per day.

So, what is a 'net carb'? Your net carbs are your total dietary carbohydrates, minus the total fiber. In other words, they are the carbs you've eaten subtracted by the fiber you've eaten. Let's use the example of a cup of broccoli.

- In total, there are 6g carbohydrates.
- Also, there's 2g of fiber.
- The 6g (total carbs) is subtracted by the 2g (dietary fiber).
- So your net carbs are 4g.

What Are the Benefits?

- **Losing Weight.** Your body burns your fat, using it as the main source of energy. This means that you will essentially be in a fasting state and using your fat stores as an energy source.
- **Better Energy.** You'll feel a lot more energized because you're providing your body with a better energy source that is more reliable. Fats are occasionally shown to be the most effective molecule to burn as fuel.
- **Cholesterol.** Keto diets improve triglyceride and cholesterol levels that are most associated with arterial buildup.
- **Lower Blood Sugar.** Studies state that the decrease of LDL cholesterol eliminate diseases such as type 2 diabetes.
- **Reduced Hunger.** By eating fat, you're more satiated for long, as it's naturally more satisfying.
- **Better Skin.** Skin inflammation and acne lesions are shown to be reduced over a twelve-week period.

Tips Before Starting

Before we get into the plan, there are some other points worth discussing.

Some argue that in counting calories when you're on a ketogenic diet isn't right, but I am one of the few that thinks it is okay. For the majority of normal people, eating enough fats and protein to keep you satiated will naturally keep you within a calorie deficit. That's assuming the average American is normal, though!

There are a lot of things to take into account, including many hormone, endocrine, and deficiency problems. What's more, no diet can work if you're consuming more than your body is expending.

The term "macros" is a shortened version of the word "macronutrients." These are what we call the "big three": fats, carbs, and proteins. There are lots of online calculators you can use to discover how much or how little of each you need—but you should know.

Many people think that macros are set in stone, but please don't worry about hitting them exactly every day. It doesn't matter if you're a few calories over or under—ultimately, it will even itself out over time. It should be about making a long-term diet plan that's right for you. Another thing worth noting is that I produced this plan with women in mind. I looked at the statistics and macros of an average of 150 women, and developed the meal plan from that. This resulted in a plan of 1,600 daily calories, divided into 136g fat, 74g protein, and 20g net carbs a day. Most of us live sedentary lives these days, so this plan is based around that sort of lifestyle. Thus, you may need to factor in your own needs, increasing and decreasing calories on your own terms.

If you need to increase your calories, simple increase the amount of fat you eat. Olive oil, macadamia nuts, coconut oil, and butter are all great ways to increase the fats in your diet without increase your other macros. You can melt it over your veggies or drizzle it on salads—whatever you can to make this plan work for you.

It's a little more complicated to decrease your calories, as you have to consider what you need and what you can lose. Chances are, you'll need to reduce your protein intake. One thing to keep in mind is to reduce your portion sizes. The most important thing, though, is to stick to the diet! Ketosis is a process, and you need to stick with it for it to work. You simple can't have "one" cheat meal, no matter how much you want. If you cheat, even a little, it can slow your progress for up to a week until the ketosis process kicks in again.

Cheating is an absolute no-no. The best way to do that? Stay prepared. Make sure you stay satiated and satisfied—but with the right foods. If you've got to force yourself to eat something you don't like or don't want, this will never work.

Finally, remember: this is a guideline on the keto diet. Change it up to fit with you and what you like, just make sure you stick to plan!

30 Days on a Ketogenic Diet

For all the recipes in this plan, I have scaled them to the best of my ability but scaling doesn't always work, meaning some recipes will leave you with leftovers. For that reason, leftovers are sometimes used later on in the plan—so make sure you look a day or two ahead so you know what to keep, what to freeze, and what to discard.

Likewise, some foods—such as the Not Your Caveman's Chili—is used in the first and last weeks. To save time, energy, and money, you can batch-cook in the first week and freeze what's left. Simply take it out and defrost it when it comes up again!

I had planned to balance the net carbs to around 20g a day but when I had finished the plan, I realized it was even better than that! The 28-day average for the net carbs works out at 11.2g per day. The average total carbs works out at 19.6g per day. Even if you decide to not count the net carbs, this plan is a great, simple way to kick-start your ketosis.

The 28-day average for all your macros works out as 1,597 calories, divided into 136g fats, 8.4g fiber, 19.6g carbs, 11.2g net carbs, and 74.9g protein.

A lot of people ask about the health and weight-loss benefits of intermittent fasting. It certainly does have benefits. It is useful for both the mental clarity and energy it can offer, but there are more benefits.

When you plateau, intermittent fasting can break through that. Likewise, intermittent fasting can benefit nutrient uptake in exercise. There's further details on intermittent fasting in weeks three and four, so keep your eyes peeled!

Finally, the first week's shopping list will be long. I have made the assumption you have none of these products, but many of the items are everyday foods that you may have already. They are keto-staples, and although stocking up may be expensive, it is an investment in your health. Besides, once you've stocked up, there won't be much to buy.

Remember, as you move forward, you may need to restock some things. It might be chicken, beef, or vegetables. One thing is for sure—you'll need plenty of spinach so keep your pantry stocked!

There are a number of specialty items that it's worth buying straight away. Some, you'll find in shops but others, you'll only find online and by time you need them, you may not have the time to order them. There are no specialty items in Week 1, so you can get started right away, but order these immediately to ensure you don't have any holdups!

Specialty Items
Liquid Stevia
Almond Flour
Coconut Flour
Milled Flaxseed Meal
Erythritol

Week 1

The primary goal of the first week is to keep things simple. Simplicity is key for anything new. It's important for the transition to be as easy as possible—it will be hard enough to get rid of your cravings!

Like we've already discussed, leftovers will be considered too—this means you won't have the hassle of cooking things more than once. I like to do breakfast in leftover-style, because if you're anything like me, you won't want to run around and stress in the mornings! I like to simply grab something from the fridge and run out the door. Simple!

Your first week will be hard, not only because of the cravings. The first signs of ketosis that you'll notice are commonly called the "keto flu." You may experience headaches, brain fogginess, fatigue. Keep drinking lots of water and maintaining a high salt intake. The ketogenic diet is a natural diuretic, so you'll be urinating more than usual, so take into account that you'll be losing electrolytes this way. Maintaining high salt and water intakes is important to give your body a chance to rehydrate and fill up on electrolytes again. That will help with—if not eradicate—your headaches.

If necessary, you can sprinkle a little salt in a glass of water. Just keep drinking water—at least four liters a day—and consuming salt. It will help! And don't worry about the effects of salt on your blood pressure, as studies show they're not correlated as previously believed.

Breakfast.
For breakfast, Keep it easy, quick, tasty, and leaving you with leftovers. I recommend you start on a weekend, so that you can make something that'll last you all week. Remember: the first week is about simplicity! You don't want to be rushing about making breakfast before work, so we won't be doing that.

Lunch.
Lunch is going to be simple too. There'll be lots of salad and meat—of course, slathered in high-fat dressings. Also, you can use leftovers from the night before, or easy canned chicken or fish. If you do decide to go for something canned, check for additives—the less, the better! Try adding spices and seasonings to make your lunch a bit more interesting—just be careful about onion and garlic powder, as they can sometimes have high carbs.

Dinner.
Can you guess what the aim for dinner will be? That's right, simple again. It will normally be a combination of leafy greens (spinach and broccoli feature highly) and meat. It'll be high-fat, moderate protein again.

PS. There'll be no dessert for the first two weeks of the plan.

Week 1 - SHOPPING LIST

MEAT

Bacon
Bacon and Cheddar
Canned Chicken
Chicken Sausage
Chicken Thighs
Pork Rinds

Chorizo Sausage
Eggs
Shrimp
Ground Beef
Stew Meat

VEGETABLES

3 Onions
1 Green Pepper
6 Lemons
Cauliflower
Sugar Snap Peas

Broccoli
Green Beans
Parsley
Orange
Spinach (lots of this)

FATS

Unsalted and Salted Butter
Bottle Olive Oil
Coconut Oil
Bacon Fat (just save the fat from the bacon you cook)

Heavy Cream
Half 'n' Half
Pecans

SAUCES

Chicken Stock
Beef Broth
Coconut Milk
Ranch Dressing (full-fat)
Dijon Mustard
Rao's Tomato Sauce (or other low-carb brand)
Worcestershire

Red Wine
Red Boat Fish Sauce (gluten-free)
Tomato Paste
Soy Sauce

CHEESE

Parmesan Cheese
Cheddar Cheese (full-fat)
Queso Fresco Cheese

SPICES

Bay Leaf
Allspice
Black Pepper
Cayenne Pepper
Cardamom
Chili Powder
Coconut Flour
Chives

Coriander
Ginger
Cumin
Minced Garlic
Oregano
Onion Powder
Paprika
Rosemary

Red Pepper Flakes
Yellow Curry Powder
Sage
Thyme
Salt
Xanthan Gum

Breakfast
(Recipe 20)
Frittata Muffins with Cheese
- 2 Muffins
    410 Calories, 2.5g Net Carbs, 32.3g Fats, 27.3g Protein

Lunch
(Recipe 30)
Simple Lunch Salad
- 2 cups spinach, 3tbsp. olive oil, and 1/3 cup canned chicken
- Add seasonings of your choice—but be careful of using too much onion or garlic powder.
    450 Calories, 0.5g Net Carbs, 44g Fats, 13.5g Protein

Dinner
(Recipe 2) (Recipe 27)
Inside-Out Bacon Burger
- 1½ Patties - refrigerate leftovers
Red Pepper and Spinach Salad
- Add a tablespoon of butter
    641 Calories, 4.7g Net Carbs, 52.5g Fats, 37g Protein

DAY TOTALS: 1601 Calories, 7.7g Net Carbs, 139.8g Fats, 77.8g Protein

Breakfast
(Recipe 11)
Scrambled Eggs with Cheese
    453 Calories, 1.2g Net Carbs, 43g Fats, 19g Protein

Lunch
Leftover Inside Out Bacon Burger & Spinach Salad
- 4 cups spinach, 4 tablespoons olive oil, and 3 tablespoons leftover meant
- Add seasonings of your choice.
    624 Calories, 1.2g Net Carbs, 63.9g Fats, 10.8g Protein

Dinner
(Recipe 16)
Beef Stew with Orange and Cinnamon
- Eat 80% of the stew, and reserve the rest
    519 Calories, 35.6g Fats, 4.1g Net Carbs, and 42.8g Protein

DAY TOTALS: 1596 Calories, 142.5g Fats, 6.5g Net Carbs, and 72.6g Protein

Breakfast
(Recipe 20)
Cheesy Frittata Muffins
- 2 Muffins
  410 Calories, 2.5g Net Carbs, 32.3g Fats, 27.3g Protein

Lunch
(Recipe 30)
Meat-Free Spinach Salad
- 4 cups spinach and 4 tablespoons olive oil
- Add the seasonings of your choice.
  537 Calories, 1g Net Carbs, 57g Fats, 5g Protein

Dinner
(Recipe 18) (Recipe 21)
Curried Chicken Thigh
- 1 chicken thigh
Fried Queso Fresco
- A quarter of the fried queso recipe
  657 Calories, 0.6g Net Carbs, 44.7g Fats, 40.3g Protein

DAY TOTAL: 1604 Calories, 4.1g Net Carbs, 134g Fats, 72.6g Protein

Week 1 / Day 4

Breakfast
(Recipe 11)
Scrambled Eggs with Cheese
  453 Calories, 1.2g Net Carbs, 43g Fats, 19g Protein

Lunch
Leftover Curried Chicken and Spinach Salad
- 4 tablespoons olive oil, 4 cups spinach, and a third-cup leftover chicken
- Add your choice of seasonings or spices.
  586 Calories, 1g Net Carbs, 58g Fats, 15g Protein

Dinner
(Recipe 33)
Chicken, Bacon, and Sausage Stir Fry
- Eat a third of the recipe, then freeze the leftovers as two separate portions.
- Add a quarter-cup of grated cheddar to the meal, but don't add the cheese to the leftovers.
  541 Calories, 8.3g Net Carbs, 38.3g Fats, 42.7g Protein

DAY TOTAL: 1580 Calories, 10.5g Net Carbs, 140g Fats, 76.7g Protein

Breakfast
(Recipe 20)
Frittata Muffins
- 2 Muffins
    410 Calories, 2.5g Net Carbs, 32.3g Fats, 27.3g Protein

Lunch
Leftover Stir Fry and Spinach Salad
- 2 tablespoons olive oil with 4 cups spinach, plus a half-portion of leftover stir fry
- Add the seasonings and spices of your choice
    742 Calories, 4.7g Net Carbs, 70.2g Fats, 20.8g Protein

Dinner
(Recipe 29)
Cauliflower and Shrimp Curry
- Divide the curry into six portions. Eat one with a tablespoon of coconut oil, freeze the rest individually.
    451 Calories, 5.6g Net Carbs, 33.5g Fats, 27.4g Protein

DAY TOTAL: 1602 Calories, 12.8g Net Carbs, 136g Fats, 75.5g Protein

Week 1 / Day 6

Breakfast
(Recipe 11)
Scrambled Eggs with Cheese
    453 Calories, 1.2g Net Carbs, 43g Fats, 19g Protein

Lunch
(Recipe 30)
Spinach Salad with Canned Chicken
- 2 cups of spinach with 2 tablespoons olive oil and a third-cup of leftover chicken
- Add the spices and seasonings of your choice
    351 Calories, 0.5g Net Carbs, 31g Fats, 15.5g Protein

Dinner
(Recipe 10) (Recipe 28)
Cheddar and Chorizo Meatballs
- Eat five meatballs, freezing the remaining meatballs
Roasted Green Beans with Pecans
- Eat half the serving, then save the rest as five separate portions
- As both these recipes use the oven, you can either pan-fry the green beans rather than roast them, or make the meatballs ahead of time, then reheat them in the oven.
    798 Calories, 7.1g Net Carbs, 63g Fats, 40.2g Protein

DAY TOTAL: 1602 Calories, 8.8g Net Carbs, 137g Fats, 74.7g Protein

Breakfast
(Recipe 11)
Scrambled Eggs with Cheese
- Add an extra tablespoon of butter

453 Calories, 1.2g Net Carbs, 43g Fats, 19g Protein

Lunch
(Recipe 30)
Spinach Salad with Cream Cheese
- 1oz. cream cheese, along with 4 cups spinach and 3 tablespoons olive oil
- Add your choice of spices or seasonings, using onion or garlic powder sparingly.

496 Calories, 2g Net Carbs, 51g Fats, 5g Protein

Dinner
(Recipe 24) (Recipe 4)
Not Your Caveman's Chili
- Eat a quarter of the recipe, and freeze the remainder in three separate portions

Sugar Snap Peas Infused with Bacon
- Eat a third of the recipe, then save the remainder as two separate portions

545 Calories, 9.6g Net Carbs, 31.1g Fats, 53.1g Protein

DAY TOTAL: 1594 Calories, 12.8g Net Carbs, 136.1g Fats, 77.1g Protein

Week 2

Phew! That's week one all over and done with. Fingers crossed, you're doing well and will have breezed through the diet.

Things will be simple again this week, especially for breakfast. We're going to introduce keto-proof coffee, though! It's all about adding a mix of heavy cream, butter, and coconut oil to your coffee. I know, I know! It sounds disgusting—but trust me!

It's really not as crazy as it sounds. Butter, after all, is made from cream, so all you're really doing is adding a delicious richness to your coffee that you'll love!

Breakfast.

Breakfast is where we'll be introducing this new coffee. Don't like coffee? Try adding it to tea. Don't like the taste? You're a rarity! But if you really don't like it, try mixing the ingredients together and eating them like that.

So, what's the point of keto-proof coffee?

Fat Loss. It's really simple: consuming medium-chain triglycerides (MCT) has been shown to lead to greater losses in adipose—fat—tissue.

Fats! Does this one even need an explanation? Eating fat leads to higher energy levels, more efficient energy usage and ultimately, high weight loss. This is the main component of the keto diet.

More Energy. Research shows that the fast rate of oxidation in MCFAs (Medium Chain Fatty Acids) increases energy expenditure. MCFAs are converted into ketones (what we're looking for) that are then absorbed differently in the body when compared to regular oils. This ultimately provides higher levels of energy.

Don't like the taste? You could always add sweetener or spices. Cinnamon, vanilla extract, and Stevia are all great additions. You could even change the taste daily, so you don't get bored!

If this is your first experience with keto-proof coffee, take your time drinking it—even perhaps an hour or two. A sudden, large exposure to coconut oil can cause an increase in toilet trips—so build your tolerance before you start drinking down your coffee in twenty minutes or less!

Lunch.

Again, it's simple here, but we'll add in more meat from the previous night's cooking. And again, green vegetables and high-fat salad dressings are vital to the plan. Balancing fats and proteins are important here.

Dinner.

Like lunch, dinner will consist mostly of meat, veggies, and high-fat dressings. There might even be slatherings of butter! Don't overthink things on this week, we're still keeping things simple.

P.S. Missing dessert? They're still a no-no this week, but you'll get a chance to dive into sweet treats next week!

Week 2 - SHOPPING LIST

MEAT

Chorizo Sausage   Chicken Breast

VEGETABLES

Lemons   Sugar Snap Peas
Green Beans   Spring Onion
Mushrooms

CRUNCH

Pecans   Pork Rinds
Almonds

SAUCES

Yellow Mustard   Apple Cider Vinegar
Coffee   Hot Sauce

SPECIALITY ITEMS

Milled Flaxseed   Almond Flour

CHEESE

Cheddar Cheese   Blue Cheese Crumbles
Cream Cheese   Mozzarella Cheese

SPICES

Baking Soda   Tone's Southwest Chipotle Seasoning
Baking Powder   Mrs. Dash Table Blend

Breakfast
(Recipe 7)
Keto-Proof Coffee
>   273 Calories, 1g Net Carbs, 30g Fats, 0g Protein

Lunch
(Recipe 30)
Spinach Salad and Canned Chicken
- 4 cups spinach with 2 tablespoons olive oil and two-thirds cup of leftover or canned chicken
>   416 Calories, 1g Net Carbs, 32g Fats, 27g Protein

Dinner
(Recipe 10) (Recipe 28)
Chorizo Meatball Leftovers
- Eat six meatballs

Roasted Green Beans with Pecans
- Use one of the leftover portions
>   921 Calories, 7.9g Net Carbs, 72.2g Fats, 47.5g Protein

DAY TOTAL: 1610 Calories, 9.9g Net Carbs, 134.2g Fats, 74.5g Protein

Breakfast
(Recipe 7)
Keto-Proof Coffee
>   273 Calories, 1g Net Carbs, 30g Fats, 0g Protein

Lunch
(Recipe 15)
Bacon, Chive, and Cheddar Mug Cake
>   573 Calories, 5g Net Carbs, 55g Fats, 24g Protein

Dinner
(Recipe 29)
Leftover Cauliflower and Shrimp Curry
- Have two of the leftover portions, with an added tablespoon of butter
>   661 Calories, 11.2g Net Carbs, 39g Fats, 54.8g Protein

DAY TOTAL: 1607 Calories, 17.2g Net Carbs, 135g Fats, 78.8g Protein

Breakfast
(Recipe 7)
Keto-Proof Coffee

> 273 Calories, 1g Net Carbs, 30g Fats, 0g Protein

Lunch
(Recipe 34)
Keto-Friendly Taco Tartlets
- Have two tartlets, and freeze the rest

> 481 Calories, 5.47g Net Carbs, 38.8g Fats, 26.2g Protein

Dinner
(Recipe 18) (Recipe 27)
Curried Chicken Thighs
- Make three chicken thighs, but eat two and store one

Spinach and Red Pepper Salad

> 763 Calories, 4.8g Net Carbs, 57.8g Fats, 50.3g Protein

> DAY TOTAL: 1577 Calories, 11.2g Net Carbs, 133.5g Fats, 76.4g Protein

Breakfast
(Recipe 7)
Keto-Proof Coffee

> 273 Calories, 1g Net Carbs, 30g Fats, 0g Protein

Lunch
Spinach Salad with Leftover Chicken Thigh
- Eat the leftover chicken thigh from yesterday, along with 4 cups of spinach and 2 tablespoons olive oil

> 553 Calories, 1.6g Net Carbs, 47.9g Fats, 24.1g Protein

Dinner
(Recipe 6) (Recipe 4)
Buffalo Chicken Strips
- Eat a third of the recipe, pop two strips into the fridge, and freeze everything else

Sugar Snap Peas Infused with Bacon
- Enjoy one portion

> 750 Calories, 9.1g Net Carbs, 58.7g Fats, 42.3g Protein

> DAY TOTAL: 1577 Calories, 11.8g Net Carbs, 136.5g Fats, 66.5g Protein

Breakfast
(Recipe 7)
Keto-Proof Coffee
> 273 Calories, 1g Net Carbs, 30g Fats, 0g Protein

Lunch
(Recipe 14)
Chicken Strip Sliders
- Save your almond buns
> 625 Calories, 4.3g Net Carbs, 51g Fats, 34.8g Protein

Dinner
(Recipe 25) (Recipe 6)
Omnivore Burger with Creamed Spinach and Almonds
- Eat half the recipe, then pop the rest in the fridge

Buffalo Chicken Strip Slider
- Use your leftovers along with an extra tablespoon of butter
> 773 Calories, 5.3g Net Carbs, 59.9g Fats, 49.1g Protein

DAY TOTAL: 1671 Calories, 10.6g Net Carbs, 140.8g Fats, 83.9g Protein

Breakfast
(Recipe 7)
Keto-Proof Coffee
> 273 Calories, 1g Net Carbs, 30g Fats, 0g Protein

Lunch
(Recipe 25)
Omnivore Burger with a Spinach Salad
- Enjoy have your leftover omnivore burger, along with four cups of spinach and 2 tablespoons olive oil
> 510 Calories, 2.4g Net Carbs, 42g Fats, 25.9g Protein

Dinner
(Recipe 3) (Recipe 28)
Mozzarella and Bacon Meatballs
- Enjoy six meatballs, then freeze the leftovers

Roasted Green Beans with Pecans
- Using your leftovers, eat one portion
> 821 Calories, 6.7g Net Carbs, 63.8g Fats, 54g Protein

DAY TOTAL: 1605 Calories, 10.2g Net Carbs, 135.8g Fats, 79.9g Protein

Breakfast
(Recipe 7)
Keto-Proof Coffee
273 Calories, 1g Net Carbs, 30g Fats, 0g Protein
Lunch
Leftover Meatballs and Spinach Salad
- Take four leftover mozzarella and bacon meatballs, along with 4 cups of spinach and 2 tablespoons of butter
641 Calories, 3g Net Carbs, 51.2g Fats, 35.2g Protein
Dinner
(Recipe 33)
Chicken, Bacon, and Sausage Stir Fry
- Enjoy one of your reserved leftover portions with an added quarter-cup of grated cheddar and a tablespoon of butter
641 Calories, 8.3g Net Carbs, 49.3g Fats, 42.7g Protein
DAY TOTAL: 1555 Calories, 12.4g Net Carbs, 130.5g Fats, 77.9g Protein

Week 3
Now that you're getting used to the plan, we're going to add a little fasting. Mornings will be all about fats, then fast until dinner time. There are, as discussed, a whole host of health benefits to this and also, it's a little easier on the schedule! My advice is to drink breakfast at 7am, then have dinner at 7pm, maintaining a full twelve hours between your two meals. This will help to put your body properly into a fasted state.

When in this state, extra fat stored for energy will be broken down. Ketosis mimics this fasting state as our bodies have little to no glucose in the bloodstream, meaning we use fats for energy instead.

Intermittent fasting has the same basis. Instead of burning the fats we're eating, we're burning the stored fats instead. It's not as simple as just fasting permanently though—you have to eat extra fat later on to prevent your body from going into starvation mode. That's why it's important the fasting is intermittent.

So was are the proven benefits of intermittent fasting? It includes improved blood lipid levels, increased longevity, and better mental clarity.

Find the fasting a bit too difficult? Don't worry! It's an added bonus, not an absolute necessity. Simply go back to week one, and work your lunches into your macros.

This is where the fun starts! Less worry, but more delicious food.

Breakfast.
Breakfast is all about fats! Just like last week, keto-proof coffee is key, but this week—we're doubling it! That means plenty of coconut oil, heavy cream, and butter. It'll give you a good boost of calories, and keep you full until dinner time!

Don't forget: drinking water is super important! Stay hydrated by drinking at least four liters a day.

Lunch.
No lunch, remember? Not to worry though—the fats you drank this morning will keep you going. If you hit a wall, which sometimes happens around 2pm, make sure you drink plenty of water.

Dinner.
Not much is changing at dinner this week. We'll be having the usual meats, veggies, and fats but we'll add in some bread-type products too. And of course, we'll be diving into desserts—a great reward for fasting, and much-needed after two weeks sweet free!

Week 3 - SHOPPING LIST

MEAT
Pork Tenderloin
Boneless, Skinless Chicken Thighs

VEGETABLES
Lemons

CHEESE
Halloumi or Mozzarella Cheese

SAUCES
Pesto Sauce   Liquid Smoke   Sugar-free Maple Syrup
Red Boat Fish Sauce (or Gluten Free Fish Sauce)
Red Wine Vinegar   Spicy Brown Mustard

SPECIALITY ITEMS
Liquid Stevia
Erythritol

SPICES
Dried Sage   Vanilla Extract
Dried Rosemary   Nutmeg
Ground Clove   Instant Coffee Grounds

Week 3 / Day 1

Breakfast
(Recipe 7)
Keto-Proof Coffee
       273 Calories, 1g Net Carbs, 30g Fats, 0g Protein

Lunch
Keep drinking that water!

Dinner
(Recipe 13) (Recipe 21)
Chicken Pesto Roulade
- Enjoy the whole lot!

Fried Queso
- Have a quarter-pound Queso with an added four cups of spinach
       886 Calories, 3.5g Net Carbs, 55.8g Fats, 75.5g Protein

Dessert
(Recipe 36)
Vanilla Latte Cookie
- Have a single cookie
       167 Calories, 1.4g Net Carbs, 17.1g Fats, 3.9g Protein

DAY TOTAL: 1599 Calories, 6.4g Net Carbs, 132.9g Fats, 79.4g Protein

Breakfast
(Recipe 7)
Keto-Proof Coffee
- Enjoy a double serving
    546 Calories, 1.5g Net Carbs, 60g Fats, 0g Protein

Lunch
No lunch, but keep up with the water!

Dinner
(Recipe 24)
Not Your Caveman's Chili
- Use a third-portion of leftovers
    531 Calories, 7g Net Carbs, 23.7g Fats, 69g Protein

Dessert
(Recipe 36)
Vanilla Latte Cookie
- Have three cookies
    501 Calories, 4.3g Net Carbs, 51.3g Fats, 11.7g Protein

DAY TOTAL: 1578 Calories, 12.8g Net Carbs, 135g Fats, 80.7g Protein

Week 3 / Day 3

Breakfast
(Recipe 7)
Keto-Proof Coffee
- Take a double serving
    546 Calories, 1.5g Net Carbs, 60g Fats, 0g Protein

Lunch
You're fasting here, but drink plenty!

Dinner
(Recipe 5) (Recipe 27)
Barbecue Pulled Chicken
- Eat a quarter of the recipe and freeze the rest
Red Pepper and Spinach Salad
    756 Calories, 6.3g Net Carbs, 50g Fats, 62.5g Protein

Dessert
(Recipe 36)
Vanilla Latte Cookie
- Enjoy two cookies
    334 Calories, 2.8g Net Carbs, 34.2g Fats, 7.8g Protein

DAY TOTAL: 1636 Calories, 10.6g Net Carbs, 144.2g Fats, 70.3g Protein

Breakfast
(Recipe 7)
Keto-Proof Coffee
- Have a double serving
  546 Calories, 1.5g Net Carbs, 60g Fats, 0g Protein

Lunch
Drink plenty of water during your fast.

Dinner
(Recipe 2)
Inside-Out Bacon Burger
- Eat three patties
  866 Calories, 2.3g Net Carbs, 69g Fats, 58g Protein

Dessert
(Recipe 32)
Low-Carb Spiced Cake
- Enjoy one cake
  283 Calories, 3.3g Net Carbs, 27g Fats, 7.3g Protein

DAY TOTAL: 1694 Calories, 7.1g Net Carbs, 156g Fats, 65.3g Protein

Week 3 / Day 5

Breakfast
(Recipe 7)
Keto-Proof Coffee
- Drink double
  546 Calories, 1.5g Net Carbs, 60g Fats, 0g Protein

Lunch
Drink plenty of water during your fast.

Dinner
(Recipe 9)
Bacon and Cheddar Explosion
- Eat a third of the recipes, then freeze the rest in two portions
  720 Calories, 4.9g Net Carbs, 63.7g Fats, 54.7g Protein

Dessert
(Recipe 32)
Low-Carb Spiced Cake
- Enjoy a cake
  283 Calories, 3.3g Net Carbs, 27g Fats, 7.3g Protein

DAY TOTAL: 1549 Calories, 9.7g Net Carbs, 150.7g Fats, 62g Protein

Breakfast
(Recipe 7)
Keto-Proof Coffee
- Take a double serving
  - **546 Calories, 1.5g Net Carbs, 60g Fats, 0g Protein**

Lunch
Still fasting! Get plenty of water in you.

Dinner
(Recipe 26) (Recipe 21)
Pork Tenderloin Wrapped in Bacon
- Eat 80% of the recipe

Fried Queso Fresco
- Enjoy a third of a pound Fried Queso
  - **841 Calories, 0.2g Net Carbs, 57.3g Fats, 75.2g Protein**

Dessert
(Recipe 32)
Low-Carb Spiced Cake
- Enjoy a cake
  - **283 Calories, 3.3g Net Carbs, 27g Fats, 7.3g Protein**

DAY TOTAL: 1670 Calories, 5g Net Carbs, 144.3g Fats, 82.5g Protein

Breakfast
(Recipe 7)
Keto-Proof Coffee
- Enjoy a double serving
  - **546 Calories, 1.5g Net Carbs, 60g Fats, 0g Protein**

Lunch
You're still fasting here, but drink plenty of water to keep yourself going

Dinner
Leftover Bacon and Cheddar Explosion
- Enjoy one of your leftover portions, along with four cups of spinach
  - **748 Calories, 5.9g Net Carbs, 63.7g Fats, 57.7g Protein**

Dessert
(Recipe 32)
Low-Carb Spiced Cake
- Enjoy one cake
  - **283 Calories, 3.3g Net Carbs, 27g Fats, 7.3g Protein**

DAY TOTAL: 1577 Calories, 10.7g Net Carbs, 150.7g Fats, 65g Protein

Week 4

From here on in, the fasting gets stricter! Last week, we had intermittent fasting. This week, we're skipping both breakfast and lunch. Remember: water, water, water! It really is your best friend, and you can mix it up with flavored waters, teas, and coffees. Ignore your growling stomach, and drown hunger pangs in the liquids you're going to drink! I promise you—your body will get used to it.

As I said last week, though, if fasting isn't your thing, don't worry. Simply re-do week two. That said, fasting takes a little while to get used to, and I advise you persevere—the health benefits are fantastic, and your self-control will be through the roof!

I love this week, because it is so close to my own daily routine. I normally give myself a six-hour window to eat in. When I wake, right up until 5pm, I fast. Then I can eat until 11pm, when I can eat lots and lots of food to make sure I'm all full up for the following day.

Here, you can play around with your dinner and dessert, and you can snack during your 'window.' Best of all? You get to eat a lot more protein-stacked chicken.

Breakfast.

No breakfast for us, thanks—we're fasting! Black coffee or tea are fine, and are great to get you going in the morning. You could try green tea, too. It has some amazing health benefits.

Polyphenols – Simply put: antioxidants. The most powerful antioxidant in green tea is Epigallocatechin gallate (EGCG), and this fights fatigue.

Improved Brain Function – Green tea has caffeine, plus an amino acid called L-theanine. This increases your GABA activity, ultimately improving anxiety, and increasing dopamine and alpha waves.

Increased Metabolic Rate – Your metabolic rate is improved when you drink green tea. That, combined with the caffeine, results in a 15% increase in fat oxidization.

Lunch.

You know what I'm going to say, right? Drink some water. And then some more. You haven't eaten breakfast, and you're not getting lunch, so stay hydrated!

Dinner.

This is where the fun happens! You get lots of food, and plenty of dessert! I recommend breaking your fast slowly. Try a little snack, then eat after around 45 minutes. It's likely you'll need to meals to cover all your macros.

Week 4 - SHOPPING LIST

MEAT
Ground Chicken

FATS
Sesame Oil
CRUNCH

| Pumpkin Seeds | Peanuts (or peanut butter) | Pistachios |

SAUCES
Rice Vinegar   1 Can Coors Light
Chili Garlic Paste   Reduced Sugar Ketchup

CHEESE

| Cream Cheese | Blue Cheese Crumbles | Mozzarella Cheese |

SPICES

| Five-Spice | Capers | Red Food Coloring |

Week 4 / Day 1

Breakfast

Nope—we're fasting! Have some water, and a cup of black coffee or tea with no added ingredient, or even better—green tea. Oh, and a bit more water.

Lunch

Like breakfast, we're fasting. Have a coffee or tea with nothing added to it, and plenty of water. Try not to drink more than three cups of coffee per day.

Dinner

(Recipe 23) (Recipe 28)

Keto-Style Szechuan Chicken
- Enjoy a third of the recipe, then freeze what's left in two portions.

Roasted Green Beans with Pecans
- Enjoy one of your leftover portions

    697 Calories, 8.5g Net Carbs, 55.2g Fats, 66.7g Protein

Dessert

(Recipe 1)

Lemon and Almond Sandwich Cakes
- Enjoy four cakes with an added tablespoon of butter

    819 Calories, 7.3g Net Carbs, 81g Fats, 11.2g Protein

DAY TOTAL: 1517 Calories, 15.9g Net Carbs, 136.2g Fats, 77.9g Protein

Week 4 / Day 2

Breakfast

Yep, still fasting! Black coffee or tea, or green tea, with no added ingredients. And don't forget the water.

Lunch

Fasting again. Tea or coffee, and loads and loads of water to keep you energized.

Dinner

(Recipe 12)

Leftover Meatballs
- Use five of your leftover meatballs

Cheesy Creamed Spinach
- Enjoy half the recipe and freeze the rest

    1061 Calories, 8.5g Net Carbs, 93.1g Fats, 60.6g Protein

Dessert

(Recipe 8)

Chai Spice Mug Cake
- Enjoy with two tablespoons of heavy cream

    539 Calories, 5.2g Net Carbs, 52g Fats, 12g Protein

DAY TOTALS: 1600 Calories, 13.7g Net Carbs, 145.1g Fats, 72.6g Protein

Week 4 / Day 3

Breakfast
No breakfast, we're fasting. Enjoy black coffee or tea, or green tea, and plenty of water.

Lunch
Fill up on water, or enjoy a cup of black coffee or tea, or green tea. Remember not to drink more than three cups of coffee a day.

Dinner
(Recipe 18) (Recipe 37)
Curried Chicken Thighs
- Cook and enjoy three thighs

Vegetable Medley
- Enjoy a third of the recipe, and freeze what's left

  1069 Calories, 9.3g Net Carbs, 83.7g Fats, 63g Protein

Dessert
(Recipe 1)
Lemon and Almond Sandwich Cakes
- Enjoy three cakes

  539 Calories, 5.5g Net Carbs, 52.5g Fats, 8.4g Protein

DAY TOTALS: 1609 Calories, 14.8g Net Carbs, 136.2g Fats, 71.4g Protein

Week 4 / Day 4

Breakfast
Don't forget, we're fasting! Tea or coffee with nothing added, and lots and lots of water.

Lunch
Forget your hunger by drinking plenty of water. I know I keep saying it, but that's because it's important! Have tea or coffee with nothing added to mix it up a bit.

Dinner
(Recipe 35) (Recipe 30)
Thai-Style Peanut Chicken
- Enjoy half the recipe, and freeze the rest

Simple Spinach Salad
- Drizzle two tablespoons of olive oil over two cups of spinach

  1003 Calories, 9.3g Net Carbs, 81.5g Fats, 72g Protein

Dessert
(Recipe 1)
Lemon and Almond Sandwich Cakes
- Have three cakes

  539 Calories, 5.5g Net Carbs, 52.5g Fats, 8.4g Protein

DAY TOTAL: 1543 Calories, 14.7g Net Carbs, 134g Fats, 80.4g Protein

Breakfast

Drink plenty of water during your fast, and have a cup of black coffee or a tea if you fancy.

Lunch

Water, water, water! A cup of tea or coffee for a change, and then some more water! Remember to keep your coffee to a maximum of three cups per day.

Dinner

(Recipe 17) (Recipe 30)

Beef Stew with Coffee and Wine

- Eat a quarter, and freeze the rest in three portions

Spinach Salad

- Drizzle two cups of spinach with two tablespoons olive oil

  1015 Calories, 4.5g Net Carbs, 76.3g Fats, 65.3g Protein

Dessert

(Recipe 8)

Chai Spice Mug Cake

- Enjoy with three tablespoons heavy cream

  589 Calories, 5.8g Net Carbs, 57g Fats, 12g Protein

  DAY TOTAL: 1605 Calories, 10.3g Net Carbs, 133.3g Fats, 77.3g Protein

Breakfast

Keep that fast going! Have a cup of black tea, black coffee, or green tea—making sure you don't add anything—and drink plenty of water.

Lunch

Keep well hydrated. Don't forget, you should have four liters of water a day. A coffee or tea is okay here too.

Dinner

(Recipe 19)

Drunken Five-Spice Beef

- Enjoy half the recipe, and freeze what's left

  1030 Calories, 12g Net Carbs, 70g Fats, 66.5g Protein

Dessert

(Recipe 31)

Snickerdoodle Cookies

- Enjoy four of these cookies

  528 Calories, 8g Net Carbs, 49.6g Fats, 13.7g Protein

  DAY TOTAL: 1558 Calories, 20g Net Carbs, 119.6g Fats, 80.2g Protein

Breakfast
Have a cup of coffee or tea with nothing added, and make sure you have plenty of water.

Lunch
Drink as much water as you can, and have a cup of coffee or tea to mix it up a little. Don't have more than three cups a day though!

Dinner
(Recipe 22) (Recipe 27)
Rosemary and Lemon Roasted Chicken Thighs
- Eat your way through the whole thing!

Red Pepper and Spinach Salad
- Have half the recipe
    797 Calories, 7.7g Net Carbs, 58.5g Fats, 55g Protein

Dessert
(Recipe 31)
Snickerdoodle Cookies
- Have six cookies tonight
    792 Calories, 12g Net Carbs, 74.4g Fats, 20.6g Protein

DAY TOTAL: 1589 Calories, 19.7g Net Carbs, 132.9g Fats, 75.6g Protein

Week 5

Week five? What do you need week five for? You've got this now! That's right, this is where we part ways—you're on your own. You've got plenty of leftovers in the freezer, ready and waiting, and remember to keep up making extra for the freezer—we're all busy people, after all. Try coming up with your own meal plan, first using this one as a guide at first, and then creating one all by yourself. Once you get used to it, you'll find it easy—I promise!

Did the fasting work for you? That's great! Just remember to hit your macros on a daily basis so you're not leaving yourself with a huge calorie deficit.

Fasting not for you? Not a problem. Focus on the plans from the first two weeks, switching it up with some different recipes to give yourself some variety.

Recipes

(Recipe 1) Lemon and Almond Cake Sandwiches

INGREDIENTS

Lemon and Almond Cakes

- ¼ cup coconut flour
- ¼ cup Honeyville almond flour
- ¼ cup butter
- ¼ cup erythritol
- 3 large eggs
- 1tbsp. lemon juice
- 1tsp. cinnamon
- 1tbsp. coconut milk
- ½tsp. almond extract
- ½tsp. baking soda
- ½tsp. vanilla extract
- ½tsp. apple cider vinegar
- ¼tsp. salt
- ¼tsp. liquid Stevia
- Garnishes (optional): Zest ½ lemon, 2tbsp. crushed pistachios

Sandwich 'Filling'

- 4oz. cream cheese
- ¼ cup powdered erythritol
- 4tbsp. butter
- 1tsp. red food coloring
- 2tbsp. heavy cream

METHOD

1. Preheat your oven to 325°F.
2. Combine the coconut flour, cinnamon, almond flour, salt, and baking soda.
3. Whisk together the eggs, vanilla extract, erythritol, almond extract, melted butter, lemon juice, coconut milk, stevia, vinegar, and food coloring.
4. Combine the two ingredients until fluffy and incorporated.
5. Divide between your muffin cups and bake for 17 to 18 minutes.
6. Leave to cool for ten minutes, then slice in half and fry in butter until crisp.
7. Allow to cool completely.
8. To make the filling, combine the butter, heavy cream, cream cheese, and powdered erythritol, then add the food coloring until it suits.
9. Fill the cakes and sandwich, then garnish with the toppings.

Makes ten cake sandwiches. Each cake, with icing:

180 Calories, 1.8g Net Carbs, 17.5g Fats, 2.8g Protein.

(Recipe 2) Inside-Out Bacon Burger

INGREDIENTS

- 2 slices bacon, chopped
- 1½tsp. chopped chives
- 2tbsp. cheddar cheese
- 200g ground beef
- ½tsp. minced garlic
- ¾tsp. soy sauce
- ½tsp. black pepper
- ½tsp. salt
- ¼tsp. Worcestershire
- ¼tsp. onion powder

METHOD

1. Cook your bacon in a skillet until crisp. Drain the grease and reserve.
2. Mix together the ground beef, ⅔ chopped bacon, and the spices.
3. Shape into three patties.
4. Put two tablespoons bacon fat back into the cast iron and, once hot, cook the patties for four to five minutes per side.
5. Let rest for five minutes, then serve with cheese, the remaining bacon, and some onion.

Makes one serving, or three patties. Each serving will be:

649 Calories, 1.8g Net Carbs, 51.8g Fats, 43.5g Protein.

(Recipe 3) Mozzarella and Bacon Meatballs

INGREDIENTS

- 4 slices bacon, cut into small pieces
- ¾ cup pesto sauce
- 1 cup mozzarella cheese
- 1½lb. ground beef
- ⅓ cup crushed pork rinds
- ½tsp. pepper
- 2 large eggs
- ½tsp. minced garlic
- ½tsp. salt
- ½tsp. onion powder

METHOD

1. Preheat your oven to 350°F.
2. Combine all your ingredients but the pesto sauce, then shape into meatballs.
3. Arrange on a foiled baking tray, and bake for around 45 minutes, or until the bacon is cooked. Serve with a half-tablespoon of pesto sauce per meatball.

Yields 24 medium meatballs. Per meatball:

128 Calories, 0.7g Net Carbs, 9.4g Fats, 10.1g Protein.

(Recipe 4) Sugar Snap Peas Infused with Bacon

INGREDIENTS

- ½ lemon juice
- 3 cups sugar snap peas
- 3tbsp. bacon fat
- ½tsp. red pepper flakes
- 2tsp. garlic

METHOD

1. Pop your bacon fat into a pan and heat until smoking.
2. Add the garlic, reduce the heat, and cook for a minute or two.
3. Stir in the sugar snap peas and lemon juice, and let it cook for another minute or two.
4. Garnish with red pepper flakes and lemon zest to serve.

Yields three servings. Per Serving:

147 Calories, 4.3g Net Carbs, 13.3g Fats, 1.3g Protein.

(Recipe 5) Barbecue Pulled Chicken

INGREDIENTS

- ⅓ cup salted butter
- 6 boneless, skinless chicken thighs
- ¼ cup erythritol
- ¼ cup chicken stock
- ¼ cup red wine vinegar
- ¼ cup tomato paste
- 2tbsp. spicy brown mustard
- 2tbsp. yellow mustard
- 1tbsp. liquid smoke
- 2tsp. chili powder
- 1tbsp. soy sauce
- 1tsp. cumin
- 1tsp. Red Boat fish sauce
- 1tsp. cayenne pepper

METHOD

1. Combine everything but the chicken and butter. Add your thighs to your slow cooker (fresh or frozen are fine), then pour the sauce over them.
2. Either, add the butter then cook on low for seven to ten hours, or cook on low for two hours, then add the butter and cook on high for three hours.
3. Once cooked, shred the chicken.
4. Mix together with the sauce, and leave cook on high for 45 minutes without the lid to thicken. Options: Add coarse sea salt sprinkled over the top, with chili paste, or with a sprinkle of curry powder.

Yields four servings. Per serving:

510 Calories, 2.3g Net Carbs, 30g Fats, 51.5g Protein.

(Recipe 6) Buffalo Chicken Strips

INGREDIENTS

- ¾ cup almond flour
- ¼ cup olive oil
- ½ cup hot sauce
- 5 chicken breasts, pounded to a ½-inch thickness
- 1tsp. salt
- 1tbsp. chili powder
- 2tsp. pepper
- 3tbsp. butter
- 2 large eggs
- 3tbsp. blue cheese
- 1tsp. onion powder
- 1tsp. garlic powder
- crumbles
- 1tbsp. paprika

METHOD

1. Preheat your oven to 400°F.
2. Mix together the paprika, salt, chili powder, pepper, onion powder, and garlic powder.
3. Rub a third of the spices on each side of the chicken breasts, reserving a third of the mix.
4. Mix the rest of the spices with the almond flour.
5. Beat your eggs.
6. Dip each piece of chicken in the egg then into the almond flour, coating each side well.
7. Arrange on a cooling rack over a foiled baking tray, then bake for fifteen minutes.
8. Drizzle two tablespoons of olive oil over the chicken, then broil for five minutes.
9. Flip the chicken, drizzle the rest of the oil, then broil for another five minutes.
10. Meanwhile, mix the ½ cup of hot sauce with three tablespoons butter in a saucepan.
11. Serve chicken covered with the hot sauce and topped with blue cheese crumbles.

Yields nine chicken strips, or three servings. Per serving:
683 Calories, 4.8g Net Carbs, 54g Fats, 41g Protein.

(Recipe 7) Keto-Proof Coffee

INGREDIENTS

- 1tbsp. unsalted butter
- 1 cup coffee
- 1tbsp. coconut oil
- 1tbsp. heavy cream
- Seasonings of your choice

METHOD

1. Brew a cup of coffee and pop into a large container.
2. Melt the butter into the coffee, then add the coconut oil. Finally, add the cream.
3. Add seasonings of your choice, and mix it all together using a hand blender.

Yields one serving. Per serving:
273 Calories 1g Net Carbs, 30g Fats, 0g Protein.

(Recipe 8) Chai Spiced Mug Cake

INGREDIENTS

- 2tbsp. Honeyville almond flour
- 2tbsp. butter
- 1tbsp. erythritol
- ½tsp. baking powder
- 7 drops liquid stevia
- 2tbsp. Honeyville almond flour
- ¼tsp. ginger
- ¼tsp. cinnamon
- ¼tsp. clove
- ¼tsp. vanilla extract
- ¼tsp. cardamom

METHOD

1. Grab a mug, and combine all the ingredients together.
2. Microwave on high for one minute, ten seconds.
3. Invert the cup, and tap gently to release the cake.
4. If you like, top with whipped cream and a sprinkle of cinnamon.

Yields one serving. Per serving:
439 Calories, 4g Net Carbs, 42g Fats, 12g Protein.

(Recipe 9) Cheddar and Bacon Explosion

INGREDIENTS
- 2½ cups cheddar cheese
- 30 slices of bacon
- 1-2tbsp. Tones Southwest chipotle seasoning
- 4-5 cups raw spinach
- 2tsp. Mrs. Dash table seasoning

METHOD
1. Preheat your oven to 375°F.
2. Weave your bacon together, fifteen pieces each way. Season well with the seasoning mix.
3. Add your cheese, leaving around an and a half around the edge.
4. Top with the spinach and press it down.
5. Slowly, roll your weave tightly, ensuring the fillings down fall out. You can season the outside too, if you like.
6. Line a baking sheet with aluminum foil, and cover in salt to absorb the bacon fat.
7. Add a cooling rack on top, then place the roll on top of this.
8. Bake for around sixty to seventy minutes, without opening the oven door. Once done, the bacon will be lovely and crisp.
9. Allow to cool, and slice.

Yields three servings. Per serving:

720 Calories, 4.9g Net Carbs, 63.7g Fats, 54.7g Protein.

(Recipe 10) Chorizo and Cheddar Meatballs

INGREDIENTS
- 1½lb. ground beef
- 1 cup cheddar cheese
- ½ cup chorizo sausages
- 1 cup tomato sauce
- 2 large eggs
- ⅓ cup crushed pork rinds
- 1tsp. cumin
- 1tsp. salt
- 1tsp. chili powder

METHOD
1. Preheat your oven to 350°F.
2. Break the sausage into small pieces, then combine well with the ground beef, spices, ground pork rinds, cheese, and eggs.
3. Shape into meatballs, and arrange on a foiled baking tray.
4. Bake for around half an hour, or until cooked through.
5. Serve topped with the tomato sauce.

Yields 24 medium meatballs. Per meatball with sauce:

115 Calories, 0.8g Net Carbs, 7.8g Fats, 9.9g Protein.

(Recipe 11) Scrambled Eggs with Cheese

INGREDIENTS
- 2tbsp. butter
- 2 large eggs
- 1tsp. chopped chives
- 1oz. cheddar cheese
- Spices of your choice

METHOD
1. Melt the butter in a pan, then add two beaten eggs.
2. Cook slowly, then add your seasonings.
3. Stir in the cheese, and serve.

Yields one serving. Per serving:

453 Calories, 1.2g Net Carbs, 43g Fats, 19g Protein.

(Recipe 12) Cheesy Spinach

INGREDIENTS
- 7 cups spinach
- 3tbsp. butter
- 1½ cup cheddar cheese
- ½tsp. Mrs. Dash seasoning
- ½tsp. pepper
- ½tsp. salt

METHOD
1. Melt the butter in a pan, then add the spinach and spices.
2. When the spinach is close to completely wilted, add the cheese and mix until melted.

Yields two servings. Per serving:
446 Calories, 4.8g Net Carbs, 47g Fats, 24g Protein.

(Recipe 13) Chicken Roulade

INGREDIENTS
- 1 chicken breast
- ¼tsp. olive oil
- ½tbsp. pesto
- Zest ¼ lemon
- 38g halloumi cheese
- ¼tsp. minced garlic
- Salt and pepper, to taste

METHOD
1. Pound your chicken breast until it's around an eighth of an inch.
2. Combine the pesto with a teaspoon and a quarter of olive oil, then spread this over your chicken. Season, then add the halloumi.
3. Roll tightly, and secure using butcher's string or toothpicks.
4. Preheat your oven to 450°F.
5. Meanwhile, in a skillet over a high heat, seer the chicken all over, in a teaspoon of olive oil. Bake for six to seven minutes, until the juice runs clear.

Yields one serving. Per serving:
478 Calories, 2.5g Net Carbs, 31g Fats, 53.3g Protein.

(Recipe 14) Buffalo Chicken Strip Slider

INGREDIENTS
ALMOND FLOUR BUNS
- ¼ cup flaxseed
- 2 large eggs
- 3tbsp. parmesan cheese
- ⅓ cup almond flour
- 4tbsp. butter
- 1tsp. Southwest seasoning
- 1tsp. baking soda
- 1tsp. paprika
- 8 drops liquid Stevia
- ½tsp. apple cider vinegar

FILLING
- 2 Leftover Buffalo Chicken Strips

METHOD
1. Preheat your oven to 350°F.
2. Combine all the dry ingredients, then reserve.
3. In the microwave, melt the butter then add eggs, vinegar, and Stevia.
4. Combine with the dry ingredients, then divide between eight muffin cups.
5. Bake for around sixteen minutes.
6. Cool for around five minutes, then slice in half.
7. To make a slider, stuff a bun with the strips.

Yields eight buns, or four servings. Per serving:
625 Calories, 4.3g Net Carbs, 51g Fats, 34.8g Protein.

(Recipe 15) Cheddar, Chive, and Bacon Mug Cake

INGREDIENTS

- 1tbsp. butter
- 1 Egg
- 2tbsp. almond flour
- 2 slices bacon, cooked
- ½tsp. baking powder
- 1tbsp. almond flour
- 1tbsp. shredded white cheddar
- 1tbsp. shredded cheddar cheese
- 1tbsp. chopped chives
- ¼tsp. Mrs. Dash seasonings
- Pinch of salt

METHOD

1. Combine all the ingredients in a mug, then microwave on high for a minute and ten seconds. Invert the cup, and let the cake slide out.

Yields one serving. Per serving:

573 Calories, 5g Net Carbs, 55g Fats, 24g Protein.

(Recipe 16) Beef Stew with Orange and Cinnamon

INGREDIENTS

- ¾ cup beef broth
- ½lb. Pound beef
- 1tbsp. coconut oil
- Zest of ¼ orange
- ¼ medium onion
- Juice of ¼ orange
- ¾tsp. minced garlic
- ¾tsp. fresh thyme
- ½tsp. ground cinnamon
- ½tsp. fish sauce
- ½tsp. soy sauce
- ¼tsp. rosemary
- 1 bay leaf
- ¼tsp. sage

*Double, triple, or quadruple the recipe to batch-cook and freeze for later!

METHOD

1. Cube your meat, and zest your orange.
2. Heat the coconut oil in a skillet until very hot.
3. Season your meat, then brown in the skillet in batches.
4. Pop your veggies into the pan, and cook for a minute or two.
5. Deglaze the pan with your orange juice, then add the rest of the ingredients except the sage, rosemary, and thyme. Cook for a minute.
6. Transfer to your Crock Pot, and cook on high for three hours.
7. Add the rosemary, sage, and thyme, and cook on high for another hour or two.

Yields one serving, with leftovers. Per serving:

649 Calories, 1.9g Net Carbs, 44.5g Fats, 53.5g Protein.

(Recipe 17) Beef Stew with Coffee and Wine

INGREDIENTS

- 2.5lbs stewing steak, cubed
- 1 cup beef stock
- 3 cups coffee
- 1½ cup mushrooms, thinly sliced
- 1 medium onion, thinly sliced
- ⅔ cup red wine
- 3tbsp. coconut oil
- 2tsp. garlic
- 2tbsp. capers
- Salt and pepper, to taste

METHOD

1. Heat three tablespoons coconut oil in a pan, then brown your seasoned beef in batches.
2. Once browned, cook the onion, mushrooms, and garlic in the remaining fat, until softened.
3. Stir in the coffee, red wine, beef stock, and capers, and return the beef.
4. Bring to a boil, then reduce the temperature. Cover, and cook for three hours.

Yields four servings. Per serving:

755 Calories, 4g Net Carbs, 48.3g Fats, 63.8g Protein.

(Recipe 18) Curried Chicken Thighs

INGREDIENTS

- 1tbsp. olive oil
- 2 chicken thighs
- ½tsp. yellow curry
- ¼tsp. cumin
- ½tsp. salt
- ¼tsp. paprika
- ⅛tsp. cayenne pepper
- ¼tsp. garlic powder
- ⅛tsp. allspice
- ⅛tsp. coriander
- ⅛tsp. chili powder
- Pinch cardamom
- Pinch ginger
- Pinch cinnamon

METHOD

1. Preheat your oven to 425°F.
2. Combine all the spices together.
3. Rub the chicken all over with the oil, then with the spice mixture, making sure it's all well-coated.
4. Arrange on a foil-covered baking sheet, and bake for around 45 minutes, or until cooked through.
5. Allow to cool for five minutes before serving.

Yields one serving. Per serving:

555 Calories, 1.3g Net Carbs, 39.8g Fats, 42.3g Protein.

(Recipe 19) Drunken Five-Spice Beef

INGREDIENTS

- 1½lbs. ground beef
- 150g. sliced mushrooms
- 1 can Coors Light
- 135g. chopped broccoli
- 3tbsp. ketchup
- 75g. raw spinach
- 2tbsp. soy sauce
- 2tsp. minced ginger
- 2tsp. garlic
- 1tbsp. five spice
- 1tsp. salt
- 1tbsp. pepper
- 1tsp. cumin
- ½tsp. onion powder
- 1tsp. cayenne pepper

METHOD

1. Cut up the broccoli florets, ginger, and garlic.
2. In a skillet, brown the ground beef, then stir in the ginger and garlic.
3. Add the broccoli, soy sauce, and spices. Incorporate well.
4. Pour in the can of Coors Light, then add the mushrooms and spinach.
5. Once wilted, stir in the ketchup, and serve.

Makes four servings. For each serving:

515 Calories, 6g Net Carbs, 35g Fats, 33.3g Protein.

(Recipe 20) Frittata Muffins with Cheese

INGREDIENTS

- ½ cup half 'n' half
- 8 large eggs
- 4oz. bacon, cooked and chopped
- 1tbsp. butter
- ½ cup cheddar cheese
- 2tsp. dried parsley
- ¼tsp. salt
- ½tsp. pepper
- Seasonings or sauces of your choice

METHOD

1. Preheat your oven to 375°F.
2. Combine the eggs with the half 'n' half, but not fully scrambling them.
3. Fold in the cheese, bacon, and spices. If you want to add seasonings, now is the time.
4. Divide between your muffin cups, filling them about ¾ of the way.
5. Bake for fifteen to eighteen minutes, or until puffy and golden.
6. Leave to cool before serving.

Yields eight servings. For each:

205 Calories, 1.3g Net Carbs, 16.1g Fats, 13.6g Protein.

(Recipe 21) Fried Queso Fresco

INGREDIENTS
- 1lb. Queso Fresco
- ½tbsp. olive oil
- 1tbsp. coconut oil

METHOD
1. Cub the cheese.
2. In a pan over a high heat, combine the two oils. Once smoking, add the cheese and cook until browned on each side.

Yields five servings. Per serving:

243 Calories, 0g Net Carbs, 19.5g Fats, 16g Protein.

(Recipe 22) Rosemary and Lemon Chicken

INGREDIENTS
- 1½tsp. minced garlic
- 3½ skinless, boneless chicken thighs
- 1½tsp. olive oil
- 1½tsp. fresh thyme
- 1 lemon, thinly sliced
- ¾tsp. dried rosemary
- 1tsp. salt
- ½tsp. dried ground sage

METHOD
1. Grind your garlic together with half the salt to create a paste.
2. Slowly add the oil, grinding and mixing as you go.
3. Coat the chicken in this, then leave to marinate for around two hours.
4. Preheat your oven to 425°F.
5. Cover your baking pan with slices of lemon, then add the chicken. Top with more lemon.
6. Add the rosemary, thyme, sage, and salt and pepper.
7. Bake for around a half-hour, or until cooked through.
8. Pour the drippings into a saucepan and bring to a boil.
9. Cook, stirring often, until thickened. Serve over the chicken.

Yields one serving. Per serving:

589 Calories, 4.2g Net Carbs, 40.5g Fats, 47g Protein.

(Recipe 23) Szechuan Chicken

INGREDIENTS
- 1½lbs. ground chicken
- ½ cup chicken stock
- 6 cups spinach
- 4tbsp. tomato paste
- 2tbsp. chili garlic paste
- 3tbsp. coconut oil
- 2tbsp. soy sauce
- 1tbsp. red wine vinegar
- 1tbsp. + 1tsp. erythritol
- 2tsp. spicy brown mustard
- 2tsp. pepper
- 2tsp. salt
- 1tsp. red pepper flakes
- ½tsp. minced ginger
- ½tsp. Mrs. Dash seasoning

METHOD
1. Combine the tomato paste, chili garlic paste, soy sauce, brown mustard, and ginger.
2. Heat three tablespoons coconut oil over a medium-high temperature.
3. Add the ground chicken, season with salt and pepper, and stir until cooked through.
4. Stir in ⅔ of the sauce.
5. Mix in the spinach and cook until it wilts, then stir in the salt and pepper, Mrs. Dash seasoning, and red pepper flakes.
6. Add the rest of your sauce, along with the chicken stock, red wine vinegar, and erythritol.
7. Reduce the heat, cover, and cook for around ten to fifteen minutes.

Yields three servings. Per serving:

515 Calories, 5.2g Net Carbs, 38.3g Fats, 63g Protein.

(Recipe 24) Not Your Caveman's Chili

INGREDIENTS
- 2lbs. stewing steak
- 1 medium green pepper
- 1 medium onion
- 1 cup beef broth
- 1tbsp. soy sauce
- ⅓ cup tomato paste
- 2tbsp. olive oil
- 1½tsp. cumin
- 2tbsp. + 1tsp. chili powder
- 2tsp. Red Boat fish sauce
- 2tsp. paprika
- 2tsp. minced garlic
- 1tsp. oregano
- 1tsp. Worcestershire
- ½tsp. cayenne pepper

METHOD
1. Cut half the meat into small cubes, and grind the other half in a food processor.
2. Finely chop the pepper and onion.
3. Mix together all your spices.
4. Brown both types of beef, then transfer to your Crock Pot.
5. Fry the veggies in the left over fat, until softened and fragrant.
6. Pop into the Crock Pot, and combine.
7. Cook on high for 2½ hours, then remove the lid and simmer for around thirty minutes to thicken the sauce.

Yields four servings. Per serving:
398 Calories, 5.3g Net Carbs, 17.8g Fats, 51.8g Protein.

(Recipe 25) Omnivore Burger with Creamed Spinach and Roasted Almonds

INGREDIENTS
- 1lb. ground beef
- ¼ onion
- 100g. sliced mushrooms
- ¼ bell pepper
- 2½tbsp. roasted almonds
- ½tbsp. Tone's Southwest chipotle seasoning
- 1tsp. red pepper flakes
- 1tsp. cumin
- ½ cups raw spinach
- 1tbsp. cream cheese
- ½tbsp. butter
- ½tbsp. heavy cream

METHOD
1. Preheat your oven to 450°F.
2. Pulse together the mushrooms, onions, and pepper in your food processor.
3. In a bowl, combine the meat, veggies, and seasonings, then shape into three patties.
4. Put a cooling rack over a baking sheet, then cook the patties on top.
5. Take some of the juices from the meat pan, and add to a skillet.
6. Add the spinach, add some salt and pepper and the pepper flakes, then let it wilt.
7. Stir in the almonds, butter, cream cheese, and heavy cream, and stir well.
8. After around twenty minutes, remove the burgers from the oven, and serve with spinach.

Yields two servings. Per serving:
562 Calories, 4.8g Net Carbs, 38.5g Fats, 45.3g Protein.

(Recipe 26) Pork Tenderloin Wrapped in Bacon

INGREDIENTS
- 2½ slices bacon
- ½lb. pork tenderloin
- 1½tsp. Dijon mustard
- ¾tsp. soy sauce
- 1½tsp. maple syrup
- ¼tsp. minced garlic
- ¼tsp. dried rosemary
- ¼tsp. liquid smoke
- Pinch black pepper
- Pinch dried sage
- Pinch cayenne

METHOD
1. Combine everything but the bacon together, then leave the pork to marinate for at least three hours.
2. Preheat your oven to 350°F.
3. Wrap your marinated pork in bacon, then bake for around an hour.
4. Broil for five to ten minutes, then cover with foil and leave to rest for around fifteen minutes.

Yields one serving. Per serving:
418 Calories, 0.3g Net Carbs, 20g Fats, 54g Protein.

(Recipe 27) Red Pepper and Spinach Salad

INGREDIENTS
- 2tbsp. ranch dressing
- ½tsp. red pepper flakes
- 3 cups spinach
- 1½tbsp. parmesan cheese

METHOD
1. In a bowl, mix the spinach with the ranch, then top with parmesan and red pepper flakes.

Yields one serving. Per serving:
208 Calories, 3.5g Net Carbs, 18g Fats, 8g Protein.

(Recipe 28) Roasted Green Beans with Pecans

INGREDIENTS
- 2tbsp. olive oil
- 2tbsp. parmesan cheese
- ¼ cup chopped pecans
- ½lb. green beans
- ½ lemon zest
- ½tsp. red pepper flakes
- 1tsp. minced garlic

METHOD
1. Preheat your oven to 450°F.
2. Grind the pecans in your food processor.
3. Combine the green beans, olive oil, pecans, parmesan cheese, minced garlic, the zest of the lemon, and red pepper flakes.
4. Spread out onto a foiled baking sheet, then roast for 20 to 25 minutes.
5. Leave to cool for five minutes, before serving.

Yields three servings. Per serving:
182 Calories, 3.3g Net Carbs, 16.8g Fats, 3.7g Protein.

(Recipe 29) Cauliflower and Shrimp Curry

INGREDIENTS
- 5 cups raw spinach
- 24oz. shrimp
- 4 cups chicken stock
- ½ head medium cauliflower
- 1 medium onion
- 1 cup coconut milk
- ¼ cup heavy cream

- ¼ cup butter
- 3tbsp. olive oil
- 1tbsp. coconut flour
- 2tbsp. curry powder
- 1tbsp. cumin
- 1tsp. chili powder
- 2tsp. garlic powder
- 1tsp. onion powder

- 1tsp. paprika
- 1tsp. cayenne
- ½tsp. ground ginger
- ½tsp. turmeric
- ½tsp. coriander
- ¼tsp. cardamom
- ¼tsp. xanthan gum
- ¼tsp. cinnamon

METHOD
1. Combine the spices but the xanthan gum and coconut flour. Slice your onion.
2. Over a high heat, cook the onion in three tablespoons of oil.
3. Once softened, add the butter, heavy cream, ⅛tsp. xanthan gum, and the mixed spices.
4. Sweat for a minute or two, then add four cups chicken broth and a cup of coconut milk.
5. Cover, and cook for around a half-hour.
6. Cut the cauliflower up into small florets, then stir this into the sauce. Cook for another fifteen minutes, with the lid on.
7. Meanwhile, devein the shrimp, then add them to the curry. Let cook for another twenty minutes, this time uncovered.
8. Add the coconut flour, then cook for five minutes.
9. Finally, stir in the spinach and cook for another five to ten minutes.

Yields six servings. Per serving:
331 Calories, 5.6g Net Carbs, 19.5g Fats, 27.4g Protein.

(Recipe 30) Simple Lunch Salad

INGREDIENTS
- 2-4tbsp. olive oil
- 1-2tbsp. parmesan cheese

- 2 cups spinach
- ½tsp. Dijon mustard
- Zest ¼ lemon

- ¾tsp. curry powder
- Meat, as specified in the plan.

METHOD
1. Mix together the wet ingredients. Combine the meat and spinach.
2. Pour the sauce all over the meat and spinach.

Yields one serving.
Macros depend on what meat you put in it.

(Recipe 31) Snickerdoodle Cookies

INGREDIENTS
- 2 cups almond flour
- ¼ cup maple syrup

- ¼ cup coconut oil
- 1tbsp. vanilla

- 1tbsp. cinnamon
- ¼tsp. baking soda

METHOD
1. Preheat your oven to 350°F. Combine your baking soda, almond flour, and salt.
2. Combine the coconut oil, vanilla, maple syrup, and stevia.
3. Blend the two mixtures to create a dough.
4. In a small ball, combine the cinnamon and erythritol.
5. Roll the dough into balls, then roll each ball in the cinnamon mix.
6. Arrange on a lined baking tray, flatten, then bake for around ten minutes.

Yields 14 cookies. Per cookie:
132 Calories, 2g Net Carbs, 12.4g Fats, 3.4g Protein.

(Recipe 32) Low-Carb Spiced Cakes

INGREDIENTS
Spiced Cakes
- 2 cups Honeyville almond flour
- ½ cup salted butter
- ¾ cup erythritol
- 5tbsp. water
- 2tsp. baking powder
- 4 large eggs
- 1tsp. vanilla extract
- ½tsp. nutmeg
- ½tsp. cinnamon
- ½tsp. allspice
- ¼tsp. ground clove
- ½tsp. ginger

Cream Cheese Frosting
- 8oz. cream cheese
- 1tbsp. butter
- 1tbsp. erythritol
- 1tsp. vanilla extract
- Zest of ½ Lemon

METHOD
1. Preheat your oven to 350°F.
2. Cream together the butter and sweetener, then add two eggs and combine well.
3. Add the other two eggs, and blend again.
4. Grind your spices together, then add all the dry ingredients to the batter.
5. Add the water, and blend your batter until smooth and creamy.
6. Fill a greased cupcake tray to ¾ full. Bake for around fifteen minutes.
7. Meanwhile, combine the cream cheese, sweetener, butter, vanilla, and lemon zest.
8. Cool the cupcakes completely before frosting.

Yields twelve frosted cakes. Per frosted cake:
283 Calories, 3.3g Carbs, 27g Fats, 7.3g Protein.

(Recipe 33) Chicken, Bacon, and Sausage Stir Fry

INGREDIENTS
- 4 chicken sausages
- 3 cups spinach
- 3 cups broccoli florets
- ½ cup parmesan cheese
- ¼ cup red wine
- ½ cup Rao's tomato sauce
- 2tbsp. salted butter
- ½tsp. red pepper flakes
- 2tsp. minced garlic

METHOD
1. Cut up the bacon, cheddar, and chicken sausages.
2. Bring a pan of water to a boil.
3. Meanwhile, cook the sausage over a high heat until browned.
4. Cook the broccoli in the water for three to five minutes.
5. Push all your sausages to one side of the pan, then add the butter. Cook the garlic in the butter for around a minutes.
6. Combine everything in the pan, then add the red wine, tomato sauce, and red pepper flakes.
7. Add the spinach, season well, and let it wilt. Simmer for around five to ten minutes.
8. Stir in the parmesan.

Yields three servings. Per serving:
451 Calories, 7.3g Net Carbs, 28.3g Fats, 35.7g Protein.

(Recipe 34) Taco Tartlets

INGREDIENTS
PASTRY
- 1 cup blanched almond flour
- 5tbsp. butter
- 3tbsp. coconut flour
- ¼tsp. salt
- 1tsp. oregano
- 1tsp. xanthan gum
- ¼tsp. paprika
- 2tbsp. ice water
- ¼tsp. cayenne

FILLING
- 400g. ground beef
- 3 stalks spring onion
- 80g. mushroom
- 2tbsp. tomato paste
- 2tsp. yellow mustard
- ⅓ cup cheddar cheese
- 1tbsp. olive oil
- 2tsp. garlic
- ½tsp. pepper
- 1tsp. cumin
- 1tsp. salt
- ¼tsp. cinnamon
- 1tsp. Worcestershire

METHOD
1. Pop all the dry ingredients for the pastry into your food processor, then add cubes of the cold butter.
2. Pulse until crumbly, then add a tablespoon of ice water until a dough forms.
3. Wrap in plastic, and freeze for around ten minutes.
4. Roll out, then cut into circles.
5. Put into a whoopie pan, and preheat your oven to 325°F.
6. Chop and slice all the veggies.
7. Cook the onions and garlic in the olive oil, then stir in the ground beef and brown well.
8. Stir in the dry spices and the Worcestershire.
9. Stir in the mushrooms, then the tomato paste and mustard.
10. Spoon into the pastry tartlets, sprinkle with cheese, and bake for 20-25 minutes.
11. Cool completely before removing the pastries.

Yields 11 tartlets. Per tartlet:
241 Calories, 1.7g Net Carbs, 19.4g Fats, 13.1g Protein.

(Recipe 35) Thai-Peanut Chicken

INGREDIENTS
- 1 cup peanuts
- 2tbsp. soy sauce
- ¼ cup chicken stock
- 6 boneless, skinless chicken thighs
- 1tbsp. orange juice
- 1tbsp. rice vinegar
- 1tbsp. lemon juice
- ½tbsp. coconut oil
- ½tsp. sesame oil
- ½tbsp. erythritol
- 1tsp. chili garlic paste
- ¼tsp. cayenne pepper
- ¼tsp. coriander
- Salt and pepper, to taste

METHOD
1. Blend the peanuts in your food processor until creamy, then add the coconut oil and erythritol. Blend again.
2. Combine all the ingredients but the chicken, salt, cayenne, and pepper.
3. Cube your chicken thighs, and season well.
4. Heat a tablespoon oil over a high heat, then add the chicken.
5. Cook until browned, then stir in the sauce and season again to taste.
6. Reduce the heat, and simmer for ten minutes.

Yields two servings. Per serving:
743 Calories, 8.8g Net Carbs, 53.5g Fats, 70.5g Protein.

(Recipe 36) Vanilla Latte Cookies

INGREDIENTS
- ½ cup unsalted butter
- 2 large eggs
- ⅓ cup erythritol
- 1tbsp. + 1tsp. instant coffee grounds
- ½tsp. baking soda
- 1½tsp. vanilla extract
- 1½ cups Honeyville blanched almond flour
- ½tsp. salt
- 17 drops liquid Stevia
- ¼tsp. cinnamon

METHOD
1. Preheat your oven to 350°F.
2. Mix together the almond flour, baking soda, coffee grounds, salt, and cinnamon.
3. Separate your egg whites and yolks.
4. Cream together the erythritol and butter, then beat in the egg yolks until smooth.
5. Beat in the flour mix, vanilla extra, and liquid Stevia.
6. Thoroughly beat your egg whites until they form stiff peaks, then fold into the cookie dough.
7. Divide onto a cookie sheet, and bake them for around fifteen minutes.
8. Cool for around ten minutes.

Yields 10 cookies. Per cookie:

167 Calories, 1.4g Net Carbs, 17.1g Fats, 3.9g Protein.

(Recipe 37) Vegetable Medley

INGREDIENTS
- 240g. baby bella mushrooms
- 6tbsp. olive oil
- 115g. broccoli
- 90g. bell pepper
- 100g. sugar snap peas
- 90g. spinach
- 2tsp. minced garlic
- 2tbsp. pumpkin seeds
- 1tsp. salt
- ½tsp. red pepper flakes
- 1tsp. pepper

METHOD
1. Chop all your veggies into bite-sized pieces.
2. In a pan over a high heat, cook the garlic in the oil for around a minute.
3. Stir in the mushrooms, allowing them to soak up some of the oil.
4. Next, stir in the broccoli.
5. Cook for a few minutes, the add the sugar snap peas.
6. Add the bell pepper, spices, and pumpkin seeds, and combine well.
7. Once cooked through, top with the spinach. Once it's wilted, stir it together.

Yields three servings. Per serving:

330 Calories, 7.7g Net Carbs, 30.7g Fats, 6.7g Protein.

Breakfast Recipes

Keto Green Smoothie

Serves: 2
Prep Time: 10 mins
Ingredients

- 2 tablespoons flax seed meal
- 2 cups frozen spinach
- 2 tablespoons chia seeds
- 1 scoop whey protein
- 5 cubes ice + 3 cups water

Directions
1. Put all the ingredients in a blender and blend until smooth.
2. Pour into 2 glasses and serve immediately.

Nutrition
Calories: 116 Carbs: 6g Fats: 4g Proteins: 13.6g Sodium: 54mg Sugar: 0.7g

Scrambled Eggs with Mushrooms and Cheese

Serves: 4
Prep Time: 20 mins
Ingredients

- 4 tablespoons butter
- 8 eggs
- 4 tablespoons Parmesan cheese, shredded
- Salt and black pepper, to taste
- 1 cup fresh mushrooms, chopped finely

Directions
1. Mix together eggs, salt, and black pepper in a bowl and beat well.
2. Melt butter in a non-stick pan and add the beaten eggs.
3. Cook for about 5 minutes and add Parmesan cheese and mushrooms.
4. Cook for another 5 minutes, stirring occasionally,
5. Let cool slightly and enjoy

Nutrition
Calories: 203 Carbs: 1.2g Fats: 17.5g Proteins: 11.2g Sodium: 217mg Sugar: 0.8g

Peanut Butter Chocolate Smoothie

Serves: 1
Prep Time: 5 mins
Ingredients

- 1 tablespoon unsweetened cocoa powder
- 1 cup unsweetened coconut milk
- 1 tablespoon unsweetened peanut butter
- 1 pinch sea salt
- 5 drops stevia

Directions
1. Put all the ingredients in a blender and blend until smooth.
2. Pour into a glass and serve immediately.

Nutrition
Calories: 79 Carbs: 6.4g Fats: 5.7g Proteins: 3.6g Sodium: 235mg Sugar: 1.6g

Cream Cheese Pancakes

Serves: 4
Prep Time: 12 mins
Ingredients

- 2 eggs
- ½ teaspoon cinnamon
- 2 oz cream cheese
- 1 teaspoon granulated sugar substitute
- ½ cup almond flour

Directions
1. Put all the ingredients in a blender and pulse until smooth.
2. Transfer the mixture into a medium bowl and put aside for about 3 minutes.

3. Grease a large non-stick skillet with butter and add ¼ of the mixture.
4. Tilt the pan to spread the mixture and cook for about 2 minutes until golden brown.
5. Turn the pancakes over onto the other side and cook for about 1 minute.

6.   Repeat with the remaining mixture in batches and top with your choice of berries.
Nutrition
Calories: 170 Carbs: 4.3g Fats: 14.3g Proteins: 6.9g Sodium: 81mg Sugar: 0.2g

Coconut Chia Pudding

Serves: 4
Prep Time: 25 mins
Ingredients
- 1 cup full-fat coconut milk
- ¼ cup chia seeds
- ½ tablespoon honey
- 2 tablespoons almonds
- ¼ cup raspberries

Directions
1.   Mix together coconut milk, chia seeds, and honey in a bowl and refrigerate overnight.
2.   Remove from the fridge and top with raspberries and almonds to serve.
Nutrition
Calories: 158 Carbs: 6.5g Fats: 14.1g Proteins: 2g Sodium: 16mg Sugar: 3.6g

Morning Hash

Serves: 2
Prep Time: 30 mins
Ingredients
- ½ teaspoon dried thyme, crushed
- ½ small onion, chopped
- 1 tablespoon butter
- ½ cup cauliflower florets, boiled
- ¼ cup heavy cream
- Salt and black pepper, to taste
- ½ pound cooked turkey meat, chopped

Directions
1.   Blend the cauliflower florets in a chopper and keep aside.
2.   Put butter and onions in a skillet and sauté for about 3 minutes.
3.   Add chopped cauliflower and sauté for about 3 more minutes.
4.   Add turkey and cook for about 6 minutes.
5.   Stir in heavy cream and cook for about 2 minutes, stirring constantly.
6.   Dish out to serve or refrigerate it for about 3 days for meal prep. You just have to heat it in the microwave while reusing it.
Nutrition
Calories per serving: 309 Carbs: 3.6g Protein: 34.3g Fat: 17.1g Sugar: 1.4g Sodium: 134mg

Spanish Scramble

Serves: 2
Prep Time: 20 mins
Ingredients
- 3 tablespoons butter
- 2 tablespoons scallions, sliced thinly
- 4 large organic eggs
- 1 Serrano chili pepper
- ¼ cup heavy cream
- 2 tablespoons cilantro, chopped finely
- 1 small tomato, chopped
- Salt and black pepper, to taste

Directions
1.   Combine cream, eggs, cilantro, salt and black pepper in a medium bowl.
2.   Put butter, tomatoes and Serrano pepper in a pan on medium heat and sauté for about 2 minutes.
3.   Add egg mixture in the pan and cook for about 4 minutes, continuously stirring.
4.   Garnish with scallions and dish out to immediately serve.
5.   You can refrigerate this scramble for about 2 days for meal prepping and reuse by heating it in microwave oven.
Nutrition
Calories per serving: 180 Carbs: 2g Protein: 6.8g Fat: 16.5g Sugar: 1.1g Sodium: 231mg

Cheese Waffles

Serves: 2/Prep Time: 20 mins
Ingredients
- ½ cup Parmesan cheese, shredded
- 2 organic eggs, beaten
- 1 teaspoon onion powder
- 1 cup mozzarella cheese, shredded
- 1 tablespoon chives, minced
- ½ teaspoon ground black pepper
- 1 cup cauliflower
- 1 teaspoon garlic powder

Directions

1. Combine all the ingredients in a bowl and keep aside.
2. Grease a waffle iron and heat it.
3. Pour half of the mixture into the waffle iron and cook until golden brown.
4. Repeat with the remaining half mixture and dish out to serve.
5. You can refrigerate these waffles up to 4 days for meal prepping. Place the waffles in a container and slide wax paper between each waffle.

Nutrition

Calories per serving: 149 Carbs: 6.1g Protein: 13.3g Fat: 8.5g Sugar: 2.3g Sodium: 228mg

Spinach Frittata

Serves: 2/Prep Time: 45 mins

Ingredients

- 1½ ounce dried bacon
- 2 ounces spinach, fresh
- 1½ ounce shredded cheese
- ½ tablespoon butter
- ¼ cup heavy whipped cream
- 2 eggs
- Salt and black pepper, to taste

Directions

1. Preheat the oven to 360 degrees and grease a baking dish.
2. Heat butter in a skillet and add bacon.
3. Cook until crispy and add spinach.
4. Stir thoroughly and keep aside.
5. Whisk together eggs and cream in a bowl and pour it in the baking dish.
6. Add bacon spinach mixture to the baking dish and transfer to the oven.
7. Bake for about 30 minutes and remove from the oven to serve.
8. You can refrigerate this frittata for about 2 days for meal prepping and reuse by heating it in microwave oven.

Nutrition

Calories per serving: 592 Carbs: 3.9g Protein: 39.1g Fat: 46.7g Sugar: 1.1g Sodium: 1533mg

Keto Oatmeal

Serves: 2

Prep Time: 20 mins

Ingredients

- 2 tablespoons flaxseeds
- 2 tablespoons sunflower seeds
- 2 cups coconut milk
- 2 tablespoons chia seeds
- 2 pinches of salt

Directions

1. Put all the ingredients in a saucepan and mix well.
2. Bring it to boil and allow it to simmer for about 7 minutes.
3. Dish out in a bowl and serve warm.

Nutrition

Calories per serving: 337 Carbs: 7.8g Protein: 4.9g Fat: 32.6g Sugar: 4.1g Sodium: 98mg

Baked Eggs

Serves: 2

Prep Time: 10 mins

Ingredients

- 2 eggs
- 2 ounces cheddar cheese, shredded
- 3 ounces ground beef, cooked

Directions

1. Preheat the oven to 390 degrees and grease a baking dish.
2. Arrange the cooked ground beef in a baking dish.
3. Make two holes in the ground beef and crack eggs in them.
4. Top with cheddar cheese and transfer the baking dish in the oven.
5. Bake for about 20 minutes and remove from the oven.
6. Allow it to cool for a bit and serve to enjoy.
7. For meal prepping, you can refrigerate these baked eggs for about 2 days wrapped in a foil.

Nutrition

Calories per serving: 512 Carbs: 1.4g Protein: 51g Fat: 32.8g Sugar: 1g Sodium: 531mg

Blueberry Smoothie

Serves: 2
Prep Time: 15 mins
Ingredients
- 1 cup fresh blueberries
- 1 teaspoon vanilla extract
- 28 ounces coconut milk
- 2 tablespoons lemon juice

Directions
1. Put all the ingredients in a blender and blend until smooth.
2. Pour it in the glasses to serve and enjoy.

Nutrition
Calories per serving: 152 Carbs: 6.9g Protein: 1.5g Fat: 13.1g Sugar: 4.5g Sodium: 1mg

Quick Keto Pancakes

Serves: 2/Prep Time: 30 mins
Ingredients
- 3 ounces cottage cheese
- 2 eggs
- ½ tablespoon psyllium husk powder, ground
- ½ cup whipped cream
- 1 oz butter

Directions
1. Mix together all the ingredients in a bowl except whipped cream and keep aside.
2. Heat butter in the frying pan and pour half of the mixture.
3. Cook for about 3 minutes on each side and dish out in a serving platter.
4. Add whipped cream in another bowl and whisk until smooth.
5. Top the pancakes with whipped cream on them.
6. Meal Prep Tip: These keto pancakes can also be used as a snack. They taste awesome when serve cold.

Nutrition
Calories per serving: 298 Carbs: 4.8g Protein: 12.2g Fat: 26g Sugar: 0.5g Sodium: 326mg

Spinach Quiche

Serves: 2
Prep Time: 15 mins
Ingredients
- 1½ cups Monterey Jack cheese, shredded
- ½ tablespoon butter, melted
- 5-ounce frozen spinach, thawed
- Salt and freshly ground black pepper, to taste
- 2 organic eggs, beaten

Directions
1. Preheat the oven to 350 degrees and lightly grease a 9-inch pie dish.
2. Heat butter on medium-low heat in a large skillet and add spinach.
3. Cook for about 3 minutes and set aside.
4. Mix together Monterey Jack cheese, eggs, spinach, salt and black pepper in a bowl.
5. Transfer the mixture into prepared pie dish and place in the oven.
6. Bake for about 30 minutes serve by cutting into equal sized wedges.

Nutrition
Calories per serving: 349 Carbs: 3.2g Protein: 23g Fat: 27.8g Sugar: 1.3g Sodium: 532mg

Cream Crepes

Serves: 2
Prep Time: 25 mins
Ingredients
- 1 teaspoon Splenda
- 2 tablespoons coconut oil, melted and divided
- 2 organic eggs
- 2 tablespoons coconut flour
- ½ cup heavy cream

Directions
1. Put 1 tablespoon of coconut oil, eggs, Splenda and salt in a bowl and beat until well combined.
2. Sift in the coconut flour slowly and beat constantly.
3. Stir in the heavy cream and continuously beat until the mixture is well combined.
4. Heat a non-stick pan and pour half of the mixture in it.
5. Cook for about 2 minutes on each side and repeat with the remaining mixture.
6. Dish out to serve and enjoy.
7. For meal prepping, wrap each cream crepe into wax paper pieces and place into a resealable bag. Freeze for up to 3 days and remove from the freezer. Microwave for about 2 minutes to serve.

Nutrition
Calories per serving: 298 Carbs: 8g Protein: 7g Fat: 27.1g Sugar: 2.4g Sodium: 70mg

Smoothie Bowl

Serves: 2
Prep Time: 15 mins
Ingredients
- ¼ cup unsweetened almond milk
- 1 cup frozen strawberries
- ½ cup fat-free plain Greek yogurt
- 1 tablespoon walnuts, chopped
- ½ tablespoon unsweetened whey protein powder

Directions
1. Put the strawberries in a blender and pulse until smooth.
2. Add almond milk, Greek yogurt and whey protein powder in the blender and pulse for about 2 minutes.
3. Transfer the mixture evenly into 2 bowls and top with walnuts to serve.
4. You can wrap the bowls with plastic wrap and refrigerate for 2 days for meal prepping.

Nutrition
Calories per serving: 71 Fat: 19g Carbs: 6.3g Protein: 6.8gSugar: 0.7g Sodium: 65mg

Devilish Pancakes

Serves: 2
Prep Time: 25 mins
Ingredients
- 2-ounce cream cheese, softened
- ½ packet stevia
- 2 organic eggs
- ½ teaspoon ground cinnamon

Directions
1. Blend all ingredients in a blender until smooth and keep aside for about 3 minutes.
2. Heat a skillet over medium heat and half of the mixture, spreading evenly.
3. Cook for about 2 minutes on each side until it becomes golden brown.
4. Repeat with the remaining mixture and dish out to serve.
5. For meal prepping, you can refrigerate these pancakes for about 4 days. Place them in a container and place wax paper between each pancake.

Nutrition
Calories per serving: 163 Fat: 14.3g Carbs: 1.6g Protein: 7.7g Sugar: 0.6 g Sodium: 324mg

Cheesy Muffins

Serves: 2/Prep Time: 45 mins
Ingredients
- ¼ cup raw hemp seeds
- ¼ teaspoon baking powder
- 1/8 cup nutritional yeast flakes
- ¼ cup Parmesan cheese, grated finely
- 3 organic eggs, beaten
- ¼ cup almond meal
- 1/8 cup flax seeds meal
- Salt, to taste
- ¼ cup low-fat cottage cheese
- ¼ cup scallion, sliced thinly

Directions
1. Preheat oven to 360 degrees and grease 2 muffin cups.
2. Combine almond meal, flax seeds, hemp seeds, baking powder and salt in a bowl and mix well.
3. Mix together cottage cheese, parmesan cheese, nutritional yeast flakes and egg in another bowl.
4. Combine the cheese and almond mixture and mix until well combined.
5. Fold in the scallions and pour this mixture into the greased muffin cups.
6. Transfer into the oven and bake for about 30 minutes.
7. Dish out to serve warm immediately or for meal prepping, you can refrigerate muffins in the refrigerator for 3-4 days, by covering them with paper towel and heat again before use.

Nutrition
Calories per serving: 179 Fat: 10.9g Carbs: 6.9g Protein: 15.4g Sugar: 2.3g Sodium: 311mg

Bacon Veggies Combo

Serves: 2
Prep Time: 35 mins
Ingredients
- ½ green bell pepper, seeded and chopped
- 2 bacon slices
- ¼ cup Parmesan Cheese
- ½ tablespoon mayonnaise
- 1 scallion, chopped

Directions
1. Preheat the oven to 375 degrees and grease a baking dish.
2. Place bacon slices on the baking dish and top with mayonnaise, bell peppers, scallions and Parmesan Cheese.
3. Transfer in the oven and bake for about 25 minutes.

4. Dish out to serve immediately or refrigerate for about 2 days wrapped in a plastic sheet for meal prepping.
Nutrition
Calories per serving: 197 Fat: 13.8g Carbs: 4.7g Protein: 14.3g Sugar: 1.9g Sodium: 662mg

Ham Spinach Ballet

Serves: 2
Prep Time: 40 mins
Ingredients
- 4 teaspoons cream
- ¾ pound fresh baby spinach
- 7-ounce ham, sliced
- Salt and black pepper, to taste
- 1 tablespoon unsalted butter, melted

Directions
1. Preheat the oven to 360 degrees and grease 2 ramekins with butter.
2. Put butter and spinach in a skillet and cook for about 3 minutes.
3. Add cooked spinach in the ramekins and top with ham slices, cream, salt and black pepper.
4. Bake for about 25 minutes and dish out to serve hot.
5. For meal prepping, you can refrigerate this ham spinach ballet for about 3 days wrapped in a foil.
Nutrition
Calories per serving: 188 Fat: 12.5g Carbs: 4.9g Protein: 14.6g Sugar: 0.3g

Creamy Parsley Soufflé

Serves: 2/Prep Time: 25 mins
Ingredients
- 2 fresh red chili peppers, chopped
- Salt, to taste
- 4 eggs
- 4 tablespoons light cream
- 2 tablespoons fresh parsley, chopped

Directions
1. Preheat the oven to 375 degrees and grease 2 soufflé dishes.
2. Combine all the ingredients in a bowl and mix well.
3. Put the mixture into prepared soufflé dishes and transfer in the oven.
4. Cook for about 6 minutes and dish out to serve immediately.
5. For meal prepping, you can refrigerate this creamy parsley soufflé in the ramekins covered in a foil for about 2-3 days.
Nutrition
Calories per serving: 108 Fat: 9g Carbs: 1.1g Protein: 6g Sugar: 0.5g

Vegetarian Three Cheese Quiche Stuffed Peppers

Serves: 2/Prep Time: 50 mins
Ingredients
- 2 large eggs
- ¼ cup mozzarella, shredded
- 1 medium bell peppers, sliced in half and seeds removed
- ¼ cup ricotta cheese
- ¼ cup grated Parmesan cheese
- ½ teaspoon garlic powder
- 1/8 cup baby spinach leaves
- ¼ teaspoon dried parsley
- 1 tablespoon Parmesan cheese, to garnish

Directions
1. Preheat oven to 375 degrees.
2. Blend all the cheeses, eggs, garlic powder and parsley in a food processor and process until smooth.
3. Pour the cheese mixture into each sliced bell pepper and top with spinach leaves.
4. Stir with a fork, pushing spinach leaves under the cheese mixture and cover with foil.
5. Bake for about 40 minutes and sprinkle with Parmesan cheese.
6. Broil for about 5 minutes and dish out to serve.
Nutrition
Calories: 157 Carbs: 7.3g Fats: 9g Proteins: 12.7g Sodium: 166mg Sugar: 3.7g

Avocado Baked Eggs

Serves: 2
Prep Time: 25 mins

Ingredients

- 2 eggs
- 1 medium sized avocado, halved and pit removed
- ¼ cup cheddar cheese, shredded
- Kosher salt and black pepper, to taste

Directions

1. Preheat oven to 425 degrees and grease a muffin pan.
2. Place avocado halves in muffin tins.
3. Crack open an egg into each half of the avocado and season with salt and black pepper.
4. Top with cheddar cheese and transfer the muffin pan in the oven.
5. Bake for about 15 minutes and dish out to serve.

Nutrition

Calories: 210 Carbs: 6.4g Fats: 16.6g Proteins: 10.7g Sodium: 151mg Sugar: 2.2g

Quick Keto McMuffins

Serves: 2/Prep Time: 15 mins

Ingredients

Muffins:

- ¼ cup flax meal
- ¼ cup almond flour
- ¼ teaspoon baking soda
- 1 large egg
- 2 tablespoons water
- 1 pinch salt
- 2 tablespoons heavy whipping cream
- ¼ cup cheddar cheese, grated

Filling:

- 2 slices cheddar cheese
- Salt and black pepper, to taste
- 2 large eggs
- 2 tablespoons butter
- 1 teaspoon Dijon mustard

Directions

1. **For Muffins:** Mix together all the dry ingredients for muffins in a small bowl and add egg, cream, cheese and water.
2. Combine well and pour in 2 single-serving ramekins.
3. Microwave on high for about 90 seconds.
4. **For Filling:** Fry the eggs and season with salt and black pepper.
5. Cut the muffins in half and spread butter on the inside of each half.
6. Top each buttered half with cheese slices, eggs and Dijon mustard.
7. Serve immediately.

Nutrition

Calories: 299 Carbs: 8.8g Fats: 24.3g Proteins: 13g Sodium: 376mg Sugar: 0.4g

Cheesy Thyme Waffles

Serves: 2
Prep Time: 15 mins

Ingredients

- ½ cup mozzarella cheese, finely shredded
- ¼ cup Parmesan cheese
- ¼ large head cauliflower
- ½ cup collard greens
- 1 large egg
- 1 stalk green onion
- ½ tablespoon olive oil
- ½ teaspoon garlic powder
- ¼ teaspoon salt
- ½ tablespoon sesame seed
- 1 teaspoon fresh thyme, chopped
- ¼ teaspoon ground black pepper

Directions

1. Put cauliflower, collard greens, spring onion and thyme in a food processor and pulse until smooth.
2. Dish out the mixture in a bowl and stir in rest of the ingredients.
3. Heat a waffle iron and transfer the mixture evenly over the griddle.
4. Cook until a waffle is formed and dish out in a serving platter.

Nutrition

Calories: 144 Carbs: 8.5g Fats: 9.4g Proteins: 9.3g Sodium: 435mg Sugar: 3g

Low Carb Green Smoothie

Serves: 2/Prep Time: 15 mins

Ingredients

- 1/3 cup romaine lettuce
- 1/3 tablespoon fresh ginger, peeled and chopped
- 1½ cups filtered water
- 1/8 cup fresh pineapple, chopped
- ¾ tablespoon fresh parsley
- 1/3 cup raw cucumber, peeled and sliced
- ¼ Hass avocado
- ¼ cup kiwi fruit, peeled and chopped
- 1/3 tablespoon Swerve

Directions

1. Put all the ingredients in a blender and blend until smooth.
2. Pour into 2 serving glasses and serve chilled.

Nutrition
Calories: 108 Carbs: 7.8g Fats: 8.9g Proteins: 1.6g Sodium: 4mg Sugar: 2.2g

Lunch Recipes

Salmon Stew

Serves: 2
Prep Time: 20 mins
Ingredients
- 1-pound salmon fillet, sliced
- 1 onion, chopped
- Salt, to taste
- 1 tablespoon butter, melted
- 1 cup fish broth
- ½ teaspoon red chili powder

Directions
1. Season the salmon fillets with salt and red chili powder.
2. Put butter and onions in a skillet and sauté for about 3 minutes.
3. Add seasoned salmon and cook for about 2 minutes on each side.
4. Add fish broth and secure the lid.
5. Cook for about 7 minutes on medium heat and open the lid.
6. Dish out and serve immediately.
7. Transfer the stew in a bowl and set aside to cool for meal prepping. Divide the mixture into 2 containers. Cover the containers and refrigerate for about 2 days. Reheat in the microwave before serving.

Nutrition
Calories per serving: 272 Carbs: 4.4g Protein: 32.1g Fat: 14.2g Sugar: 1.9g

Asparagus Salmon Fillets

Serves: 2
Prep Time: 30 mins
Ingredients
- 1 teaspoon olive oil
- 4 asparagus stalks
- 2 salmon fillets
- ¼ cup butter
- ¼ cup champagne
- Salt and freshly ground black pepper, to taste

Directions
1. Preheat the oven to 355 degrees and grease a baking dish.
2. Put all the ingredients in a bowl and mix well.
3. Put this mixture in the baking dish and transfer it to the oven.
4. Bake for about 20 minutes and dish out.
5. Place the salmon fillets in a dish and set aside to cool for meal prepping. Divide it into 2 containers and close the lid. Refrigerate for 1 day and reheat in microwave before serving.

Nutrition
Calories per serving: 475 Carbs: 1.1g Protein: 35.2g Fat: 36.8g Sugar: 0.5g Sodium: 242mg

Crispy Baked Chicken

Serves: 2
Prep Time: 40 mins
Ingredients
- 2 chicken breasts, skinless and boneless
- 2 tablespoons butter
- ¼ teaspoon turmeric powder
- Salt and black pepper, to taste
- ¼ cup sour cream

Directions
1. Preheat the oven to 360 degrees and grease a baking dish with butter.
2. Season the chicken with turmeric powder, salt and black pepper in a bowl.
3. Put the chicken on the baking dish and transfer it to the oven.
4. Bake for about 10 minutes and dish out to serve topped with sour cream.
5. Transfer the chicken in a bowl and set aside to cool for meal prepping. Divide it into 2 containers and cover the containers. Refrigerate for up to 2 days and reheat in microwave before serving.

Nutrition
Calories per serving: 304 Carbs: 1.4g Protein: 26.1g Fat: 21.6g Sugar: 0.1g Sodium: 137mg

Sour and Sweet Fish

Serves: 2/Prep Time: 25 mins

Ingredients
- 1 tablespoon vinegar
- 2 drops stevia
- 1 pound fish chunks
- ¼ cup butter, melted
- Salt and black pepper, to taste

Directions
1. Put butter and fish chunks in a skillet and cook for about 3 minutes.
2. Add stevia, salt and black pepper and cook for about 10 minutes, stirring continuously.
3. Dish out in a bowl and serve immediately.
4. Place fish in a dish and set aside to cool for meal prepping. Divide it in 2 containers and refrigerate for up to 2 days. Reheat in microwave before serving.

Nutrition
Calories per serving: 258 Carbs: 2.8g Protein: 24.5g Fat: 16.7g Sugar: 2.7g Sodium: 649mg

Creamy Chicken

Serves: 2/Prep Time: 25 mins

Ingredients
- ½ small onion, chopped
- ¼ cup sour cream
- 1 tablespoon butter
- ¼ cup mushrooms
- ½ pound chicken breasts

Directions
1. Heat butter in a skillet and add onions and mushrooms.
2. Sauté for about 5 minutes and add chicken breasts and salt.
3. Secure the lid and cook for about 5 more minutes.
4. Add sour cream and cook for about 3 minutes.
5. Open the lid and dish out in a bowl to serve immediately.
6. Transfer the creamy chicken breasts in a dish and set aside to cool for meal prepping. Divide them in 2 containers and cover their lid. Refrigerate for 2-3 days and reheat in microwave before serving.

Nutrition
Calories per serving: 335 Carbs: 2.9g Protein: 34g Fat: 20.2g Sugar: 0.8g Sodium: 154mg

Paprika Butter Shrimp

Serves: 2/Prep Time: 30 mins

Ingredients
- ¼ tablespoon smoked paprika
- 1/8 cup sour cream
- ½ pound shrimp
- 1/8 cup butter
- Salt and black pepper, to taste

Directions
1. Preheat the oven to 390 degrees and grease a baking dish.
2. Mix together all the ingredients in a large bowl and transfer into the baking dish.
3. Place in the oven and bake for about 15 minutes.
4. Place paprika shrimp in a dish and set aside to cool for meal prepping. Divide it in 2 containers and cover the lid. Refrigerate for 1-2 days and reheat in microwave before serving.

Nutrition
Calories per serving: 330 Carbs: 1.5g Protein: 32.6g Fat: 21.5g Sugar: 0.2g Sodium: 458mg

Bacon Wrapped Asparagus

Serves: 2/Prep Time: 30 mins

Ingredients
- 1/3 cup heavy whipping cream
- 2 bacon slices, precooked
- 4 small spears asparagus
- Salt, to taste
- 1 tablespoon butter

Directions
1. Preheat the oven to 360 degrees and grease a baking sheet with butter.
2. Meanwhile, mix cream, asparagus and salt in a bowl.
3. Wrap the asparagus in bacon slices and arrange them in the baking dish.
4. Transfer the baking dish to the oven and bake for about 20 minutes.
5. Remove from the oven and serve hot.
6. Place the bacon wrapped asparagus in a dish and set aside to cool for meal prepping. Divide it in 2 containers and cover the lid. Refrigerate for about 2 days and reheat in the microwave before serving.

Nutrition
Calories per serving: 204 Carbs: 1.4g Protein: 5.9g Fat: 19.3g Sugar: 0.5g

Spinach Chicken

Serves: 2/Prep Time: 20 mins
Ingredients
- 2 garlic cloves, minced
- 2 tablespoons unsalted butter, divided
- ¼ cup parmesan cheese, shredded
- ¾ pound chicken tenders
- ¼ cup heavy cream
- 10 ounces frozen spinach, chopped
- Salt and black pepper, to taste

Directions
1. Heat 1 tablespoon of butter in a large skillet and add chicken, salt and black pepper.
2. Cook for about 3 minutes on both sides and remove the chicken to a bowl.
3. Melt remaining butter in the skillet and add garlic, cheese, heavy cream and spinach.
4. Cook for about 2 minutes and add the chicken.
5. Cook for about 5 minutes on low heat and dish out to immediately serve.
6. Place chicken in a dish and set aside to cool for meal prepping. Divide it in 2 containers and cover them. Refrigerate for about 3 days and reheat in microwave before serving.

Nutrition Calories per serving: 288 Carbs: 3.6g Protein: 27.7g Fat: 18.3g Sugar: 0.3g

Lemongrass Prawns

Serves: 2/Prep Time: 25 mins
Ingredients
- ½ red chili pepper, seeded and chopped
- 2 lemongrass stalks
- ½ pound prawns, deveined and peeled
- 6 tablespoons butter
- ¼ teaspoon smoked paprika

Directions
1. Preheat the oven to 390 degrees and grease a baking dish.
2. Mix together red chili pepper, butter, smoked paprika and prawns in a bowl.
3. Marinate for about 2 hours and then thread the prawns on the lemongrass stalks.
4. Arrange the threaded prawns on the baking dish and transfer it in the oven.
5. Bake for about 15 minutes and dish out to serve immediately.
6. Place the prawns in a dish and set aside to cool for meal prepping. Divide it in 2 containers and close the lid. Refrigerate for about 4 days and reheat in microwave before serving.

Nutrition Calories per serving: 322 Carbs: 3.8g Protein: 34.8g Fat: 18g Sugar: 0.1g Sodium: 478mg

Stuffed Mushrooms

Serves: 2/Prep Time: 45 mins
Ingredients
- 2 ounces bacon, crumbled
- ½ tablespoon butter
- ¼ teaspoon paprika powder
- 2 portobello mushrooms
- 1 oz cream cheese
- ¾ tablespoon fresh chives, chopped
- Salt and black pepper, to taste

Directions
1. Preheat the oven to 400 degrees and grease a baking dish.
2. Heat butter in a skillet and add mushrooms.
3. Sauté for about 4 minutes and set aside.
4. Mix together cream cheese, chives, paprika powder, salt and black pepper in a bowl.
5. Stuff the mushrooms with this mixture and transfer on the baking dish.
6. Place in the oven and bake for about 20 minutes.
7. These mushrooms can be refrigerated for about 3 days for meal prepping and can be served with scrambled eggs.

Nutrition Calories per serving: 570 Carbs: 4.6g Protein: 19.9g Fat: 52.8g Sugar: 0.8g Sodium: 1041mg

Honey Glazed Chicken Drumsticks

Serves: 2/Prep Time: 30 mins
Ingredients
- ½ tablespoon fresh thyme, minced
- 1/8 cup Dijon mustard
- ½ tablespoon fresh rosemary, minced
- ½ tablespoon honey
- 2 chicken drumsticks
- 1 tablespoon olive oil
- Salt and black pepper, to taste

Directions
1. Preheat the oven at 325 degrees and grease a baking dish.
2. Combine all the ingredients in a bowl except the drumsticks and mix well.
3. Add drumsticks and coat generously with the mixture.

4. Cover and refrigerate to marinate overnight.
5. Place the drumsticks in in the baking dish and transfer it in the oven.
6. Cook for about 20 minutes and dish out to immediately serve.
7. Place chicken drumsticks in a dish and set aside to cool for meal prepping. Divide it in 2 containers and cover them. Refrigerate for about 3 days and reheat in microwave before serving.

Nutrition Calories per serving: 301 Carbs: 6g Fats: 19.7g Proteins: 4.5g Sugar: 4.5g Sodium: 316mg

Keto Zucchini Pizza

Serves: 2/Prep Time: 15 mins
Ingredients
- 1/8 cup spaghetti sauce
- ½ zucchini, cut in circular slices
- ½ cup cream cheese
- Pepperoni slices, for topping
- ½ cup mozzarella cheese, shredded

Directions
1. Preheat the oven to 350 degrees and grease a baking dish.
2. Arrange the zucchini on the baking dish and layer with spaghetti sauce.
3. Top with pepperoni slices and mozzarella cheese.
4. Transfer the baking dish to the oven and bake for about 15 minutes.
5. Remove from the oven and serve immediately.

Nutrition Calories per serving: 445 Carbs: 3.6g Protein: 12.8g Fat: 42g Sugar: 0.3g Sodium: 429mg

Omega-3 Salad

Serves: 2/Prep Time: 15 mins
Ingredients
- ½ pound skinless salmon fillet, cut into 4 steaks
- ¼ tablespoon fresh lime juice
- 1 tablespoon olive oil, divided
- 4 tablespoons sour cream
- ¼ zucchini, cut into small cubes
- ¼ teaspoon jalapeño pepper, seeded and chopped finely
- Salt and black pepper, to taste
- ¼ tablespoon fresh dill, chopped

Directions
1. Put olive oil and salmon in a skillet and cook for about 5 minutes on both sides.
2. Season with salt and black pepper, stirring well and dish out.
3. Mix remaining ingredients in a bowl and add cooked salmon to serve.

Nutrition Calories per serving: 291 Fat: 21.1g Carbs: 2.5g Protein: 23.1g Sugar: 0.6g Sodium: 112mg

Crab Cakes

Serves: 2/Prep Time: 30 mins
Ingredients
- ½ pound lump crabmeat, drained
- 2 tablespoons coconut flour
- 1 tablespoon mayonnaise
- ¼ teaspoon green Tabasco sauce
- 3 tablespoons butter
- 1 small egg, beaten
- ¾ tablespoon fresh parsley, chopped
- ½ teaspoon yellow mustard
- Salt and black pepper, to taste

Directions
1. Mix together all the ingredients in a bowl except butter.
2. Make patties from this mixture and set aside.
3. Heat butter in a skillet over medium heat and add patties.
4. Cook for about 10 minutes on each side and dish out to serve hot.
5. You can store the raw patties in the freezer for about 3 weeks for meal prepping. Place patties in a container and place parchment paper in between the patties to avoid stickiness.

Nutrition Calories per serving: 153 Fat: 10.8g Carbs: 6.7g Protein: 6.4g Sugar: 2.4 Sodium: 46mg

Salmon Burgers

Serves: 2/Prep Time: 20 mins
Ingredients
- 1 tablespoon sugar-free ranch dressing
- ½-ounce smoked salmon, chopped roughly
- ½ tablespoon fresh parsley, chopped
- ½ tablespoon avocado oil
- 1 small egg
- 4-ounce pink salmon, drained and bones removed
- 1/8 cup almond flour
- ¼ teaspoon Cajun seasoning

Directions
1. Mix together all the ingredients in a bowl and stir well.
2. Make patties from this mixture and set aside.
3. Heat a skillet over medium heat and add patties.

4. Cook for about 3 minutes per side and dish out to serve.
5. You can store the raw patties in the freezer for about 3 weeks for meal prepping. Place patties in a container and place parchment paper in between the patties to avoid stickiness.

Nutrition Calories per serving: 59 Fat: 12.7g Carbs: 2.4g Protein: 6.3g Sugar: 0.7g Sodium: 25mg

Burrito Bowl

Serves: 2/Prep Time: 40 mins
Ingredients
For Chicken:
- 1 tablespoon olive oil
- Salt and black pepper, to taste
- ½ pound grass-fed skinless, boneless chicken breasts
- 1/8 cup fresh lime juice

- ¼ cup fresh cilantro, chopped
- 1 teaspoon garlic, minced

For Cauliflower Rice:
- 1½ cups cauliflower rice
- 1 tablespoon olive oil
- 1 teaspoon garlic powder
- Salt, to taste

- 1/8 cup yellow onion, sliced thinly
- ½ teaspoon ground cumin
- ¼ cup carrot, peeled and shredded

Directions
For Chicken:
Put oil, garlic, chicken, salt and black pepper in a large skillet and cook for about 8 minutes each side.
1. Remove it from heat and allow it to cool down, shredding chicken lightly.
2. Mix together rest of the ingredients in a bowl and add chicken, tossing well.
For Cauliflower Rice:
3. Put oil, cumin and onions in a large skillet and sauté for about 3 minutes.
4. Add cauliflower rice, garlic powder and salt and cook for about 5 minutes.
5. Stir in carrots and remove from heat to cool down.
6. Combine chicken and cauliflower rice in a serving bowl and serve.
7. You can store both chicken and cauliflower rice in separate containers up to 5 days for meal prepping. Reheat before serving it.

Nutrition Calories per serving: 303 Fat: 18.3g Carbs: 8.8g Protein: 27.6g Sugar: 3.4g Sodium: 135mg

Chicken Meal

Serves: 2/Prep Time: 35 mins
Ingredients
- ½ medium zucchini, chopped
- ½ small yellow onion, chopped
- 1 (6-ounce) skinless, boneless chicken breasts, cut into ½-inch pieces
- ½ cup fresh broccoli florets

- 1 garlic clove, minced
- ¼ teaspoon paprika
- 1 tablespoon olive oil
- ½ teaspoon Italian seasoning
- Salt and black pepper, to taste

Directions
1. Preheat the oven to 450 degree and line a baking dish with foil.
2. Put all the ingredients in a bowl and toss to coat well.
3. Place the chicken mixture in the baking dish and transfer to the oven.
4. Bake for about 20 minutes and dish out to serve hot.
5. For meal prepping, cool the mixture and wrap it with plastic wrap. Refrigerate for up to 5 days.

Nutrition Calories per serving: 195 Fat: 10.6g Carbs: 5.6g Protein: 20.5g Sugar: 2.1g Sodium: 134mg

Tangy Chicken

Serves: 2/Prep Time: 25 mins
Ingredients
- ¾ pound skinless, boneless chicken thighs
- 1/8 cup onion, chopped finely
- 1 tablespoon unsalted butter, divided
- Freshly ground black pepper, to taste
- ½ cup chicken broth

- ½ tablespoon fresh lemon juice
- 1 tablespoon maple syrup
- 1 tablespoon fresh ginger, minced
- ½ cup fresh cranberries

Directions
1. Put butter, chicken, salt and black pepper in a large skillet and cook for about 5 minutes per side.
2. Dish out the chicken in a bowl and wrap it with foil to keep it warm.
3. Put onions, ginger and lemon juice in the same skillet and sauté for about 4 minutes.
4. Stir in broth and bring it to boil while continuously stirring.
5. Add cranberries and cook for about 5 minutes.
6. Stir in maple syrup and black pepper and cook for about 2 minutes.
7. Unwrap the chicken and pour this mixture over it.

8. Serve hot.
9. For meal prepping, you can store this cranberry mixture for 2 days and reheat in microwave when you want to use it again.

Nutrition
Calories per serving: 199 Fat: 8g Carbs: 4.2g Protein: 25.9g Sugar: 1.4g Sodium: 78mg

Garlic and Chive Cauliflower Mash

Serves: 2/Prep Time: 25 mins
Ingredients
- 1/6 cup avocado mayonnaise
- ½ tablespoon water

- ½ clove garlic, peeled
- ¼ teaspoon Kosher salt
- 1/8 teaspoon lemon juice

- 2 pinches black pepper
- 2 cups cauliflower florets

- ½ tablespoon fresh chives, chopped
- ¼ teaspoon lemon zest

Directions
1. Mix together cauliflower, avocado mayonnaise, water, garlic, salt and black pepper in a large microwave safe bowl.
2. Microwave on high for about 15 minutes and transfer the cooked mixture to a food processor.
3. Puree until smooth and add lemon juice, zest and chives.
4. Pulse until combined and dish out on a platter to serve.

Nutrition Calories: 160 Carbs: 5.7g Fats: 16.1g Proteins: 2.1g Sodium: 474mg Sugar: 2.4g

Spinach & Artichoke Dip Cauliflower Casserole

Serves: 2/Prep Time: 45 mins
Ingredients
- 4 tablespoons butter
- 2 oz full fat cream cheese
- 2 pinches ground nutmeg
- 1/8 teaspoon smoked paprika
- ¼ cup frozen artichoke hearts, drained and chopped
- 1 cup raw cauliflower florets, roughly chopped

- 1/8 cup Silk Cashew Milk, unsweetened
- Kosher salt and black pepper, to taste
- 1/8 teaspoon garlic powder
- ¼ cup frozen spinach, chopped
- ½ cup whole milk mozzarella cheese, shredded
- 1/8 cup parmesan cheese, grated

Directions
1. Preheat the oven to 400 degrees F and grease a casserole.
2. Mix together the cauliflower, Silk Cashew Milk, butter, cream cheese, nutmeg, garlic powder, salt, black pepper and paprika in a microwave safe dish.
3. Microwave for 10 minutes on high and add spinach, artichoke hearts, half of the mozzarella cheese and parmesan cheese.
4. Stir well and dish out the mixture in an ovenproof casserole dish.
5. Sprinkle the remaining mozzarella cheese over the top and transfer in the oven.
6. Bake for about 20 minutes at 400 degrees F and dish out to serve hot.

Nutrition Calories: 357 Carbs: 6.8g Fats: 34.2g Proteins: 8.9g Sodium: 697mg Sugar: 2.7g

Zucchini and Sweet Potato Latkes

Serves: 4/Prep Time: 5 mins
Ingredients
- 1 cup shredded zucchini
- 1 cup shredded sweet potato
- 1 egg, beaten
- 1 Tbsp coconut flour
- 1/2 tsp garlic powder

- 1/4 tsp ground cumin
- 1/2 tsp dried parsley
- Salt & pepper to taste
- 1 Tbsp butter
- 1 Tbsp EV olive oil

Directions
1. Combine the zucchini, sweet potato and egg in a medium bowl.
2. In a small bowl, mix the coconut flour and spices together. Add the dry ingredients to the zucchini mixture and stir until fully combined.
3. Heat the butter and olive oil in a medium nonstick pan. Divide the mixture into four equal portions and drop into the pan, pressing down with a fork until a 1/2-inch-thick cake is formed. Cook on medium heat until golden and crisp, then flip carefully and cook the other side. Remove to a plate lined with paper towels to drain.
4. Season with an additional sprinkle of kosher salt. Serve hot.

Nutrition
Calories: 109 Carbs: 6.2g Fats: 9.6g Proteins: 0.9g Sodium: 227mg Sugar: 1.8g

Cheesy Spaghetti Squash with Pesto

Serves: 2
Prep Time: 25 mins
Ingredients
- ½ tablespoon olive oil
- 1/8 cup basil pesto
- 1 cup cooked spaghetti squash, drained
- ¼ cup whole milk ricotta cheese
- Salt and black pepper, to taste
- 2 oz fresh mozzarella cheese, cubed

Directions
1. Preheat the oven to 375 degrees and grease a casserole dish.
2. Mix together squash and olive oil in a medium-sized bowl and season with salt and black pepper.
3. Put the squash in the casserole dish and top with ricotta and mozzarella cheese.
4. Bake for about 10 minutes and remove from the oven.
5. Drizzle the pesto over the top and serve hot.

Nutrition Calories: 169 Carbs: 6.2g Fats: 11.3g Proteins: 11.9g Sodium: 217mg Sugar: 0.1g

Cheesy Spinach Puffs

Serves: 2
Prep Time: 25 mins
Ingredients
- ½ cup almond flour
- 1 large egg
- ¼ cup feta cheese, crumbled
- ½ teaspoon kosher salt
- ½ teaspoon garlic powder
- 1½ tablespoons heavy whipping cream

Directions
1. Preheat the oven to 350 degrees and grease a cookie sheet.
2. Put all the ingredients in a blender and pulse until smooth.
3. Allow to cool down and form 1-inch balls from this mixture.
4. Arrange on a cookie sheet and transfer into the oven.
5. Bake for about 12 minutes and dish out to serve,

Nutrition Calories: 294 Carbs: 7.8 Fats: 24g Proteins: 12.2g Sodium: 840mg Sugar: 1.1g

Dinner Recipes

Luncheon Fancy Salad

Serves: 2
Prep Time: 40 mins
Ingredients
- 6-ounce cooked salmon, chopped
- 1 tablespoon fresh dill, chopped
- Salt and black pepper, to taste
- 4 hard-boiled eggs, peeled and cubed
- 2 celery stalks, chopped
- ½ yellow onion, chopped
- ¾ cup avocado mayonnaise

Directions
1. Put all the ingredients in a bowl and mix until well combined.
2. Cover with a plastic wrap and refrigerate for about 3 hours to serve.
3. For meal prepping, put the salad in a container and refrigerate for up to 3 days.

Nutrition
Calories per serving: 303 Carbs: 1.7g Protein: 10.3g Fat: 30g Sugar: 1g Sodium: 314mg

Cheese Casserole

Serves: 2
Prep Time: 46 mins
Ingredients
- 2½ ounce marinara sauce
- ½ tablespoon olive oil
- 4 ounces parmesan cheese, shredded
- ½ pound sausages, scrambled
- 4 ounces mozzarella cheese, shredded

Directions
1. Preheat the oven to 375 degrees and grease a baking dish with olive oil.
2. Place half of the sausage scramble in it and top with half of marinara sauce, mozzarella cheese and parmesan cheese.
3. Place the remaining sausage scramble in the baking dish and top again with marinara sauce, mozzarella cheese and parmesan cheese.
4. Transfer to the oven and bake for about 20 minutes.

5. Place the casserole in a dish and set aside to cool for meal prepping. Divide it in 6 containers and refrigerate for 1-2 days. Reheat in microwave before serving.

Nutrition

Calories per serving: 353 Carbs: 5.5g Protein: 28.4g Fat: 24.3g Sugar: 5g Sodium: 902mg

Air Fried Simple Steak

Serves: 2
Prep Time: 15 mins
Ingredients
- ½ pound quality cut steaks
- Salt and black pepper, to taste

Directions
1. Preheat the Air fryer to 385 degrees.
2. Rub the steaks evenly with salt and black pepper.
3. Place the steak in an Air fryer basket and cook for about 15 minutes.
4. Dish out and serve immediately.
5. Divide the steaks in 2 containers and refrigerate for about 3 days for meal prepping purpose. Reheat in microwave before serving.

Nutrition

Calories per serving: 301 Carbs: 0g Fats: 25.1g Proteins: 19.1 Sugar: 0g

Creamy Turkey Breasts

Serves: 2
Prep Time: 1 hour
Ingredients
- ¼ cup sour cream
- ¼ cup butter
- Salt and black pepper, to taste
- ¾ pound turkey breasts
- ½ cup heavy whipping cream
- 2 garlic cloves, minced

Directions
1. Preheat the oven to 390 degrees F and grease the baking dish with some butter.
2. Marinate the turkey breasts with butter, garlic, salt and black pepper in a bowl.
3. Place the marinated turkey breasts on a baking dish and top with heavy whipping cream and sour cream.
4. Bake for about 45 minutes and dish out in a platter.
5. For meal prepping, place the creamy turkey breasts on a dish and keep aside to cool. Divide it in 2 containers and refrigerate for about 2 days. Reheat in microwave before serving.

Nutrition

Calories per serving: 304 Carbs: 4.8g Protein: 20.3g Fat: 23.1g Sugar: 4.1g Sodium: 246mg Sodium: 315mg

Chicken Wraps

Serves: 2/Prep Time: 45 mins
Ingredients
- ¼ pound lean ground chicken
- ¼ green bell pepper, seeded and chopped
- 1/8 cup yellow squash, chopped
- ½ tablespoon low-sodium soy sauce
- Freshly ground black pepper, to taste
- ½ cup Parmesan cheese, shredded
- ½ tablespoon unsalted butter
- ¼ onion, chopped
- 1 garlic clove, minced
- ¼ cup carrot, peeled and chopped
- 1/8 cup zucchini, chopped
- ¼ teaspoon curry powder
- 2 large lettuce leaves

Directions
1. Put butter and chicken in a skillet and cook for about 5 minutes.
2. Break the lumps and stir in the vegetables.
3. Cook for about 5 minutes and add curry powder, soy sauce and black pepper.
4. Cook for 5 more minutes and set aside.
5. Arrange the lettuce leaves in serving plates and place chicken mixture over them.
6. Sprinkle with cheese and serve.
7. You must place the mixture on the leaves evenly for meal prepping purpose. You can refrigerate it in a container for about 2 days.

Nutrition

Calories per serving: 71 Fat: 6.7g Carbs: 4.2g Protein: 4.8g Sugar: 30.5g Sodium: 142mg

Tofu in Purgatory

Serves: 2
Prep Time: 25 mins

Ingredients
- 4 large garlic cloves
- Salt and black pepper, to taste

- 2 teaspoons dried herbs
- 1 block medium tofu, not pressed and cut into rounds

- 1 tablespoon olive oil
- 1 can diced tomatoes

- ½ teaspoon dried chili flakes

Directions
1. Heat olive oil in a skillet over medium heat and add garlic.
2. Sauté for about 1 minute and add tomatoes, chili flakes, herbs, salt and black pepper.
3. Simmer for about 5 minutes over a medium heat and add the tofu.
4. Reduce the heat to medium-low and simmer for about 15 minutes.
5. Dish out and serve with a baguette.

Nutrition Calories: 123 Carbs: 8.3g Fats: 8.9gProteins: 4.8g Sodium: 10mg Sugar: 1.3g

Four Cheese Pesto Zoodles

Serves: 2/Prep Time: 20 mins
Ingredients
- 1/8 cup parmesan cheese, grated
- ¼ teaspoon kosher salt
- 2 pinches ground nutmeg
- ½ cup mozzarella cheese, grated
- 4 ounces Mascarpone cheese

- 1/8 cup Romano cheese, grated
- ½ teaspoon ground black pepper
- 1/8 cup basil pesto
- 4 cups raw zucchini noodles

Directions
1. Preheat the oven to 400 degrees and grease a casserole dish.
2. Microwave the zucchini noodles for 3 minutes on high and keep aside.
3. Mix together the parmesan cheese, mascarpone cheese, Romano cheese, nutmeg, salt and black pepper in a large microwave safe bowl.
4. Microwave for 1 minute on high and whisk together until smooth.
5. Fold in the basil pesto, mozzarella cheese and cooked zoodles.
6. Transfer to a casserole dish and place in the oven.
7. Bake for about 10 minutes and serve immediately.

Nutrition Calories: 139 Carbs: 3.3g Fats: 9.7g Proteins: 10.2g Sodium: 419mg Sugar: 0.2g

Roasted Baby Eggplant with Ricotta

Serves: 2/Prep Time: 45 mins
Ingredients
- ¼ tablespoon olive oil
- 1 eggplant, halved
- ¼ teaspoon Wild Fennel Pollen

To serve:
- 1/8 cup ricotta cheese
- Sea salt and black pepper, to taste

- ¼ teaspoon black pepper
- ¼ teaspoon sea salt

- ¼ tablespoon extra-virgin olive oil

Directions
1. Preheat the oven to 350 degrees and grease a cookie sheet.
2. Place the eggplant halves on a cookie sheet, cut side up and top with olive oil, fennel pollen, salt and black pepper.
3. Transfer in the oven and bake for about 45 minutes, until lightly browned.
4. Remove from the oven and allow to cool slightly.
5. Serve warm topped with ricotta cheese, olive oil, salt and black pepper.

Nutrition Calories: 69 Carbs: 3.4g Fats: 5.5g Proteins: 2.4g Sodium: 247mg Sugar: 1.6g

Moroccan Roasted Green Beans

Serves: 2/Prep Time: 45 mins
Ingredients
- 1/3 teaspoon kosher salt
- 2 cups raw green beans, trimmed
- ¼ teaspoon ground black pepper

- 2 tablespoons olive oil
- 1/3 tablespoon seasonings

Directions
1. Preheat the oven to 400 degrees and grease a roasting pan.
2. Mix together green beans, olive oil and seasonings in a bowl and transfer into the roasting pan.
3. Roast for about 20 minutes and remove from the oven.
4. Return to the oven and roast for another 10 minutes.

5. Dish out and serve warm.
Nutrition Calories: 160 Carbs: 8.5g Fats: 14.1g Proteins: 2g Sodium: 437mg Sugar: 1.5g

Spinach Artichoke Stuffed Portobello

Serves: 8
Prep Time: 30 mins
Ingredients
- 1 medium portobello mushroom, stems and gills removed
- ¼ can artichoke hearts drained and chopped, 14 ounce can
- ½ tablespoon sour cream
- 1 clove garlic, chopped
- ½ tablespoon olive oil
- ¼ package (10 ounces) frozen spinach, chopped, cooked and drained
- 1-ounce cream cheese
- ¼ cup Parmesan cheese, grated
- Salt and black pepper, to taste
- ¾-ounce mozzarella cheese, shredded

Directions
1. Preheat the oven to 375 degrees and line a baking pan with foil.
2. Brush the mushrooms with olive oil and transfer to baking pan.
3. Broil for about 5 minutes each side and dish out.
4. Mix together the spinach, cream cheese, artichoke, sour cream, garlic, Parmesan cheese, salt and black pepper until well combined.
5. Stuff each mushroom cap with the spinach mixture and sprinkle with mozzarella cheese.
6. Transfer into the oven and bake for about 12 minutes.
7. Dish out and serve warm.
Nutrition Calories: 143 Carbs: 4g Fats: 11.9g Proteins: 6.8g Sodium: 218mg Sugar: 0.5g

Grilled Halloumi Bruschetta

Serves: 2
Prep Time: 20 mins
Ingredients
- 2 tablespoons fresh basil, chopped
- ½ tablespoon olive oil
- 1/3 medium tomatoes, chopped
- ½ clove garlic, minced
- Salt and black pepper, to taste
- 1½-ounce package Halloumi cheese, sliced

Directions
1. Mix together tomatoes, basil, garlic, olive oil, salt and black pepper in a bowl.
2. Refrigerate for about 1 hour.
3. Grill the Halloumi cheese for about 2 minutes on each side and transfer to a serving platter.
4. Top with tomato basil mixture and serve chilled.

Nutrition Calories: 84 Carbs: 1.6g Fats: 7.2g Proteins: 3.8g Sodium: 1mg Sugar:

Cheesy Ranch Roasted Broccoli

Serves: 2
Prep Time: 45 mins
Ingredients
- 1/8 cup ranch dressing
- 1½ cups broccoli florets
- ¼ cup sharp cheddar cheese, shredded
- Kosher salt and black pepper, to taste
- 1/8 cup heavy whipping cream

Directions
1. Preheat the oven to 375 degrees and grease oven proof casserole dish.
2. Mix together all the ingredients in a medium-sized bowl and transfer to the casserole dish.
3. Place in the oven and bake for about 30 minutes.
4. Dish out in a platter and serve hot.
Nutrition Calories: 111 Carbs: 5.7g Fats: 7.7g Proteins: 5.8g Sodium: 198mg Sugar: 1.6g

Easy Low-Carb Cauliflower Fried Rice

Serves: 2
Prep Time: 15 mins
Ingredients
- 6 ounces cauliflower fresh or frozen, riced
- 1 large green onion, sliced with white and green parts separated
- 1 tablespoon butter
- 1/8 cup carrots, finely diced
- 1 clove garlic, crushed
- 1 tablespoon soy sauce
- 1 small egg, beaten
- ½ teaspoon toasted sesame oil

Directions
1. Melt butter in a large heavy skillet over medium-high heat and add carrots and riced cauliflower.
2. Cook for about 5 minutes and stir in garlic and white part of the green onions.
3. Cook for about 3 minutes and whisk in the egg.
4. Cook for about 2 minutes and stir in the soy sauce, green part of green onions, and the sesame oil.
5. Dish out and serve hot.
Nutrition Calories: 123 Carbs: 7.3g Fats: 8.9g Proteins: 5g Sodium: 484mg Sugar: 2.8g

Creamy Avocado Pasta with Shirataki

Serves: 2/Prep Time: 5 mins
Ingredients
- ½ avocado
- ½ teaspoon dried basil
- ½ packet shirataki noodles
- 1/8 cup heavy cream
- ½ teaspoon black pepper
- ½ teaspoon salt

Directions
1. Boil some water and cook the shirataki for about 2 minutes.
2. Mash avocado in a bowl and add cream, basil, salt and black pepper.
3. Transfer into a blender and blend until smooth.
4. Put shirataki noodles in the frying pan and add blended mixture.
5. Cook for about 2 minutes and dish out to serve hot.
Nutrition Calories: 131 Carbs: 4.9g Fats: 12.6g Proteins: 1.2g Sodium: 588mg Sugar: 0.3g

Cheesy Broccoli & Cauliflower Rice

Serves: 2/Prep Time: 15 mins
Ingredients
- ½ cup broccoli, riced
- ¼ teaspoon kosher salt
- 1½ cups cauliflower, riced
- ½ tablespoon butter
- ¼ teaspoon ground black pepper
- Pinch of ground nutmeg
- 1/8 cup mascarpone cheese
- ¼ teaspoon garlic powder
- ¼ cup sharp cheddar cheese, shredded

Directions
1. Mix together cauliflower, butter, broccoli, garlic powder, nutmeg, salt and black pepper in a medium sized microwave safe bowl.
2. Microwave for about 5 minutes on high and add the cheddar cheese.
3. Microwave for 2 more minutes and stir in the mascarpone cheese until creamy.
4. Dish out and serve hot.
Nutrition Calories: 138 Carbs: 6.6g Fats: 9.8g Proteins: 7.5g Sodium: 442mg Sugar: 2.4g

Zucchini Noodle Alfredo

Serves: 2/Prep Time: 25 mins
Ingredients
- ½ tablespoon olive oil
- ½ pound zucchini, spiralized into noodles
- ¾ ounces cream cheese
- ¼ cup Parmesan cheese, grated
- ½ tablespoon sour cream

Directions
1. Heat olive oil in a large pan over medium heat and add zucchini noodles.
2. Sauté for about 5 minutes and add cream cheese, sour cream and Parmesan cheese.
3. Stir well and pour this mixture over noodles.
4. Dish out and serve hot.
Nutrition Calories: 103 Carbs: 4.3g Fats: 8.8g Proteins: 3.4g Sodium: 77mg Sugar: 2g

Creamy Mushroom and Cauliflower Risotto

Serves: 2
Prep Time: 5 mins
Ingredients
- 1 garlic clove, sliced
- ½ cup cream
- ½ cup cauliflower, riced
- ½ cup mushrooms, sliced
- Coconut oil
- Parmesan cheese, for topping

Directions
1. Heat coconut oil over medium-high heat in a frying pan and add garlic and mushrooms.
2. Sauté for about 4 minutes and add cauliflower and cream.
3. Simmer for about 12 minutes and dish out in a bowl.
4. Top with Parmesan cheese and serve.
Nutrition Calories: 179 Carbs: 4.4g Fats: 17.8g Proteins: 2.8g Sodium: 61mg Sugar: 2.1g

KETO SMOOTHIES

Chia Seed & Blueberry Smoothie

Yield: 4 Servings /Prep Time: 5 Minutes
Ingredients
- 1 cup unsweetened almond milk
- 1 cup full fat Greek yogurt
- 1 cup frozen blueberries
- 2 tablespoons chia seed, ground
- 1/2 cup coconut cream
- 2 tablespoons coconut oil
- 2 tablespoons Swerve
- 1 scoop protein powder, optional

Directions
Combine all ingredients in a blender and blend until very smooth. Enjoy!
Nutritional Information Per Serving
Calories: 249; Total Fat: 21.1 g; Carbs: 7.7 g; Dietary fiber: 3.5 g; Sugars: 1.9g; Protein: 16.2 g; Cholesterol: 18 mg; Sodium: 182 mg

Blackberry Avocado Chia Seed Smoothie

Yield: 1 Serving/Prep Time: 5 Minutes
Ingredients
- 1/4 avocado
- 1 1/4 cups coconut milk
- 1 teaspoon peanut butter
- 1 teaspoon chia seeds
- 1/2 cup blackberries
- 1 teaspoon Stevia
- 2 tsp unsweetened cocoa powder

Directions
Combine all ingredients in a blender and blend until very smooth. Serve topped with more chia seeds!
Nutritional Information Per Serving
Calories: 353; Total Fat: 27 g; Carbs: 7 g; Dietary fiber: 2 g; Sugars: 2.2 g; Protein: 8 g; Cholesterol: 3 mg; Sodium: 39 mg

Spiced Low Carb Coconut Milk Avocado Smoothie

Yield: 2 Servings /Prep Time: 5 Minutes
Ingredients
- 2 tablespoons fresh lemon juice
- 1/2 avocado
- 1/4 cup almond milk
- 3/4 cup full-fat coconut milk
- 1 teaspoon fresh grated ginger
- 1 scoop protein powder
- 1/2 teaspoon turmeric
- 1 cup crushed ice
- Stevia

Directions
Combine all ingredients in a blender and blend until very smooth. Enjoy!
Nutritional Information Per Serving
Calories: 208; Total Fat: 21 g; Carbs: 5 g; Dietary fiber: 1.1 g; Sugars: 2.2 g; Protein: 11.9 g; Cholesterol: 9 mg; Sodium: 3 mg

Superfood Keto Smoothie

Yield: 2 Servings /Prep Time: 5 Minutes
Ingredients
- 1 tablespoon peanut butter
- 1 tablespoon MCT Oil
- 1 cup unsweetened almond milk
- 2 teaspoons acai powder
- 2 teaspoons maca powder
- 2 teaspoons chia seeds
- 1 handful ice

Directions
Combine all ingredients in a blender and blend until very smooth. Enjoy!
Nutritional Information Per Serving
Calories: 287; Total Fat: 28.2 g; Carbs: 6.5g; Dietary fiber: 1.6 g; Sugars: 1.8 g; Protein: 11.1 g; Cholesterol: 0 mg; Sodium: 113 mg

Creamy Low-Carb Chia Seed Avocado Smoothie

Yield: 2 Servings /Prep Time: 5 Minutes
Ingredients
- 1/2 avocado
- 3/4 cup heavy cream
- 1 tablespoon almond butter
- 1 tablespoon chia seeds, soaked
- 2 scoops chocolate collagen
- 1 1/4 cup water
- 5 ice cubes

Directions
Combine all ingredients in a blender and blend until very smooth. Enjoy!
Nutritional Information Per Serving
Calories: 500; Total Fat: 49.4 g; Carbs: 7.3 g; Dietary fiber: 2.; g; Sugars: 2.2 g; Protein: 13.6 g; Cholesterol: 0 mg; Sodium: 123 mg

Creamy Peanut Butter Smoothie

Yield: 1 Serving/Prep Time: 5 Minutes
Ingredients
- 2 tablespoons peanut butter
- 3 large fresh strawberries
- 1 cup unsweetened almond milk
- 1 scoop vanilla protein powder

Directions
Combine all ingredients in a blender and blend until very smooth. Enjoy!
Nutritional Information Per Serving
Calories: 372; Total Fat: 26 g; Carbs: 12 g; Dietary fiber: 7 g; Sugars: 5 g; Protein: 15 g; Cholesterol: 4 mg; Sodium: 97 mg

Low Carb Chocolate Smoothie

Yield: 2 Servings /Prep Time: 5 Minutes
Ingredients
- 1/3 coconut yogurt
- 3 large egg yolks
- 1/4 cup cocoa powder
- 1 tablespoon tahini
- 2 scoops protein powder
- 20 drops Stevia
- 1 cup water

Directions
Combine all ingredients in a blender and blend until very smooth. Enjoy!
Nutritional Information Per Serving
Calories: 207; Total Fat: 9.4 g; Carbs: 10 g; Dietary fiber: 3.6 g; Sugars: 2.2 g; Protein: 8.1 g; Cholesterol: 78 mg; Sodium: 172 mg

Dairy-Free Coconut Chocolate Smoothie

Yield: 2 Servings /Prep Time: 5 Minutes
Ingredients
- 1/2 cup Coconut Milk
- 1 scoop vanilla protein powder
- 1/2 avocado
- 1 tablespoon dark chocolate chips
- 2 tablespoon coconut cream
- 1/8 teaspoon peppermint extract
- 8 ice cubes

Directions
Combine all ingredients in a blender and blend until very smooth. Enjoy!
Nutritional Information Per Serving
Calories: 259; Total Fat: 14.1 g; Carbs: 7.7 g; Dietary fiber: 5 g; Sugars: 2.2 g; Protein: 26.4 g; Cholesterol: 4 mg; Sodium: 256 mg

Minty Matcha Chocolate Smoothie

Yield: 2 Servings /Prep Time: 5 Minutes
Ingredients
- 3 tablespoons coconut cream
- 1 cup unsweetened almond milk
- 1 tablespoon cacao nibs
- 1/8 teaspoon mint extract
- 1/2 scoop chocolate protein powder
- 1 scoop vanilla protein powder
- 1 scoop Matcha powder
- 1/2 cup ice cubes

Directions
Combine all ingredients in a blender and blend until very smooth. Enjoy!
Nutritional Information Per Serving
Calories: 295; Total Fat: 22.8 g; Carbs: 3.7 g; Dietary fiber: 2.8 g; Sugars: 1.2 g; Protein: 22.3 g; Cholesterol: 4 mg; Sodium: 195 mg

Chocolate Avocado Smoothie

Yield: 2 Servings /Prep Time: 5 Minutes
Ingredients
- 1 cup almond milk
- 1 avocado
- 1 tablespoon cacao powder
- 1 scoop chocolate protein powder
- 1 cup ice

Directions
Combine all ingredients in a blender and blend until very smooth. Enjoy!
Nutritional Information Per Serving
Calories: 239; Total Fat: 18.9 g; Carbs: 11 g; Dietary fiber: 7 g; Sugars: 1 g; Protein: 13 g; Cholesterol: 4 mg; Sodium: 401 mg

Creamy Cucumber Smoothie

Yield: 2 Servings /Prep Time: 5 Minutes
Ingredients
- 1 cup sliced cucumber
- 1 avocado
- 2 teaspoon Match Green Tea powder
- 1 teaspoon lemon juice
- 1/2 cup heavy cream
- 1/2 cup water
- 1/2 teaspoon lemon liquid Stevia
- 1/2 cup ice

Directions
Combine all ingredients in a blender and blend until very smooth. Enjoy!
Nutritional Information Per Serving
Calories: 169; Total Fat: 14.6 g; Carbs: 6.8 g; Dietary fiber: 3.4 g; Sugars: 1.3 g; Protein: 8 g; Cholesterol: 11 mg; Sodium: 3 mg

Strawberry Cucumber Keto Smoothie

Yield: 2 Servings /Prep Time: 5 Minutes
Ingredients
- 1/2 cup cucumber, with peel
- 2 large strawberries
- 1/2 cup kale
- 1 avocado
- 1/2 cup unsweetened almond milk
- 1 teaspoon vanilla extract
- 1/2 teaspoon salt
- 1 teaspoon Stevia

Directions
Combine all ingredients in a blender and blend until very smooth. Enjoy!
Nutritional Information Per Serving
Calories: 141; Total Fat: 11.1 g; Carbs: 6.9 g; Dietary fiber: 5.5 g; Sugars: 1.9 g; Protein: 2.8 g; Cholesterol: 0 mg; Sodium: 109 mg

Keto Choco Peanut Butter Smoothie

Yield: 3 Servings /Prep Time: 5 Minutes
Ingredients
- 1 cup heavy cream
- 1/4 cup peanut butter
- 1 1/2 cup unsweetened almond milk
- 3 tablespoons cocoa powder
- 1/8 tsp sea salt
- 6 tablespoons Erythritol

Directions
Combine all ingredients in a blender and blend until very smooth. Enjoy!
Nutritional Information Per Serving
Calories: 435; Total Fat: 41 g; Carbs: 10 g; Dietary fiber: 4 g; Sugars: 3 g; Protein: 9 g; Cholesterol: 19 mg; Sodium: 119 mg

Low Carb Cinnamon Smoothie

Yield: 2 Servings /Prep Time: 5 Minutes
Ingredients
- 1/2 cup coconut milk
- 1 tablespoon ground chia seeds
- 1/2 teaspoon cinnamon
- 1 tablespoon MCT oil or coconut oil
- 1/2 cup water
- 1/4 cup vanilla whey protein

Directions
Combine all ingredients in a blender and blend until very smooth. Sprinkle with more cinnamon to serve!
Nutritional Information Per Serving
Calories: 467; Total Fat: 40.3 g; Carbs: 4.7 g; Dietary fiber: 1.; g; Sugars: 2.5 g; Protein: 23.6 g; Cholesterol: 4 mg; Sodium: 110 mg

Creamy Strawberry Coconut Milk Smoothie

Yield: 2 Servings /Prep Time: 5 Minutes

Ingredients
- 2 tablespoons almond butter
- 1 cup unsweetened coconut milk
- 1 cup strawberries frozen
- 2 packets Stevia

Directions
Combine all ingredients in a blender and blend until very smooth. Enjoy!

Nutritional Information Per Serving
Calories: 397; Total Fat: 37 g; Carbs: 5 g; Dietary fiber: 5 g; Sugars: 8 g; Protein: 6 g; Cholesterol: 0 mg; Sodium: 19 mg

Low Carb Tropical Smoothie

Yield: 2 Servings /Prep Time: 5 Minutes

Ingredients
- 1/2 cup fresh diced mango
- 1/2 cup frozen blueberries
- 1/2 banana, diced
- 1 tablespoon MCT Oil
- 2 tablespoons flaxseed meal
- 1/4 cup sour cream
- 3/4 cup unsweetened coconut milk
- 7 large ice cubes
- 20 drops liquid Stevia

Directions
Combine all ingredients in a blender and blend until very smooth. Enjoy!

Nutritional Information Per Serving
Calories: 356; Total Fat: 32.3 g; Carbs: 7.4 g; Dietary fiber: 3 g; Sugars: 4.4 g; Protein: 6.4 g; Cholesterol: 0 mg; Sodium: 341 mg

Choco Berry Spinach Smoothie

Yield: 1 Serving/Prep Time: 5 Minutes

Ingredients
- 1/4 cup raspberries
- 1/4 cup blueberries
- 1/2 cup spinach
- 1 tablespoon cocoa powder
- 1/2 cup heavy cream
- 1/2 cup water
- 1 tablespoon Erythritol
- 1/2 cup ice cubes

Directions
Combine all ingredients in a blender and blend until very smooth. Enjoy!

Nutritional Information Per Serving
Calories: 442; Total Fat: 45 g; Carbs: 10.5 g; Dietary fiber: 4.1 g; Sugars: 6.4 g; Protein: 4.3 g; Cholesterol: 44 mg; Sodium: 289 mg

Low Carb Superfood Detox Smoothie

Yield: 1 Serving/Prep Time: 5 Minutes

Ingredients
- 1 cup Greek yogurt
- 1 Tablespoon coconut flakes
- 1 Tablespoon cacao nibs
- 1 Tablespoon goji berries
- 1 Tablespoon chia seeds
- 1 scoop protein powder
- 1 teaspoon matcha powder
- Stevia

Directions
Combine all ingredients in a blender and blend until very smooth. Enjoy!

Nutritional Information Per Serving
Calories: 420; Total Fat: 28 g; Carbs: 15 g; Dietary fiber: 8 g; Sugars: 6 g; Protein: 13 g; Cholesterol: 4 mg; Sodium: 337 mg

Chia Seed Keto Smoothie

Yield: 2 Servings /Prep Time: 5 Minutes

Ingredients
- 1/2 avocado
- 1/2 cup coconut milk
- 1 tablespoon coconut oil
- 1 tablespoon cacao powder
- 1 tablespoon chopped mint
- 1 scoop collagen protein
- 1/2 cup frozen cauliflower
- 1/2 cup water
- 1 teaspoon vanilla extract
- Dash cinnamon
- Dash sea salt
- 1 tablespoon chia seeds

Directions
Combine all ingredients in a blender and blend until very smooth. Enjoy!

Nutritional Information Per Serving

Calories: 397; Total Fat: 23.1 g; Carbs: 6.8 g; Dietary fiber: 2.7 g; Sugars: 2.9 g; Protein: 19.8 g; Cholesterol: 4 mg; Sodium: 352 mg

Low Carb Mocha Smoothies

Yield: 3 Servings /Prep Time: 5 Minutes
Ingredients
- 1 1/2 cups unsweetened almond milk
- 1/2 cup coconut milk
- 1 avocado
- 3 tablespoons unsweetened cocoa powder
- 2 teaspoons instant coffee
- 3 tablespoons Stevia
- 1 teaspoon vanilla extract

Directions
Combine all ingredients in a blender and blend until very smooth. Enjoy!
Nutritional Information Per Serving
Calories: 176; Total Fat: 16 g; Carbs: 10 g; Dietary fiber: 3 g; Sugars: 4 g; Protein: 3 g; Cholesterol: 0 mg; Sodium: 63 mg

Creamy Strawberry Avocado Smoothie

Yield: 2 Servings /Prep Time: 5 Minutes
Ingredients
- 1 large Avocado
- 1 cup Frozen strawberries
- 1 1/2 cups Unsweetened almond milk
- 1/4 cup heavy cream
- 1 scoop protein powder
- 1/4 cup Erythritol

Directions
Combine all ingredients in a blender and blend until very smooth. Enjoy!
Nutritional Information Per Serving
Calories: 106; Total Fat: 17.8 g; Carbs: 8.7 g; Dietary fiber: 5 g; Sugars: 2.4 g; Protein: 11.9 g; Cholesterol: 9 mg; Sodium: 85 mg

Low Carb Chai Pumpkin Smoothie

Yield: 2 Servings /Prep Time: 5 Minutes
Ingredients
- ½ fresh avocado
- ½ teaspoon pumpkin pie spice
- 1 teaspoon chai tea
- 1 tablespoon MCT oil
- 3 tablespoons pumpkin puree
- 3/4 cup full-fat coconut milk
- 1 teaspoon vanilla

Directions
Combine all ingredients in a blender and blend until very smooth. Enjoy!
Nutritional Information Per Serving
Calories: 726; Total Fat: 69.8 g; Carbs: 11.3 g; Dietary fiber: 4.2 g; Sugars: 5.6 g; Protein: 5.5 g; Cholesterol: 0 mg; Sodium: 54 mg

Dairy-Free Lemony Avocado Berry Smoothie

Yield: 2 Servings /Prep Time: 5 Minutes
Ingredients
- 1/2 cup frozen berries
- 1 avocado
- 3 tablespoons lemon juice
- 1 1/3 cups water
- 2 tablespoons Stevia

Directions
Combine all ingredients in a blender and blend until very smooth. Enjoy!
Nutritional Information Per Serving
Calories: 227; Total Fat: 20.1 g; Carbs: 12.8 g; Dietary fiber: 8.8 g; Sugars: 1.9 g; Protein: 2.5 g; Cholesterol: 0 mg; Sodium: 17 mg

Low-Carb Blueberry Coconut Milk Smoothie

Yield: 1 Serving/Prep Time: 5 Minutes
Ingredients
- 1/4 cup blueberries
- 1 cup coconut milk
- 1 teaspoon coconut or MCT oil
- 30 g protein powder
- 1 teaspoon vanilla extract

Directions
Combine all ingredients in a blender and blend until very smooth. Enjoy!

Calories: 231; Total Fat: 10.1 g; Carbs: 5.9 g; Dietary fiber: 2.8 g; Sugars: 2.5 g; Protein: 21.3 g; Cholesterol: 9 mg; Sodium: 90 mg

Low Carb Blueberry Smoothie

Yield: 2 Servings /Prep Time: 5 Minutes
Ingredients
- 1/4 cup fresh blueberries
- 1 cup coconut milk
- 1 teaspoon coconut oil
- 30g protein powder
- 1 teaspoon vanilla extract

Directions
Combine all ingredients in a blender and blend until very smooth. Enjoy!
Nutritional Information Per Serving
Calories: 215; Total Fat: 10.1 g; Carbs: 7 g; Dietary fiber: 3.6 g; Sugars: 2.2 g; Protein: 23 g; Cholesterol: 9 mg; Sodium: 182 mg

Keto Almond Butter & Acai Smoothie

Yield: 1 Serving/Prep Time: 5 Minutes
Ingredients
- 1/4 of an avocado
- 3/4 cup unsweetened almond milk
- 1 tablespoon almond butter
- 2 tablespoons acai powder
- 1 tablespoon coconut oil
- 3 tablespoons protein powder
- 2 drops liquid Stevia
- 1/2 teaspoon vanilla extract

Directions
Combine all ingredients in a blender and blend until very smooth. Enjoy!
Nutritional Information Per Serving
Calories: 345; Total Fat: 20.1 g; Carbs: 8.1 g; Dietary fiber: 2 g; Sugars: 3.2 g; Protein: 15.3 g; Cholesterol: 4 mg; Sodium: 112 mg

Low Carb Green Smoothie

Yield: 2 Servings /Prep Time: 5 Minutes
Ingredients
- 1 cup almond milk
- 1 tablespoon almond butter
- 1/4 small cucumber
- 1/2 avocado
- 10g fresh mint leaves
- 1 tablespoon protein powder unsweetened
- 15g kale
- 1 celery stick
- 1/2 lemon, juiced

Directions
Combine all ingredients in a blender and blend until very smooth. Enjoy!
Nutritional Information Per Serving
Calories: 137; Total Fat: 10 g; Carbs: 5.7 g; Dietary fiber: 4.4 g; Sugars: 1.1 g; Protein: 6.7 g; Cholesterol: 4 mg; Sodium: 31 mg

Low Carb Chocolate & Coconut Smoothie Bowl

Yield: 1 Serving /Prep Time: 5 Minutes
Ingredients:
- 3/4 cup full-fat coconut milk
- 2 scoops collagen protein
- 2 tablespoons unsweetened cocoa powder
- Handful of ice
- 20 drops liquid coconut Stevia

Directions
Combine all ingredients in a blender and blend until very smooth. Serve in a bowl!
Nutritional Information Per Serving
Calories: 500; Total Fat: 38 g; Carbs: 8 g; Dietary fiber: 4 g; Sugars: 3 g; Protein: 26 g; Cholesterol: 12 mg; Sodium: 120 mg

Low Carb Spinach Avocado Smoothie

Yield: 2 Servings /Prep Time: 5 Minutes
Ingredients
- 1 cup frozen avocado
- 1 cup baby spinach
- 3/4 English cucumber peeled
- 1 inch ginger, peeled
- 1/2 cup cilantro
- 1 lemon peeled
- 1 scoop protein powder
- 1 cup cold water

Directions

Combine all ingredients in a blender and blend until very smooth. Enjoy!
Nutritional Information Per Serving
Calories: 148; Total Fat: 11 g; Carbs: 8.2 g; Dietary fiber: 6 g; Sugars: 2 g; Protein: 12 g; Cholesterol: 4 mg; Sodium: 28 mg

Turmeric Keto Smoothie

Yield: 1 Serving/Prep Time: 5 Minutes
Ingredients
- 1/2 cup unsweetened almond milk
- 1/2 cup full fat coconut milk
- 1 tablespoon coconut oil
- 1 teaspoon ground ginger
- 1 teaspoon ground cinnamon
- 1 tablespoon ground turmeric
- 1 scoop protein powder
- 1 teaspoon granulated sweetener
- 1 tablespoon Chia seeds

Directions
Combine all ingredients in a blender and blend until very smooth. Serve topped with chia seeds.
Nutritional Information Per Serving
Calories: 250; Total Fat: 28.1 g; Carbs: 4 g; Dietary fiber: 1.4 g; Sugars: 2.3 g; Protein: 17 g; Cholesterol: 4 mg; Sodium: 91 mg

Minty Chocolate & Mint Avocado Smoothie

Yield: 1 Serving/Prep Time: 5 Minutes
Ingredients:
- 1/2 avocado, frozen
- 1/2 cup coconut milk
- 1 tablespoon crushed cacao butter
- 4 mint leaves
- 2 scoops chocolate protein powder
- 1 cup water
- 1/2 cup ice
- 2 tablespoons shredded coconut

Directions
Combine all ingredients in a blender and blend until very smooth. Serve topped with coconut flakes.
Nutritional Information Per Serving
Calories: 552; Total Fat: 44.4 g; Carbs: 10.4 g; Dietary fiber: 9.1 g; Sugars: 2 g; Protein: 26 g; Cholesterol: 0 mg; Sodium: 100 mg

Cinnamon & Chocolate Low-Carb Smoothie

Yield: 1 Serving /Prep Time: 5 Minutes
Ingredients
- 1/2 ripe avocado
- 3/4 cup coconut milk
- 1 scoop protein powder
- 1 teaspoon coconut oil
- 1/4 teaspoon vanilla extract
- 1 teaspoon cinnamon powder
- 2 teaspoons unsweetened cacao powder
- Stevia

Directions
Combine all ingredients in a blender and blend until very smooth. Enjoy!
Nutritional Information Per Serving
Calories: 300; Total Fat: 30.7 g; Carbs: 12.2 g; Dietary fiber: 9.8 g; Sugars: 2.1 g; Protein: 9.1 g; Cholesterol: 4 mg; Sodium: 22 mg

Minty Avocado Green Smoothie

Yield: 2 Servings /Prep Time: 5 Minutes
Ingredients
- 1/2 cup unsweetened almond milk
- 1 cup fresh spinach
- 1/2 avocado
- 1 scoop whey protein powder
- 1/4 teaspoon peppermint extract
- 12 drops Stevia
- 1 cup ice

Directions
Combine all ingredients in a blender and blend until very smooth. Enjoy!
Nutritional Information Per Serving
Calories: 293; Total Fat: 15.4 g; Carbs: 11.7 g; Dietary fiber: 7.3 g; Sugars: 3.1 g; Protein: 28.3 g; Cholesterol: 4 mg; Sodium: 181 mg

Healthy Green Tea Detox Smoothie

Yield 2 Servings/Prep Time 5 minutes
Ingredients

- 2 tsp Match Green Tea powder
- 1 cup water
- 1 tablespoons lemon juice
- 1/2 ripe avocado
- 1/2 tsp liquid Stevia
- 1 cup sliced cucumber
- 1/2 cup ice

Directions

In a blender, blend together green tea powder and water until well combined; add the remaining ingredients and blend until very smooth. Serve right away.

Nutritional Information Per Serving

Calories: 230; Total Fat: 16.7 g; Carbs: 12.2 g; Dietary fiber: 9.8 g; Sugars: 2.7 g; Protein: 4.7 g; Cholesterol: 0 mg; Sodium: 22 mg

Healthy Keto Green Smoothie

Yield: 1 Serving/Prep Time: 5 Minutes

Ingredients

- ½ cup coconut milk
- ½ cup chopped spinach
- ½ medium avocado, diced
- 1 tbsp. extra virgin coconut oil
- ½ tsp. vanilla powder
- ½ cup water
- Handful of ice cubes
- ¼ cup chocolate whey protein
- 1 tsp. matcha powder
- 5 drops liquid Stevia

Directions

In a blender, combine all ingredients; blend until very smooth. Enjoy!

Nutritional Information per Serving:

Calories: 468; Total Fat: 48.3 g; Carbs: 6 g; Dietary Fiber: 4.5 g; Sugars: 1.2 g; Protein: 14.2 g; Cholesterol: 0 mg; Sodium: 109 mg

Keto Creamy Almond Smoothie

Yield: 2-3 Servings/Prep Time: 10 Minutes

Ingredients

- 500ml almond milk, unsweetened
- ¼ cup frozen strawberries, unsweetened
- 1 scoop protein powder
- 100ml heavy cream
- Stevia, to taste

Directions

Combine all the ingredients in a blender and process until smooth.
Serve immediately.

Nutritional Information per Serving:

Calories: 304; Total Fat: 25 g; Carbs: 7 g; Dietary Fiber: 2.5 g; Sugars: 3.9 g; Protein: 15 g; Cholesterol: 71 mg; Sodium: 107 mg

Peanut Butter Protein Smoothie

Yield: 2 Servings /Prep Time: 5 Minutes

Ingredients

- 4 tablespoons peanut butter
- 1 cup cottage cheese
- 1/2 cup unsweetened almond milk
- 1 scoop whey protein powder
- 2 drops liquid Sstevia
- 1 cup ice cubes
- Drizzle of peanut butter and cacao nibs
- Pinch of chicory powder

Directions

In a blender, blend together peanut butter, cottage cheese, almond milk, whey protein, Stevia and ice until very smooth. Serve over ice drizzled with peanut butter and sprinkled with cacao nibs and chicory powder.

Nutritional Information per Serving:

Calories: 218; Total Fat: 28.2 g; Carbs: 6.4 g; Dietary Fiber: 0.9 g; Sugars: 7.1 g; Protein: 21.4 g; Cholesterol: 37 mg; Sodium: 319 mg

Keto Almond-Strawberry Smoothie

Yield: 2-3 Servings /Prep Time: 10 Minutes

Ingredients

- 500ml almond milk, unsweetened
- ¼ cup frozen strawberries, unsweetened
- 1 scoop vegetarian protein powder
- 100ml heavy cream
- Stevia, to taste

Directions

Combine all the ingredients in a blender and process until smooth.
Serve immediately.

Nutritional Information per Serving:

Calories: 304; Total Fat: 25 g; Carbs: 7.2 g; Dietary Fiber: 3.3 g; Sugars: 2.8 g; Protein: 15 g; Cholesterol: 17 mg; Sodium: 332 mg

Low Carb Berry-Spinach Smoothie

Yield: 3 Servings /Prep Time: 7 Minutes

Ingredients
- ½ cup reduced fat, plain Greek yogurt
- 1 cup baby spinach
- ¼ cup frozen blueberries, unsweetened
- 1/3 cup almond milk, unsweetened
- 1 scoop vegetarian protein powder
- ¼ cup ice

Directions

Combine all the ingredients in a blender and process until smooth or desired consistency is achieved. Serve.

Nutritional Information per Serving:

Calories: 270; Total Fat: 13.9g; Carbs: 6.2 g; Dietary Fiber: 4.1 g; Sugars: 2.1 g; Protein: 11.6 g; Cholesterol: 11 mg; Sodium: 185 mg

Chocolate Peanut Butter Smoothie

Yield: 1 Serving/Prep Time: 5 Minutes

Ingredients
- 1 tablespoon natural peanut butter
- 1 tablespoon unsweetened cocoa powder
- 1/2 cup almond milk
- Pinch of sea salt
- 1 teaspoon liquid Stevia
- 1 scoop protein powder

Directions

Blend all ingredients together until smooth. Enjoy!

Nutritional Information per Serving: *Calories: 414; Total Fat: 34 g; Carbs: 13.3 g; Dietary Fiber: 2.4 g; Sugars: 4.6 g; Protein: 22.7 g; Cholesterol: 0 mg; Sodium: 219 mg*

Low Carb Pomegranate-Blueberry Smoothie

Yield: 1 Servings/Prep Time: 10 Minutes

Ingredients
- 2 pomegranates, chopped
- 1/2 apple, chopped
- 1 cup blueberries
- 1 scoop protein powder
- 1 banana, chopped
- 2 tablespoons coconut oil
- 1 avocado

Directions

Add the pomegranate arils and the apple to a juicer and process them together to make the juice. Combine this juice with the remaining ingredients in your blender and pulse until smooth. Enjoy!

Nutritional Information per Serving: *Calories: 203; Total Fat: 25.6g; Carbs: 17.2 g; Dietary Fiber: 5.5 g; Sugars: 9.4 g; Protein: 11.6g; Cholesterol: 0 mg; Sodium: 2 mg*

Red Grape & Fish Oil Smoothie

Yield: 1 Serving/Prep Time: 10 Minutes

Ingredients
- 1 cup seedless red grapes
- ½ banana, chopped
- ½ avocado, chopped
- 2 fish oil capsules
- 1 vitamin C capsule
- 1 cup unsweetened coconut water

Directions

Combine all the ingredients apart from the capsules in your blender. Open and empty the capsules into the blender and pulse until smooth.

Serve in a tall glass and enjoy!

Nutritional Information per Serving:

Calories: 126; Total Fat: 34.3 g; Carbs: 13.5 g; Dietary Fiber: 1.5 g; Sugars: 7.2 g; Protein: 0.6 g; Cholesterol: 0 mg; Sodium: 1 mg

Protein Rich Pumpkin Smoothie

Yield: 2 Servings/Prep Time: 8 Minutes

Ingredients
- 1/4 cup pumpkin puree
- 1 avocado
- 1 cup heavy cream
- ½ cup ice water
- 1 scoop protein powder
- ½ teaspoon pumpkin pie spice
- 2 tablespoons flax meal

Directions

Combine all the smoothie ingredients in your blender and pulse until super smooth. Serve immediately and enjoy!

Nutritional Information per Serving:*Calories: 152; Total Fat: 22.7 g; Carbs: 10.9 g; Dietary Fiber: 3.8 g; Sugars: 5.4 g; Protein: 12.4 g; Cholesterol: 4 mg; Sodium: 8 mg*

Creamy Blackberry Lemonade Smoothie

Yield: 2 Servings /Prep Time: 5 Minutes

Ingredients
- 1/2 cup blackberries
- 1/4 cup lemon juice
- 2/3 cup unsweetened almond milk
- 2 tablespoons coconut oil
- 2 pinches Himalayan salt
- ½ teaspoon Stevia
- 1 teaspoon vanilla extract
- 1 tablespoon collagen
- 3 cups ice cubes

Directions
Combine all ingredients in a blender and blend until very smooth. Enjoy!

Nutritional Information Per Serving:*Calories: 298; Total Fat: 19.1 g; Carbs: 5.9 g; Dietary fiber: 3 g; Sugars: 2.2 g; Protein: 17 g; Cholesterol: 4 mg; Sodium: 223 mg*

Creamy Chia Seed Almond Milk Smoothie

Yield: 2 Servings /Prep Time: 5 Minutes

Ingredients
- 2 tablespoons heavy cream
- 1 tablespoon chia seeds
- 1 tablespoon MCT Oil
- ½ cup ice cubes
- 1 1/2 cups unsweetened almond milk
- 1/8 teaspoon Stevia
- 1 teaspoon vanilla extract

Directions
Combine all ingredients in a blender and blend until very smooth. Enjoy!

Nutritional Information Per Serving: *Calories: 344; Total Fat: 32 g; Carbs: 7 g; Dietary fiber: 5 g; Sugars: 0 g; Protein: 4 g; Cholesterol: 41 mg; Sodium: 502 mg*

Creamy Raspberry Almond Milk Smoothie

Yield: 2 Servings /Prep Time: 5 Minutes

Ingredients
- 1/4 cup fresh raspberries
- 1/4 cup heavy whipping cream
- 1 cup unsweetened plain almond milk
- 1 tablespoon cream cheese
- 1/2 teaspoon vanilla extract
- 2 tablespoons confectioners Swerve
- pinch of salt
- 1 cup crushed ice

Directions
Combine all ingredients in a blender and blend until very smooth. Enjoy!

Nutritional Information Per Serving: *Calories: 150; Total Fat: 15 g; Carbs: 3.5 g; Dietary fiber: 1.5 g; Sugars: 1.5 g; Protein: 2 g; Cholesterol: 41 mg; Sodium: 250 mg*

Choco Macadamia Smoothie

Yield: 2 Servings /Prep Time: 5 Minutes

Ingredients
- 2 tablespoons macadamia nuts
- 1 cup vanilla almond milk
- 1 tablespoon cacao powder
- 2 tablespoons chia seed
- 1 tablespoon coconut butter
- 1 teaspoon MCT oil

Directions
Combine all ingredients in a blender and blend until very smooth. Enjoy!

Nutritional Information Per Serving: *Calories: 460; Total Fat: 41 g; Carbs: 17 g; Dietary fiber: 1; g; Sugars: 8 g; Protein: 10 g; Cholesterol: 29 mg; Sodium: 335 mg*

Gingery Strawberry Smoothie

Yield: 2 Servings /Prep Time: 5 Minutes

Ingredients
- 1 cup coconut milk
- 1/2 cup coconut yogurt
- 1 cup blueberries
- 1 teaspoon MCT oil
- 2 slices of apple
- 1/2 tablespoon collagen powder
- 3 slices of ginger
- Stevia

Directions
Combine all ingredients in a blender and blend until very smooth. Enjoy!

Nutritional Information Per Serving

Calories: 215; Total Fat: 10.1 g; Carbs: 7 g; Dietary fiber: 3.6 g; Sugars: 2.2 g; Protein: 23 g; Cholesterol: 9 mg; Sodium: 182 mg

Minty Strawberry Smoothie

Yield: 2 Servings /Prep Time: 5 Minutes

Ingredients
- 1 cup unsweetened coconut milk
- 1/2 cup cream
- 1/4 cup cream cheese
- 1 cup strawberries
- 2 tablespoons chopped mint leaves
- Stevia

Directions
Combine all ingredients in a blender and blend until very smooth. Enjoy!

Nutritional Information Per Serving
Calories: 291; Total Fat: 30.1 g; Carbs: 6.7 g; Dietary fiber: 1; g; Sugars: 5 g; Protein: 2 g; Cholesterol: 43 mg; Sodium: 129 mg

Low Carb Key Lime Cashew & Spinach Smoothie

Yield: 2 Servings /Prep Time: 5 Minutes

Ingredients
- 1/4 cup cashews, soaked
- 2 cups coconut milk
- 4 tablespoons lime juice
- 2 tablespoons chia seeds
- 2 tablespoons coconut butter
- 2 handfuls spinach
- 1/2 avocado
- 1 tablespoon lime zest
- 20 drops liquid Stevia
- ½ teaspoon vanilla extract
- 2 tablespoons collagen

Directions
Combine all ingredients in a blender and blend until very smooth. Enjoy!

Nutritional Information Per Serving
Calories: 340; Total Fat: 21 g; Carbs: 17 g; Dietary fiber: 8 g; Sugars: 2 g; Protein: 12 g; Cholesterol: 0 mg; Sodium: 46 mg

Hearty Soups and Salads Recipes

Sausage Kale Soup with Mushrooms

Serves: 6
Prep Time: 1 hour 10 mins
Ingredients
- 2 cups fresh kale, cut into bite sized pieces
- 6.5 ounces mushrooms, sliced
- 6 cups chicken bone broth
- 1 pound sausage, cooked and sliced
- Salt and black pepper, to taste

Directions
1. Heat chicken broth with two cans of water in a large pot and bring to a boil.
2. Stir in the rest of the ingredients and allow the soup to simmer on low heat for about 1 hour.
3. Dish out and serve hot.

Nutrition
Calories: 259 Carbs: 4g Fats: 20g Proteins: 14g Sodium: 995mg Sugar: 0.6g

Cheesy Broccoli Soup

Serves: 4
Prep Time: 30 mins
Ingredients
- ½ cup heavy whipping cream
- 1 cup broccoli
- 1 cup cheddar cheese
- Salt, to taste
- 1½ cups chicken broth

Directions
1. Heat chicken broth in a large pot and add broccoli.
2. Bring to a boil and stir in the rest of the ingredients.
3. Allow the soup to simmer on low heat for about 20 minutes.
4. Ladle out into a bowl and serve hot.

Nutrition
Calories: 188 Carbs: 2.6g Fats: 15.5g Proteins: 9.8g Sodium: 514mg Sugar: 0.8g

Creamy Keto Cucumber Salad

Serves: 2
Prep Time: 5 mins
Ingredients
- 2 tablespoons mayonnaise
- Salt and black pepper, to taste
- 1 cucumber, sliced and quartered
- 2 tablespoons lemon juice

Directions
1. Mix together the mayonnaise, cucumber slices, and lemon juice in a large bowl.
2. Season with salt and black pepper and combine well.
3. Dish out in a glass bowl and serve while it is cold.

Nutrition
Calories: 84 Carbs: 9.3g Fats: 5.2g Proteins: 1.2g Sodium: 111mg Sugar: 3.8g

Egg, Avocado and Tomato Salad

Serves: 4
Prep Time: 40 mins
Ingredients
- 2 boiled eggs, chopped into chunks
- 1 ripe avocado, chopped into chunks
- 1 medium-sized tomato, chopped into chunks
- Salt and black pepper, to taste
- 1 lemon wedge, juiced

Directions
1. Mix together all the ingredients in a large bowl until well combined.
2. Dish out in a glass bowl and serve immediately.

Nutrition
Calories: 140 Carbs: 5.9g Fats: 12.1g Proteins: 4g Sodium: 35mg Sugar: 1.3g

Snap Pea Salad

Serves: 2
Prep Time: 15 mins
Ingredients
- 1/8 cup lemon juice
- ½ clove garlic, crushed
- 4 ounces cauliflower riced
- 1/8 cup olive oil
- ¼ teaspoon coarse grain Dijon mustard
- ½ teaspoon granulated stevia
- ¼ cup sugar snap peas, ends removed and each pod cut into three pieces
- 1/8 cup chives
- 1/8 cup red onions, minced
- Sea salt and black pepper, to taste
- ¼ cup almonds, sliced

Directions
1. Pour water in a pot fitted with a steamer basket and bring water to a boil.
2. Place riced cauliflower in the steamer basket and season with sea salt.
3. Cover the pot and steam for about 10 minutes until tender.
4. Drain the cauliflower and dish out in a bowl to refrigerate for about 1 hour.
5. Meanwhile, make a dressing by mixing olive oil, lemon juice, garlic, mustard, stevia, salt and black pepper in a bowl.
6. Mix together chilled cauliflower, peas, chives, almonds and red onions in another bowl.
7. Pour the dressing over this mixture and serve.

Nutrition Calories: 203 Carbs: 7.6g Fats: 18.8g Proteins: 4.2g Sodium: 28mg Sugar: 2.9g

Simple Greek Salad

Serves: 2
Prep Time: 15 mins
Ingredients
- ½ pint grape tomatoes, halved
- 1 cucumber, peeled and chopped
- 2 oz feta cheese, cubed
- 1 tablespoon extra-virgin olive oil
- 1 tablespoon fresh dill

Directions
1. Mix together all the ingredients in a bowl except olive oil.
2. Drizzle with the olive oil and mix well to serve.

Nutrition Calories: 178 Carbs: 11g Fats: 13.5g Proteins: 6.1g Sodium: 327mg Sugar: 6g

Crispy Tofu and Bok Choy Salad

Serves: 2
Prep Time: 15 mins

Ingredients

- 7 ounces extra firm tofu, pressed and chopped

For Marinade

- ½ tablespoon soy sauce
- ½ tablespoon sesame oil
- 1 teaspoon garlic, minced
- ½ teaspoon lemon juice
- ½ tablespoon water
- ½ tablespoon rice wine vinegar

For Salad

- ½ stalk green onion
- 1½ tablespoons coconut oil
- 4 ounces bok choy, sliced
- 1 tablespoon cilantro, chopped
- 1 tablespoon soy sauce
- ½ tablespoon peanut butter
- 3 drops liquid stevia
- ½ tablespoon sambal olek
- ½ teaspoon lemon juice

Directions

1. Preheat the oven to 350 degrees and line a baking sheet with parchment paper.
2. Mix together all the ingredients for the marinade in a bowl.
3. Place the tofu in a plastic bag along with marinade, allowing it to marinate overnight.
4. Transfer the marinated tofu on the baking sheet and place in the oven.
5. Bake for about 30 minutes and dish out.
6. Mix together all the salad ingredients except bok choy in a bowl.
7. Top the salad with baked tofu and bok choy to serve.

Nutrition Calories: 230 Carbs: 5.2g Fats: 19.9g Proteins: 10.9g Sodium: 745mg Sugar: 1.9g

Keto Asian Noodle Salad with Peanut Sauce

Serves: 2
Prep Time: 10 mins
Ingredients
For the salad:

- ½ cup green cabbage, shredded
- 1/8 cup cilantro, chopped
- 1/8 cup peanuts, chopped
- 2 cups shirataki noodles, drained and rinsed
- ½ cup red cabbage, shredded
- 1/8 cup scallions, chopped

For the dressing:

- ½ teaspoon garlic, minced
- ½ tablespoon lime juice
- 1 tablespoon ginger, minced
- ¼ cup filtered water
- ½ tablespoon toasted sesame oil
- ½ tablespoon coconut amino
- ¼ teaspoon cayenne pepper
- ½ tablespoon granulated erythritol sweetener
- ½ tablespoon wheat-free soy sauce
- 1/8 cup sugar free peanut butter
- ¼ teaspoon kosher salt

Directions

1. Mix together all the salad ingredients in a large bowl.
2. Put all the dressing ingredients in a blender and blend until smooth.
3. Pour the dressing over the salad and mix well to coat.
4. Serve immediately in a serving bowl.

Nutrition Calories: 118 Carbs: 8.2g Fats: 12.9g Proteins: 3.8g Sodium: 250mg Sugar: 5.7g

Zucchini Noodles Salad with Parmesan & Walnuts

Serves: 2
Prep Time: 15 mins
Ingredients
For the salad:

- ½ cup fresh radicchio, shredded
- 2 cups zucchini noodles, spiralized
- 1/8 cup fresh parsley, roughly chopped
- 1/8 cup walnuts, roughly chopped
- ½ oz parmesan cheese, shaved

For the vinaigrette:

- 1/8 cup fresh lemon juice
- ½ cup avocado oil
- ½ teaspoon fresh garlic, minced
- Kosher salt and black pepper, to taste
- ¼ teaspoon granulated Swerve

Directions

1. Mix together all the salad ingredients in a bowl.
2. Whisk together the vinaigrette ingredients in a small bowl.
3. Drizzle the vinaigrette over the salad and toss to coat well.
4. Serve immediately in a serving bowl.

Nutrition Calories: 173 Carbs: 9.4g Fats: 13.6g Proteins: 6.6g Sodium: 87mg Sugar: 2.6g

Zoodles Greek Salad

Serves: 2/Prep Time: 10 mins
Ingredients
- 1/3 tablespoon balsamic vinegar
- 1/3 teaspoon fresh oregano, minced
- 1 medium zucchini, peeled and spiralized
- 1 oz. feta cheese, crumbled
- 4 tablespoons lemon juice
- 1/3 tablespoon olive oil
- Kosher salt and black pepper, to taste
- ½ cup cherry tomatoes, halved
- ¼ cup pitted kalamata olives, halved

Directions
1. Whisk together the balsamic vinegar, lemon juice, olive oil, oregano, salt and black pepper in a small bowl to make a dressing.
2. Mix together the dressing, zucchini noodles, tomatoes, olives and feta cheese in a large bowl until coated evenly.

Nutrition Calories: 109 Carbs: 7.5g Fats: 7.7g Proteins: 4g Sodium: 323m Sugar: 4.1g

"Anti" Pasta Cauliflower Salad

Serves: 2/Prep Time: 15 mins
Ingredients
- 1/8 cup radicchio, chopped
- 1/8 cup fresh basil, chopped
- ½ cup raw cauliflower, chopped
- 1/8 cup artichoke hearts, chopped
- 1/8 cup parmesan cheese, freshly grated
- ¾ tablespoon kalamata olives, chopped
- ¾ tablespoon balsamic vinegar
- Salt and black pepper, to taste
- ¾ tablespoon sundried tomatoes, chopped
- ½ clove garlic, minced
- ¾ tablespoon extra-virgin olive oil

Directions
1. Cook chopped cauliflower in the microwave for about 5 minutes.
2. Mix together the radicchio, basil, artichoke hearts, parmesan, olives, sundried tomatoes and garlic in a bowl.
3. Whisk together the olive oil and vinegar in another bowl and drizzle it over the salad.
4. Season with salt and pepper and toss well to serve.

Nutrition Calories: 71 Carbs: 3.6g Fats: 6.1g Proteins: 1.7g Sodium: 86mg Sugar: 1.2g

Clear Soups Recipes

Clear Chicken Soup

Serves: 4/Prep Time: 25 mins
Ingredients
- ¼ cup onions, chopped
- ¾ pound chicken with bones
- 4 garlic cloves, smashed
- 2bay leaves
- 4cupswater
- ¼ teaspoon black pepper, freshly cracked
- ¼ cup carrots, chopped
- 3sprigsthyme
- Salt, to taste

Directions
1. Put the chicken, garlic, onions, carrot, thyme, bay leaves and water in a pressure cooker.
2. Season with salt and black pepper and pressure cook on high heat until one whistle.
3. Cook on low heat for about 12 minutes and release the pressure naturally.
4. Strain the soup using a soup strainer and shred the chicken pieces.
5. Place the shredded chicken pieces in each serving bowl and pour clear soup on top.
6. Dish out and serve hot.

Nutrition: Calories: 194 Carbs: 3.1g Fats: 12.9g Proteins: 15.5g Sodium: 77mg Sugar: 0.7g

Chinese Clear Vegetable Soup

Serves: 6
Prep Time: 15 mins
Ingredients
- ¾ cup cabbage
- 3 sticks celery
- 1 carrot, thinly sliced
- 3 lettuce leaves
- 5 cups boiling water
- 3 spring onions with greens, chopped
- 5 oz cauliflower, sliced
- Pinch of baking powder
- 2 teaspoons soy sauce
- 4 tablespoons olive oil
- Pinch of citric acid
- Salt to taste

Directions

1. Heat oil in a pot and add baking powder, citric acid and vegetables.
2. Cook for about 4 minutes on high flame and add boiling water, salt and soy sauce.
3. Boil for about 4 minutes and dish out to serve hot.

Nutrition Calories: 109 Carbs: 6.2g Fats: 9.6g Proteins: 0.9g Sodium: 227mg Sugar: 1.8g

Hot Mushroom Clear Soup

Serves: 2/Prep Time: 15 mins
Ingredients
- ½ cup mushrooms, finely chopped
- 2 cups water
- 2 teaspoons butter
- Salt and black pepper, to taste

Directions
1. Put butter and mushrooms in a deep non-stick pan and cook for about 5 minutes on a low flame.
2. Stir in water, salt and black pepper and cook for another 5 minutes, stirring occasionally.
3. Dish out and serve hot.

Nutrition Calories: 37 Carbs: 0.6g Fats: 3.9g Proteins: 0.6g Sodium: 35mg Sugar: 0.3g

Spinach and Mushrooms Clear Soup

Serves: 3/Prep Time: 10 mins
Ingredients
- 1 cup spinach, torn into small pieces
- 3 cups clear vegetable stock
- ½ cup mushrooms, chopped
- 1 tablespoon olive oil
- ½ teaspoon soy sauce
- 1 teaspoon sesame seeds, roasted
- 1 teaspoon garlic, finely chopped
- Salt and black pepper, to taste

Directions
1. Heat olive oil in a deep non-stick pan and add garlic.
2. Sauté for 30 seconds on a high flame and add the mushrooms and spinach.
3. Sauté for about 1 minute and stir in clear vegetable stock, soy sauce, salt and black pepper.
4. Cook for about 3 minutes on a medium flame, stirring occasionally and serve topped with sesame seeds.

Nutrition Calories: 62 Carbs: 3.4g Fats: 7.2g Proteins: 1g Sodium: 778mg Sugar: 2.3g

Cream Soups Recipes

Creamy Roasted Butternut Squash Soup

Serves: 4/Prep Time: 55 mins
Ingredients
- 1 potato, peeled and chopped
- 1 onion, chopped
- 1 large butternut squash, peeled and cubed
- 3 tablespoons extra-virgin olive oil
- 2 tablespoons butter
- 1 cup heavy cream
- 1 stalk celery, thinly sliced
- 1 tablespoon fresh thyme leaves
- 1 quart low-sodium chicken broth
- Salt and black pepper, to taste

Directions
1. Preheat oven to 400 degrees and grease a large baking sheet.
2. Toss potatoes and butternut squash with olive oil and season generously with salt and black pepper.
3. Transfer on the baking sheet and roast for about 25 minutes.
4. Meanwhile, melt butter over medium heat in a large pot and add onion, carrots and celery.
5. Cook for about 10 minutes until softened and season generously with salt, black pepper and thyme.
6. Add potatoes, chicken broth and roasted squash and allow it to simmer for about 10 minutes.
7. Transfer the mixture into an immersion blender and blend soup until creamy.
8. Dish out and serve garnished with thyme.

Nutrition Calories: 214 Carbs: 11g Fats: 18.3g Proteins: 2.8g Sodium: 87mg Sugar: 1.6g

Creamy Garlic Chicken Soup

Serves: 4/Prep Time: 20 mins
Ingredients
- 1 large chicken breast
- 2 tablespoons butter
- 4 ounces cream cheese, cubed
- 14.5 oz chicken broth
- ½ cup heavy cream
- 2 tablespoons Garlic Gusto Seasoning
- Salt to taste

Directions
1. Melt butter over medium heat in a saucepan and add shredded chicken.
2. Sauté for about 2 minutes and add Garlic Gusto seasoning and cream cheese.
3. Cook for about 3 minutes and add chicken broth and heavy cream.

4. Bring to a boil and reduce heat to low.
5. Simmer for about 4 minutes and season with salt to serve.
Nutrition Calories: 247 Carbs: 7g Fats: 22.4g Proteins: 9.9g Sodium: 470mg Sugar: 0.4g

Creamy Curried Cauliflower Soup

Serves: 4/Prep Time: 35 mins
Ingredients
- 2 tablespoons avocado oil
- 1-inch ginger, chopped
- 2 teaspoons curry powder
- 1 large cauliflower, cut into florets
- 1 white onion, chopped
- 4 garlic cloves, chopped
- ½ Serrano pepper, seeds removed and chopped
- 1 teaspoon salt
- ¼ teaspoon turmeric powder
- 1 cup chicken broth
- ½ teaspoon black pepper
- 1 cup water
- 1 can full fat coconut milk
- Cilantro, for garnishing

Directions
1. Put oil and onions over medium heat in a heavy bottomed pot and sauté for about 3 minutes.
2. Add Serrano pepper, garlic and ginger and stir-fry for about 2 minutes.
3. Add curry powder, turmeric, salt and black pepper and stir fry for 1 minute.
4. Add cauliflower florets and water and cover with a lid.
5. Cook for about 10 minutes, stirring occasionally.
6. Turn off heat and allow it to cool.
7. Transfer into the blender and blend until smooth.
8. Pour blended cauliflower back into pot and add coconut milk and broth.
9. Cook for another 10 minutes then garnish with cilantro and serve.
Nutrition Calories: 263 Carbs: 8.9g Fats: 23.9g Proteins: 3.3g Sodium: 838mg Sugar: 4.1g

Cream of Zucchini Soup

Serves: 4/Prep Time: 25 mins
Ingredients
- 2 garlic cloves
- ½ small onion, quartered
- 2 medium zucchinis, cut in large chunks
- 4 tablespoons sour cream
- 1 cup Parmesan cheese, freshly grated
- 2 tablespoons butter
- 32 oz chicken broth
- Salt and black pepper, to taste

Directions
1. Mix together chicken broth, onion, garlic and zucchini over medium heat in a pot and bring to a boil.
2. Lower the heat and simmer for about 20 minutes until tender.
3. Remove from heat and transfer into an immersion blender.
4. Add the sour cream and purée until smooth.
5. Season with salt and black pepper and serve hot.
Nutrition Calories: 179 Carbs: 6.5g Fats: 7.6g Proteins: 10.9g Sodium: 909mg Sugar: 2.8g

Cream of Asparagus Soup

Serves: 6/Prep Time: 30 mins
Ingredients
- 4 tablespoons unsalted butter
- 6 cups reduced sodium chicken broth
- 2 pounds asparagus, cut in half
- 1 small onion, chopped
- ½ cup sour cream
- Salt and black pepper, to taste

Directions
1. Heat butter in a large pot over low heat and add onions.
2. Sauté for about 2 minutes until soft and add asparagus, chicken broth and black pepper.
3. Bring to a boil, cover and cook for about 20 minutes on low heat.
4. Remove from heat and transfer into blender along with sour cream.
5. Pulse until smooth and dish out to serve.
Nutrition Calories: 161 Carbs: 8.7g Fats: 11.9g Proteins: 7.4g Sodium: 623mg Sugar: 3.9g

Creamy Broccoli Cheddar Soup

Serves: 6
Prep Time: 40 mins

Ingredients

- 1 small white onion, diced
- 4 cups vegetable broth
- 3 tablespoons unsalted butter
- 2 garlic cloves, minced
- 3 tablespoons almond flour
- 2 cups half-and-half
- 1½ cups cheddar cheese, grated
- Pinch of nutmeg
- 2 small heads broccoli, cut into florets
- Salt and black pepper, to taste
- 4 tablespoons sour cream, for garnishing

Directions

1. Melt butter in a large pot over medium-high heat and add onions.
2. Cook for about 5 minutes until soft and add garlic.
3. Sauté for about 1 minute and add almond flour.
4. Cook for about 3 minutes, stirring constantly and add half-and-half and broth.
5. Bring to a boil and reduce heat to medium.
6. Add broccoli and simmer for about 20 minutes.
7. Transfer into an immersion blender and blend until smooth.
8. Pulse until smooth and dish out in a bowl.
9. Whisk in cheddar cheese and season with nutmeg, salt and pepper.
10. Garnish with sour cream and serve.

Nutrition Calories: 345 Carbs: 8g Fats: 28.8g Proteins: 14.3g Sodium: 769mg Sugar: 1.5g

Creamy Low-Carb Red Gazpacho

Serves: 10/Prep Time: 30 mins

Ingredients

- 1 large red pepper, halved
- 2 medium avocados
- 2 tablespoons fresh lemon juice
- 2 tablespoons basil, freshly chopped
- 2 medium spring onions, diced
- 1 cup extra virgin olive oil
- 1 large green pepper, halved
- 1 small red onion
- 4 medium tomatoes
- 2 garlic cloves
- 2 tablespoons apple cider vinegar
- 1 large cucumber, diced
- Salt and black pepper, to taste
- 20 oz feta cheese

Directions

1. Preheat the oven to 400 degrees and line a baking sheet with parchment paper.
2. Transfer in the oven and roast for about 20 minutes.
3. Peel the skin of roasted bell peppers and transfer into a blender along with red onions, tomatoes, fresh herbs, cucumber, spring onions, lemon juice, vinegar, garlic, olive oil, salt and black pepper.
4. Pulse until smooth and season with more salt and black pepper.
5. Top with feta cheese and serve.

Nutrition: Calories: 293 Carbs: 8.4g Fats: 28.6g Proteins: 4.3g Sodium: 230mg Sugar: 4.2g

Creamy Keto Taco Soup with Ground Beef

Serves: 8/Prep Time: 30 mins

Ingredients

- ½ cup onions, chopped
- 1 tablespoon ground cumin
- 1-pound ground beef
- 2 garlic cloves, minced
- 1 teaspoon chili powder
- 2 (14.5 ounce) cans beef broth
- ½ cup heavy cream
- 1 (8 ounce) package cream cheese, softened
- 2 (10 ounce) cans diced tomatoes and green chilies
- 2 teaspoons salt

Directions

1. Mix together ground beef, onions and garlic over medium-high heat in a large soup pot.
2. Cook for about 7 minutes until beef is browned and add cumin and chili powder.
3. Cook for about 2 more minutes and add cream cheese into the pot.
4. Mash it into the beef with a big spoon for about 5 minutes until no white spots remain.
5. Stir in broth, diced tomatoes, heavy cream and salt and cook for about 10 more minutes.
6. Dish out and serve.

Nutrition Calories: 262 Carbs: 4.3g Fats: 17g Proteins: 22.4g Sodium: 1175mg Sugar: 0.7g

Creamy Tomato Basil Soup

Serves: 4/Prep Time: 45mins

Ingredients

- 4 cups tomato juice
- 14 leaves fresh basil
- 1 cup butter
- 3 tomatoes, peeled, seeded and diced
- 2 cups water
- 1 cup heavy whipping cream
- Salt and black pepper, to taste

Directions

1. Place tomatoes, water and tomato juice over medium heat in a pot.
2. Simmer for about 30 minutes and transfer into blender along with basil leaves.
3. Blend until smooth and return to the pot.
4. Place the pot over medium heat and stir in heavy cream and butter.
5. Season with salt and black pepper and stir until the butter is melted.

Nutrition Calories: 284 Carbs: 7.4g Fats: 28.7g Proteins: 1.9g Sodium: 500mg Sugar: 5.6g

Vegetable Soups Recipes

Cream of Broccoli and Cheddar Soup

Serves: 2/Prep Time: 15 mins

Ingredients

- ¾ cup vegetable stock
- ¼ teaspoon garlic powder
- ¼ teaspoon mustard powder
- Salt and black pepper, to taste
- 1/8 cup butter
- 1 cup broccoli florets
- 1/3 cup sharp cheddar cheese, shredded
- ¼ teaspoon onion powder
- 1 pinch nutmeg
- ¼ cup heavy whipping cream

Directions

1. Place the broccoli florets in the microwave for about 4 minutes on high.
2. Transfer the broccoli in a blender along with other ingredients and blend until smooth.
3. Place this mixture in the microwave for about 2 minutes on high.
4. Stir well and cook for another 4 minutes to serve hot.

Nutrition Calories: 264 Carbs: 4.8g Fats: 24.1g Proteins: 8.4g Sodium: 506mg Sugar: 1.4g

Anti-Inflammatory Egg Drop Soup

Serves: 2/Prep Time: 15 mins

Ingredients

- 1/3 teaspoon ground turmeric
- 1 clove garlic, minced
- ¾ quart vegetable stock
- 1/3 teaspoon ground ginger
- 1/3 small chili pepper, sliced
- ¾ cup brown mushrooms, sliced
- 1 cup Swiss chard, chopped
- 1 small spring onion, sliced
- 1/3 teaspoon salt
- 2 tablespoons extra-virgin olive oil
- ¾ tablespoon coconut amino
- 1 large egg
- ¾ tablespoon cilantro, freshly chopped
- Black pepper, to taste

Directions

1. Heat vegetable stock in a large pot and simmer for about 3 minutes.
2. Place the ginger, garlic, turmeric, chili pepper, chard stalks, coconut amino and mushrooms into the pot and let it simmer for about 5 minutes.
3. Add chard leaves and cook for about 1 minute.
4. Whisk the eggs and pour them slowly into the simmering soup.
5. Cook for about 3 minutes and add cilantro and spring onions.
6. Season with salt and pepper and dish out in a bowl.
7. Drizzle with olive oil and serve immediately

Nutrition Calories: 184 Carbs: 5.4g Fats: 16.9g Proteins: 4.7g Sodium: 489mg Sugar: 1.7g

Ginger Zucchini Noodle Egg Drop Soup

Serves: 2/Prep Time: 25 mins

Ingredients

- 1 tablespoon extra-virgin olive oil
- 1¼ cups portobello mushrooms, sliced
- ½ cup plus ½ tablespoon water, divided
- 1¼ tablespoons low-sodium soy sauce
- 1 medium zucchini, spiralized
- ½ tablespoon ginger, minced
- 2 cups vegetable broth, divided
- ¼ teaspoon red pepper flakes
- ½ cup scallions, thinly sliced and divided
- 1 large egg, beaten
- Salt and black pepper, to taste
- ¾ tablespoon corn starch

Directions

1. Heat olive oil in a large pot over medium-high heat and add ginger.
2. Sauté for about 2 minutes and add shiitake mushrooms and ½ tablespoon of water.
3. Cook for about 4 minutes and add 1½ cup vegetable broth, ½ cup water, ½ cup scallions, red pepper flakes and tamari sauce.
4. Bring to a boil, stirring occasionally and pour in the beaten eggs slowly.
5. Meanwhile, mix ½ cup of vegetable broth with the corn starch.
6. Add this mixture to the soup while continuously stirring and cook for about 5 minutes.

7. Season with salt and black pepper and add zucchini noodles.
8. Cook for about 2 minutes until the noodles are soft and top with the remaining scallions to serve.
Nutrition Calories: 193 Carbs: 11g Fats: 11.3g Proteins: 11.8g Sodium: 1366mg Sugar: 4.8g

Hearty Veggies Low-Carb Miso Soup

Serves: 2/Prep Time: 25 mins
Ingredients
- 1 clove garlic, chopped
- 1 small rainbow carrot, peeled and diced
- ¼ head Romanesco, florets chopped
- ¾ small zucchini, sliced and halved
- 1¼ oz baby spinach
- 2 tablespoons coconut oil
- ¼ medium purple onion, peeled and diced
- 3 cups water
- ¼ head purple cauliflower, florets chopped
- ¾ tablespoon Bouillon
- 1/8 cup mellow white miso
- Fresh dill
- Salt and black pepper, to taste
- Fresh parsley

Directions
1. Put coconut oil in a large pot over medium-high heat and add garlic and onions.
2. Cook for about 3 minutes and add carrots and water.
3. Bring to a boil and cook for about 14 minutes.
4. Add cauliflower and Romanesco and cook for about 5 minutes.
5. Stir in spinach, miso and bouillon and mix until miso is dissolved.
6. Stir in dill and parsley and season with salt and black pepper to serve.
Nutrition Calories: 173 Carbs: 11.7g Fats: 14.1g Proteins: 4.4g Sodium: 102mg Sugar: 3.4g

Cauliflower Parmesan Soup

Serves: 2/Prep Time: 35 mins
Ingredients
- Salt and black pepper, to taste
- 2¾ tablespoons butter
- ½ onion, sliced
- 1/3 head cauliflower, chopped
- ½ cup water
- 1/3 cup Parmesan cheese
- ½ leek, sliced
- ¾ cup vegetable broth
- ¾ tablespoon thyme, chopped

Directions
1. Melt ¾ tablespoon butter in large pot and add onion, leek and salt.
2. Cook for about 3 minutes and add remaining butter, cauliflower, broth and water.
3. Allow it to simmer for about 15 minutes and add thyme.
4. Simmer for about 10 minutes until cauliflower is tender and transfer to a blender along with cheese.
5. Blend until smooth and dish out in a bowl to serve.
Nutrition Calories: 208 Carbs: 9.2g Fats: 17.6g Proteins: 5.1g Sodium: 463mg Sugar: 3.4g

Cheesy Keto Zucchini Soup

Serves: 2/Prep Time: 20 mins
Ingredients
- ½ medium onion, peeled and chopped
- 1 cup bone broth
- 1 tablespoon coconut oil
- 1½ zucchinis, cut into chunks
- ½ tablespoon nutritional yeast
- Dash of black pepper
- ½ tablespoon parsley, chopped, for garnish
- ½ tablespoon coconut cream, for garnish

Directions
1. Melt the coconut oil in a large pan over medium heat and add onions.
2. Sauté for about 3 minutes and add zucchinis and bone broth.
3. Reduce the heat to simmer for about 15 minutes and cover the pan.
4. Add nutritional yeast and transfer to an immersion blender.
5. Blend until smooth and season with black pepper.
6. Top with coconut cream and parsley to serve.
Nutrition Calories: 154 Carbs: 8.9g Fats: 8.1g Proteins: 13.4g Sodium: 93mg Sugar: 3.9g

Spring Soup with Poached Egg

Serves: 2/Prep Time: 20 mins
Ingredients
- 32 oz vegetable broth
- 2 eggs
- 1 head romaine lettuce, chopped
- Salt, to taste

Directions
1. Bring the vegetable broth to a boil and reduce the heat.
2. Poach the eggs for 5 minutes in the broth and remove them into 2 bowls.
3. Stir in romaine lettuce into the broth and cook for 4 minutes.

4. Dish out in a bowl and serve hot.
Nutrition Calories: 158 Carbs: 6.9g Fats: 7.3g Proteins: 15.4g Sodium: 1513mg Sugar: 3.3g

Easy Butternut Squash Soup

Serves: 4/Prep Time: 1 hour 45 mins
Ingredients
- 1 small onion, chopped
- 4 cups chicken broth
- 1 butternut squash
- 3 tablespoons coconut oil
- Salt, to taste
- Nutmeg and pepper, to taste

Directions
1. Put oil and onions in a large pot and add onions.
2. Sauté for about 3 minutes and add chicken broth and butternut squash.
3. Simmer for about 1 hour on medium heat and transfer into an immersion blender.
4. Pulse until smooth and season with salt, pepper and nutmeg.
5. Return to the pot and cook for about 30 minutes.
6. Dish out and serve hot.
Nutrition Calories: 149 Carbs: 6.6g Fats: 11.6g Proteins: 5.4g Sodium: 765mg Sugar: 2.2g

Cauliflower, Leek & Bacon Soup

Serves: 4/ Time: 10 mins
Ingredients
- 4 cups chicken broth
- ½ cauliflower head, chopped
- 1 leek, chopped
- Salt and black pepper, to taste
- 5 bacon strips

Directions
1. Put the cauliflower, leek and chicken broth into the pot and cook for about 1 hour on medium heat.
2. Transfer into an immersion blender and pulse until smooth.
3. Return the soup into the pot and microwave the bacon strips for 1 minute.
4. Cut the bacon into small pieces and put into the soup.
5. Cook on for about 30 minutes on low heat.
6. Season with salt and pepper and serve.
Nutrition Calories: 185 Carbs: 5.8g Fats: 12.7g Proteins: 10.8g Sodium: 1153mg Sugar: 2.4g

Swiss Chard Egg Drop Soup

Serves: 4/Prep Time: 20 mins
Ingredients
- 3 cups bone broth
- 2 eggs, whisked
- 1 teaspoon ground oregano
- 3 tablespoons butter
- 2 cups Swiss chard, chopped
- 2 tablespoons coconut amino
- 1 teaspoon ginger, grated
- Salt and black pepper, to taste

Directions
1. Heat the bone broth in a saucepan and add whisked eggs while stirring slowly.
2. Add the swiss chard, butter, coconut amino, ginger, oregano and salt and black pepper.
3. Cook for about 10 minutes and serve hot.
Nutrition
Calories: 185 Carbs: 2.9g Fats: 11g Proteins: 18.3g Sodium: 252mg Sugar: 0.4g

Mushroom Spinach Soup

Serves: 4/Prep Time: 25 mins
Ingredients
- 1 cup spinach, cleaned and chopped
- 10 oz mushrooms chopped
- 1 onion
- 6 garlic cloves
- ½ teaspoon red chili powder
- Salt and black pepper, to taste
- 3 tablespoons buttermilk
- 1 teaspoon almond flour
- 2 cups chicken broth
- 3 tablespoons butter
- ¼ cup fresh cream for garnish

Directions
1. Heat butter in a pan and add onions and garlic.
2. Sauté for about 3 minutes and add spinach, salt and red chili powder.
3. Sauté for about 4 minutes and add mushrooms.
4. Transfer into a blender and blend to make a puree.
5. Return to the pan and add buttermilk and almond flour for creamy texture.
6. Mix well and simmer for about 2 minutes.
7. Garnish with fresh cream and serve hot.

Nutrition
Calories: 160 Carbs: 7g Fats: 13.3g Proteins: 4.7g Sodium: 462mg Sugar: 2.7g

Squash Soup

Serves: 5/Prep Time: 45 mins
Ingredients
- 1½ cups beef bone broth
- 1 small onion peeled and grated.
- ½ teaspoon sea salt
- ¼ teaspoon poultry seasoning
- 2 small squash, chopped
- 2 garlic cloves, minced
- 2 tablespoons olive oil
- ¼ teaspoon black pepper
- 1 small lemon, juiced
- 5 tablespoons sour cream

Directions
1. Put squash and water in a medium pan and bring to a boil.
2. Reduce the heat and cook for about 20 minutes.
3. Drain and set aside.
4. Put olive oil, onions, garlic and poultry seasoning in a small saucepan.
5. Cook for about 2 minutes and add broth.
6. Allow it to simmer for 5 minutes and remove from heat.
7. Whisk in the lemon juice and transfer the mixture in a blender.
8. Pulse until smooth and top with sour cream.

Nutrition Calories: 109 Carbs: 4.9g Fats: 8.5g Proteins: 3g Sodium: 279mg Sugar: 2.4g

Broccoli Soup

Serves: 6
Prep Time: 10 mins
Ingredients
- 3 tablespoons ghee
- 5 garlic cloves
- 1 teaspoon sage
- ¼ teaspoon ginger
- 2 cups broccoli
- 1 small onion
- 1 teaspoon oregano
- ½ teaspoon parsley
- Salt and black pepper, to taste
- 6 cups vegetable broth
- 4 tablespoons butter

Directions
1. Put ghee, onions, spices and garlic in a pot and cook for 3 minutes.
2. Add broccoli and cook for about 4 minutes.
3. Add vegetable broth, cover and allow it to simmer for about 30 minutes.
4. Transfer into a blender and blend until smooth.
5. Add the butter to give it a creamy delicious texture and flavor

Nutrition Calories: 183 Carbs: 5.2g Fats: 15.6g Proteins: 6.1g Sodium: 829mg Sugar: 1.8g

Keto French Onion Soup

Serves: 6
Prep Time: 40 mins
Ingredients
- 5 tablespoons butter
- brown onion medium
- 4 drops liquid stevia
- 4 tablespoons olive oil
- 3 cups beef stock

Directions
1. Put the butter and olive oil in a large pot over medium low heat and add onions and salt.
2. Cook for about 5 minutes and stir in stevia.
3. Cook for another 5 minutes and add beef stock.
4. Reduce the heat to low and simmer for about 25 minutes.
5. Dish out into soup bowls and serve hot.

Nutrition Calories: 198 Carbs: 6g Fats: 20.6g Proteins: 2.9g Sodium: 883mg Sugar: 1.7g

Cauliflower and Thyme Soup

Serves: 6
Prep Time: 30 mins
Ingredients
- 2 teaspoons thyme powder
- 1 head cauliflower
- 3 cups vegetable stock
- ½ teaspoon matcha green tea powder
- 3tablespoonsolive oil
- Salt and black pepper, to taste
- 5garlic cloves chopped

Directions

1. Put the vegetable stock, thyme and matcha powder to a large pot over medium-high heat and bring to a boil.
2. Add cauliflower and cook for about 10 minutes.
3. Meanwhile, put the olive oil and garlic in a small saucepan and cook for about 1 minute.
4. Add the garlic, salt and black pepper and cook for about 2 minutes.
5. Transfer into an immersion blender and blend until smooth.
6. Dish out and serve immediately.

Nutrition Calories: 79 Carbs: 3.8g Fats: 7.1g Proteins: 1.3g Sodium: 39mg Sugar: 1.5g

Chicken Soups Recipes

Chicken Kale Soup

Serves: 6
Prep Time: 6 hours 10 mins
Ingredients
- 2 pounds chicken breast, skinless
- 1/3 cup onion
- 1 tablespoon olive oil
- 14 ounces chicken bone broth
- ½ cup olive oil
- 4 cups chicken stock
- ¼ cup lemon juice
- 5 ounces baby kale leaves
- Salt, to taste

Directions
1. Season chicken with salt and black pepper.
2. Heat olive oil over medium heat in a large skillet and add seasoned chicken.
3. Reduce the temperature and cook for about 15 minutes.
4. Shred the chicken and place in the crock pot.
5. Process the chicken broth and onions in a blender and blend until smooth.
6. Pour into crock pot and stir in the remaining ingredients.
7. Cook on low for about 6 hours, stirring once while cooking.

Nutrition Calories: 261 Carbs: 2g Fats: 21g Proteins: 14.1g Sodium: 264mg Sugar: 0.3g

Chicken Mulligatawny Soup

Serves: 10
Prep Time: 30 mins
Ingredients
- 1½ tablespoons curry powder
- 3 cups celery root, diced
- 2 tablespoons Swerve
- 10 cups chicken broth
- 5 cups chicken, chopped and cooked
- ¼ cup apple cider
- ½ cup sour cream
- ¼ cup fresh parsley, chopped
- 2 tablespoons butter
- Salt and black pepper, to taste

Directions
1. Combine the broth, butter, chicken, curry powder, celery root and apple cider in a large soup pot.
2. Bring to a boil and simmer for about 30 minutes.
3. Stir in Swerve, sour cream, fresh parsley, salt and black pepper.
4. Dish out and serve hot.

Nutrition Calories: 215 Carbs: 7.1g Fats: 8.5g Proteins: 26.4g Sodium: 878mg Sugar: 2.2g

Buffalo Ranch Chicken Soup

Serves: 4
Prep Time: 40 mins
Ingredients
- 2 tablespoons parsley
- 2 celery stalks, chopped
- 6 tablespoons butter
- 1 cup heavy whipping cream
- 4 cups chicken, cooked and shredded
- 4 tablespoons ranch dressing
- ¼ cup yellow onions, chopped
- 8 oz cream cheese
- 8 cups chicken broth
- 7 hearty bacon slices, crumbled

Directions
1. Heat butter in a pan and add chicken.
2. Cook for about 5 minutes and add 1½ cups water.
3. Cover and cook for about 10 minutes.
4. Put the chicken and rest of the ingredients into the saucepan except parsley and cook for about 10 minutes.
5. Top with parsley and serve hot.

Nutrition Calories: 444 Carbs: 4g Fats: 34g Proteins: 28g Sodium: 1572mg Sugar: 2g

Chicken Cabbage Soup

Serves: 8/Prep Time: 35 mins
Ingredients
- 2 celery stalks
- 2garlic cloves, minced
- 4 oz butter
- 6 oz mushrooms, sliced
- 2 tablespoons onions, dried and minced
- 1 teaspoon salt
- 8 cups chicken broth
- 1medium carrot
- 2 cups green cabbage, sliced into strips
- 2 teaspoons dried parsley
- ¼ teaspoon black pepper
- 1½ rotisserie chickens, shredded

Directions
1. Melt butter in a large pot and add celery, mushrooms, onions and garlic into the pot.
2. Cook for about 4 minutes and add broth, parsley, carrot, salt and black pepper.
3. Simmer for about 10 minutes and add cooked chicken and cabbage.
4. Simmer for an additional 12 minutes until the cabbage is tender.
5. Dish out and serve hot.

Nutrition Calories: 184 Carbs: 4.2g Fats: 13.1g Proteins: 12.6g Sodium: 1244mg Sugar: 2.1g

Green Chicken Enchilada Soup

Serves: 5/Prep Time: 20 mins
Ingredients
- 4 oz. cream cheese, softened
- ½ cup salsa verde
- 1 cup cheddar cheese, shredded
- 2 cups cooked chicken, shredded
- 2 cups chicken stock

Directions
1. Put salsa verde, cheddar cheese, cream cheese and chicken stock in an immersion blender and blend until smooth.
2. Pour this mixture into a medium saucepan and cook for about 5 minutes on medium heat.
3. Add the shredded chicken and cook for about 5 minutes.
4. Garnish with additional shredded cheddar and serve hot.

Nutrition Calories: 265 Carbs: 2.2g Fats: 17.4g Proteins: 24.2g Sodium: 686mg Sugar: 0.8g

Seafood Soups Recipes

Spicy Halibut Tomato Soup

Serves: 8/Prep Time: 1-hour 5mins
Ingredients
- 2garlic cloves, minced
- 1 tablespoon olive oil
- ¼ cup fresh parsley, chopped
- 10 anchovies canned in oil, minced
- 6 cups vegetable broth
- 1 teaspoon black pepper
- 1-pound halibut fillets, chopped
- 3 tomatoes, peeled and diced
- 1teaspoon salt
- 1 teaspoon red chili flakes

Directions
1. Heat olive oil in a large stockpot over medium heat and add garlic and half of the parsley.
2. Add anchovies, tomatoes, vegetable broth, red chili flakes, salt and black pepper and bring to a boil.
3. Reduce the heat to medium-low and simmer for about 20 minutes.
4. Add halibut fillets and cook for about 10 minutes.
5. Dish out the halibut and shred into small pieces.
6. Mix back with the soup and garnish with the remaining fresh parsley to serve.

Nutrition Calories: 170 Carbs: 3g Fats: 6.7g Proteins: 23.4g Sodium: 2103mg Sugar: 1.8g

Spicy Shrimp and Chorizo Soup

Serves: 8/Prep Time: 55 mins
Ingredients
- 2 tablespoons butter
- 1 medium onion, diced
- 3 celery ribs, diced
- 4 garlic cloves, sliced
- 12 ounces chorizo, diced
- 2 tomatoes, diced
- 1½ teaspoons smoked paprika
- 1 teaspoon ground coriander
- 1 teaspoon sea salt
- 1-quart chicken broth
- 1-pound shrimp, peeled, deveined and chopped
- 2tablespoons fresh cilantro, minced
- 1avocado,diced
- Chopped fresh cilantro for garnish

Directions

1. Heat half of butter over medium-high heat in a large pot and add celery, bell pepper and onions.
2. Cook for about 8 minutes, stirring occasionally and add tomato paste, half of chorizo, garlic, coriander, smoked paprika and salt.
3. Cook for about 1 minute, stirring continuously and add the tomatoes and broth.
4. Cook for about 20 minutes and heat remaining butter in a small pan.
5. Add remaining chorizo and cook for about 5 minutes until crispy.
6. Add smoked paprika, shrimp, coriander and simmer for about 4 minutes.
7. Remove from the heat and stir in minced cilantro.
8. Top with the crispy chorizo and chopped cilantro and serve.

Nutrition Calories: 374 Carbs: 7.9g Fats: 25.9g Proteins: 26.8g Sodium: 1315mg Sugar: 2.1g

Creamy Leek & Salmon Soup

Serves: 4/Prep Time: 30 mins
Ingredients
- 2 tablespoons butter
- 2 leeks, washed, trimmed and sliced
- 3 garlic cloves, minced
- 6 cups seafood broth
- 2 teaspoons dried thyme leaves
- 1-pound salmon, in bite size pieces
- 1½ cups coconut milk
- Salt and black pepper, to taste

Directions
1. Heat butter at a low-medium heat in a large saucepan and add garlic and leeks.
2. Cook for about 3 minutes and add stock and thyme.
3. Simmer for about 15 minutes and season with salt and black pepper.
4. Add salmon and coconut milk to the pan and simmer for about 5 minutes.
5. Dish out and serve immediately.

Nutrition Calories: 332 Carbs: 9.1g Fats: 24.3g Proteins: 21.5g Sodium: 839mg Sugar: 3.9g

Thai Coconut Shrimp Soup

Serves: 5/Prep Time: 40 mins
Ingredients
BROTH
- 4 cups chicken broth
- 1½ cups full fat coconut milk
- 1 organic lime zest
- 1 teaspoon dried lemongrass
- 1 cup fresh cilantro
- 1 jalapeno pepper, sliced
- 1-inch piece fresh ginger root
- 1 teaspoon sea salt

SOUP
- 100 grams raw shrimp
- 1 tablespoon coconut oil
- 30 grams mushrooms, sliced
- 1 red onion, thinly sliced
- 1 anchovy, finely smashed
- 1 lime, juiced
- 1 tablespoon cilantro, chopped

Directions
1. Broth: Mix together all the ingredients in a saucepan and simmer for about 20 minutes.
2. Strain the mixture through a fine mesh colander and pour back into the pan.
3. Soup: Simmer the broth again and add shrimp, onions, mushrooms and anchovy.
4. Allow it to simmer for about 10 minutes and add lime juice.
5. Garnish with cilantro and serve hot.

Nutrition Calories: 247 Carbs: 7.7g Fats: 19g Proteins: 11.5g Sodium: 1061mg Sugar: 3.2g

Carrot Ginger Halibut Soup

Serves: 6/Prep Time: 45 mins
Ingredients
- 1 large onion, chopped
- 2 tablespoons fresh ginger, peeled and minced
- 1 tablespoon coconut oil
- 4 carrots, peeled and sliced
- 2 cups chicken broth
- 1 cup water
- ½ teaspoon black pepper
- 1-pound halibut, cut into 1" chunks
- Sea salt, to taste

Directions
1. Heat coconut oil over medium heat in a large pot and add onions.
2. Sauté for about 8 minutes and add ginger, carrots, broth and water.
3. Bring to a boil, reduce heat and simmer for about 20 minutes.
4. Transfer into an immersion blender and blend until smooth.
5. Return the soup to the pot and add halibut, sea salt and black pepper.
6. Allow to simmer for 5 more minutes and serve.

Nutrition
Calories: 246 Carbs: 8g Fats: 16.3g Proteins: 16.3g Sodium: 363mg Sugar: 3.4g

Cheesy Shrimp Soup

Serves: 8
Prep Time: 30 mins
Ingredients
- 8 oz cheddar cheese, shredded
- 24 oz extra small shrimp
- 2 cups mushrooms, sliced
- 32 oz chicken broth
- ½ cup butter
- 1 cup heavy whipping cream

Directions
1. Put chicken broth and mushrooms to a large soup pot and bring to a boil.
2. Reduce heat and stir in butter, heavy whipping cream and cheese.
3. Add shrimp and allow it to simmer for about 15 minutes.
4. Dish out and serve hot.

Nutrition
Calories: 395 Carbs: 3.3g Fats: 28.7g Proteins: 29.8g Sodium: 1428mg Sugar: 0.8g

Thai Hot and Sour Shrimp Soup

Serves: 6/Prep Time: 55 mins
Ingredients
- 3 tablespoons butter
- 1-inch piece ginger root, peeled
- 1/2teaspoon fresh lime zest
- 5 cups chicken broth
- 1 small green zucchini
- 1-pound shrimp, peeled and deveined
- 1 medium onion, diced
- 4 garlic cloves
- 1 lemongrass stalk
- 1 red Thai chili, roughly chopped
- ½ pound cremini mushrooms, sliced into wedges
- 2 tablespoons fresh lime juice
- 2 tablespoons fish sauce
- 1/ fresh Thai basil, coarsely chopped
- ¼ bunch fresh cilantro, coarsely chopped
- Salt and black pepper, to taste

Directions
1. Heat butter in a large pot over medium heat and add shrimp.
2. Stir well and add garlic, onions, ginger, lemongrass, lime zest, Thai chilies, salt and black pepper.
3. Cook for about 3 minutes and add chicken broth to the pot.
4. Simmer for about 30 minutes and strain it.
5. Heat a large sauté pan over high heat and add coconut oil, mushrooms, zucchini, salt and black pepper.
6. Sauté for about 3 minutes and add to the shrimp mixture.
7. Simmer for about 2 minutes and add fish sauce, lime juice, salt and black pepper.
8. Cook for about 1 minute and add fresh cilantro and basil.
9. Dish out and serve hot.

Nutrition
Calories: 223 Carbs: 8.7g Fats: 10.2g Proteins: 23g Sodium: 1128mg Sugar: 3.6g

Beef and Pork Soup Recipes

Creamy Pulled Pork Soup

Serves: 6
Prep Time: 55 mins
Ingredients
- 1 medium onion
- 1-pound cauliflower
- ½ cup butter
- 8 garlic cloves
- 1 teaspoon sea salt
- 7 cups chicken broth
- 1½ cups pulled pork
- 2 teaspoons dried oregano
- 3 tablespoons sour cream

Directions
1. Heat butter in a saucepan and add onions and garlic.
2. Sauté for about 3 minutes and add cauliflower, chicken broth and sea salt.
3. Cook for about 20 minutes and transfer it to an immersion blender.
4. Blend until smooth and add dried oregano.
5. Return to the saucepan and simmer for about 5 minutes.
6. Add sour cream and pulled pork and cook for about 15 minutes.
7. Dish out and serve hot.

Nutrition
Calories: 257 Carbs: 8.7g Fats: 19.1g Proteins: 13.6g Sodium: 1351mg Sugar: 3.5g

Thai Beef and Broccoli Soup

Serves: 8
Prep Time: 50 mins
Ingredients

- 1 onion, chopped
- 2 garlic cloves, minced
- 2 tablespoons avocado oil
- 2 tablespoons Thai green curry paste
- 2-inch ginger, minced
- 1 Serrano pepper, minced
- 3 tablespoons coconut amino
- ½ teaspoon salt
- 4 cups beef bone broth
- 1 cup full-fat coconut milk
- 1-pound ground beef
- 2 teaspoons fish sauce
- ½ teaspoon black pepper
- 2 large broccoli stalks, cut into florets
- Cilantro, garnish

Directions

1. Put avocado oil and onions into a large pot and sauté for about 4 minutes.
2. Add ginger, garlic, Serrano pepper and curry paste and cook for about 1 minute.
3. Add coconut amino, fish sauce, ground beef, salt and black pepper.
4. Cook for about 6 minutes and add bone broth.
5. Reduce the heat to low and cook, covered for about 20 minutes.
6. Add coconut milk and broccoli florets to the pot and cover.
7. Cook for another 10 minutes and increase heat to high.
8. Simmer for about 5 minutes and garnish with cilantro to serve.

Nutrition Calories: 240 Carbs: 8.5g Fats: 13.5g Proteins: 22g Sodium: 547mg Sugar: 2.2g

Good Ole' Southern Pot Licker Soup

Serves: 6
Prep Time: 10 mins
Ingredients

- 1 large onion, diced
- 2 garlic cloves, minced
- 6 cups chicken broth
- 4 tablespoons butter
- 1-pound ham steaks, cubed
- 2 celery stalks, chopped
- 1 cup kale, chopped
- 1 tablespoon apple cider vinegar
- 6 cups collards, chopped
- 1 tablespoon Sriracha
- Salt and black pepper, to taste

Directions

1. Put butter, ham, garlic, onions, carrots and celery in a heavy-bottomed pot.
2. Cook for about 3 minutes over medium heat and add rest of the ingredients.
3. Bring to a boil and reduce the heat.
4. Simmer for about 90 minutes and dish out to serve.

Nutrition
Calories: 160 Carbs: 7.6g Fats: 10.3g Proteins: 9.4g Sodium: 1055mg Sugar: 2g

Pot Sticker Meatball Asian Noodle Soup

Serves: 6
Prep Time: 35 mins
Ingredients
For the meatballs:

- 1 egg
- 1-pound ground pork
- 1/3 cup almond flour
- ½ teaspoon garlic powder
- 1 teaspoon ginger, minced
- 1 tablespoon gluten free soy sauce
- ½ teaspoon kosher salt

For the broth:

- 2 tablespoons ginger, minced
- 1 teaspoon sesame oil
- 1 teaspoon garlic, minced
- 2 cups water
- 1 tablespoon fish sauce
- ½ teaspoon kosher salt
- 4 cups chicken broth
- 1 tablespoon gluten free soy sauce
- ½ teaspoon red pepper flakes

To assemble the soup:

- 2 cups Napa cabbage, shredded
- 3 cups shirataki noodles, drained and rinsed
- ¼ cup radish sticks
- 6 lime wedges
- ½ cup cilantro, chopped

Directions

1. *For the meatballs:* Mix together all the ingredients for meatballs in a medium bowl.
2. Make meatballs out of this mixture and transfer onto a baking sheet.
3. Bake for about 12 minutes at 375 degrees and dish out.

4. *For the broth:* Heat sesame oil and add ginger and garlic
5. Cook for about 1 minute and add water, soy sauce, chicken broth, red pepper flakes, fish sauce and salt.
6. Bring to a boil and simmer for about 10 minutes.
7. Strain the broth and return to the pan.
8. Bring to a boil right before serving.
9. *To assemble the soup:* Place about ½ cup shirataki noodles in a soup bowl and top with a handful of cabbage, four meatballs, a pinch of radish and cilantro.
10. Ladle about 1 cup of hot broth into each bowl and squeeze a lime wedge over it.

Nutrition Calories: 226 Carbs: 7.9g Fats: 8.7g Proteins: 27.4g Sodium: 1476mg Sugar: 1.3g

Beef Noodle Soup with Shitake Mushrooms and Baby Bok Choy

Serves: 1/Prep Time: 25 mins
Ingredients

- 2 teaspoons garlic, minced
- ¼ teaspoon crushed red pepper flakes
- ½ large zucchini, peeled and spiralized
- 3 oz beef steaks, cut into 1" cubes
- 2 tablespoons olive oil
- 1 cup chicken broth, homemade
- 1 head of baby bok choy, roughly chopped
- ¼ cup green onions, chopped
- ¼ cup water
- 1 tablespoon coconut amino
- ½ cup mushrooms
- Salt and black pepper, to taste

Directions

1. Season the beef cubes with 1 teaspoon olive oil, salt and black pepper.
2. Heat 1 tablespoon of olive oil over medium heat in a large saucepan and add garlic.
3. Sauté for about 1 minute and add beef.
4. Cook for about 2 minutes on each side and dish out.
5. Add remaining oil in the same saucepan and add mushrooms, bok choy and red pepper flakes.
6. Stir to combine and cook for about 2 minutes.
7. Add chicken broth and water and bring to a boil.
8. Add coconut amino and reduce heat to low.
9. Simmer for about 5 minutes and add zucchini noodles, beef and half of the green onions.
10. Cook for about 2 minutes and dish out into a bowl.
11. Top with remaining green onions and serve.

Nutrition Calories: 252 Carbs: 7.2g Fats: 17.6g Proteins: 17.7g Sodium: 262mg Sugar: 2.6g

Thai Tom Saap Pork Ribs Soup

Serves: 6/Prep Time: 2 hours
Ingredients

- 1 red shallot, chopped
- 1-pound pork spareribs
- 4 small lemongrass stalks, chopped
- 8 cups water
- 1 lime, juiced
- 2 tablespoons fish sauce
- 3 tablespoons ginger
- 10 kaffir lime leaves
- Salt to taste

Directions

1. Put the pork spareribs into a large pot of water and bring to a boil.
2. Cook for about 10 minutes and pour out the liquid with the froth.
3. Pour water, lemongrass, shallots, ginger and salt to the pot and simmer for about 1 hour on low heat.
4. Add kaffir lime leaves, fish sauce, lime juice and salt and dish out to serve.

Nutrition Calories: 232 Carbs: 8.9g Fats: 16.4g Proteins: 12.2g Sodium: 424mg Sugar: 0.3g

Creamy Cauliflower & Ham Soup

Serves: 10/Prep Time: 10 mins
Ingredients

- 6 cups chicken broth
- ½ teaspoon onion powder
- 2 tablespoons apple cider vinegar
- 24 oz cauliflower florets
- 2 cups water
- ½ teaspoon garlic powder
- 3 cups ham, chopped
- 1 tablespoon fresh thyme leaves
- 3 tablespoons butter
- Salt and black pepper, to taste

Directions

1. Mix together garlic powder, chicken broth, cauliflower, water and onion powder in a large soup pot.
2. Bring to a boil and simmer for about 30 minutes.
3. Transfer into an immersion blender and blend until smooth.
4. Return to the pot and stir in ham and thyme leaves.
5. Simmer for about 10 minutes and add butter and apple cider vinegar.
6. Remove from the heat and season with salt and black pepper.
7. Dish out and serve hot.

Bacon and Pumpkin Soup

Serves: 6/Prep Time: 4 hours 15 mins
Ingredients
- 400g pumpkin diced
- 3 cups bacon hock, diced
- Boiling water

Directions
1. Place pumpkin, boiling water and bacon hock in the slow cooker.
2. Cook on HIGH for about 4 hours and pull the meat away from the bones.
3. Return the meat to the slow cooker and allow it to simmer for 5 minutes before serving.

Nutrition Calories: 116 Carbs: 3.2g Fats: 5.9g Proteins: 12.1g Sodium: 27mg Sugar: 1.3g

Quick Italian Sausage and Pepper Soup

Serves: 10/Prep Time: 6 hours 20 mins
Ingredients
- 2 pounds hot Italian sausage cut into bite size pieces
- 2 sweet bell peppers, chopped
- 2 cups chicken broth low sodium
- 2 tablespoons extra virgin olive oil
- 4 garlic cloves, minced
- 1 onion, chopped
- 2 tablespoons red wine vinegar
- 2 cups water
- 1 teaspoon dried parsley
- 4 ounces fresh spinach leaves
- 1 (28 ounce) can diced tomatoes with juice
- 1 teaspoon dried basil
- ½ cup Parmesan cheese, grated

Directions
1. Heat olive oil in a large skillet and add sausages.
2. Cook for about 5 minutes until browned and transfer into a slow cooker.
3. Add the remaining ingredients except spinach and fresh herbs.
4. Cook on LOW for about 6 hours.
5. Add fresh herbs and spinach and serve.

Nutrition Calories: 373 Carbs: 6.9g Fats: 29.4g Proteins: 20.4g Sodium: 845mg Sugar: 3.8g

Pork and Tomato Soup

Serves: 8/Prep Time: 45 mins
Ingredients
- 2 tablespoons olive oil
- ½ cup onions, chopped
- 2 pounds boneless pork ribs, cut into 1-inch pieces
- 1 tablespoon garlic, chopped
- ½ cup dry white wine
- 1 cup chicken stock
- 1 cup water
- 2 cups cauliflower, finely chopped
- 2 cups fresh tomatoes, chopped
- 2 tablespoons fresh oregano, chopped
- Salt and black pepper, to taste

Directions
1. Season the pork generously with salt and black pepper.
2. Heat olive oil in a heavy saucepan and add seasoned pork.
3. Cook for about 3 minutes per side until browned and add garlic and onions.
4. Cook for about 2 minutes and add the chicken stock, white wine, fresh tomatoes and water.
5. Bring to a boil and pour into a slow cooker.
6. Cook on HIGH for about 4 hours until the meat is tender.
7. Stir in the cauliflower and fresh oregano and cook for another 20 minutes.
8. Dish out and serve hot.

Nutrition Calories: 228 Carbs: 5.3g Fats: 7.8g Proteins: 31g Sodium: 172mg Sugar: 2.4g

Cold Soups Recipes

Mint Avocado Chilled Soup

Serves: 2/Prep Time: 10 mins
Ingredients
- 2 romaine lettuce leaves
- 1 medium ripe avocado
- 1 cup coconut milk, chilled
- 20 fresh mint leaves
- 1 tablespoon lime juice
- Salt, to taste

Directions
1. Put all the ingredients into a blender and blend until smooth.
2. Refrigerate for about 10 minutes and serve chilled.

Chilled Zucchini Soup

Serves: 5/Prep Time: 10 mins
Ingredients
- 1 medium zucchini, cut into ½ inch pieces
- 4 cups chicken broth
- 8ozcream cheese cut into cubes
- ½ teaspoon ground cumin
- Salt and black pepper, to taste

Directions
1. Mix chicken broth and zucchini in a large stockpot.
2. Bring to a boil and reduce heat to low.
3. Simmer for about 10 minutes and add cream cheese
4. Stir well and transfer to an immersion blender.
5. Blend until smooth and season with cumin, salt and black pepper.
6. Refrigerate to chill for about 2 hours and serve.

Nutrition Calories: 196 Carbs: 3.4g Fats: 17g Proteins: 7.8g Sodium: 749mg Sugar: 1.3g

Super Food Keto Soup

Serves: 7/Prep Time: 30 mins
Ingredients
- 1 medium white onion, diced
- 1 bay leaf, crumbled
- 200 g fresh spinach
- 1 medium head cauliflower
- 2 garlic cloves
- 150 g watercress
- 4 cups vegetable stock
- ¼ cup ghee
- 1 cup coconut cream
- Salt and black pepper, to taste

Directions
1. Put ghee, onions and garlic in a soup pot over medium-high heat.
2. Cook until golden brown and add cauliflower and bay leaf.
3. Cook for about 5 minutes and add the spinach and watercress.
4. Cook for about 3 minutes and pour in the vegetable stock.
5. Bring to a boil and add coconut cream.
6. Season with salt and black pepper and transfer to an immersion blender.
7. Pulse until smooth and refrigerate for about an hour before serving.

Nutrition Calories: 187 Carbs: 9.4g Fats: 15.8g Proteins: 4.3g Sodium: 115mg Sugar: 4.4g

Chilled Guacamole Soup

Serves: 6/Prep Time: 10 mins
Ingredients
- 2 avocados, peeled and pitted
- ¼ cup red onion, chopped
- 1 tablespoon fresh cilantro, chopped
- ¼ teaspoon black pepper
- ¼ cup whipping cream
- 2½ cups low-sodium chicken broth, divided
- 6 tablespoons cheddar cheese, shredded
- 2 garlic cloves, coarsely chopped
- 1 jalapeno, seeded and coarsely chopped
- 1 tablespoon lime juice
- ½ teaspoon salt
- ¼ teaspoon cayenne
- 2 tablespoons sour cream

Directions
1. Put 1 cup of chicken broth, garlic, jalapeño, avocados, lime juice, cilantro and onions in a food processor.
2. Pulse until smooth and add remaining broth, cayenne salt and black pepper.
3. Puree until smooth and transfer to a large bowl.
4. Stir in whipping cream and chill for at least 1 hour before serving.
5. Ladle into bowls and top with sour cream and shredded cheese.

Nutrition Calories: 188 Carbs: 7.7g Fats: 15.3g Proteins: 6g Sodium: 317mg Sugar: 0.6g

Spinach Mint Soup with Sumac

Serves: 3/Prep Time: 10 mins
Ingredients
- 350 g spinach leaves
- 400 ml chicken stock
- ½ cup mint leaves
- 4spring onion chopped
- 4 tablespoons heavy cream
- Pinch of sumac
- 1 tablespoon olive oil
- 2 garlic cloves
- Salt and black pepper, to taste

Directions
1. Heat oil in a pot and add spring onions and garlic.

2. Sauté for about 3 minutes and add spinach leaves.
3. Cook for about 4 minutes and add chicken stock and mint leaves.
4. Transfer into a blender and blend until smooth.
5. Stir in heavy cream, salt, black pepper and a pinch of sumac.
6. Refrigerate and serve chilled.

Nutrition Calories: 157 Carbs: 8.6g Fats: 13g Proteins: 5.1g Sodium: 538mg Sugar: 1.4g

Vegan Gazpacho

Serves: 6
Prep Time: 10 mins
Ingredients
- ½ red onion, finely chopped
- 2 tomatoes, finely chopped
- ½ medium cucumber, finely chopped
- ½ green pepper, seeded and finely chopped
- 6 celery stalks, finely chopped
- 1 garlic clove, crushed
- 2 cups tomato juice
- 1/3 cup extra virgin olive oil
- ¼ cup white wine vinegar
- ¼ cup fresh parsley, finely chopped
- 1 scoop stevia
- Salt and black pepper, to taste

Directions
1. Put all the ingredients into a blender and blend until smooth.
2. Refrigerate for about 3 hours and serve chilled.

Nutrition
Calories: 133 Carbs: 8.2g Fats: 11.4g Proteins: 1.6g Sodium: 237mg Sugar: 5.3g

Chilled Avocado Arugula Soup

Serves: 6/Prep Time: 10 mins
Ingredients
- 2 medium ripe Hass avocados, diced
- 65 grams arugula
- 1/3 cup mint leaves, roughly chopped
- 1 teaspoon sea salt
- 1 lemon, juiced
- 1 scoop stevia
- 1/3 cup heavy cream
- 3 cups spring water, ice cold
- 1 tablespoon olive oil
- 3 tablespoons goat cheese, for topping

Directions
1. Put all the ingredients into a blender and blend until smooth.
2. Dish out into bowls and top with goat cheese.

Nutrition
Calories: 167 Carbs: 6.2g Fats: 15.5g Proteins: 3.2g Sodium: 341mg Sugar: 0.6g

Chowder Recipes

Manhattan Clam Chowder

Serves: 9/Prep Time: 30 mins
Ingredients
- 1/3 pound bacon, diced
- 4 oz onions, diced
- 2 large garlic cloves, rough chopped
- 10 oz celery root, peeled and diced
- ½ cup dry white wine
- 2 tablespoons tomato paste
- ½ teaspoon dried thyme
- 2 bay leaves
- 4 cups unsalted chicken broth
- 14 oz can whole plum tomatoes and juice
- 20 oz whole baby clams
- 8 oz bottle clam juice
- 6 tablespoons butter
- ¼ cup fresh parsley, chopped
- Salt and black pepper, to taste

Directions
1. Heat butter in a pot and add bacon.
2. Cook for about 6 minutes until crispy, stirring occasionally.
3. Reduce the heat to low and add the garlic, onions and celery root.
4. Sauté for about 3 minutes and pour in the wine, thyme, bay leaves, plum tomatoes, chicken broth, clam juice and tomato paste.
5. Bring to a boil and reduce the heat to simmer for about 15 minutes.
6. Add the clams, parsley, salt and pepper to serve.

Nutrition Calories: 249 Carbs: 8.9g Fats: 16.1g Proteins: 15.6g Sodium: 1071mg Sugar: 2.6g

Chipotle Chicken Chowder

Serves: 8/Prep Time: 35 mins
Ingredients
- 1 medium onion, chopped
- 2 garlic cloves, minced
- 6 bacon slices, chopped
- 4 cups jicama, cubed
- 3 cups chicken stock
- 1 teaspoon salt
- 2 cups heavy cream
- 1 tablespoon olive oil
- 2 tablespoons fresh cilantro, chopped
- 1¼ pounds chicken thighs, boneless, skinless, cut into 1-inch chunks
- ½ teaspoon black pepper
- 1 chipotle pepper in adobo, minced

Directions
1. Heat olive oil over medium heat in a large saucepan and add bacon.
2. Cook until crispy and add onions, garlic and jicama.
3. Cook for about 7 minutes and add chicken stock and chicken.
4. Bring to a boil and reduce temperature to low.
5. Simmer for about 10 minutes and season with salt and black pepper.
6. Add heavy cream and chipotle and simmer for about 5 minutes.
7. Sprinkle with chopped cilantro and dish out into serving bowls.

Nutrition
Calories: 350 Carbs: 8.4g Fats: 22.7g Proteins: 27.4g Sodium: 1023mg Sugar: 2g

Smoky Bacon & Turkey Chowder

Serves: 8/Prep Time: 40 mins
Ingredients
- 1 large shallot, peeled and chopped
- 8 cups turkey (or chicken) stock
- ½ cup extra sharp cheddar cheese, shredded
- 8 oz bacon, crumbled
- ½ cup celery, chopped
- ½ cup heavy whipping cream
- 1 cup potatoes, peeled and chopped
- 1 teaspoon dried parsley
- ½ teaspoon liquid smoke
- 1 tablespoon fresh thyme leaves
- 4 cups cooked turkey meat, shredded or chopped
- 1 teaspoon xanthan gum
- 1 tablespoon olive oil
- Salt and black pepper, to taste

Directions
1. Put olive oil, bacon, shallots and celery in a pot and cook for about 5 minutes.
2. Add the turkey stock, cheddar cheese and whipping cream and cook for about 3 minutes.
3. Add the sweet potato, parsley, turkey and liquid smoke and simmer for about 20 minutes.
4. Whisk in the xanthan gum and cook for 5 more minutes.
5. Add fresh thyme, salt and black pepper.
6. Garnish with fresh thyme leaves and serve hot.

Nutrition:
Calories: 295 Carbs: 7.4g Fats: 17.3g Proteins: 26.8g Sodium: 1106mg Sugar: 1.1g

Thai Seafood Chowder

Serves: 8
Prep Time: 35 mins
Ingredients
- ¼ cup onions, diced
- 2 celery stalks chopped
- 3cupschicken broth
- ½ head cabbage, roughly chopped
- ½ pound raw shrimp peeled and deveined
- 2tablespoonsavocado oil
- Salt and black pepper, to taste
- 1jalapeño,seeded and diced
- 2tablespoonsgreen Thai curry paste
- 1 (15-ounce)can full fat coconut milk
- 1poundwild pacific cod cut into 1-inch chunks
- 2 tablespoons fish sauce
- ¼ cup fresh cilantro, chopped
- 2 tablespoons fresh lime juice

Directions
1. Heat oil over medium heat in a large stock pot and add onions, salt and black pepper.
2. Sauté for about 4 minutes and add celery and jalapeño.
3. Cook for about 3 minutes and stir in curry paste for about 30 seconds.
4. Add coconut milk, chicken broth and cabbage and simmer for about 10 minutes.
5. Add shrimp, cod chunks and continue to simmer for 10 more minutes.
6. Remove from heat and stir in lime juice and fish sauce.
7. Top with fresh cilantro and serve.

Nutrition
Calories: 206 Carbs: 5.8g Fats: 11.6g Proteins: 18.3g Sodium: 938mg Sugar: 3.1g

Hearty Fish Chowder

Serves: 6/Prep Time: 35 mins
Ingredients
- 4 bacon slices chopped
- 1 medium onion chopped
- 3 cups daikon radish, chopped
- 2½ cups chicken stock
- ½ teaspoon dried thyme
- Salt and black pepper, to taste
- 2 cups heavy cream
- 1 pound tilapia, chopped
- 2 tablespoons butter

Directions
1. Heat butter over medium heat in a large saucepan and add bacon.
2. Cook until crisp and add onions and daikon radish.
3. Cook for about 5 minutes and add chicken stock.
4. Simmer for about 10 minutes and season with thyme, salt and pepper.
5. Add cream and tilapia and simmer for about 4 minutes.
6. Dish out and serve immediately.

Nutrition Calories: 319 Carbs: 4.4g Fats: 24.9g Proteins: 20.6g Sodium: 686mg Sugar: 1.6g

Smoked Salmon Chowder

Serves: 6/Prep Time: 1 hour
Ingredients
- 1 small onion, diced
- 4 garlic cloves, minced
- 4 slices raw bacon, crumbled
- 1 teaspoon smoked paprika
- 2 cups chicken broth
- 2 celery stalks, diced
- 1 bay leaf
- 1 cup squash, cut into ½ inch cubes
- 2½ cups cream, heavy whipping
- 8 oz smoked salmon, cut into cubes
- Salt and black pepper, to taste

Directions
1. Put chicken stock, celery, onions, bay leaf and garlic in a soup pot and bring to a simmer.
2. Add squash, bell peppers, paprika, salt and black pepper and cook for about 5 minutes.
3. Reduce temperature to low and add cream, salmon and bacon to the chowder.
4. Simmer on low for about 45 minutes and dish out to serve.

Nutrition Calories: 203 Carbs: 6.4g Fats: 13.1g Proteins: 14.6g Sodium: 1343mg Sugar: 3.2g

Lobster Chowder

Serves: 6/Prep Time: 10 mins
Ingredients
- ½ cup onions, chopped
- 2 cups lobster broth
- 3 cups unsweetened almond milk
- 4 strips raw bacon, chopped
- ¼ cup salted butter
- 2 cups raw cauliflower florets
- 2 cups cooked lobster, cut into chunks
- ¼ teaspoon ground black pepper
- ¼ teaspoon garlic powder
- 2 tablespoons apple cider vinegar
- 2 tablespoons fresh parsley, chopped
- 1½ teaspoons kosher salt
- ¼ teaspoon xanthan gum
- 3 tablespoons Cointreau
- 1 tablespoon butter, to finish

Directions
1. Put butter, bacon and onion over low heat in a large pan and cook for about 4 minutes.
2. Add lobster broth and cauliflower, cover and simmer for about 8 minutes.
3. Add almond milk and lobster and cook for about 5 minutes.
4. Remove ½ cup of broth to a small bowl and stir in the xanthan gum.
5. Return it to the chowder and stir in the Cointreau, apple cider vinegar, parsley and 1 tablespoon butter.
6. Dish out and serve hot.

Nutrition Calories: 264 Carbs: 7.5g Fats: 16.1g Proteins: 20.7g Sodium: 1725mg Sugar: 1.6g

Turkey Chowder

Serves: 12/Prep Time: 1-hour 30mins
Ingredients
- ½ cup green onions, sliced into small rounds
- 1 cup celery, diced
- 1 cup cauliflower, broken into small pieces
- ½ cup oat bran
- ½ cup butter
- ½ cup carrots, diced
- 1 cup broccoli, diced
- 2 cups turkey, diced, cooked and smoked
- 1 teaspoon salt
- ½ teaspoon pepper
- 1 tablespoon parsley
- 2 cups heavy cream
- ½ cup frozen corn
- ½ teaspoon thyme
- 4 cups chicken stock
- 1 cup cheddar cheese, shredded

Directions
1. Put butter and vegetables in a pot over medium heat and cook for about 5 minutes.
2. Add the turkey, oat bran and seasonings and cook for about 4 minutes.
3. Add chicken stock and cream and simmer for about 15 minutes.
4. Add the corn and cheese and cook for at least 10 minutes.
5. Dish out and serve hot.
Nutrition: Calories: 236 Carbs: 4.7g Fats: 19.8g Proteins: 10.8g Sodium: 607mg Sugar: 1.4g

Creamy Chicken Bacon Chowder

Serves: 12/Prep Time: 40 mins
Ingredients
- 8 ounces full fat cream cheese
- ½ cup frozen onions
- 6 boneless chicken thighs, cubed
- 4 teaspoons garlic, minced
- 6 ounces mushrooms, sliced
- 1 teaspoon thyme
- 3 cups chicken broth
- 1-pound cooked bacon chopped
- 4 tablespoons butter
- Salt and black pepper, to taste
- 1cupheavy cream
- 2cupsfresh spinach

Directions
1. Put all the ingredients in a zipper bag except chicken broth, spinach, cream and bacon and zip to seal.
2. Refrigerate for about 2 hours and then, pour into Instant Pot with chicken broth.
3. Cook for about 30 minutes and add spinach and cream.
4. Cover and allow it to sit for 10 minutes.
5. Top with bacon and serve hot.
Nutrition
Calories: 330 Carbs: 3.6g Fats: 24.5g Proteins: 23.6g Sodium: 1113mg Sugar: 1.3g

Bay Scallop Chowder

Serves: 6/Prep Time: 35mins
Ingredients
- 1medium onion chopped
- 2½ cups chicken stock
- 4 slices bacon chopped
- 3 cups chopped daikon radish
- ½ teaspoon dried thyme
- 2 cups heavy cream
- 1 tablespoon butter
- Salt and black pepper, to taste
- 1-pound bay scallops

Directions
1. Heat butter over medium heat in a large saucepan and add bacon.
2. Cook until crisp and add onions and daikon radish.
3. Cook for about 5 minutes and add chicken stock.
4. Simmer for about 8 minutes and season with thyme, salt and pepper.
5. Add heavy cream and bay scallops and simmer for about 4 minutes.
6. Dish out and serve immediately.
Nutrition
Calories: 307 Carbs: 6.2g Fats: 22.8g Proteins: 19.2g Sodium: 767mg Sugar: 1.6g

Stew Recipes

Brazilian Shrimp Stew

Serves: 6/Prep Time: 25 mins
Ingredients
- 1 garlic clove, minced
- ¼ cup onions, diced
- ¼ cup olive oil
- 1½ pounds raw shrimp, peeled & deveined
- ¼ cup red pepper, roasted and diced
- 1 (14 oz) can diced tomatoes with chilies
- 2 tablespoons lemon juice
- 2 tablespoons Sriracha hot sauce
- 1 cup coconut milk
- ¼ cup fresh cilantro, chopped
- Salt and black pepper, to taste

Directions
1. Heat olive oil in a medium saucepan and add garlic and onions.
2. Sauté for about 3 minutes and add peppers, tomatoes, shrimp and cilantro.
3. Simmer for about 5 minutes and add coconut milk and Sriracha sauce.
4. Cook for about 5 minutes and stir in lime juice, salt and black pepper.
5. Garnish with fresh cilantro and serve hot.
Nutrition
Calories: 316 Carbs: 7.4g Fats: 19.9g Proteins: 26.9g Sodium: 593mg Sugar: 3.7g

Bacon Cabbage Chuck Beef Stew

Serves: 6
Prep Time: 7 hours 10 mins
Ingredients

- ½ pound bacon strips
- 2 pounds grass-fed chuck roast, cut in 2" pieces
- 2 small red onions, peeled and sliced
- 1 garlic clove, minced
- 1 small Napa cabbage
- Salt and black pepper, to taste
- 1 sprig fresh thyme
- 1 cup homemade beef bone broth

Directions

1. Put bacon slices, onion slices and garlic at the bottom of the slow cooker.
2. Layer with the chuck roast, followed by the cabbage slices, thyme and broth.
3. Season with salt and black pepper and cook on LOW for 7 hours.
4. Dish out and serve hot.

Nutrition

Calories: 170 Carbs: 3.7g Fats: 9g Proteins: 19.6g Sodium: 164mg Sugar: 1.2g

Belizean Stewed Chicken

Serves: 6/Prep Time: 40 mins
Ingredients

- 2 tablespoons white vinegar
- 2 tablespoons recadorojo seasoning
- 1 tablespoon coconut oil
- 4 whole chicken legs
- 3 tablespoons Worcestershire sauce
- 1 teaspoon dried oregano
- 1 tablespoon erythritol
- 1 teaspoon ground cumin
- ½ cup cilantro
- 2 cups chicken stock
- 3 garlic cloves
- 1 cup yellow onions, sliced
- ½ teaspoon black pepper

Directions

1. Mix together the vinegar, recadorojo paste, Worcestershire sauce, oregano, cumin, erythritol and pepper in a large bowl.
2. Add chicken pieces and rub the marinade into it.
3. Marinate overnight and transfer into an Instant Pot.
4. Select "Sauté" and add coconut oil and chicken.
5. Sauté for about 2 minutes per side and dish out.
6. Add garlic and onions and sauté for about 3 minutes.
7. Return chicken pieces to the Instant Pot and stir in broth.
8. Lock the lid and set to "Manual" at high pressure for about 20 minutes.
9. Release the pressure naturally and garnish with cilantro to serve.

Nutrition

Calories: 184 Carbs: 7g Fats: 11.9g Proteins: 14.7g Sodium: 526mg Sugar: 5.1g

Garlic Beef Stew with Olives, Capers and Tomatoes

Serves: 10
Prep Time: 4 hours 30 mins
Ingredients

- 1 cup garlic cloves, peeled
- 1 can (14.5 oz.) diced tomatoes with juice
- 2 tablespoons olive oil
- 3 bay leaves
- 2 tablespoons tomato paste
- 2 pounds beef chuck roast, cut into 1-inch pieces
- 1 cup Kalamata olives, cut in half lengthwise
- 1 teaspoon dried Greek oregano
- 3 tablespoons red wine vinegar
- 1 cup low-sodium beef broth
- 2 tablespoons capers, rinsed
- 1 small can (8 oz.) tomato sauce
- Black pepper, to taste

Directions

1. Heat 1 tablespoon olive oil in a heavy frying pan over medium-high heat and add beef cubes.
2. Cook for about 6 minutes and transfer into crockpot.
3. Heat more oil and add garlic and Kalamata olives.
4. Sauté for about 2 minutes and transfer into crockpot.
5. Add beef broth, bay leaves, oregano, capers, canned tomatoes and juice, red wine vinegar, tomato sauce, tomato paste and black pepper to the crockpot.
6. Cook for about 4 hours on HIGH and dish out to serve hot.

Nutrition

Calories: 398 Carbs: 6.8g Fats: 29.6g Proteins: 25.3g Sodium: 311mg Sugar: 0.8g

Kimchi Beef Stew

Serves: 6/Prep Time: 40 mins

Ingredients

- 1-pound beef cubes, cut into 2-inch pieces
- 1 cup mushrooms
- 2 cups Kimchi
- 1 cup onions, chopped
- 1 tablespoon garlic, minced
- 1 tablespoon sesame oil
- 1 tablespoon dark soy sauce
- 1 tablespoon gochujang
- 2 cups water
- ½ cup green onions, diced
- 1 tablespoon ginger, minced
- ½ teaspoon cayenne pepper
- ¼ teaspoon Splenda
- Salt, to taste

Directions

1. Put all the ingredients in an Instant Pot and lock the lid.
2. Set to "Manual" at high pressure for about 15 minutes.
3. Release the pressure naturally and dish out to serve hot.

Nutrition Calories: 157 Carbs: 6.1g Fats: 6.4g Proteins: 17.8g Sodium: 327mg Sugar: 2.4g

West African Chicken and Peanut Stew with Chilies, Ginger, And Green Onions

Serves: 6/Prep Time: 30 mins

Ingredients

- ¼ cup red onion, finely diced
- 2 teaspoons jalapeno, finely minced
- 2 tablespoons olive oil
- 1 tablespoon ginger root, finely minced
- Salt and black pepper, to taste
- 1 cup chicken stock
- 2 tablespoons tomato paste
- 3 cups chicken, cooked and diced
- 3 green onions, thinly sliced
- 1 teaspoon chili powder
- ½ cup chunky peanut butter
- 1 tablespoon cider vinegar

Directions

1. Heat olive oil in a heavy pan and add ginger, red onions and jalapenos.
2. Season with salt and chili powder and sauté for about 2 minutes.
3. Stir in peanut butter, chicken stock, tomato paste, apple cider vinegar and tomato paste.
4. Bring to a boil and add chicken.
5. Simmer for about 15 minutes and dish out.
6. Garnish with green onions and serve.

Nutrition Calories: 285 Carbs: 7.2g Fats: 17.7g Proteins: 26.1g Sodium: 287mg Sugar: 3g

Beef Chuck Roast Stew

Serves: 8/Prep Time: 2 hours 45 mins

Ingredients

- 8 ounces whole mushrooms, quartered
- 4 ounces onions, trimmed and peeled
- 3 ounces carrots, roll-cut
- 2 tablespoons tomato paste
- 1 large bay leaf
- Salt and black pepper, to taste
- 1¼ pounds beef chuck roast, cubed into 1-inch pieces
- 6 ounces celery root, peeled and cubed into ¾ inch pieces
- 2 celery sticks, sliced
- 2 garlic cloves, sliced
- 2 tablespoons olive oil
- 5 cups beef broth
- ½ teaspoon dried thyme

Directions

1. Heat 1 tablespoon of oil in a heavy bottomed pot over medium heat and add mushrooms.
2. Sauté for about 2 minutes and mix in a bowl with other vegetables.
3. Heat 1 tablespoon of oil in the pot and brown the beef in batches.
4. Stir in the tomato paste, bay leaf and thyme and cook for about 2 minutes.
5. Add broth and reduce the heat to low.
6. Simmer gently for about 1½ hours and add the vegetables.
7. Simmer for about 1 hour and season with salt and pepper.

Nutrition Calories: 343 Carbs: 7.4g Fats: 24.3g Proteins: 23.4g Sodium: 565mg Sugar: 3g

Easy Crockpot Chicken Stew

Serves: 6

Prep Time: 2 hours 5mins

Ingredients

- 2 cups chicken stock
- ½ cup carrots, peeled and finely diced
- 2 celery sticks, diced
- ½ onion, diced
- 28 ounces skinless and deboned chicken thighs, diced into 1" pieces
- ½ teaspoon dried rosemary
- 3 garlic cloves, minced
- ¼ teaspoon dried thyme
- ½ teaspoon dried oregano
- 1 cup fresh spinach
- ½ cup heavy cream
- Salt and black pepper, to taste
- ½ teaspoon xanthan gum

Directions

1. Place the onions, chicken thighs, carrots, chicken stock, celery, garlic, rosemary, oregano and thyme into a crockpot.
2. Cook on LOW for about 4 hours and season with salt and pepper.
3. Stir in the heavy cream, spinach and xanthan gum.
4. Cook for another 10 minutes, while stirring continuously.
5. Dish out and serve hot.

Nutrition

Calories: 239 Carbs: 4.6g Fats: 15.6g Proteins: 23.2g Sodium: 401mg Sugar: 1.3g

Beef Vegetables Keto Stew

Serves: 6/Prep Time: 10 mins

Ingredients

- 2 cups beef broth
- 100 grams onions
- 100 grams radishes
- 1-pound beef short rib
- 4 cloves garlic, minced
- 100 grams carrots
- ¼ teaspoon pink salt
- ½ teaspoon xanthan gum
- 1 tablespoon coconut oil
- ¼ teaspoon pepper
- 1 tablespoon butter

Directions

1. Heat coconut oil on medium-high heat in a large saucepan and add beef short rib.
2. Cook for about 4 minutes until brown on all sides and add onions, garlic and butter.
3. Cook for about 3 minutes and add the broth and xanthan gum.
4. Bring to a boil and simmer for about 30 minutes.
5. Add the carrots and radishes and cook for 30 more minutes, stirring repeatedly.
6. Dish out and serve hot.

Nutrition

Calories: 224 Carbs: 5.8g Fats: 11.5g Proteins: 24.1g Sodium: 366mg Sugar: 2.1g

Spicy Crockpot Double Beef Stew

Serves: 6

Prep Time: 6 hours 10 mins

Ingredients

- 1 (14.5 oz) can chili-ready diced tomatoes
- 1½ pounds stew beef
- 1 tablespoon chili mix
- 2 teaspoons hot sauce
- Salt, to taste
- 1 cup beef broth
- 1 tablespoon Worcestershire sauce

Directions

1. Put all the ingredients in crockpot and mix well.
2. Cook for about 6 hours on HIGH and break up meat with a fork.
3. Season with more salt if needed and cook for about 2 hours on LOW.
4. Dish out and serve hot.

Nutrition

Calories: 197 Carbs: 5.6g Fats: 7.1g Proteins: 26.5g Sodium: 425mg Sugar: 4.2g

Beef Stew with Herby Dumplings

Serves: 8

Prep Time: 4 hours

Ingredients

- 1 carrot
- 1 red onion, chopped
- 3 bay leaves
- 2 tablespoons olive oil
- 2 pounds stew beef
- 100 g pumpkin
- 2 cloves garlic, minced
- ½ cup dry red wine
- 3 sprigs of fresh rosemary
- ¼ teaspoon black pepper
- ¾ teaspoon sea salt
- 2 tablespoons tomato puree
- 2 cups beef stock

Dumplings:
- 1 cup water, boiling
- ¾ cup almond flour
- 1½ teaspoons gluten-free baking powder
- 1 teaspoon fresh lemon zest
- 1 large egg
- 3 large egg whites
- ¼ cup coconut flour
- 1 tablespoon chopped rosemary
- 1/3 cup sesame seed flour
- ¼ teaspoon sea salt
- 1 pinch black pepper
- Fresh parsley, for topping
- 1 tablespoon psyllium husk powder
- 1 tablespoon fresh thyme

Directions
1. Preheat the oven to 320 °F.
2. Heat 1 tablespoon of olive oil in a pan and add meat.
3. Cook for about 5 minutes on a medium heat until brown.
4. Heat 1 tablespoon of olive oil in a pan and add vegetables.
5. Cook for about 10 minutes on a medium heat and add rosemary, beef, bay leaves, garlic and tomato puree.
6. Sauté for about 2 minutes and add the red wine.
7. Reduce the heat to low and simmer for about 5 minutes.
8. Add the stock and season with salt and black pepper.
9. Bring to a boil and transfer into a casserole dish.
10. Place in the oven and roast for about 3 hours.
11. Dish out and change the temperature to about 350 °F.
12. Mix together all the ingredients for dumplings and make dumplings shape out of this mixture.
13. Grease cupcake tins with olive oil and place dumplings in the cupcake holes.
14. Transfer in the oven and bake for about 25 minutes.
15. Flip with a spoon and place back in the oven to cook for another 5 minutes.
16. Add the dumplings to the stew and serve.

Nutrition
Calories: 333 Carbs: 9.9g Fats: 17.1g Proteins: 31.6g Sodium: 612mg Sugar: 1.6g

Keto Chicken Curry Stew

Serves: 8/Prep Time: 10 mins
Ingredients
- 2 tablespoons curry powder
- ¼ cup coconut oil
- 1 green bell pepper
- 1.5 pounds boneless chicken thighs
- 2 teaspoons garlic powder
- - pound cauliflower
- 14 oz coconut milk
- ¼ cup fresh cilantro
- Salt and black pepper, to taste

Directions
1. Heat coconut oil in a wok pan and add curry powder and garlic powder.
2. Sauté for about 1 minute and add chicken, salt and black pepper.
3. Sauté for about 5 minutes and dish out the chicken mixture.
4. Add cauliflowers and bell peppers to the same wok pan and cook for about 3 minutes.
5. Add coconut milk and simmer for about 10 minutes.
6. Season with salt and black pepper and add fried chicken to the stew.
7. Garnish with fresh cilantro and serve hot.

Nutrition
Calories: 314 Carbs: 8.4g Fats: 23.9g Proteins: 19.5g Sodium: 99mg Sugar: 4g Per serving

Low Carb Lamb Stew

Serves: 3
Prep Time: 6 hours 15 mins
Ingredients
- 8 oz turnips peeled and chopped
- 14 oz can of beef broth
- 1 teaspoon garlic paste
- 1-pound boneless lamb stewing meat
- 8 oz mushrooms sliced or quartered
- 1 teaspoon onion powder
- Salt and black pepper, to taste
- ¼ cup fresh flat-leaf parsley, chopped

Directions
1. Put turnips, mushrooms, lamb, beef broth, garlic paste, onion powder, salt and black pepper in a slow cooker.
2. Cook on LOW for about 6 hours and dish out.
3. Garnish with fresh flat-leaf parsley and serve.

Nutrition
Calories: 360 Carbs: 8.7g Fats: 20.7g Proteins: 33g Sodium: 597mg Sugar: 4.5g

Leftover Turkey Stew

Serves: 12/Prep Time: 35 mins

Ingredients
- 2 cups turkey, cooked and cubed
- 3 tablespoons butter
- 15 ounce can mixed vegetables
- 14 ounce can chicken broth

Directions
1. Put all the ingredients in a large saucepan and bring to a boil.
2. Reduce heat to low and simmer for about 25 minutes.
3. Dish out and serve hot.

Nutrition Calories: 143 Carbs: 3.5g Fats: 6.8g Proteins: 16.2g Sodium: 134mg Sugar: 0.9g

Spicy Pork Stew with Spinach

Serves: 4/Prep Time: 45 mins

Ingredients
- 4 garlic cloves
- 1 large onion
- 1 teaspoon dried thyme
- 1-pound pork butt meat cut into 2-inch chunks
- 4 cups baby spinach, chopped
- 2 teaspoons Cajun seasoning blend
- ½ cup heavy whipping cream

Directions
1. Blend together onions and garlic and put into the pressure cooker.
2. Add Cajun Seasoning blend and pork and lock the lid.
3. Cook for about 20 minutes at high pressure.
4. Release the pressure naturally for about 10 minutes and add baby spinach and cream.
5. Select "Sauté" and cook for about 5 minutes.
6. Dish out and serve hot.

Nutrition Calories: 376 Carbs: 6.2g Fats: 24.7g Proteins: 31.5g Sodium: 140mg Sugar: 1.8g

Side Dishes and Snacks Recipes

Keto Gin Cocktail

Serves: 1/Prep Time: 10 mins

Ingredients
- 4 blueberries
- 2 ounces dry gin
- 1 teaspoon erythritol, powdered
- 1 can club soda
- ½ ounce fresh lime juice

Directions
1. Put the blueberries and mint into a cocktail shaker.
2. Shake well and add the gin, lime juice, erythritol and ice.
3. Shake again and strain into a cocktail glass.
4. Top with club soda and serve chilled.

Nutrition Calories: 161 Carbs: 7.3g Fats: 0.1g Proteins: 0.2g Sodium: 76mg Sugar: 1.7g

Parmesan and Garlic Keto Crackers

Serves: 4/Prep Time: 40 mins

Ingredients
- 1 cup Parmesan cheese, finely grated
- 1 cup almond flour, blanched
- ½ teaspoon garlic powder
- 1 large egg, whisked
- 1 tablespoon butter, melted

Directions
1. Preheat the oven to 350 degrees F and grease 2 large baking sheets.
2. Mix together the parmesan cheese, almond flour, chives and garlic powder in a large bowl until well incorporated.
3. Whisk together the eggs and butter in a separate bowl.
4. Mix together the dry and wet ingredients until a dough is formed.
5. Divide the dough into two halves and press until ¼ inch thick.
6. Cut each sheet of dough with a pastry cutter into 25 crackers of equal size.
7. Arrange the crackers on the baking sheets and transfer into the oven.
8. Bake for about 15 minutes and allow them to stay in the off oven.
9. Remove from the oven and serve.

Nutrition
Calories: 304 Carbs: 7.4g Fats: 23.5g Proteins: 16.8g Sodium: 311mg Sugar: 0.2g

Keto Sausage Balls

Serves: 6
Prep Time: 30 mins
Ingredients
- 1 cup almond flour, blanched
- 1-pound bulk Italian sausage
- 1¼ cups sharp cheddar cheese, shredded
- 2 teaspoons baking powder
- 1 large egg

Directions
1. Preheat the oven to 360 degrees F and grease a baking sheet.
2. Mix together all the ingredients in a large bowl until well incorporated.
3. Make equal sized balls from this mixture and arrange on the baking sheet.
4. Transfer in the oven and bake for about 20 minutes until golden brown.

Nutrition
Calories: 477 Carbs: 5.1g Fats: 39g Proteins: 25.6g Sodium: 732mg Sugar: 0.2g

Creamy Basil Baked Sausage

Serves: 12
Prep Time: 45 mins
Ingredients
- 8 oz cream cheese
- ¼ cup basil pesto
- 8 oz mozzarella cheese
- 3 pounds Italian chicken sausages
- ¼ cup heavy cream

Directions
1. Preheat the oven to 400 degrees and grease a large casserole dish.
2. Put the sausages in the casserole dish and transfer to the oven.
3. Bake for about 30 minutes and dish out.
4. Mix together the pesto, cream cheese and heavy cream in a bowl.
5. Top the sausage with the pesto mixture, followed by mozzarella cheese.
6. Bake for 10 more minutes and remove from the oven to serve.

Nutrition
Calories: 342 Carbs: 8.9g Fats: 23.3g Proteins: 21.6g Sodium: 624mg Sugar: 0.5g

Low Carb Tortilla Chips

Serves: 4
Prep Time: 25 mins
Ingredients
- 2 tablespoons olive oil
- 3 tablespoons lime juice
- 1 tablespoon taco seasoning
- 6 tortillas, low carb

Directions
1. Preheat the oven to 350 degrees and grease a cookie sheet.
2. Cut each tortilla into small wedges and arrange on a cookie sheet.
3. Mix together the olive oil and lime juice and spray each tortilla wedge.
4. Sprinkle with the taco seasoning and transfer into the oven.
5. Bake for about 8 minutes and rotate the pan.
6. Bake for another 8 minutes and dish out to serve.

Nutrition
Calories: 147 Carbs: 17.8g Fats: 8g Proteins: 2.1g Sodium: 174mg Sugar: 0.7g

Broccoli Cheese Soup

Serves: 6/Prep Time: 5 hours 10 mins
Ingredients
- 1 cup heavy whipping cream
- 2 cups chicken broth
- 2 cups broccoli
- Salt, to taste
- 2 cups cheddar cheese

Directions
1) Place the cheddar cheese, broccoli, chicken broth, heavy whipping cream and salt in a crock pot.
2) Set the crock pot on LOW and cook for about 5 hours.
3) Ladle out in a bowl and serve hot.

Nutrition
Calories: 244 Carbs: 3.4g Fats: 20.4g Proteins: 12.3g Sodium: 506mg Sugar: 1g

Mediterranean Spinach with Cheese

Serves: 6/Prep Time: 25 mins
Ingredients
- 2 pounds spinach, chopped
- ½ cup black olives, halved and pitted
- Salt and black pepper, to taste
- 4 tablespoons butter
- 1½ cups feta cheese, grated
- 4 teaspoons fresh lemon zest, grated

Directions
1) Preheat the Air fryer to 400 degrees and grease an Air fryer basket.
2) Cook spinach for about 4 minutes in a pan of boiling water. Drain well.
3) Mix together butter, spinach, salt, and black pepper in a bowl.
4) Transfer the spinach mixture into an air fryer basket.
5) Cook for about 15 minutes, tossing once in the middle way.
6) Dish into a bowl and stir in the olives, cheese, and lemon zest to serve.

Nutrition
Calories: 215 Carbs: 8g Fats: 17.5g Proteins: 9.9g Sodium: 690mg Sugar: 2.3g

Cheesy Cauliflower

Serves: 6
Prep Time: 30 mins
Ingredients
- 2 tablespoons mustard
- ½ cup butter, cut into small pieces
- 2 cauliflower heads, chopped
- 1 cup Parmesan cheese, grated
- 2 teaspoons avocado mayonnaise

Directions
1) Preheat the oven to 400 degrees F and grease a baking dish.
2) Mix together mustard and avocado mayonnaise in a bowl.
3) Coat the cauliflower with the mustard mixture and transfer into a baking dish.
4) Top with Parmesan cheese and butter and bake for about 25 minutes.
5) Pull from the oven and serve hot.

Nutrition
Calories: 201 Carbs: 6.2g Fats: 18.9g Proteins: 4.3g Sodium: 192mg Sugar: 2.4g

Parmesan Roasted Bamboo Sprouts

Serves: 6
Prep Time: 25 mins
Ingredients
- 2 cups Parmesan cheese, grated
- 2 pounds bamboo sprouts
- 4 tablespoons butter
- ½ teaspoon paprika
- Salt and black pepper, to taste

Directions
1) Preheat the oven to 365 degrees and grease a baking dish.
2) Marinate the bamboo sprouts with paprika, butter, salt, and black pepper, and keep aside.
3) Transfer the seasoned bamboo sprouts in the baking dish and place in the oven.
4) Bake for about 15 minutes and dish to serve.

Nutrition
Calories: 162 Carbs: 4.7g Fats: 11.7g Proteins: 7.5g Sodium: 248mg Sugar: 1.4g

Mexican Cheesy Veggies

Serves: 4
Prep Time: 40 mins
Ingredients
- 1 onion, thinly sliced
- 1 tomato, thinly sliced
- 1 zucchini, sliced
- 1 teaspoon mixed dried herbs
- Salt and black pepper, to taste
- 1 teaspoon olive oil
- 1 cup Mexican cheese, grated

Directions
1) Preheat the oven to 370 degrees and grease a baking dish.
2) Layer the vegetables in the baking dish and drizzle with olive oil.
3) Top evenly with cheese and sprinkle with herbs, salt, and black pepper.
4) Bake for about 30 minutes and dish to serve hot.

Nutrition
Calories: 305 Carbs: 8.3g Fats: 22.3g Proteins: 15.2g Sodium: 370mg Sugar: 4.2g

Cauliflower Mash

Serves: 4
Prep Time: 20 mins
Ingredients
- 1 tablespoon full-fat coconut milk
- 3 garlic cloves, minced
- 1 teaspoon green chilies, chopped
- 3 tablespoons butter
- ½ cup feta cheese
- 1 head cauliflower stems, completely removed
- Salt and black pepper, to taste

Directions
1) Preheat the oven to 360 degrees and grease a baking dish.
2) Place cauliflower pieces in the baking dish and transfer into the oven.
3) Bake for about 10 minutes and dish out the cauliflower pieces.
4) Mix with the remaining ingredients and blend with an immersion hand blender to achieve the desired texture.

Nutrition
Calories: 154 Carbs: 5.3g Fats: 13.5g Proteins: 4.3g Sodium: 292mg Sugar: 2.5g

Bacon Wrapped Asparagus

Serves: 3/Prep Time: 30 mins
Ingredients
- 6 small asparagus spears
- 3 bacon slices
- 2 tablespoons butter
- ¼ cup heavy whipping cream
- Salt and black pepper, to taste

Directions
1) Preheat the oven to 370 degrees and grease the baking dish with butter.
2) Sprinkle the asparagus spears with salt and black pepper.
3) Add heavy whipping cream to the asparagus and wrap with bacon slices.
4) Place the wrapped asparagus in the baking dish and transfer into the oven.
5) Bake for about 20 minutes and dish out to serve hot.

Nutrition Calories: 176 Carbs: 1.2g Fats: 13.4g Proteins: 0.8g Sodium: 321mg Sugar: 0.5g

Cheesy Brussels Sprout

Serves: 5/Prep Time: 35 mins
Ingredients
- 1-pound Brussels sprouts
- 3 tablespoons olive oil
- ½ cup cream
- Salt and black pepper, to taste
- 2 tablespoons butter
- ½ cup parmesan cheese, grated

Directions
1) Preheat the oven to 360 degrees and grease a baking dish.
2) Mix together Brussels sprouts, olive oil, parmesan cheese, salt, and black pepper in a bowl.
3) Transfer the Brussels sprouts in the baking dish and drizzle with butter.
4) Transfer it into the oven and bake for about 25 minutes.
5) Dish to serve hot.

Nutrition
Calories: 190 Carbs: 8.5g Fats: 16.8g Proteins: 5g Sodium: 124mg Sugar: 2g

Tomato Soup

Serves: 4/Prep Time: 30 mins
Ingredients
- 2 cups low-sodium vegetable broth
- ¼ cup fresh basil, chopped
- 1 garlic clove, minced
- 1 teaspoon dried parsley, crushed
- Freshly ground black pepper, to taste
- 1 teaspoon dried basil, crushed
- 2 tablespoons Erythritol
- ½ tablespoon balsamic vinegar
- ½ tablespoon olive oil
- 1-pound fresh tomatoes, chopped
- 1 cup cheddar cheese

Directions
1) Put the oil in a pot and add tomatoes, garlic, herbs, black pepper, and broth.
2) Cover the lid and cook for about 18-20 minutes on medium-low heat.
3) Stir in sugar and vinegar and place the mixture in an immersion blender.
4) Blend until smooth and ladle into a bowl.
5) Garnish with basil and serve immediately.

Nutrition
Calories: 194 Carbs: 5.6g Fats: 15.4g Proteins: 9.2g Sodium: 257mg Sugar: 3.2g

Spinach Quiche

Serves: 6
Prep Time: 45 mins
Ingredients

- 1 tablespoon butter, melted
- Salt and black pepper, to taste
- 1 (10-ounce) package frozen spinach, thawed
- 5 organic eggs, beaten
- 3 cups Monterey Jack cheese, shredded

Directions

1) Preheat the oven to 360 degrees and grease a 9-inch pie dish lightly.
2) Put butter and spinach in a large skillet on medium-low heat.
3) Cook for about 3 minutes and set aside.
4) Mix together Monterey Jack cheese, spinach, eggs, salt, and black pepper in a bowl.
5) Put the mixture into prepared pie dish and transfer into the oven.
6) Bake for about 30 minutes and remove from the oven.
7) Cut into equal sized wedges and serve hot.

Nutrition

Calories: 349 Carbs: 3.2g Fats: 27.8g Proteins: 23g Sodium: 532mg Sugar: 1.3g

Broccoli Pops

Serves: 6
Prep Time: 20 mins
Ingredients

- 1/3 cup Parmesan cheese, grated
- 2 cups cheddar cheese, grated
- Salt and black pepper, to taste
- 3 eggs, beaten
- 3 cups broccoli florets
- 1 tablespoon olive oil

Directions

1) Preheat the oven to 360 degrees and grease a baking dish with olive oil.
2) Pulse the broccoli in a food processor until finely crumbed.
3) Add broccoli and stir in rest of the ingredients in a large bowl.
4) Make small equal-sized balls from the mixture.
5) Put the balls in a baking sheet and refrigerate for at least 30 minutes.
6) Place balls in the baking dish and transfer the dish into the oven.
7) Bake for about 13 minutes and dish out to serve.

Nutrition

Calories: 162 Carbs: 1.9g Fats: 12.4g Proteins: 11.2g Sodium: 263mg Sugar: 0.5g

Keto Onion Rings

Serves: 4/Prep Time: 20 mins
Ingredients

- 2 large onions, cut into ¼ inch slices
- 2 teaspoons baking powder
- Salt, to taste
- 2 cups cream cheese
- 2 eggs

Directions

1) Preheat the oven to 375 degrees and separate the onion slices into rings.
2) Mix together salt and baking powder in a bowl.
3) Whisk together cream cheese and eggs in another dish.
4) Dredge the onion rings into baking powder mixture and dip into cream cheese mixture.
5) Place the onion rings in the oven and bake for about 10 minutes.
6) Dish out to serve hot.

Nutrition

Calories: 266 Carbs: 9.9g Fats: 22.5g Proteins: 8g Sodium: 285mg Sugar: 3.5g

Zucchini Cream Cheese Fries

Serves: 4/Prep Time: 20 mins
Ingredients

- 1 cup cream cheese
- 1-pound zucchini, sliced into 2 ½-inch sticks
- 2 tablespoons olive oil
- Salt, to taste

Directions

1) Preheat the oven to 380 degrees and grease a baking dish with olive oil.
2) Season the zucchini with salt and coat with cream cheese.
3) Place zucchini in the baking dish and transfer into the oven.
4) Bake for about 10 minutes and dish out to serve.

Nutrition

Calories: 374 Carbs: 7.1g Fats: 36.6g Proteins: 7.7g Sodium: 294mg Sugar: 2.8g

Asparagus Bites

Serves: 6/Prep Time: 20 mins
Ingredients
- 1 cup desiccated coconut
- 2 cups asparagus
- 1 cup feta cheese

Directions
1) Preheat the oven to 400 degrees and grease a baking dish with cooking spray.
2) Place the desiccated coconut in a shallow dish and coat asparagus evenly with coconut.
3) Arrange the coated asparagus in the baking dish and top with cheese.
4) Transfer into the oven and bake for about 10 minutes to serve.

Nutrition Calories: 135 Carbs: 5g Fats: 10.3g Proteins: 7g Sodium: 421mg Sugar: 3.1g

Fish and Seafood Recipes

Lemon Garlic Shrimp

Serves: 3/Prep Time: 25 mins
Ingredients
- 3 tablespoons butter
- 1-pound large raw shrimp
- 2 lemons, sliced
- 1 teaspoon paprika
- 4 garlic cloves

Directions
1. Heat the butter in a skillet and add garlic.
2. Sauté for about 1 minute and add shrimp, paprika, and lemon slices.
3. Cook for about 10 minutes on medium low heat and dish out to serve hot.

Nutrition
Calories: 271 Carbs: 5.3g Fats: 13.4g Proteins: 32.5g Sodium: 422mg Sugar: 1.1g

Cheesy and Creamy Tilapia

Serves: 4/Prep Time: 40 mins
Ingredients
- 1 cup Parmesan cheese, grated
- 4 tilapia fillets
- ¼ cup mayonnaise
- Salt and black pepper, to taste
- ¼ cup fresh lemon juice

Directions
1. Preheat the oven to 350 degrees and grease 2 baking dishes.
2. Marinate tilapia fillets with mayonnaise, fresh lemon juice, salt and black pepper.
3. Put the marinated fillets in the baking dishes and top with cheese.
4. Transfer into the oven and bake for about 30 minutes.
5. Remove from the oven and serve hot.

Nutrition Calories: 245 Carbs: 4.9g Fats: 12.1g Proteins: 30.4g Sodium: 411mg Sugar: 1.3g

Roasted Mahi-Mahi Fish

Serves: 3/Prep Time: 45 mins
Ingredients
- ½ cup fresh lemon juice
- 1-pound mahi-mahi fillets
- 4 tablespoons butter
- Salt and black pepper, to taste
- 1 teaspoon dried rosemary, crushed

Directions
1. Preheat the oven to 350 degrees and grease 2 baking dishes.
2. Season the mahi-mahi fish fillets with salt and black pepper.
3. Put the seasoned fillets in the baking dishes and top with dried oregano, dried rosemary, and fresh lemon juice.
4. Bake for about 30 minutes and remove from the oven to serve hot.

Nutrition Calories: 267 Carbs: 1.1g Fats: 15.7g Proteins: 28.6g Sodium: 245mg Sugar: 0.9g

Sweet and Sour Fish

Serves: 6/Prep Time: 25 mins
Ingredients
- ¼ cup butter
- 2 pounds fish chunks
- 2 tablespoons vinegar
- Salt and black pepper, to taste
- 4 drops liquid stevia

Directions

1. Put the butter and fish in a skillet and sauté for about 4 minutes.
2. Pour in the stevia, vinegar, salt and black pepper.
3. Cook for about 10 minutes on medium low heat and dish out to serve hot.

Nutrition

Calories: 190 Carbs: 2.8g Fats: 9g Proteins: 27.1g Sodium: 595mg Sugar: 2.7g

Mahi Mahi Cakes

Serves: 4/Prep Time: 30 mins

Ingredients

- 2 teaspoons primal palate seafood seasoning
- 12 oz mahi mahi, canned
- ¼ cup onions minced
- 3 tablespoons organic palm oil
- 2 teaspoons parsley garnish
- 3pasture egg yolks
- 1 teaspoon chives garnish
- 4 lemon wedges, for garnish

Directions

1) Preheat the oven at 360 degrees and grease a baking tray.
2) Mix together seafood seasoning, salmon, onions, and egg yolks in a bowl.
3) Make small patties out of this mixture and arrange them on the baking tray.
4) Transfer it to the oven and bake for about 15 minutes.
5) Dish out the patties and set aside.
6) Put palm oil in a skillet on a medium-high heat and add patties.
7) Flip the sides of the patties and dish onto a plate.
8) Garnish with parsley, lemon wedges, and chives to serve.

Nutrition

Calories: 248 Carbs: 1.8g Fats: 18.9g Proteins: 18.7g Sodium: 464mg Sugar: 0.6g

Salmon Stew

Serves: 3/Prep Time: 20 mins

Ingredients

- 1 cup homemade fish broth
- 1 medium onion, chopped
- 1-pound salmon fillet, cubed
- Salt and black pepper, to taste
- 1 tablespoon butter

Directions

1) Season the salmon fillets with salt and black pepper.
2) Put butter and onions in a skillet and sauté for about 3 minutes.
3) Add salmon and cook for about 2 minutes on each side.
4) Stir in the fish broth and cover the lid.
5) Cook for about 7 minutes and dish out to serve hot.

Nutrition

Calories: 272 Carbs: 4.4g Fats: 14.2g Proteins: 32.1g Sodium: 275mg Sugar: 1.9g

Paprika Shrimp

Serves: 6/Prep Time: 25 mins

Ingredients

- 6 tablespoons butter
- 1 teaspoon smoked paprika
- 2 pounds tiger shrimps
- Salt, to taste

Directions

1) Preheat the oven to 395 degrees and grease a baking dish with butter.
2) Season the shrimps with smoked paprika and salt.
3) Arrange the seasoned shrimp in the baking dish and transfer the baking dish in oven.
4) Bake for about 15 minutes and dish out to serve.

Nutrition Calories: 173 Carbs: 0.1g Fats: 8.3g Proteins: 23.8g Sodium: 332mg Sugar: 0g

Shrimp Magic

Serves: 3/Prep Time: 25 mins

Ingredients

- 2 tablespoons butter
- ½ teaspoon smoked paprika
- 1-pound shrimps, peeled and deveined
- Lemongrass stalks
- 1 red chili pepper, seeded and chopped

Directions

1) Place all the ingredients in a bowl, except lemongrass, and mix well to marinate for about 2 hours.
2) Preheat the oven to 400 degrees and thread the shrimps onto lemongrass stalks.
3) Bake for about 15 minutes and serve immediately.

Nutrition

Calories: 251 Carbs: 3g Fats: 10.3g Proteins: 34.6g Sodium: 424mg Sugar: 0.1g

Sweet and Sour Fish

Serves: 3/Prep Time: 25 mins
Ingredients
- ¼ cup butter
- 2 drops liquid stevia
- 1-pound fish chunks
- Salt and black pepper, to taste
- 1 tablespoon vinegar

Directions
1) Heat butter in a large skillet and add fish chunks.
2) Cook for about 3 minutes and add liquid stevia and vinegar.
3) Cook for about 1 minute and add salt and black pepper.
4) Stir continuously at medium-low heat for about 10 minutes.
5) Place onto a serving bowl and serve hot.

Nutrition Calories: 274 Carbs: 2.8g Fats: 15.4g Proteins: 33.2g Sodium: 604mg Sugar: 0g

Buttered Scallops

Serves: 6/Prep Time: 25 mins
Ingredients
- 4 tablespoons fresh rosemary, chopped
- 4 garlic cloves, minced
- 2 pounds sea scallops
- Salt and black pepper, to taste
- ½ cup butter

Directions
1) Put butter, rosemary and garlic on medium-high heat and sauté for about 1 minute.
2) Stir in the sea scallops, salt, and black pepper and cook for about 2 minutes per side.
3) Add garlic and rosemary and sauté for about 3 minutes.
4) Dish out in a bowl and serve hot.

Nutrition Calories: 279 Carbs: 5.7g Fats: 16.8g Proteins: 25.8g Sodium: 354mg Sugar: 0g

BBQ Trout

Serves: 4/Prep Time: 20 mins
Ingredients
- 2 garlic cloves, crushed
- Salt and black pepper, to taste
- 2 small lemons, seeded, sliced thinly and divided
- 1½ tablespoons olive oil
- 4 rainbow trout fillets
- 1 small onion, sliced thinly

Directions
1) Preheat the grill to medium-high heat and grease the grill grate.
2) Rub the trout slices with garlic and arrange each trout slice over a piece of foil.
3) Arrange lemon and onion slices evenly over fillets and sprinkle with salt and black pepper.
4) Drizzle with olive oil and fold the foil pieces in order to seal the trout slices.
5) Grill the trout for about 6 minutes and serve hot.

Nutrition
Calories: 190 Carbs: 7g Fats: 13.4g Proteins: 13.5g Sodium: 361mg Sugar: 2.3g

Salmon with Orange Ginger Sauce

Serves: 2/Prep Time: 20 mins
Ingredients
- 1-pound salmon
- 1 tablespoon dark soy sauce
- 2 teaspoons minced ginger
- 1 teaspoon minced garlic
- .5-1 teaspoon salt
- 1-1.5 teaspoon ground pepper
- 2 tablespoons low sugar marmalade.

Directions
1. Place salmon in a 6-inch pan.
2. Toss all the ingredients for the sauce then pour it over the salmon.
3. Let it marinate for 30 minutes at room temperature.
4. Pour about 2 cups of water into the insert of the Instant Pot.
5. Place the trivet over the water and place the marinated salmon over it.
6. Pour the marinade over it liberally
7. Seal the Instant Pot lid and turn the pressure valve to sealing position.
8. Select Manual mode for 3 minutes at high pressure
9. Once done, release the pressure completely then remove the lid.
10. Serve warm.

Nutrition Calories per serving: 236 Carbohydrate: 3.2g Protein: 22.2g Fat: 10.6g Sugar: 1.4g Sodium: 53mg

Coconut Fish Curry

Serves: 2/Prep Time: 30 mins
Ingredients
- 1-1.5 lb. fish steaks, rinsed and cut into bite-size pieces
- 1 tomato, chopped
- 2 green chilies, sliced into strips
- 2 medium onions, sliced into strips
- 2 garlic cloves, squeezed
- 1 tablespoon freshly grated ginger,
- 6 curry leaves, or bay leaves
- 1 tablespoon ground coriander
- 2 teaspoons ground cumin
- ½ teaspoon ground turmeric
- 1 teaspoon chili powder,
- ½ teaspoon ground fenugreek
- 2 cups unsweetened coconut milk
- salt to taste
- lemon juice to taste

Directions
1. Preheat oil in the insert of the Instant Pot.
2. Add curry leaves and sauté for 1 minute.
3. Toss in ginger, onion, and ginger, sauté until soft.
4. Add all the spices including fenugreek, chili powder, cumin, coriander, and turmeric.
5. Sauté for 2 minutes then add coconut milk and deglaze the pot.
6. Stir in fish pieces, tomatoes, and green chilies.
7. Seal the Instant Pot lid and turn the pressure valve to sealing position.
8. Select Manual mode for 5 minutes at low pressure
9. Once done, release the pressure completely then remove the lid.
10. Adjust seasoning with lemon juice and salt.
11. Enjoy.

Nutrition Calories per serving: 270 Carbohydrate: 1.1g Protein: 22.5g Fat: 20.3g Sugar: 0.3g Sodium: 117mg

Poultry Recipes

Stuffed Chicken with Asparagus and Bacon

Serves: 4/Prep Time: 50 mins
Ingredients
- ½ teaspoon salt
- 1-pound chicken tenders
- ¼ teaspoon black pepper
- 8 bacon slices
- 12 asparagus spears

Directions
1. Preheat the oven to 400 degrees and grease a baking sheet.
2. Lay bacon slices on a baking sheet and top with chicken tenders.
3. Season with salt and black pepper and add asparagus spears.
4. Wrap the bacon around the chicken and asparagus.
5. Bake for about 40 minutes and dish out to serve hot.

Nutrition Calories: 377 Carbs: 3g Fats: 25g Proteins: 32g Sodium: 798mg Sugar: 1g

Crock-Pot Whole Roasted Turkey

Serves: 6/Prep Time: 40 mins
Ingredients
- 1 cup mozzarella cheese, shredded
- 1 (2-pound) whole chicken, cleaned, pat dried
- 2 tablespoons fresh lemon juice
- Salt and black pepper, to taste
- 4 whole garlic cloves, peeled

Directions
1. Stuff the turkey cavity with garlic cloves and season with salt and black pepper.
2. Place the turkey into a non-stick skillet and squeeze the lemon juice onto it.
3. Cook for about 30 minutes and dish out to serve hot.

Nutrition Calories: 310 Carbs: 0.5g Fats: 12.8g Proteins: 45.3g Sodium: 230mg Sugar: 0.1g

Ketogenic Italian Turkey

Serves: 5/Prep Time: 35 mins
Ingredients
- ¾ cup cream cheese
- ¾ cup parmesan cheese, grated
- 1½ pounds turkey breasts, sliced
- 1 teaspoon butter
- 1 teaspoon Italian seasoning

Directions
1. Mix the cream cheese, parmesan cheese and Italian seasoning.

2. Put the butter and turkey breasts in a non-stick skillet.
3. Cook for about 5 minutes on medium heat and add the cheese mixture.
4. Cook for about 25 minutes and dish out to serve hot.

Nutrition
Calories: 336 Carbs: 7.5g Fats: 19.7g Proteins: 32.3g Sodium: 1674mg Sugar: 4.9g

Mushroom Garlic Chicken

Serves: 6/Prep Time: 40 mins
Ingredients
- 2 tablespoons butter
- 2 pounds chicken thighs
- 1 cup mushrooms, sliced
- Salt and black pepper, to taste
- 3 garlic cloves

Directions
1. Season the chicken thighs with salt and black pepper.
2. Put the butter in a skillet and add seasoned chicken.
3. Sauté for about 2 minutes and stir in garlic and mushrooms.
4. Sauté for about 30 minutes on medium-low heat and dish out to serve hot.

Nutrition
Calories: 326 Carbs: 0.9g Fats: 15.1g Proteins: 44.3g Sodium: 158mg Sugar: 0.2g

Chili Lime Turkey

Serves: 6/Prep Time: 20 mins
Ingredients
- ¼ cup cooking wine
- ½ teaspoon paprika
- 5 garlic cloves, minced
- 1 tablespoon lime juice
- ¼ cup butter
- 1 onion, diced
- 1 teaspoon sea salt
- ½ cup organic chicken broth
- 2 pounds turkey thighs
- 1 teaspoon dried parsley
- 3 green chilies, chopped

Directions
1) Put butter, onions, and garlic in a large skillet and sauté for about 3 minutes.
2) Add rest of the ingredients and cook for about 20 minutes.
3) Dish out in a platter and serve hot.

Nutrition Calories: 282 Carbs: 6.3g Fats: 15.2g Proteins: 27.4g Sodium: 2117mg Sugar: 3.3g

Stuffed Whole Chicken

Serves: 6/Prep Time: 8 hours 10 mins
Ingredients
- 1 cup Monterey Jack cheese
- 4 whole garlic cloves, peeled
- 1 (2-pound) whole chicken, cleaned, pat dried
- Salt and black pepper, to taste
- 2 tablespoons fresh lemon juice

Directions
1) Stuff the chicken cavity with Monterey Jack cheese and garlic cloves.
2) Season the chicken with salt and black pepper.
3) Transfer the chicken into the slow cooker and drizzle with lemon juice.
4) Set the slow cooker on LOW and cook for about 8 hours.
5) Dish out and serve hot.

Nutrition Calories: 309 Carbs: 1.6g Fats: 12.1g Proteins: 45.8g Sodium: 201mg Sugar: 0.7g

Mediterranean Turkey Cutlets

Serves: 4/Prep Time: 25 mins
Ingredients
- 2 tablespoons olive oil
- 1-pound turkey cutlets
- ½ cup almond flour
- 1 teaspoon turmeric powder
- 1 teaspoon Greek seasoning

Directions
1) Mix together Greek seasoning, almond flour, and turmeric powder in a bowl and coat turkey cutlets with this mixture.
2) Heat oil in a skillet and add the turkey cutlets.
3) Cover the lid and cook for about 20 minutes on medium-low heat.
4) Dish out in a serving platter and serve.

Nutrition
Calories: 340 Carbs: 3.7g Fats: 19.4g Proteins: 36.3g Sodium: 124mg Sugar: 0g

Caprese Hasselback Chicken

Serves: 4/Prep Time: 25 mins

Ingredients

- 4 large chicken breasts
- 2 tablespoons butter
- 1 cup fresh mozzarella cheese, thinly sliced
- 2 large Roma tomatoes, thinly sliced
- Salt and freshly ground black pepper, to taste

Directions

1) Make slits in the chicken breasts and season with salt and black pepper.
2) Stuff the mozzarella cheese slices and tomatoes in the chicken slits.
3) Preheat the oven to 365 degrees and grease the baking dish with butter.
4) Arrange the stuffed chicken breasts in the baking dish and transfer into the oven.
5) Bake for about 1 hour and dish to serve.

Nutrition Calories: 287 Carbs: 3.8g Fats: 15g Proteins: 33.2g Sodium: 178mg Sugar: 2.4g

Keto Garlic Turkey Breasts

Serves: 4/Prep Time: 25 mins

Ingredients

- 4 tablespoons butter
- ½ teaspoon garlic powder
- ¼ teaspoon dried oregano
- ½ teaspoon salt
- 1-pound turkey breasts, boneless
- ¼ teaspoon dried basil
- 1 teaspoon black pepper

Directions

1) Preheat the oven to 420 degrees and grease a baking tray.
2) Season the turkey with garlic powder, dried oregano, salt, dried basil, and black pepper.
3) Put butter and seasoned turkey in a skillet and cook for about 4 minutes on each side.
4) Transfer the turkey to the oven and bake for about 15 minutes.
5) Dish out in a platter and serve hot.

Nutrition Calories: 223 Carbs: 5.4g Fats: 13.4g Proteins: 19.6g Sodium: 1524mg Sugar: 4.1g

Creamy Turkey Breast

Serves: 6/Prep Time: 2 hours 10 mins

Ingredients

- 2 tablespoons butter
- ½ cup sour cream
- 1½ cups Italian dressing
- 1 (2-pound) bone-in turkey breast
- 2 garlic cloves, minced
- Salt and black pepper, to taste

Directions

1) Preheat the oven to 360 degrees and grease a baking dish with butter.
2) Mix together garlic cloves, salt, and black pepper. Then rub the turkey breast with this mixture.
3) Transfer the turkey breast in the baking dish and top with sour cream and Italian dressing.
4) Bake for about 2 hours, coating with pan juices intermittently.
5) Dish out and serve immediately.

Nutrition Calories: 369 Carbs: 6.5g Fats: 23.2g Proteins: 35.4g Sodium: 990mg Sugar: 4.9g

Chicken Pho

Serves: 6/Prep Time: 45 mins

Ingredients

- 14 oz of rice noodles
- 1 tablespoon olive oil extra virgin
- 1 large yellow onion halved
- 1 2-inch piece ginger cut into 1/4-inch slices
- 3 cardamom pods lightly smashed
- 1 cinnamon stick
- 1 tablespoon coriander seeds
- 1 fuji apple peeled, cored and diced

Garnish

- 1 lime cut into wedges
- 2 jalapenos thinly sliced
- 1/2 red onion thinly sliced
- Fresh herbs (mint, cilantro, basil)
- 1/2 cup coarsely chopped cilantro leaves
- 6 chicken thighs bone-in, skin-on
- 3 tablespoons fish sauce
- 3-star anise pods
- 1 tablespoon sugar
- 5 cloves
- 8 cups of water
- 1 1/2 teaspoon salt

- Bean sprouts
- Sriracha sauce
- Daikon radish sprouts (optional)

Directions

1. Soak noodles in a large bowl filled with hot water for 45 minutes.
2. Heat oil in the insert of the Instant Pot on Sauté mode.
3. Add onion and ginger. Sauté them for 4 minutes.
4. Stir in cinnamon, cardamom, star anise cloves, and coriander.

5. Cook for 1 minute then add water, cilantro, apple, fish sauce, sugar, and chicken.
6. Seal and secure the Instant Pot lid of the Instant Pot.
7. Press the Manual button with high pressure and 15 minutes of cooking time.
8. Once done, release the pressure completely then remove the lid.
9. Remove the chicken from the Instant Pot and keep it aside.
10. Strain the remaining broth and mix it with salt and pepper.
11. Shred the chicken using a fork and discard all the bones.
12. Divide the chicken shreds in the serving bowls.
13. Strain the cooked noodles then add them to the serving bowls.
14. Pour in the broth and garnish as desired.
15. Serve warm.

Nutrition Calories per serving: 220 Carbohydrate: 12.9g Protein: 12.3g Fat: 13.4g Sugar: 6.1g Sodium: 804mg

Chicken Paprikash

Serves: 4/Prep Time: 25 mins
Ingredients

- 1 large onion, diced
- 2 garlic cloves, minced
- 3 tablespoons olive oil
- 2 lb. skinless chicken thighs, bone in
- 1 teaspoon salt
- ¼ teaspoon black pepper
- 2 tablespoons sweet paprika
- 1 bay leaf
- 1½ cup chicken stock
- 1 cup heavy cream
- 2 tablespoons sour cream
- 5 tablespoon corn starch
- ½ lemon or more to taste

Directions
1. Select Sauté mode on your Instant Pot.
2. Add 3 tablespoons to the Instant Pot and preheat it.
3. Stir in garlic and onion, sauté for 3 minutes until soft.
4. Toss in chicken thighs and cook them for 3 minutes per side.
5. Add sweet paprika, pepper, and salt. Mix well.
6. Pour in chicken stock and add the bay leaf.
7. Seal and secure the Instant Pot lid then select the Manual mode for 5 minutes at high pressure.
8. Once done, release the pressure completely then remove the lid.
9. Switch your Instant pot to Sauté mode.
10. Mix corn-starch with 1 tablespoon water and pour this mixture into the pot.
11. Stir in sour cream and heavy cream.
12. Cook until the sauce thickens then add juice from the ½ lemon.
13. Adjust seasoning as desired.
14. Serve warm.

Nutrition Calories per serving: 270 Carbohydrate: 6.6g Protein: 17.9g Fat: 20.1g Sugar: 2.8g Sodium: 50mg

Chicken Carnitas

Serves: 4/Prep Time: 20 mins
Ingredients

- 1 tablespoon cumin
- 1 tablespoon oregano

- 1 teaspoon chili powder
- 1 tablespoon olive oil
- 1 medium onion, chopped
- 4 cloves garlic, minced
- 1/4 cup pineapple juice
- 1 teaspoon salt
- 1 teaspoon black pepper

- 1/4 cup lime juice
- 1/4 cup chicken stock
- 1-pound boneless, skinless chicken breasts
- fresh cilantro for topping

Directions
1. Thoroughly mix oregano, cumin, chili powder, salt and pepper in a small bowl.
2. Preheat olive oil in the insert of the Instant Pot on Sauté mode.
3. Add onion to the oil and sauté for 3 minutes until soft.
4. Stir in garlic and stir cook for 1 minute.
5. Add lime juice, pineapple juice, spice mixture, and chicken stock.
6. Mix well then place the chicken in it.
7. Seal and secure the Instant Pot lid then select Manual mode for 8 minutes at high pressure.
8. Once done, release the pressure completely then remove the lid.
9. Shred the chicken using a fork.
10. Mix gently then serve warm.
11. Devour.

KETO VEGAN RECIPES

Sweet Superfood Vegan Porridge

Yield: 1 Serving/Total Time: 10 Minutes/Prep Time: 10 Minutes/Cook Time: 10 Minutes

Ingredients
- ¼ cup unsweetened almond milk
- 1 tablespoon chopped almonds or walnuts
- 1 teaspoon ground flaxseed
- 1 tablespoon chia seeds
- 1 tablespoon shredded unsweetened coconut
- 1 teaspoon pure vanilla extract

Toppings:
- 1 teaspoon peanut butter
- 1 teaspoon toasted coconut

Directions
1. In a large bowl, mix all ingredients together; cover and refrigerate overnight. Divide porridge into serving bowls and top with peanut butter, and toasted coconut.

Nutritional Information per Serving:
Calories: 293; Total Fat: 27.5 g; Carbs: 10.7 g; Dietary Fiber: 4.3 g; Sugars: 5.6 g; Protein: 4.6 g; Cholesterol: 0 mg; Sodium: 35 mg

Scrumptious Mushroom & Tofu Scramble

Yield: 3 Servings/Total Time: 35 Minutes/ Prep Time: 20 Minutes /Cook Time: 15 Minutes

Ingredients
- 3 tablespoons olive oil
- 1 pound firm or extra firm tofu, drained and pressed
- 1 1/2 cups mushrooms (sliced)
- 1/4 onion (diced)
- 1/2 cup halved cherry tomatoes
- 1 garlic clove (minced)
- 2 tsp dried parsley
- 1/2 teaspoon dry mustard
- 1/2 teaspoon smoked paprika
- 1/4 teaspoon turmeric
- 1/4 teaspoon cumin
- 1/2 teaspoon salt
- 1/8 teaspoon pepper

Directions
1. Heat a tablespoon of oil in a skillet set over medium heat; sauté garlic and onion for about 2 minutes or until fragrant. Stir in mushrooms and cook for about 5 minutes or until lightly browned.
2. Crumble in tofu and stir in spices, salt and pepper; cook for about 5 minutes or until heated through. Remove from heat and stir in tomatoes. Serve hot!

Nutritional Information per Serving:
Calories: 231; Total Fat: 22.7 g; Carbs: 8.1 g; Dietary Fiber: 7 g; Sugars: 3 g; Protein: 14 g; Cholesterol: 0 mg; Sodium: 402 mg

Healthy Vegan Scramble

Yield: 3 servings/Total Time: 20 minutes/Prep time: 10 minutes/Cook time: 10 minutes

Ingredients
- 1 cauliflower, cut into florets
- 1 tofu block, cut into cubes
- 1 broccoli, divided into florets
- 1 large onion, chopped
- 2 tbsp. dark soy sauce
- 2 tbsp. extra virgin olive oil, divided into 1+1
- ½ tsp. onion powder
- ½ tsp. garlic powder
- 1 tsp. turmeric powder
- Ground pepper to taste

Directions
1. Start by marinating the tofu in 1 tablespoon of olive oil, onion, garlic, turmeric, and onion powders then set aside.
2. Cook the tofu in the remaining olive oil for 5 minutes, breaking it up using a wooden spatula.
3. Toss the broccoli and cauliflower florets in the leftover marinade and olive oil. In case it's too little, drizzle with some soy sauce and toss to ensure all the florets are evenly covered, then add to the tofu and cook for another 5 minutes until the veggies are soft.
4. Serve hot.

Nutritional Information per Serving:
Calories: 139; Total Fat: 12.6 g; Carbs: 8g; Dietary Fiber: 6 g; Sugars: 3 g; Protein: 11 g; Cholesterol: 0 mg; Sodium: 181 mg

Delicious Breakfast Porridge

Yield: 4 servings/Total Time: 25 minutes/Prep time: 5 minutes/Cook time: 20 minutes

Ingredients
- ½ cup pecans
- ½ cup walnuts
- ¼ cup unsweetened coconut flakes
- 4 tablespoons chia seeds
- ¼ cup raw sunflower seeds
- 2 cups unflavored almond milk
- 1 teaspoon maple syrup
- ½ teaspoon cinnamon powder

Directions
1. Combine the pecans, sunflower seeds, and walnuts in a food processor or blender and pulse until crumbled.
2. Next, combine all the ingredients in a large saucepan over medium to high heat, stirring constantly. Once the pot starts boiling, lower the heat and simmer for 20 minutes.
3. Serve hot!

Nutritional Information per Serving:
Calories: 311; Total Fat: 34.59 g; Carbs: 12.37 g; Dietary Fiber: 9. 1g; Sugars: 1.58 g; Protein: 9.25 g; Cholesterol: 0 mg; Sodium: 182 mg

Keto Vegan Smoothie Bowl w/ Greens

Yield: 2 servings/Total Time: 15 minutes/Prep time: 15 minutes

Ingredients
- ¼ cup zucchini, frozen
- 1 cup frozen wild blueberries
- 1 cup frozen raspberries
- 2 tablespoons hemp hearts
- 1 cup frozen spinach
- 2 tablespoons raw almond butter
- 1 cup almond milk
- 1 teaspoon cinnamon powder
- Grain free granola, for serving
- ½ cup mixed berries, for serving

Directions
1. Add all the ingredients, apart from the granola and mixed berries, into your blender and pulse until cream.
2. Divide the smoothie into two bowls and top with grain free granola and mixed berries.

Nutritional Information per Serving:
Calories: 243; Total Fat: 17.6 g; Carbs: 9.4 g; Dietary Fiber: 8 g; Sugars: 6.9 g; Protein: 12 g; Cholesterol: 0 mg; Sodium: 142 mg

Healthy Breakfast Parfait

Yield: 4 Servings/Total Time: 15 Minutes /Prep Time: 15 Minutes

Ingredients

Seeds and Nuts
- ½ cup pumpkin seeds
- ¼ cup flax seeds
- ¼ cup chia seeds
- 1 cup raw walnuts
- 1 cup raw almonds

Cashew Cream
- 1 cup raw cashews, soaked for about 2 hours
- ¼ teaspoon cinnamon
- ½ teaspoon vanilla
- 1 teaspoon maple syrup
- ⅓ cup water
- ¼ teaspoon salt
- Blackberries and strawberries to garnish

Directions
Seeds and Nuts: combine all nuts and seeds in a food processor and process into coarse meal.
Cashew Cream: combine all cream ingredients in a blender and blend until very smooth and creamy.
Assemble: In a serving glass, layer berries, then seeds and nut meal, and finally top with the cashew cream.
Sprinkle with more seeds and nut meal and garnish with berries.
Serve.

Nutritional Information per Serving:
Calories: 559 Total Fat: 46.3 g; Carbs: 16.6 g; Dietary Fiber: 8.8 g; Sugars: 3.4 g; Protein: 23.3 g; Cholesterol: 0 mg; Sodium: 159 mg

Power Breakfast Chia Pudding with Blueberries

Yield: 4 Servings /Total Time: 5 Minutes/Prep Time: 5 Minutes

Ingredients
- ½ cup chia seeds
- 1 ½ cups almond milk
- 1 teaspoon ground cinnamon
- 1 teaspoon vanilla essence
- 1 teaspoon agave
- ¼ cup frozen berries

Directions

1. In a bowl, stir together all ingredients until well combined.
2. Let sit overnight to soak well.
3. When ready to serve, divide into serving bowls.
4. Garnish each serving with berries.
5. Enjoy!

Nutritional Information per Serving:
Calories: 216 Total Fat: 21.5 g; Carbs: 6.7 g; Dietary Fiber: 1.1 g; Sugars: 1.3 g; Protein: 13.1 g; Cholesterol: 26 mg; Sodium: 40 mg

Spiced Low Carb Vegan Pancakes

Yield: 4 Servings/Total Time: 26 Minutes/Prep Time: 10 Minutes /Cook Time: 16 Minutes
Ingredients

- 4 tablespoons coconut oil
- 1 cup coconut milk
- 1/4 cup tapioca flour
- 1/4 cup almond flour
- 1 teaspoon salt
- ½ teaspoon chili powder
- ¼ teaspoon turmeric powder
- ¼ teaspoon black pepper
- ½ inch ginger, grated
- 1 serrano pepper, minced
- 1 handful cilantro, chopped
- ½ red onion, chopped

Directions
1. In a bowl, combine coconut milk, tapioca flour, almond flour and spices until well blended; stir in ginger, serrano pepper, cilantro, and red onion until well combined.
2. Melt coconut oil in a saucepan over medium low heat; add about ¼ cup of batter and spread out in the pan.
3. Cook for about 4 minutes per side or until golden brown. Transfer to a plate and keep warm; repeat with the remaining batter and oil.
4. Serve the pancakes with freshly squeezed orange juice.

Nutritional Information per Serving:
Calories: 386; Total Fat: 33.9 g; Carbs: 10.5 g; Dietary Fiber: 3.5 g; Sugars: 3.2 g; Protein: 4.1 g; Cholesterol: 0 mg; Sodium: 596 mg

Tasty Chickpea Vegan Omelet

Yield: 2 Servings/Total Time: 15 Minutes/Prep Time: 10 Minutes /Cook Time: 5 Minutes
Ingredients
For the batter:

- 4 tablespoons coconut oil
- 1/2 cup coconut milk
- 1/4 cup chickpea flour
- 2 teaspoons apple cider vinegar
- ¼ teaspoon onion powder
- ¼ teaspoon garlic powder
- ¼ teaspoon turmeric powder
- ¼ teaspoon baking soda
- 1/4 teaspoon sea salt

Stuffing options:

- 2 garlic cloves, minced
- 1 red onion, chopped
- ¼ cup small broccoli florets
- ¼ cup tomatoes, chopped

Directions
1. In a bowl, whisk together coconut milk, chickpea flour, 2 tablespoons coconut oil, apple cider vinegar, onion powder, garlic powder, turmeric powder, baking soda, and salt until well blended; let sit for about 10 minutes.
2. In a nonstick skillet set over medium heat, heat a tablespoon of coconut oil until melted; stir in onion garlic and red onion and sauté for about 4 minutes or until lightly browned and fragrant. Add broccoli and cook for about 5 minutes or until tender; transfer to a plate.
3. Add coconut oil to the skillet and pour in half of batter; add half of the broccoli mixture and tomatoes onto the batter and cook for about 2 minutes. Gently fold one side of the pancake to cover the filling and cover the skillet; cook for about 5 minutes. Transfer the pancake to a plate and keep warm. Repeat with the remaining batter and filling ingredients.
4. To serve, garnish with sliced avocado, lime wedges, and more red onion. Sprinkle with salt and pepper. Enjoy!

Nutritional Information per Serving:
Calories: 472; Total Fat: 31.1 g; Carbs: 15.4 g; Dietary Fiber: 11.6 g; Sugars: 10.5 g; Protein: 12.1 g; Cholesterol: 0 mg; Sodium: 418 mg

Low Carb Vegan Thai Soup

Yield: 4 Servings/Total Time: 25 Minutes /Prep Time: 10 Minutes /Cook Time: 15 Minutes

Ingredients

- 3 sliced mushrooms
- 1/2 julienned red bell pepper
- 1/2-inch ginger root, chopped
- 2 cloves of garlic, chopped
- 1/2 julienned red onion
- 1/2 Thai chili, finely chopped
- 275g tofu, cubed
- 1 ½ cups of canned coconut milk
- 2 cups vegetable broth
- 1 tablespoon tamari
- 1/4 cup fresh lime juice
- 1 tablespoon coconut sugar
- A handful of fresh cilantro, chopped

Directions

1. In a large pot, combine mushrooms, red bell pepper, onion, ginger, garlic, Thai chili, sugar, coconut milk and broth; bring to a rolling boil and then simmer for about 5 minutes. Stir in tofu and continue cooking for 5 minutes more. Remove the pot from the heat and then stir in cilantro, lime juice, and tamari. Serve hot!

Nutritional Information per Serving:
Calories: 339; Total Fat: 27.6 g; Carbs: 12.5 g; Dietary Fiber: 3.2 g; Sugars: 5.3 g; Protein: 14.8 g; Cholesterol: 11 mg; Sodium: 297 mg

Red Onion, Avocado & Cucumber Salad

Yield: 4 Servings/Total Time: 10 Minutes/Prep Time: 10 Minutes

Ingredients

- 2 avocados, diced
- 2 large cucumbers, sliced
- ½ cup chopped red onion
- 1 large tomato, diced
- 2 tablespoons olive oil
- 2 tablespoons fresh lemon juice
- 1/8 sea salt
- 1/8 teaspoon pepper

Directions

1. In a salad bowl, mix cucumbers, avocado, chopped red onion and chopped tomatoes; drizzle with lemon juice and olive oil; sprinkle with salt and pepper. Toss to combine well. Enjoy!

Nutritional Information per Serving:
Calories: 139; Total Fat: 19.3 g; Carbs: 8.8 g; Dietary Fiber: 1.7 g; Sugars: 4.5 g; Protein: 4.6 g; Cholesterol: 0 mg; Sodium: 7 mg

Nutty Collard Wraps

Yield: 4 Servings/Total Time: 20 Minutes /Prep Time: 20 Minutes

Ingredients

- 4 good quality collard leaves
- 1 cup pecans, raw
- 1 ripe avocado, sliced
- 1/3 cup alfalfa sprouts
- 1 red pepper, sliced
- ½ lemon
- 1 tablespoon extra-virgin olive oil
- 1 teaspoon cumin
- ½ teaspoon grated ginger
- 1 tablespoon tamari

Directions

1. Cut off the stems of the collard leaves and rinse them under running water to remove any grit. Soak them in warm water with the juice of half a lemon for about 10 minutes then dry the leaves using paper towels.
2. Shave of the central root so the leaves become easier to roll.
3. Add the nuts, cumin, and tamari, ginger, and olive oil to your food processor and pulse until the mixture forms a ball-like shape.
4. Spread out the collard leaves and divide the pecan mix among the leaves. Top with sliced red pepper, avocado, alfalfa sprouts and drizzle lime juice on top.
5. Fold the top and bottom parts then roll up the sides. Slice the wrap in two, if desired, and serve immediately. Enjoy!

Nutritional Information per Serving:
Calories: 375; Total Fat: 36.2 g; Carbs: 14.3 g; Dietary Fiber: 8 g; Sugars: 3.4 g; Protein: 5.8 g; Cholesterol: 0 mg; Sodium: 257 g

Ginger and Leafy Greens Stir-Fry

Yield: 4 Servings/Total Time: 20 Minutes /Prep Time: 10 Minutes /Cook Time: 10 Minutes

Ingredients:

- 3 tablespoons coconut oil
- 1 onion, finely sliced
- 2 garlic cloves, peeled and chopped
- 1 piece of ginger, chopped
- 1/4 squash, seeded, diced
- 2 handfuls of chopped leafy greens (spinach, kale, or chard)
- 1/4 Savoy cabbage
- 1 red or green chili, finely chopped
- Fresh juice of ½ a lemon
- A dash of Braggs liquid aminos
- A pinch of sea salt
- 1 pinch of freshly ground pepper
- A little water

Directions

1. In a large frying pan set over medium heat, heat coconut oil; sauté onion for about 4 minutes or until fragrant.
2. Stir in garlic, ginger, and chili; cook for about 5 minutes, stirring.
3. Add squash and salt and cook until squash is tender.
4. Toss in the leafy greens, lemon juice, Braggs Liquid Aminos, salt and pepper; cook for 1 minute.

Nutritional Information Per Serving:

Calories: 195; Total Fat: 17 g; Carbs: 6.2 g; Dietary Fiber: 1.3 g; Sugars: 3.9 g; Protein: 1 g; Cholesterol: 0 mg; Sodium: 63 mg

Buckwheat Pasta with Broccoli & Bell Pepper

Yield: 4 Servings/Total Time: 25 Minutes /Prep Time: 10 Minutes /Cook Time: 15 Minutes

Ingredients

- 5 tablespoons coconut oil
- 300g buckwheat pasta
- 2 garlic cloves, diced
- 1 medium white onion, cut into rings
- 3 carrots, sliced
- 1 head broccoli
- 1 red bell pepper, chopped into strips
- 3 medium tomatoes, diced
- 1 teaspoon vegetable broth
- 1 tablespoon fresh lemon juice
- 1 teaspoon oregano
- A pinch of sea salt
- A pinch of pepper

Directions

1. Chop all the veggies so they are ready to cook.
2. Cook buckwheat pasta in boiling saltwater. In a separate pot, boil broccoli in boiling saltwater.
3. Meanwhile, heat two tablespoons of oil in a pan and sauté garlic and onion until fragrant and translucent. Remove from pan and set aside.
4. Heat the remaining oil in the same pan and cook veggies for a few minutes until tender. Add broccoli and onions to the pan and stir in broth, lemon juice, oregano, salt and pepper. Stir to mix well and serve the veggie mix over the buckwheat pasta.

Nutritional Information Per Serving:

Calories: 278; Total Fat: 14 g; Carbs: 9.8 g; Dietary Fiber: 3.4 g; Sugars: 7.5 g; Protein: 2 g; Cholesterol: 0 mg; Sodium: 101 mg

Tres Verdures Kale Salad

Yield: 4 Servings/Total Time: 15 Minutes /Prep Time: 15 Minutes

Ingredients

- 250g Lacinato kale, rinsed thoroughly and chopped with stems removed
- ½ cup snow peas, chopped
- 2 cloves garlic, minced
- 2 teaspoons flaxseed oil
- 2 teaspoons sesame oil
- ½-inch ginger, minced
- 1 ½ teaspoons aged balsamic vinegar
- 1 tablespoon orange zest
- 2 teaspoons coconut aminos
- 2 tablespoons green onions
- 1 avocado, sliced
- Coarse sea salt, to taste
- Hemp seeds, for serving

Directions

1. Combine the chopped kale, flaxseed and sesame oil, ginger, garlic and salt in a large bowl and massage the kale.
2. Add in all the remaining ingredients and toss well until evenly combined. Serve immediately or chilled.

Nutritional Information Per Serving:

Calories: 135; Total Fat: 18 g; Carbs: 10 g; Dietary Fiber: 3 g; Sugars: 1 g; Protein: 3 g; Cholesterol: 0 mg; Sodium: 48 mg

Tangy Broccoli Rice

Yield: 4 Servings/Total Time: 15 Minutes /Prep Time: 10 Minutes /Cook Time: 5 Minutes

Ingredients

- 2 heads broccoli, riced in a food processor
- 1 tablespoon minced garlic
- ½-inch ginger, frozen
- 1 tablespoon coconut aminos
- 1 tablespoon organic avocado oil
- 2 teaspoons sesame oil
- Juice from quarter of a lemon
- ¼ cup chopped green onions
- 2 tablespoons parsley, chopped
- Chopped almonds, for serving
- Sea salt and freshly ground black pepper, to taste
- Lemon wedges for serving

Directions

1. Add the avocado oil to a medium skillet over medium-high heat. Lightly sauté the broccoli rice and garlic for about 1 minute. Stir in the coconut aminos, salt and sesame oil and cook for another minute or two, careful not to overcook the broccoli.

2. Remove from heat and grate the ginger over the broccoli and drizzle with lemon juice.
3. Lightly toss with parsley, green onions and chopped almonds and serve with lemon wedges. Enjoy!

Nutritional Information Per Serving:
Calories: 135; Total Fat: 18 g; Carbs: 10 g; Dietary Fiber: 3 g; Sugars: 1 g; Protein: 3 g; Cholesterol: 0 mg; Sodium: 48 mg

Masala Cauliflower Head

Yield: 4 Servings/Total Time: 30 Minutes /Prep Time: 10 Minutes /Cook Time: 20 Minutes

Ingredients
- 1 medium cauliflower head
- ½ cup cashew nuts, soaked overnight in almond milk then blended
- 2 cloves garlic, minced
- ½-inch ginger, minced
- 1 onion, chopped
- 4 tomatoes, chopped
- 2 tablespoons vegetable oil
- 2 tablespoons olive oil
- ½ teaspoon garam masala
- ½ teaspoon turmeric powder
- 4 peppercorns
- 1 bay leaf
- 3 cardamoms
- 1 teaspoon toasted sesame seeds
- 1 teaspoon coriander powder
- ½ teaspoon cumin seeds
- 3 cloves
- 1 teaspoon red chili powder
- 2 cups hot water
- Sea salt and black pepper, to taste

Directions
1. Place a saucepan over medium heat and add the cloves, cumin seeds, bay leaf, cardamoms, peppercorns and oil and give a good stir.
2. Add in garlic, ginger and onions and cook for 2 minutes, then stir in chili powder, turmeric and coriander powder and cook for 2 more minutes.
3. Next, add in the tomatoes and cook until soft and the oil starts to separate.
4. Pour in the blended cashews and 1 cup hot water, little by little and season with salt and pepper
5. Meanwhile, rub olive oil on the cauliflower and roast for 5-10 minutes in your oven at 350° F or until it starts browning slightly.
6. Place the roasted cauliflower on a serving platter and drizzle with the masala sauce. Garnish with toasted sesame seeds. Yum!

Nutritional Information Per Serving:
Calories: 306 Total Fat: 22 g; Carbs: 13 g; Dietary Fiber: 7 g; Sugars: 3 g; Protein: 9 g; Cholesterol: 0 mg; Sodium: 121 mg

Fried Rice, Vegan Style!

Yield: 4 Servings/Total Time: 20 Minutes /Prep Time: 10 Minutes /Cook Time: 10 Minutes

Ingredients
- 1 ½ cauliflower heads, riced in a food processor
- 1 red onion, chopped
- ½ broccoli head, separated into florets
- 1 carrot, julienned
- 4 tablespoons coconut oil
- 1-inch ginger, minced
- ¼ cup scallions, thinly sliced
- Salt and pepper, to taste
- ¼ cup tamari
- 3 tablespoons water
- Cilantro, for garnish

Directions
1. Cook the onions in coconut oil in a large pan until soft. Add the broccoli, carrots and water to the pan. Cover and let steam for 3-5 minutes or until soft but not mushy.
2. Next, push the veggies in the pan to one side and add the riced cauliflower, tamari and ginger to the empty side of the pan. Stir well and cook for 5 minutes or until soft. Mix all the contents of the pan and season with salt and pepper.
3. Remove from heat and garnish with sliced scallions and cilantro. Enjoy!

Nutritional Information Per Serving:
Calories: 152 Total Fat: 18 g; Carbs: 11.9 g; Dietary Fiber: 5 g; Sugars: 7 g; Protein: 6 g; Cholesterol: 0 mg; Sodium: 300 mg

Crunchy French Beans

Yield: 4 Servings/Total Time: 20 Minutes/Prep Time: 10 Minutes/Cook Time: 10 Minutes

Ingredients
- 400g French Beans, trimmed and steamed
- 1 tbsp. chopped almonds
- 1 tbsp. rice vinegar
- 2 tbsp. sriracha sauce
- 1/4 cup gluten free soy sauce
- 2 tbsp. sesame oil
- 1/2 tbsp. cayenne pepper
- 1 tbsp. smoked paprika
- 1 tsp. onion powder
- 2 tsp. garlic powder
- 1 tsp. red pepper flakes
- Salt and pepper

Directions

1. Place a pan on medium heat and cook the almonds for 3 minutes then stir in all the remaining ingredients. Cook for 2-5 minutes until heated through.Serve hot. Enjoy!

Nutritional Information Per Serving:

Calories: 162 Total Fat: 13.6 g; Carbs: 9.2 g; Dietary Fiber: 8 g; Sugars: 3 g; Protein: 7 g; Cholesterol: 0 mg; Sodium: 201 mg

Power Roasted Roots Soup

Yield: 5 Servings/Total Time: 1 Hour/Prep Time: 10 Minutes /Cook Time: 50 Minutes

Ingredients

- 2 tablespoons extra virgin olive oil
- 2 red onions, quartered
- 2 red peppers, deseeded, chopped
- 3 tomatoes, halved
- 3 carrots, peeled, diced
- ½ sweet potato, peeled, diced
- 2 cans light coconut milk
- 1 teaspoon ground cumin
- 1 tablespoon smoked paprika, plus extra for garnish
- 2 inches fresh root ginger, peeled, minced
- 1 bay leaf
- Salt and black pepper
- Chopped coriander to garnish
- Lime wedges

Directions

1. In a baking pan, mix all the veggies and oil and roast in the oven at 350° F for 30 minutes or until cooked.
2. Chop the roasted vegetables and place them in a saucepan; add the remaining ingredients and stir to mix well; season with salt and bring the mixture to a gentle boil in a saucepan and then simmer for about 20 minutes.
3. Divide the soup among six serving bowls and sprinkle each with coriander, black pepper and smoked paprika. Garnish with lime wedges and enjoy!

Nutritional Information Per Serving:

Calories: 162 Total Fat: 13.6 g; Carbs: 9.2 g; Dietary Fiber: 8 g; Sugars: 3 g; Protein: 7 g; Cholesterol: 0 mg; Sodium: 201 mg

Healthy Vegetable Sauté

Yield: 4 Servings/Total Time: 25 Minutes /Prep Time: 10 Minutes/Cook Time: 15 Minutes

Ingredients:

- 2 tablespoons coconut oil
- 1 tablespoon minced garlic
- 1 large shallot, sliced
- 1 cup mushrooms, sliced
- 1 cup broccoli florets
- 1 cup artichoke hearts
- 1 bunch asparagus, sliced into 3-inch pieces
- 1 cup baby peas
- 1 cup cherry tomatoes, halved
- 1/2 teaspoon sea salt

Vinaigrette

- 3 tablespoons white wine vinegar
- 6 tablespoons extra-virgin olive oil
- 1/2 teaspoon sea salt
- 1 teaspoon ground oregano
- handful fresh parsley, chopped

Directions

1. Add oil to a pan and set over medium heat. Stir in garlic and shallots and sauté for about 2 minutes.
2. Stir in mushrooms for about 3 minutes or until golden. Stir in broccoli, artichokes, and asparagus and continue cooking for 3 more minutes. Stir in peas, tomatoes and salt and transfer to the air fryer and cook for 5-8 more minutes.
3. Prepare vinaigrette: mix together vinegar, oil, salt, oregano and parsley in a bowl until well combined.
4. Serve vegetable sauté in a serving bowl and drizzle with vinaigrette. Toss to combine and serve.

Nutritional Information Per Serving:

Calories: 284 Total Fat: 11.5 g; Carbs: 8.6 g; Dietary Fiber: 7 g; Sugars: 4 g; Protein: 11.2 g; Cholesterol: 0 mg; Sodium: 119 mg

Delicious Kale Salad w/Grapefruit & Avocado

Yield: 4 Servings/Total Time: 15 Minutes/Prep Time: 15 Minutes

Ingredients

- 2 tablespoons fresh orange juice
- 1 tablespoon fresh grapefruit juice
- 1 clove garlic, minced
- A pinch of sea salt
- A pinch of pepper
- 1/2 cup extra virgin olive oil
- 3 cups shredded kale leaves
- 1 cup chopped lettuce
- 1 avocado, sliced
- 1 pink grapefruit, sectioned
- 2 tablespoons sunflower seeds, toasted

Directions

1. Make Dressing: in a small bowl, whisk together orange juice, grapefruit juice, garlic, salt and pepper; let sit for at least 10 minutes. Gradually whisk in extra virgin olive oil: set aside.
2. Add kale and lettuce to another bowl and drizzle with a splash of the dressing; massage for about 2 minutes and let sit until tender.
3. Divide kale among serving plates and top each serving with avocado and grapefruit; sprinkle with toasted sunflower seeds and drizzle generously with the dressing. Enjoy!

Nutritional Information per Serving:
Calories: 368; Total Fat: 35.8 g; Carbs: 13.8 g; Dietary Fiber: 4.7 g; Sugars: 3.8 g; Protein: 3.1 g; Cholesterol: 0 mg; Sodium: 84 mg

Coconut Milk Mushroom Soup

Yield: 4 Servings/Total Time: 15 Minutes/Prep Time: 10 Minutes/Cook Time: 5 Minutes

Ingredients

- 1 ½ pounds mushrooms, trimmed
- 3 tablespoons olive oil
- 1 clove garlic, minced
- 2 red onions, chopped
- 4 cups vegetable stock
- 2 cups coconut milk
- 1 tablespoon fresh thyme
- 1/8 teaspoon sea salt
- Thyme sprigs
- 1/8 teaspoon pepper

Directions

1. Grill the mushrooms, turning frequently, for about 5 minutes or until charred and tender; set aside.
2. In a soup pot, sauté red onion in olive oil. Stir in vegetable stock and cook for a few minutes.
3. Place the onions and half of mushrooms in a blender; blend until very smooth; add coconut milk, garlic, and thyme and continue blending until very smooth and creamy.
4. Return the soup to the pot and season with salt, thyme sprigs and pepper.
5. To serve, top with the remaining mushrooms and enjoy!

Nutritional Information per Serving:
Calories: 338; Total Fat: 29.2 g; Carbs: 16.1 g; Dietary Fiber: 5.8 g; Sugars: 9.3 g; Protein: 8.8 g; Cholesterol: 0 mg; Sodium: 89 mg

Mixed Veggie Salad with Edamame & Avocado

Yield: 2 Servings/Total Time: 15 Minutes/Prep Time: 15 Minutes

Ingredients

- 1 bunch curly kale, chopped into bite-sized pieces
- 1 cup snow peas, chopped
- 1 red pepper, chopped
- 1 carrot, peeled and cut into ribbons using a julienne peeler
- 1 cup edamame
- 1 shallot, finely sliced
- A handful each of basil and cilantro, chopped
- 1 avocado, cubed
- Fine sea salt, to taste

For the vinaigrette:

- ¼ cup extra virgin olive oil
- 1 tablespoon very finely grated fresh ginger
- 2 teaspoons freshly squeezed lime juice
- 3 cloves garlic minced
- 2 tablespoons rice vinegar

Directions

1. Place the kale in a large bowl and sprinkle with the sea salt. Gently massage the kale using your hands until soft and fragrant.
2. Toss in the remaining salad ingredients until well combined.
3. Whisk the vinaigrette ingredients then drizzle over the salad and toss well to combine.

Nutritional Information per Serving:
Calories: 345; Total Fat: 26.9 g; Carbs: 11.8 g; Dietary Fiber: 8.0 g; Sugars: 4.1 g; Protein: 11.1 g; Cholesterol: 0 mg; Sodium: 84 mg

Lemony Green Soup w/Cayenne

Yield: 4-6 Servings/Total Time: 1 Hour 15 Minutes/Prep Time: 15 Minutes/Cook Time: 60 Minutes

Ingredients

- 1 pound curly kale, torn
- 12 ounces baby spinach
- 1/4 cup brown Arborio rice, rinsed
- 2 yellow onions, chopped
- 4 tablespoons olive oil
- 3 cups plus 2 tablespoons water
- 4 cups homemade vegetable broth
- 1 tablespoon fresh lemon juice
- 1 large pinch of cayenne pepper
- Salt, to taste

Directions

1. Add olive oil in a large pan and cook the onions over medium heat. Sprinkle with salt and cook for 5 minutes until they start browning.

2. Lower the heat and add two tablespoons of water. Cover and lower the heat, then cook for 25 minutes until the onions caramelize, stirring frequently.
3. Meanwhile, add the remaining water and some salt to a Dutch oven and stir in the rice. Bring to a boil then lower the heat and simmer for about 15 minutes until tender. Stir the kale into the cooked rice, cover and cook for 10 more minutes.
4. Add the onions to the rice mixture together with the broth, spinach and cayenne and simmer for 5 minutes.
5. Use an immersion blender to puree the rice mixture until smooth, then stir in the lemon juice.
6. Serve in soup bowls and drizzle each with some olive oil.

Nutritional Information per Serving:
Calories: 202; Total Fat: 19.4 g; Carbs: 8.3 g; Dietary Fiber: 3.1 g; Sugars: 2.8 g; Protein: 3.1 g; Cholesterol: 0 mg; Sodium: 109 mg

Easy Detox Salad with Tahini Dressing

Yield: 4 Servings /Total Time: 10 Minutes/Prep Time: 10 Minutes

Ingredients
- 4 cup mixed greens
- 4 cups chopped kale
- 3 tablespoons dried cranberries
- 1 ripe avocado, thinly sliced
- 1 tablespoon roasted sunflower seeds
- 4 radishes, thinly sliced
- ¼ cup diced red onion
- 2 tablespoons olive oil
- ¼ cup fresh lemon juice
- ¼ cup tahini

Directions
1. In a large serving bowl, combine greens, kale, dried cranberries, avocado, sunflower seeds, radishes, and red onion; drizzle with olive oil, lemon juice, and tahini then season with salt and pepper. Toss to coat and serve immediately.

Nutrition Information per Serving
Calories: 293; Total Fat: 29.2 g; Carbs: 16.7 g; Dietary Fiber; 6 g; Sugars: 1.4 g; Protein: 8.8 g Cholesterol: 0 mg; Sodium: 49 mg

Detox Salad with Lemony Poppy Seed Dressing

Yield: 6 Servings/Total Time: 10 Minutes /Prep Time: 10 Minutes

Ingredients
For Lemony Poppy Seed Dressing
- ½ cup fresh lemon juice
- 6 tablespoons water
- ½-inch knob of ginger, minced
- 1 tablespoon Dijon mustard
- 4 tablespoons olive oil
- 1 teaspoon stevia
- 1 clove garlic, chopped
- ¼ teaspoon salt
- ¼ teaspoon Pepper
- 1 tablespoon poppy seeds

For the Salad
- 1 cup carrots, roughly chopped
- 2 cups red cabbage, roughly chopped
- 2 cups Brussels sprouts, roughly chopped
- 2 cups broccoli florets
- 2 cups kale
- 2 tablespoons toasted sunflower seeds
- ½ cup almonds, chopped
- ½ cup chopped parsley

Directions
1. In a blender, blend together all the ingredients, except poppy seeds until smooth; add poppy seeds and set aside.
2. Mix all the salad ingredients in a large bowl; drizzle with the dressing and toss to coat well. Serve.

Nutrition Information per Serving
Calories: 275; Total Fat: 31.8 g; Carbs: 12.4 g; Dietary Fiber; 4.7 g; Sugars: 5.6 g; Protein: 7.3 g Cholesterol: 0 mg; Sodium: 27 mg

Freekeh, Roasted Cauliflower w/ Tahini Sauce

Yield: 6 Servings/Total Time: 1 Hour 20 Minutes/Prep Time: 20 Minutes/Cook Time: 60 Minutes

Ingredients
For the freekeh:
- 1 ¼ - 1 ½ cups cracked freekeh
- ¼ cup sliced almonds
- 2 cloves garlic, minced
- 1 tablespoon olive oil
- ¼ teaspoon coriander
- ½ teaspoon salt
- ¼ teaspoon cumin
- 3 ½ cups water or homemade vegetable stock

For the cauliflower:
- 1 large cauliflower, cut into florets
- 3 tablespoons olive oil
- Black pepper and salt to taste

Tahini sauce:
- 1/3 cup tahini

Toppings:
- Sesame seeds
- Chopped cilantro

- 2 cloves garlic, minced
- 3 tablespoons freshly squeezed lime juice
- 1/3 cup water
- A large pinch of red pepper flakes
- Black pepper and salt to taste

- Raisins

Directions
1. Preheat your oven to 425° F.
2. Arrange the cauliflower in a baking sheet and toss with salt, pepper and olive oil. Spread them in one layer and roast for half an hour, until they start turning golden, turning them halfway through cook time.
3. Meanwhile, add a tablespoon of olive oil to a heavy bottomed saucepan over medium heat and cook the almonds for 3 minutes or until they start browning. Toss in the freekeh and cook for 2 minutes then add the remaining dry ingredients and cook for a minute.
4. Pour in the broth or water and bring to a boil. Lower the heat and simmer for 25 minutes until tender. Drain any excess liquid and remove from heat. Season with salt and pepper and fluff using a fork.
5. Whisk the dressing ingredients until smooth then set aside.
6. To serve, start with the freekeh followed by the roasted cauliflower and top with the tahini sauce. Garnish with the desired toppings and serve immediately.

Nutritional Information per Serving:
Calories: 278; Total Fat: 27.8 g; Carbs: 6.6 g; Dietary Fiber: 2.7 g; Sugars: 0 g; Protein: 4.9 g; Cholesterol: 0 mg; Sodium: 321 mg

Raw Zucchini Pasta with Tasty Avocado Sauce

Yield: 1 Serving/Total Time: 30 Minutes/Prep Time: 30 Minutes
Ingredients
- 1 large zucchini, spiralized
- 2 tablespoons homemade cashew butter
- 1 avocado

- ½ teaspoon fresh lemon juice
- ½ teaspoon salt
- ¼ teaspoon ground pepper

Directions
1. Add zucchini to a large bowl and sprinkle with salt; set aside for at least 20 minutes.
2. In a blender, blend together the remaining ingredients until smooth and creamy.
3. Drain the zucchini and stir in avocado cream; mix to coat well and serve.

Nutrition Information per Serving
Calories: 463; Total Fat: 39.8 g; Carbs: 16.9 g; Dietary Fiber: 17.1 g; Sugars: 6.9 g; Protein: 7.8 g Cholesterol: 0 mg; Sodium: 1208 mg

Scrumptious Vegan Ratatouille

Yield: 5 Servings/Total Time: 1 Hour 20 Minutes/Prep Time: 20 Minutes/Cook Time: 1 Hour
Ingredients
- 1/4 teaspoon apple cider vinegar
- 4 tablespoons extra-virgin olive oil
- 1 cup crushed tomatoes
- 1/4 teaspoon chili powder
- 1 teaspoon herbs de Provence
- 1 tablespoon chopped fresh basil

- 1 teaspoon minced garlic
- 1/4 teaspoon salt & pepper
- 3 large fresh tomatoes, sliced
- 1 large Japanese eggplant, sliced
- 2 large zucchinis, sliced
- 1 red onion, chopped

Directions
1. Preheat your oven to 350°F and lightly grease a 6 x 9-inch baking dish.
2. In a bowl, mix together vinegar, oil and crushed tomatoes until well combined; stir in chili powder, herbs de Provence, basil, garlic and salt and pour the mixture into the prepared baking dish. Spread it into a single layer and smooth the top.
3. In alternating pattern, layer vegetable slices on top of the tomato mixture in rows repeating the layers until you have used all the veggies. Spray the veggies with oil and bake in the oven for about 1 hour or until the tomato sauce is bubbly and veggies tender. Garnished with chopped basil and serve hot.

Nutritional Information per Serving:
Calories: 206; Total Fat: 24 g; Carbs: 11.3 g; Dietary Fiber: 5.2 g; Protein:5.3 g; Cholesterol: 0 mg; Sodium: 295 mg; Sugars: 9.7 g

Fried Tofu with Tender Spring Greens

Yields: 3 Servings/Total Time: 35 Minutes /Prep Time: 10 Minutes/Cook Time: 25 Minutes

Ingredients
- 3 tablespoons extra virgin olive oil
- 14 ounces extra-firm tofu, sliced
- 1 medium onion, thinly sliced
- 1 medium yellow or red bell pepper, chopped
- 2 teaspoons grated fresh ginger
- 12 ounces spring greens, chopped
- 2 tablespoons teriyaki sauce
- 1/4 cup toasted cashews, chopped

Directions
1. Add half the oil to a pan set over medium heat. Add tofu and fry until golden. Transfer to a plate.
2. Add the remaining oil to the pan and sauté onion until translucent. Stir in bell pepper and continue sautéing until onion is tender and golden. Stir in ginger and greens until wilted.
3. Stir in tofu and season with teriyaki sauce. Top with toasted cashews to serve.

Nutritional Information per Serving:
Calories: 338; Total Fat: 22.7 g; Carbs: 10.8 g; Dietary Fiber: 6.9 g; Protein: 19.3 g; Cholesterol: 0 mg; Sodium: 962 mg; Sugars: 7.6 g

Sage Infused Butternut Squash Zucchini Noodles

Yield: 4 Servings/Total Time: 50 Minutes/Prep Time: 15 Minutes/Cook Time: 35 Minutes

Ingredients
- 3 large zucchinis, spiralized or julienned into noodles
- 3 cups cubed butternut squash
- 2 cloves garlic, finely chopped
- 1 yellow onion, chopped
- 2 tablespoons olive oil
- 2 cups homemade vegetable broth
- ¼ teaspoon red pepper flakes
- Freshly ground black pepper
- 1 tablespoon fresh sage, finely chopped
- Salt, to taste and smoked salt for garnish

Directions
1. Add the oil to a pan over medium heat. Once the oil is hot, sauté the sage until it turns crisp. Transfer to a small bowl and season lightly with salt then set aside.
2. Add the onion, butternut, garlic and pepper flakes to the pan and cook for about 10 minutes. Season with salt and pepper and pour in the broth. Bring to a boil then simmer for 20 minutes until the butternut becomes soft.
3. Meanwhile, steam the zucchini noodles in your microwave or steamer until crisp and tender.
4. Once the butternut mixture is ready, remove from heat and let cool off slightly, then transfer to a blender and process until smooth.
5. Combine the zucchini noodles and the butternut puree in the skillet over medium heat and cook until heated through and evenly coated for 2 minutes.
6. Sprinkle with fried sage and smoked salt, then serve hot.

Nutritional Information per Serving:
Calories: 301; Total Fat: 28.5 g; Carbs: 13.8 g; Dietary Fiber: 3.4 g; Sugars: 4.8 g; Protein: 1.9 g; Cholesterol: 0 mg; Sodium: 161 mg

Satisfying Grilled Mushrooms

Yield: 4 Servings/Total Time: 20 Minutes /Prep Time: 10 Minutes/Cook Time: 10 Minutes

Ingredients
- 2 cups shiitake mushrooms
- 1 tablespoon balsamic vinegar
- 1/4 cup extra virgin olive oil
- 1-2 garlic cloves, minced
- A handful of parsley
- 1 teaspoon salt

Directions
1. Rinse the mushrooms and pat dry; put in a foil pan and drizzle with balsamic vinegar and extra virgin olive oil.
2. Sprinkle the mushroom with garlic, parsley, and salt.
3. Grill for about 10 minutes or until tender and cooked through. Serve warm.

Nutritional Information per Serving:
Calories: 171; Total Fat: 22.8 g; Carbs: 14.9 g; Dietary Fiber: 2.4 g; Protein: 1.8 g; Cholesterol: 0 mg; Sodium: 854 mg; Sugars: 4.1 g

Vegan Creamy Mushroom and Leek Risotto

Yield: 4 Servings /Total time: 30 Minutes/Prep Time 5 minutes/Cook Time 25 minutes

Ingredients
- 1 cup riced cauliflower
- 3/4 cup thinly sliced leeks
- 8 ounces cremini mushrooms, sliced
- 2 tablespoons olive oil
- 4 cups vegetable broth
- 1/4 cup vegan parmesan cheese
- 1 tablespoon vegan butter
- 1/4 cup dry white wine
- Fresh chopped parsley
- Salt & pepper

Directions

1. In a saucepan, bring vegetable broth to a simmer and then turn heat to low.
2. Meanwhile, heat half of olive oil in a large saucepan set over medium heat; sauté mushrooms for about 4 minutes or until browned. Stir in salt and pepper and remove from heat; transfer the mushroom to a dish and set aside.
3. Return the pan to heat and add the remaining oil; sauté leeks for about 2 minutes or until lightly browned. Stir in cauliflower rice and cook for about 1 minute. Stir in wine and cook for about 2 minutes or until absorbed.
4. Ladle in ½ cup of the vegetable broth one ladle at a time while stirring until risotto comes back to a simmer. Make sure the risotto does not boil to avoid it getting gummy. Repeat adding in stock and cooking for about 20 minutes or until cauliflower is tender. Remove the pan from heat and stir in butter, cheese and two-thirds of the sautéed mushrooms. Stir to coat well and adjust the seasoning.
5. Serve the risotto topped with the remaining mushrooms, more cheese and parsley.

Nutritional Information per Serving:
Calories: 407; Total Fat: 43.7 g; Carbs: 15.8 g; Dietary Fiber: 2.7 g; Protein:11.7 g; Cholesterol: 0 mg; Sodium: 774 mg; Sugars: 2.5 g

Healthy Green Bean & Zucchini Sauté

Yield: 2 Servings/Total Time: 15 Minutes/Prep Time: 5 Minutes /Cook Time: 10 Minutes

Ingredients
- 3 tablespoons extra virgin olive oil, divided
- 1/2 cup green beans - cut into small pieces
- 1/2 small zucchini, thinly sliced
- A pinch of salt
- 2 tablespoons lemon juice
- 2 tablespoons sliced scallions

Directions
1. Add half of the oil to a skillet set over medium heat.
2. Stir in green beans, zucchini, and salt and sauté, stirring, for about 9 minutes or until the veggies are crisp tender.
3. Remove the pan from heat and stir in lemon juice and scallions.
4. Serve immediately.

Nutritional Information per Serving:
Calories: 46; Total Fat: 13.7 g; Carbs: 3.4 g; Dietary Fiber: 1.4 g; Protein: 1 g; Cholesterol: 0 mg; Sodium: 200 mg; Sugars: 1.1 g

Mung-Spinach Stew

Yield: 3 Servings/Total Time: 20 Minutes/Prep Time: 5 Minutes/Cook Time: 15 Minutes

Ingredients
- 2 tablespoons sesame oil
- ½ cup diced carrots
- ½ cup chopped celery
- 1 cup chopped leeks or onions
- 2 garlic cloves, minced
- 1 teaspoon minced ginger
- 1 tablespoon date paste
- 2 tablespoons nut paste (walnuts and pumpkin seeds)
- 1-2 teaspoons lemon/lime juice
- 1 teaspoon allspice
- 1/4 teaspoon cardamom powder
- 2 teaspoons cumin powder
- A pinch of red chili flakes
- 1/2 teaspoon crushed black pepper
- Salt
- 4 cups vegetable broth
- ½ cup coarsely chopped spinach
- 1 cup cooked yellow mung beans

Directions
1. Heat oil in a stock pot over medium high heat.
2. Sauté chopped veggies and seasonings except spinach and beans.
3. Cook for about 10 minutes and then stir in, vegetable broth, spinach and mung beans; simmer for about 3 minutes and remove from heat.
4. Serve the stew with small avocado cubes, garnished with tomatoes and parsley.

Nutritional Information per Serving:
Calories: 437; Total Fat: 38.7 g; Carbs: 16.2 g; Dietary Fiber: 8.9 g; Sugars: 5.2 g; Protein: 9.1 g; Cholesterol: 0 mg; Sodium: 153 mg

Avocado w/Sriracha, Sea Salt and Fresh Lime Juice

Yield: 2 Servings/Total Time: 5 Minutes/Prep Time: 5 Minutes

Ingredients
- 1 avocado, peeled and cut in half
- 1 tablespoon sriracha
- 2 tablespoons freshly squeezed lime juice
- Freshly ground black pepper and sea salt to taste

Directions
1. Top the halved avocadoes with lime juice, sriracha, black pepper and sea salt. Enjoy!

Calories: 213; Total Fat: 19.6 g; Carbs: 10.1 g; Dietary Fiber: 6.7 g; Sugars: 0.5 g; Protein: 1.9 g; Cholesterol: 0 mg; Sodium: 59 mg

Blissful Matcha-Pistachio Balls

Yield: 4 Servings /Total Time: 20 Minutes /Prep Time: 5 Minutes

Ingredients
- ½ cup shredded coconut, unsweetened
- 2 Medjool dates, pitted
- ¼ cup raw pistachios, shelled
- ¾ cup raw cashews
- 2 teaspoons matcha powder
- ¼ pistachios, chopped

Directions
1. In a food processor, process together coconut, dates, cashews, ¼ cup pistachios, and matcha powder until finely chopped.
2. Roll into small balls and then roll the balls into the remaining chopped pistachios, pressing the pistachios firmly into the balls.
3. Refrigerate the balls for about 15 minutes before serving.

Nutrition Information per Serving
Calories: 213; Total Fat: 17.9 g; Carbs: 9.4 g; Dietary Fiber: 2.2 g; Sugars: 2.3 g; Protein: 5.4 g Cholesterol: 0 mg; Sodium: 36 mg

Healthy Pea Guacamole

Yield: 2 Servings/Total Time: 10 Minutes/Prep Time: 10 Minutes

Ingredients
- 1 avocado
- 2 tablespoons avocado oil
- 1 cup thawed frozen green peas
- ¼ cup fresh lime juice
- 1 teaspoon crushed garlic
- ½ teaspoon cumin
- 1/8 teaspoon hot sauce
- ½ cup chopped cilantro
- 4 green onions, chopped
- 1 tomato, chopped
- Sea salt

Directions
1. In a food processor, blend together peas, lime juice, garlic, and cumin until very smooth; transfer to a large bowl and stir in hot sauce, cilantro, green onion, tomato and sea salt. Refrigerate, covered, for about 30 minutes for flavors to blend. Enjoy!

Nutrition Information per Serving
Calories: 137; Total Fat: 30.8 g; Carbs: 13.2 g; Dietary Fiber: 8.8 g; Sugars: 9.9 g; Protein: 10.9 g Cholesterol: 0 mg; Sodium: 90 mg

Roasted Chili-Vinegar Peanuts

Yield: 4 Servings/Total Time: 10 Minutes /Prep Time: 10 Minutes

Ingredients
- 2 tablespoons coconut oil
- 2 cups raw peanuts, unsalted
- 2 teaspoon sea salt
- 2 tablespoon apple cider vinegar
- 1 teaspoon chili powder
- 1 teaspoon fresh lime zest

Directions
1. Preheat oven to 350°F.
2. In a large bowl, toss together coconut oil, peanuts, and salt until well coated.
3. Transfer to a rimmed baking sheet and roast in the oven for about 15 minutes or until fragrant.
4. Transfer the roasted peanuts to a bowl and add vinegar, chili powder and lime zest.
5. Toss to coat well and serve.

Nutritional Information per Serving:
Calories: 447; Total Fat: 39.5g; Carbs: 11.3 g; Dietary Fiber: 6.5 g; Sugars: 3 g; Protein: 18.9 g; Cholesterol: 0 mg; Sodium: 956 mg

Raw Guilt Free Keto Cake Bars

Yield: 8 Servings /Total Time: 25 Minutes + Chilling Time /Prep Time: 10 Minutes /Cook Time: 15 Minutes

Ingredients:
- 1 cup vanilla protein powder
- 1/3 cup almond flour
- 1/3 cup peanut flour
- 1/3 cup oat flour
- 1/3 cup almond milk
- 1/2 cup Stevia
- 1/2 cup peanut butter

For Frosting Layer
- 2 tablespoons chocolate chips
- 1 tablespoon shredded coconut
- 3 tablespoons coconut cream
- 2 tablespoons coconut oil

For Ganache
- 2 tablespoon coconut oil
- 1/4 cup dark chocolate chips

Directions:
1. Prepare a square cake pan by lining with aluminum foil.
2. In a bowl, mix all dry ingredients; in another bowl, stir together butter and Stevia until well combined; pour over the dry ingredients and then stir in almond milk. Mix to form a dough like ball.
3. Press the dough into the prepared pan and refrigerate for at least 30 minutes.
4. Make the frosting: Microwave coconut oil for 20 seconds or until melted; stir in coconut cream, chocolate chips and coconut until well combined. Spread the mixture over the dough and then continue refrigerating for another 30. minutes.
5. Make Ganache: combine all ganache ingredients in a microwave safe bowl and microwave until melted; pour over the bar and refrigerate for about an hour. Remove the bar from the fridge and slice into 16 bars. Serve.

Nutritional Information per Serving:
Calories: 501; Total Fat: 33.6 g; Carbs: 15.2 g; Protein: 28.8 g; Dietary Fiber: 4.6 g; Sugars: 3.8 g; Cholesterol: 0 mg; Sodium: 349 mg

Raw Chocolate Chip Cookie Protein Bars

Yield: 6 Servings/Total Time: 20 Minutes + Chilling Time /Prep Time: 20 Minutes

Ingredients
- 1 cup vanilla almond milk
- 5 tablespoons melted coconut oil
- 1 cup coconut flour
- 3/4 cup whey protein
- 1 tsp vanilla extract
- 2 tablespoons mini chocolate chips
- 1/4 teaspoon salt
- 5 teaspoons powered Stevia

Directions
1. Line a loaf pan with baking paper and set aside.
2. In a bowl, whisk together protein powder, coconut flour and salt until well combined. In another bowl, whisk together milk, coconut oil and vanilla; stir in Stevia and then pour into the flour mixture. Stir until well blended and then fold in the chocolate chips.
3. Pour the batter into the loaf pan, pressing into the bottom of the pan. Press in the remaining chocolate chips and refrigerate for at least 2 hours. Cut into bars and serve, refrigerating the rest.

Nutritional Information per Serving:
Calories: 266; Total Fat: 20.7 g; Carbs: 8.6 g; Protein: 16.9 g; Dietary Fiber: 3.4 g; Sugars: 3.3 g; Cholesterol: 0 mg; Sodium: 332 mg

Coconut Yogurt & Red Onion Dip

Yield: 8 Servings/Total Time: 40 Minutes /Prep Time: 20 Minutes /Cook Time: 20 Minutes

Ingredients
- 2 cups coconut yogurt
- 1 cup coconut cream
- 2 tablespoons olive oil
- 2 red onions, thinly sliced
- A pinch kosher salt
- A pinch pepper
- 1 tablespoon apple cider vinegar
- 2 teaspoons fresh thyme leaves

Directions
1. Heat olive oil in a skillet set over medium-low heat until hot, but not smoky; stir in thyme and onions, salt and pepper and sauté for about 20 minutes or until caramelized. Stir in the vinegar and cook for 1 minute; remove the onions from heat.
2. In a bowl, stir together Greek yogurt and caramelized onions until well blended. Serve the dip with celery or carrot sticks.

Nutritional Information per Serving:
Calories: 247; Total Fat: 20.7 g; Carbs: 9.4 g; Protein: 8.8 g; Dietary Fiber: 1.8 g; Sugars: 3.9 g; Cholesterol: 0 mg; Sodium: 221 mg

Chocolate & Pumpkin Protein Pudding

Yield: 6 Servings/Total Time: 5 Minutes /Prep Time: 5 Minutes

Ingredients
- 1 cup almond milk
- 2 cups unsweetened pumpkin puree
- 3 tablespoons coconut oil
- ½ cup chocolate protein powder
- ¼ cup unsweetened cocoa powder
- ½ teaspoon ground cinnamon
- 1 teaspoon vanilla extract
- 1 teaspoon Stevia

Directions
1. In a blender, blend together pumpkin puree, coconut oil, protein powder, cinnamon, and vanilla until smooth; add in half of the milk and blend until smooth. Add in the remaining milk and Stevia, then blend until very smooth. Refrigerate the shake for at least 2 hours before serving. Enjoy!

Nutritional Information per Serving:

Calories: 234; Total Fat: 15.1 g; Carbs: 5.9 g; Protein: 11.8 g; Dietary Fiber: 1.8 g; Sugars: 1.5 g; Cholesterol: 1 mg; Sodium: 15 mg

Low Carb Superfood Cereal

Yield: 6 Servings/Total Time: 45 Minutes /Prep Time: 10 Minutes /Cook Time: 35 Minutes
Ingredients
- 2 tablespoons chia seeds
- 2 tablespoons flax seeds
- 1/4 cup sesame seeds
- 1 tablespoon olive oil
- 1 cup walnuts, chopped
- 1 cup almonds, chopped
- 1 cup unsweetened coconut flakes
- 1 teaspoon vanilla extract
- 1 1/2 teaspoons cinnamon
- 1/2 teaspoon ground clove
- 1/4 cup melted coconut oil
- 1/2 teaspoon kosher salt

Directions
1. Preheat your oven to 350° F and prepare a baking sheet by greasing with olive oil.
2. In a bowl, mix together chia seeds, sesame seeds, flax seeds, walnuts, almonds, and coconut flakes. Stir in vanilla, cinnamon, cloves and salt. Stir in coconut oil until well coated. Spread the seed mixture over the baking sheet and bake for about 25 minutes or until golden brown. Remove from oven and let cool before serving.

Nutritional Information per Serving:
Calories: 422; Total Fat: 38.4 g; Carbs: 11.4 g; Protein: 16.4 g; Dietary Fiber: 7.3 g; Sugars: 6.4 g; Cholesterol: 0 mg; Sodium: 239 mg

Chocolate Protein Fudge

Yield: 6 Servings/Total Time: 10 Minutes + Refrigerating Time /Prep Time: 10 Minutes
Ingredients
- 2 tablespoons almond butter
- 1/4 cup dark chocolate chips
- 3 tablespoons coconut oil
- 2 tablespoons coconut flour
- 4 scoops protein powder
- 1 teaspoon cocoa powder
- 1 teaspoon vanilla
- 1 tablespoon Stevia
- A pinch of sea salt

Directions
1. In a bowl, mix together all ingredients, except a tablespoon of coconut oil and chocolate chips. Press the mixture into a glass container and refrigerate.
2. In a pan over low heat, melt the remaining coconut oil and chocolate chips; stir well and then pour over the fudge. Continue refrigerating for at least 30 minutes before slicing to serve.

Nutritional Information per Serving:
Calories: 213; Total Fat: 16.3 g; Carbs: 7.2 g; Protein: 10.2 g; Dietary Fiber: 1.9 g; Sugars: 3.2 g; Cholesterol: 2 mg; Sodium: 52 mg

Lime & Coconut Avocado Popsicles

Yield: 3 Servings/Total Time: 5 Minutes + Freezing Time /Prep Time: 5 Minutes
Ingredients
- 2 avocados
- 2 tablespoons lime juice
- 1 1/2 cups coconut milk
- 1/4 cup Stevia

Directions
1. In a blender, blend together all ingredients until smooth and creamy; distribute the mixture into 6 popsicle molds and then freeze for at least 2 hours or until firm. Enjoy!

Nutritional Information per Serving:
Calories: 493; Total Fat: 48.3 g; Carbs: 10.9 g; Protein: 8.4 g; Dietary Fiber: 2.6 g; Sugars: 6.5 g; Cholesterol: 0 mg; Sodium: 28 mg

Homemade Keto Nutella

Yield: 6 Servings/Total Time: 10 Minutes /Prep Time: 10 Minutes
Ingredients
- 3/4 cup toasted hazelnuts
- 3 tablespoons melted coconut oil
- 2 tablespoons cocoa powder
- 3 scoops protein powder
- 1/2 teaspoon vanilla extract
- 2 tablespoons powdered sweetener
- Pinch salt

Directions
1. In the food processor, process hazelnuts until finely ground; add in coconut oil and process the mixture into butter; add in the remaining ingredients and process until creamy and smooth. Serve with celery or carrot sticks.

Nutritional Information per Serving:

Calories: 219; Total Fat: 18.8 g; Carbs: 6.7 g; Protein: 10.1 g; Dietary Fiber: 2.4 g; Sugars: 1.1 g; Cholesterol: 1 mg; Sodium: 32 mg

Warm Lemon Rosemary Olives

Yields: 12 Servings /Total Time: 35 Minutes/Prep Time: 53 Minutes/Cook Time: 20 Minutes

Ingredients
- 1 teaspoon extra-virgin olive oil
- 1 teaspoon grated lemon peel
- 1 teaspoon crushed red pepper flakes
- 2 sprigs fresh rosemary
- 3 cups mixed olives
- Lemon twists, optional

Directions
1. Preheat your oven to 400° F. Place pepper flakes, rosemary, olives and grated lemon peel onto a large sheet of foil; drizzle with oil and fold the foil, pinching the edges of the sheet to tightly seal.
2. Bake in the oven for about 30 minutes. Remove from the sheet and place the mixture to serving dish. Serve warm garnished with lemon twists.

Nutritional Information Per Serving:

Calories: 289 Total Fat: 24.2 g; Carbs: 11.7 g; Dietary Fiber: 9.4 g; Sugars: 1 g; Protein: 4.5 g; Cholesterol: 0 mg; Sodium: 239 mg

Vegetable Recipes

Zucchini Noodles

Serves: 4/Prep Time: 25 mins

Ingredients
- ¼ cup butter
- 1-pound zucchini, spiralized
- ½ cup cream cheese
- ¼ cup Parmesan cheese, grated
- 1 tablespoon sour cream

Directions
1. Mix together cream cheese, sour cream and Parmesan cheese in a bowl.
2. Put the butter in the skillet and add zucchini noodles.
3. Cook for about 5 minutes and stir in the cheese mixture.
4. Cook for 8 minutes and dish out to serve hot.

Nutrition

Calories: 250 Carbs: 5g Fats: 24g Proteins: 6.1g Sodium: 246mg Sugar: 2g

Bacon Wrapped Asparagus

Serves: 6/Prep Time: 35 mins

Ingredients
- 6 bacon slices
- 24 small spears asparagus
- 4 tablespoons butter
- Salt and black pepper, to taste
- 1 cup heavy whipping cream

Directions
1. Season the asparagus spears with salt and black pepper.
2. Add heavy whipping cream to the asparagus.
3. Wrap the asparagus in the bacon slices.
4. Put the butter and wrapped asparagus in the skillet.
5. Cook for about 20 minutes on medium-low heat, rotating every 5 minutes.
6. Dish out and serve hot.

Nutrition

Calories: 249 Carbs: 2.7g Fats: 23.1g Proteins: 8.6g Sodium: 502mg Sugar: 0.9g

Roasted Cauliflower and Broccoli

Serves: 3/Prep Time: 22 mins

Ingredients
- 1 cup broccoli florets
- ¼ cup butter
- Salt and black pepper, to taste
- 1 cup cauliflower florets
- ½ cup Parmesan cheese, grated

Directions
1. Preheat the oven to 360 degrees and grease a baking tray.
2. Mix together broccoli florets, cauliflower florets, butter, salt and black pepper in a bowl.
3. Put the veggie mixture on the baking tray and top with Parmesan cheese.
4. Bake for about 20 minutes and remove from the oven to serve hot.

Nutrition Calories: 215 Carbs: 4.5g Fats: 19.5g Proteins: 7.7g Sodium: 305mg Sugar: 1.3g

Mushroom Bacon Skewers

Serves: 4
Prep Time: 20 mins
Ingredients
- 1-pound mushrooms
- 6 bacon strips
- 2 cups cheddar cheese, shredded
- Skewers
- 2 tablespoons mesquite seasoning

Directions
1. Preheat the oven to 395 degrees and grease a baking tray.
2. Season the mushrooms with mesquite seasoning.
3. Pierce one end of the bacon strip in the skewer, followed by the mushroom.
4. Spear the other end of the bacon strip above the mushroom on the skewer.
5. Put the skewers on the baking tray and top with cheddar cheese.
6. Bake for about 15 minutes and remove from oven to serve.

Nutrition
Calories: 409 Carbs: 5.6g Fats: 32.7g Proteins: 23.9g Sodium: 1482mg Sugar: 2.2g

Roasted Brussels Sprouts

Serves: 3
Prep Time: 35 mins
Ingredients
- ½ cup butter
- ¾ pound brussels sprouts
- ½ teaspoon ginger-garlic paste
- Salt and black pepper, to taste
- ½ tablespoon Dijon mustard

Directions
1. Preheat the oven to 395 degrees and grease a baking tray.
2. Marinate the brussels sprouts with Dijon mustard, ginger-garlic paste, butter, salt and black pepper.
3. Arrange the marinated brussels sprouts on the baking tray and transfer in the oven.
4. Roast for about 20 minutes and dish out to serve hot.

Nutrition
Calories: 328 Carbs: 10.7g Fats: 31.7g Proteins: 4.3g Sodium: 276mg Sugar: 2.5g

Creamed Peas

Serves: 3
Prep Time: 15 mins
Ingredients
- 1 cup water
- 1 cup fresh green peas
- 3 tablespoons butter
- Salt, to taste
- 1 cup heavy cream

Directions
1. Heat the butter in the skillet and add fresh peas.
2. Sauté for about 3 minutes and add salt, water, and heavy cream.
3. Cook for about 5 minutes on medium-low heat and dish out to serve hot.

Nutrition
Calories: 279 Carbs: 8.1g Fats: 26.5g Proteins: 3.6g Sodium: 152mg Sugar: 2.8g

Spinach Balls

Serves: 6
Prep Time: 40 mins
Ingredients
- 1 cup cheddar cheese, grated
- 6 cup fresh spinach leaves, trimmed
- ½ cup butter
- ½ teaspoon garlic salt
- ¼ cup fresh parsley, finely chopped

Directions
1. Preheat the oven to 400 degrees F and lightly grease a baking tray.
2. Put the butter, garlic salt, cheddar cheese, fresh spinach leaves. and fresh parsley in a skillet.
3. Cook for about 20 minutes on medium-low heat and dish out.
4. Mold the spinach mixture into small-sized balls and arrange on the baking tray.
5. Transfer in the oven and bake for about 10 minutes.
6. Dish out and serve warm.

Nutrition
Calories: 220 Carbs: 1.7g Fats: 21.7g Proteins: 5.8g Sodium: 251mg Sugar: 0.3g

Cheesy Cauliflowers

Serves: 4
Prep Time: 35 mins
Ingredients

- ¾ cup sour cream
- 1-pound cauliflower florets
- ¾ cup cheddar cheese, grated
- Salt and black pepper, to taste
- 3 tablespoons butter

Directions

1. Preheat the oven to 400 degrees and lightly grease a baking dish.
2. Put the sour cream, cauliflower, salt and black pepper in a food processor.
3. Process until coarse and transfer to the baking dish.
4. Top with cheddar cheese and melted butter.
5. Bake for about 20 minutes and remove from oven to serve.

Nutrition
Calories: 282 Carbs: 8.2g Fats: 24.8g Proteins: 9g Sodium: 250mg Sugar: 2.9g

Tofu with Mushrooms

Serves: 6
Prep Time: 30 mins
Ingredients

- 2 cups fresh mushrooms, chopped finely
- 8 tablespoons Parmesan cheese, shredded
- 2 blocks tofu, pressed and cubed into 1-inch pieces
- 8 tablespoons butter
- Salt and freshly ground black pepper, to taste

Directions

1) Mix together tofu, salt and black pepper in a bowl.
2) Put butter and seasoned tofu in a pan over medium-low heat.
3) Cook for about 5 minutes and stir in the mushrooms and Parmesan cheese.
4) Cook for about 4 minutes, occasionally stirring and dish onto a serving plate.

Nutrition
Calories: 211 Carbs: 2g Fats: 18.5g Proteins: 11.5g Sodium: 346mg Sugar: 0.5g

Bacon Veggies Combo

Serves: 4
Prep Time: 35 mins
Ingredients

- 1 green bell pepper, seeded and chopped
- 2 scallions, chopped
- 4 bacon slices
- 3 garlic cloves, minced
- ½ cup Parmesan Cheese
- 1 tablespoon avocado mayonnaise

Directions

1) Preheat the oven to 380 degrees F and grease a baking dish.
2) Arrange the bacon slices in the baking dish and top with scallions, bell peppers, avocado mayonnaise, and Parmesan Cheese.
3) Bake for about 25 minutes and serve immediately.

Nutrition
Calories: 197 Carbs: 4.7g Fats: 13.8g Proteins: 14.3g Sodium: 662mg Sugar: 1.9g

Onion Tofu Scramble

Serves: 4
Prep Time: 20 mins
Ingredients

- 4 tablespoons butter
- 2 blocks tofu, pressed and cubed into 1-inch pieces
- 1 cup cheddar cheese, grated
- Salt and black pepper, to taste
- 2 medium onions, sliced

Directions

1) Season tofu with salt and black pepper in a bowl.
2) Put butter and onions in a pan over medium-low heat.
3) Cook for about 3 minutes and add tofu mixture.
4) Cook for about 2 minutes and add cheddar cheese.
5) Cover with lid and cook for about 5 minutes on low heat.
6) Dish in a bowl to serve for breakfast.

Nutrition
Calories: 184 Carbs: 6.3g Fats: 7.3g Proteins: 12.2g Sodium: 222mg Sugar: 2.7g

Ham Spinach Blast

Serves: 4/Prep Time: 40 mins
Ingredients
- ¼ cup cream
- Salt and black pepper, to taste
- 1½ pounds fresh baby spinach
- 14-ounce ham, sliced
- 2 tablespoons butter, melted

Directions
1) Preheat the oven to 375 degrees F and grease 4 ramekins with butter.
2) Put butter and spinach in a pan over medium-low heat.
3) Cook for about 3 minutes and drain the liquid from the spinach completely.
4) Return spinach in the pan and top with ham slices, cream, salt, and black pepper.
5) Bake for about 25 minutes and dish into a large serving bowl to serve hot.

Nutrition
Calories: 188 Carbs: 4.9g Fats: 12.5g Proteins: 14.6g Sodium: 1098mg Sugar: 0.3g

Bacon Bok Choy Samba

Serves: 6/Prep Time: 25 mins
Ingredients
- 2 tablespoons olive oil
- 4 bacon slices
- 8 tablespoons cream
- 8 bok choy, sliced
- Salt and black pepper, to taste
- 1 cup Parmesan cheese, grated

Directions
1) Season bok choy with salt and black pepper.
2) Put olive oil and bacon slices in a skillet on medium-high heat.
3) Sauté for about 5 minutes and stir in cream and bok choy.
4) Sauté for about 6 minutes and sprinkle with Parmesan cheese.
5) Cook for about 4 minutes on low heat and dish out in a serving platter.

Nutrition
Calories: 112 Carbs: 1.9g Fats: 4.9g Proteins: 3g Sodium: 355mg Sugar: 0.8g

Garlic Parmesan Fried Eggplant

Serves: 12/Prep Time: 30 mins
Ingredients
- 1 teaspoon salt
- 2 medium eggplants, cut into 1/3-inch-thick slices
- 2 large eggs
- 2 cups almond flour
- 4 teaspoons garlic powder
- 1 teaspoon black pepper
- 2 cups Parmesan cheese grated
- 1 teaspoon salt
- ½ cup butter

Directions
1) Arrange the eggplants in a single layer in a dish and season with salt.
2) Whisk together eggs in a shallow bowl.
3) Mix together Parmesan, almond flour, garlic powder, salt, and black pepper in another bowl.
4) Heat butter in a large skillet over medium heat.
5) Dip each slice of eggplant in egg and then coat with almond flour mixture.
6) Drop the eggplant slices in a skillet in batches and fry until browned.
7) Dish out and serve with your favorite dip.

Nutrition
Calories: 271 Carbs: 10g Fats: 22g Proteins: 12g Sodium: 696mg Sugar: 2.6g

Whole Garlic Roast

Serves: 4
Prep Time: 25 mins
Ingredients
- 4 tablespoons herbed butter
- 1 cup water
- Salt and black pepper, to taste
- 4 large garlic bulbs

Directions
1) Preheat the oven to 395 degrees F and grease a baking dish.
2) Season the garlic bulbs with salt and pepper.
3) Transfer in the baking dish and top with herbed butter.
4) Place the baking dish in the oven and bake for about 15 minutes.
5) Remove from the oven and serve hot.

Nutrition
Calories: 117 Carbs: 3g Fats: 11.5g Proteins: 0.1g Sodium: 84mg Sugar: 0g

Pork and Beef Recipes

Pork Carnitas

Serves: 4
Prep Time: 35 mins
Ingredients
- 1 tablespoon ghee
- 1-pound bone-in pork shoulder
- ½ teaspoon garlic powder
- Salt and black pepper, to taste
- 1 orange, juiced

Directions
1. Season the pork with garlic powder, salt and black pepper.
2. Put the seasoned pork, ghee and orange in the pressure cooker.
3. Cook for about 25 minutes on HIGH pressure.
4. Release the pressure naturally and dish out to serve.

Nutrition
Calories: 284 Carbs: 6.7g Fats: 19.4g Proteins: 19.7g Sodium: 274mg Sugar: 5.4g

Easy Beef Brisket

Serves: 6
Prep Time: 45 mins
Ingredients
- 1 tablespoon butter
- 2 pounds beef brisket
- 2 garlic cloves, minced
- Salt and black pepper, to taste
- 1 small onion, sliced

Directions
1. Heat butter in a large wok and add onions and garlic.
2. Sauté for about 3 minutes and add beef briskets, salt and black pepper.
3. Cover the lid and cook for about 30 minutes on medium-low heat.
4. Dish out the brisket and cut into desired slices on a cutting board to serve.

Nutrition
Calories: 304 Carbs: 1.4g Fats: 11.4g Proteins: 46.1g Sodium: 114mg Sugar: 0.5g

Bacon Swiss Pork Chops

Serves: 8/Prep Time: 55 mins
Ingredients
- 12 bacon strips, cut in half
- 8 pork chops, bone-in
- 2 tablespoons butter
- Salt and black pepper, to taste
- 1 cup Swiss cheese, shredded

Directions
1. Season the pork chops with salt and black pepper.
2. Put the butter and seasoned pork chops in a wok.
3. Cook for about 3 minutes on each side and add bacon.
4. Cook, covered for about 15 minutes on medium-low heat and add cheese.
5. Cover the lid again and cook for about 5 minutes until the cheese is melted.
6. Stir well and dish out to serve.

Nutrition
Calories: 483 Carbs: 0.7g Fats: 40g Proteins: 27.7g Sodium: 552mg Sugar: 0.2g

Jamaican Pork Roast

Serves: 4/Prep Time: 2 hours
Ingredients
- 1 tablespoon butter
- 1-pound pork shoulder
- ¼ cup beef broth
- Salt and black pepper, to taste
- ¼ cup Jamaican Jerk spice blend

Directions
1. Preheat the oven to 360 degrees and lightly grease a baking dish.
2. Keep the pork soaked in the beef broth for about 1 hour.
3. Brush the pork with the melted butter and sprinkle with Jamaican Jerk spice blend, salt and black pepper.
4. Place on the baking dish and transfer in the oven.
5. Bake for about 1 hour and dish out to serve.

Nutrition
Calories: 359 Carbs: 0.1g Fats: 27.2g Proteins: 26.7g Sodium: 145mg Sugar: 0g

Citrus Pork

Serves: 8/Prep Time: 45 mins
Ingredients
- 2 tablespoons butter
- 2 pounds pork shoulder roast, boneless
- 1 tablespoon lemon juice
- Salt and black pepper, to taste
- 1 tablespoon lemon zest, freshly grated

Directions
1. Preheat the oven to 380 degrees and lightly grease a baking dish.
2. Mix together butter, lemon juice, lemon zest, salt and black pepper in a bowl.
3. Scrub the pork with this mixture and place on the baking dish.
4. Transfer in the oven and bake for about 30 minutes.
5. Dish out to serve hot.

Nutrition Calories: 317 Carbs: 0.2g Fats: 26g Proteins: 19.1g Sodium: 96mg Sugar: 0.1g

Paprika Mushroom Pork

Serves: 8/Prep Time: 35 mins
Ingredients
- 2 tablespoons butter
- 2 pounds pork loin
- ¾ cup sour cream
- Salt and black pepper, to taste
- 1 cup white mushrooms

Directions
1. Season the pork with salt and black pepper.
2. Heat butter in a wok and add pork.
3. Sauté for about 3 minutes and add sour cream and mushrooms.
4. Cover the lid and cook for about 15 minutes.
5. Dish out and serve hot.

Nutrition Calories: 348 Carbs: 1.2g Fats: 23.2g Proteins: 32g Sodium: 103mg Sugar: 0.2g

Pesto Parmesan Pork Chops

Serves: 6/Prep Time: 7 hours 40 mins
Ingredients
- 1 cup Parmesan cheese, shredded
- ½ cup parsley, chopped
- 6 pork chops, boneless
- 6 tablespoons pesto sauce
- Salt and black pepper, to taste

Directions
1. Season the pork chops with parsley, salt and black pepper.
2. Drizzle with pesto sauce and place in the slow cooker.
3. Cover the lid and cook on LOW for about 7 hours.
4. Open the lid and top with parsley and Parmesan cheese.
5. Cook for about 30 minutes and dish out to serve hot.

Nutrition Calories: 386 Carbs: 2g Fats: 30.5g Proteins: 25.7g Sodium: 329mg Sugar: 1g

Beef Fajitas

Serves: 5/Prep Time: 45 mins
Ingredients
- 2 bell peppers, sliced
- 2 tablespoons fajita seasoning
- 1½ pounds beef, sliced
- 1 onion, sliced
- 2 tablespoons butter

Directions
1. Heat butter in the skillet and add onions and bell peppers.
2. Sauté for about 3 minutes and add beef and fajita seasoning.
3. Cover the lid and cook on medium-low heat for about 30 minutes.
4. Dish out and serve hot.

Nutrition Calories: 330 Carbs: 8.2g Fats: 13.2g Proteins: 42.1g Sodium: 334mg Sugar: 3.3g

Mustard Pork Chops

Serves: 4/Prep Time: 1 hour
Ingredients
- 2 tablespoons butter
- 4 pork chops
- 2 tablespoons Dijon mustard
- Salt and black pepper, to taste
- 1 tablespoon fresh rosemary, coarsely chopped

Directions
1. Preheat the oven to 360 degrees F and lightly grease a baking dish.

2. Marinate the pork chops with rosemary, Dijon mustard, salt and black pepper.
3. Drizzle with butter and place on the baking dish.
4. Bake for about 45 minutes and dish out to serve warm.

Nutrition

Calories: 315 Carbs: 1g Fats: 26.1g Proteins: 18.4g Sodium: 186mg Sugar: 0.1g

Ground Beef and Brussels Sprouts

Serves: 2/Prep Time: 1 hour 40 mins

Ingredients

- 5 oz ground beef
- 4½ oz Brussels sprouts
- ¼ cup mayonnaise
- 1½ oz butter
- Salt and black pepper, to taste

Directions

1. Heat 3 tablespoons of butter in a large pan on medium heat and stir in beef.
2. Cook until brown in color and season with salt and black pepper.
3. Decrease the heat and add remaining butter, Brussels sprouts, salt and black pepper.
4. Cook for about 8 minutes, stirring occasionally and top with mayonnaise to serve.

Nutrition

Calories: 356 Carbs: 5.5g Fats: 26.9g Proteins: 23.5g Sodium: 202mg Sugar: 0.9g

Pork with Carrots

Serves: 8/Prep Time: 7 hours 20 mins

Ingredients

- 1 large onion, thinly sliced
- 2 pounds pork shoulder roast, boneless
- 4 medium carrots, peeled and sliced lengthwise
- Salt and black pepper, to taste
- 1 teaspoon dried oregano, crushed

Directions

1. Sprinkle the pork shoulder with salt, black pepper and dried oregano.
2. Transfer the seasoned pork in a bowl and keep aside for about 3 hours.
3. Place onions and carrots in a slow cooker and add the pork.
4. Cover the lid and set the slow cooker on LOW.
5. Cook for about 7 hours and dish out to serve hot.

Nutrition

Calories: 312 Carbs: 4.9g Fats: 23.1g Proteins: 19.6g Sodium: 97mg Sugar: 2.3g

Garlic Creamy Beef Steak

Serves: 6/Prep Time: 45 mins

Ingredients

- 4 garlic cloves, minced
- ½ cup butter
- 2 pounds beef top sirloin steaks
- 1½ cup cream
- Salt and freshly ground black pepper, to taste

Directions

1) Rub the beef top sirloin steaks with garlic, salt and black pepper.
2) Marinate the beef with cream and butter and keep aside.
3) Preheat the grill and transfer the steaks on it.
4) Grill for about 15 minutes on each side and serve hot.

Nutrition

Calories: 353 Carbs: 3.9g Fats: 24.1g Proteins: 31.8g Sodium: 298mg Sugar: 1.2g

Ketogenic Beef Sirloin Steak

Serves: 3/Prep Time: 35 mins

Ingredients

- ½ teaspoon garlic powder
- 3 tablespoons butter
- 1-pound beef top sirloin steaks
- 1 garlic clove, minced
- Salt and freshly ground black pepper, to taste

Directions

1) Put butter and beef sirloin steaks in a large grill pan.
2) Cook for about 2 minutes on each side to brown the steaks.
3) Add garlic clove, garlic powder, salt, and black pepper and cook for about 15 minutes on each side on medium-high heat.
4) Transfer the steaks in a serving platter and serve hot.

Nutrition

Calories: 246 Carbs: 2g Fats: 13.1g Proteins: 31.3g Sodium: 224mg Sugar: 0.1g

Beef Roast

Serves: 6/Prep Time: 1 hour
Ingredients
- 1 cup onion soup
- 2 pounds beef roast
- 1 cups beef broth
- Salt and freshly ground black pepper, to taste

Directions
1) Put the beef roast in the pressure cooker and then add beef broth, onion soup, salt, and black pepper.
2) Secure the lid and cook at high pressure for about 50 minutes.
3) Release the pressure naturally and dish onto a serving platter.

Nutrition Calories: 349 Carbs: 2.9g Fats: 18.8g Proteins: 39.9g Sodium: 480mg Sugar: 1.2g

Keto Minced Meat

Serves: 4/Prep Time: 30 mins
Ingredients
- 1 pound ground lamb meat
- 2 tablespoons butter
- 1 cup onions, chopped
- ½ teaspoon turmeric powder
- 1 teaspoon salt
- ½ teaspoon cayenne pepper
- 1 tablespoon garlic, minced
- 1 tablespoon ginger, minced
- ½ teaspoon ground coriander
- ½ teaspoon cumin powder

Directions
1) Put the butter, garlic, ginger, and onions in a pot and sauté for about 3 minutes.
2) Add ground meat and all the spices. Next, lock the lid.
3) Cook for about 20 minutes on medium-high heat and present in a large serving bowl.

Nutrition Calories: 304 Carbs: 4.8g Fats: 21.1g Proteins: 21.8g Sodium: 705mg Sugar: 1.3g

2-Meat Chili

Serves: 8/Prep Time: 45 mins
Ingredients
- 1-pound grass-fed ground beef
- ½ of small yellow onion, chopped
- 2 garlic cloves, minced
- 1 tablespoon ground cumin
- Salt and freshly ground black pepper, to taste
- ½ cup cheddar cheese, shredded
- 1 tablespoon olive oil
- 1-pound ground pork
- 3 medium tomatillos, chopped
- 2 jalapeño peppers, chopped
- 1 (6-ounce) can sugar-free tomato sauce
- 1 tablespoon chili powder
- ¼ cup water

Directions
1) Heat the oil in a pressure cooker and add beef and pork.
2) Cook for about 5 minutes on medium heat and add the remaining ingredients, except cheese.
3) Lock the lid and cook for about 30 minutes at high pressure.
4) Release the pressure naturally and top with cheddar cheese.

Nutrition Calories: 259 Carbs: 5.4g Fats: 12.5g Proteins: 29.9g Sodium: 253mg Sugar: 1.2g

Mustard Pork Chops

Serves: 4/Prep Time: 40 mins
Ingredients
- 2 tablespoons Dijon mustard
- 2 tablespoons butter
- 4 pork chops
- 1 tablespoon fresh rosemary, coarsely chopped
- Salt and freshly ground black pepper, to taste

Directions
1) Marinate the pork chops with fresh rosemary, Dijon mustard, salt, and black pepper for about 3 hours.
2) Put the butter and marinated pork chops in a non-stick skillet and cover the lid.
3) Cook for about 30 minutes on medium-low heat and dish to serve hot.

Nutrition Calories: 315 Carbs: 1g Fats: 26.1g Proteins: 18.4g Sodium: 186mg Sugar: 0.1g

Zesty Pork Chops

Serves: 4/Prep Time: 35 mins
Ingredients
- 3 tablespoons lemon juice
- 4 tablespoons butter
- 4 pork chops, bone-in
- 1 cup picante sauce
- 2 tablespoons low-carb flour mix

Directions
1) Mix picante sauce and orange in a bowl and keep aside.
2) Coat the chops with flour and keep aside.

3) Put the oil and pork chops in the pressure cooker.
4) Close the lid and cook for about 15 minutes at high pressure.
5) Naturally release the pressure for 10 minutes and dish to serve hot.
Nutrition Calories: 284 Carbs: 1g Fats: 19.5g Proteins: 24.8g Sodium: 150mg Sugar: 0.3g

Greek Pork Gyros

Serves: 4
Prep Time: 40 mins
Ingredients
- 1-pound pork meat, ground
- 4 garlic cloves
- 1 teaspoon rosemary
- ¾ teaspoons salt
- ¼ teaspoon black pepper
- ½ small onion, chopped
- 1 teaspoon dried oregano
- 1 teaspoon ground marjoram
- ¾ cup water

Directions
1) Put onions, ground lamb meat, garlic, marjoram, rosemary, salt, and black pepper in a food processor and process until well combined.
2) Press Meat mixture into the Loaf Pan until very tight and compact.
3) Cover tightly with tin foil and poke some holes in the foil.
4) Preheat the oven to 390 degrees F and transfer the loaf pan in the oven.
5) Bake for about 25 minutes and dish to serve hot.
Nutrition Calories: 242 Carbs: 2.4g Fats: 15.2g Proteins: 21.4g Sodium: 521mg Sugar: 0.4g

Crispy Parmesan Crusted Pork Chops

Serves: 4/Prep Time: 30 mins
Ingredients
- ½ teaspoon salt
- ½ teaspoon onion powder
- 4 thick pork chops, center cut boneless
- ¼ teaspoon pepper
- 1 teaspoon smoked paprika
- ¼ teaspoon chili powder
- 1 cup pork rind crumbs
- 2 large eggs
- 3 tablespoons parmesan cheese, grated

Directions
1) Preheat the Air fryer to 400 degrees.
2) Season pork chops with salt and black pepper.
3) Mix together parmesan cheese, pork rind crumbs, and seasonings in a bowl.
4) Whisk the eggs in another bowl and dip each pork chop into the egg mixture first, and then in the crumb mixture.
5) Place pork chops in the air fryer basket and cook for about 20 minutes.
6) Dish out and serve with your favorite dip.
Nutrition Calories: 271 Carbs: 1.2g Fats: 12.3g Proteins: 38.5g Sodium: 605mg Sugar: 0.4g

Roasted Pork

Serves: 12 Prep Time: 2 hours 25 mins
Ingredients
- 2 teaspoons garlic powder
- ½ teaspoon sea salt
- 4 pounds pork
- 3 teaspoons thyme, dried
- 1 tablespoon Chimichurri sauce, for serving

Directions
1) Preheat the oven at 360 degrees F and wrap a baking sheet with foil.
2) Season the lamb breast with garlic powder, dried thyme, and salt.
3) Arrange the lamb onto the baking sheet and bake for about 1 hour.
4) Increase the temperature of the oven to 440 degrees F and transfer the baking sheet inside the oven.
5) Cook for about 1 hour and dish out the lamb breast onto a serving plate.
6) Top with lemon wedges and chimichurri sauce before serving hot.
Nutrition Calories: 286 Carbs: 0.6g Fats: 11.3g Proteins: 42.6g Sodium: 200mg Sugar: 0.1g

Beef Barbacoa

Serves: 4
Prep Time: 60 mins

Ingredients

- 2 tablespoons vegetable oil
- 2 lb. beef stew meat
- 1 cup beef broth
- 2 tablespoons canned chipotle chili in adobo, finely chopped
- 3 cloves garlic, finely chopped
- 1 package (1 oz) taco seasoning mix
- 1 teaspoon ground cumin
- 1 teaspoon ground coriander
- ¼ teaspoon salt
- 2 cups chopped red onions

Directions

1. Preheat oil in the insert of the Instant Pot on sauté mode.
2. Add beef and sear it for 4 minutes per side until brown.
3. Stir in chili, broth, taco seasoning, garlic, coriander, salt, and cumin.
4. Seal the Instant Pot lid and turn the pressure valve to sealing position.
5. Select Manual mode for 45 minutes at high pressure
6. Once done, release the pressure completely then remove the lid.
7. Shred the beef using 2 forks and cook the mixture on sauté mode until it is reduced slightly.
8. Serve warm.

Nutrition Calories per serving: 343 Carbohydrate: 4.8g Protein: 28.7g Fat: 22.5g Sugar: 1.3g Sodium: 676mg

Pork Tenderloin with Gravy

Serves: 6 Prep Time: 50 mins

Ingredients

- 3-pound Smithfield prime pork tenderloin
- 1/2 teaspoon garlic powder
- 1/2 teaspoon kosher salt
- 1/4 teaspoon ground ginger
- 1/4 teaspoon dried thyme
- 1/4 teaspoon black pepper
- 1 tablespoon olive oil
- 2 cups chicken broth
- 2 tablespoons fresh lemon juice
- 1 tablespoon low sodium soy sauce
- 3 tablespoons cornstarch + 3 tablespoons cold water
- salt and pepper

Directions

1. Pat dry the tenderloin with paper towel then cut it into half.
2. Thoroughly mix salt, ginger, thyme, garlic powder, and pepper in a small bowl.
3. Rub this mixture liberally over the pork.
4. Preheat oil in the insert of the Instant Pot on sauté mode.
5. Cook one half of the pork at a time in the heated oil for 3 minutes per side.
6. Transfer the cooked pork to the cutting board.
7. Add broth to the pot and deglaze the insert.
8. Stir in soy sauce and lemon juice.
9. Place the trivet over broth mixture and arrange seared pork over it.
10. Seal the Instant Pot lid and turn the pressure valve to sealing position.
11. Select Manual mode for 6 minutes at high pressure
12. Once done, release the pressure completely then remove the lid.
13. Transfer the pork to the cutting board and slice it.
14. Switch the Instant pot to sauté mode.
15. Mix corn-starch with water and pour this slurry into the pot.
16. Cook the mixture until it thickens.
17. Add the sliced pork then serve.
18. Enjoy.

Nutrition Calories per serving: 381 Carbohydrate: 6.3g Protein: 39.1g Fat: 21.5g Sugar: 3.5g Sodium: 628mg

Sweet Balsamic Pork

Serves: 4
Prep Time: 40 mins

Ingredients

- 1 1.5-2 lb. pork tenderloin, cut into four pieces

Sauce

- 3 garlic cloves, chopped
- 1/4 cup brown sugar
- 1/4 cup balsamic vinegar
- 1/4 cup water
- 1 tablespoon olive oil
- 1 tablespoon tamari
- 1 tablespoon rosemary, chopped
- 1 tablespoon corn starch

Directions

1. Combine all the ingredients for pork sauce in a bowl except for corn-starch.
2. Preheat olive oil in the insert of your Instant Pot.
3. Rub the pork with salt and pepper then place it in the Instant Pot.

4. Sear the meat for 2 3 minutes per side. Pour in the prepared sauce.
5. Seal the Instant Pot lid and turn the pressure valve to sealing position.
6. Select Meat/ Stew mode for 20 minutes at high pressure
7. Once done, release the pressure naturally then remove the lid.
8. Mix corn-starch with 1 tablespoon water in a bowl then pour it into the pot.
9. Cook more on sauté mode for few minutes until it thickens.
10. Enjoy.

Nutrition Calories per serving: 340 Carbohydrate: 7.1g Protein: 29.5g Fat: 21.3g Sugar: 4.3g Sodium: 179mg

Barbecue Pulled Pork Sandwiches

Serves: 6
Prep Time: 1hr. 30 mins
Ingredients

- 3 tablespoons light brown sugar
- 2 teaspoons hot paprika
- 1 teaspoon mustard powder
- 1/2 teaspoon ground cumin
- kosher salt and freshly ground pepper
- one 4-pound boneless pork shoulder, cut into 6 chunks

- 2 teaspoons vegetable oil
- 1/2 cup apple cider vinegar, plus more to taste
- 3 tablespoons tomato paste
- 12 hamburger potato buns
- 1 cup barbecue sauce, for serving
- 4 cups coleslaw, for serving

Directions
1. Mix mustard powder, paprika, 1 tablespoon brown sugar, cumin, salt and pepper in a bowl.
2. Season the pork with this spice's mixture liberally.
3. Preheat oil in the insert of the Instant Pot on Sauté mode.
4. Add pork to the pot in batches and cook each for 5 minutes per side.
5. Transfer the seared pork to a plate and keep it aside.
6. Add 2 ¾ cups water, vinegar, 2 tablespoons brown sugar, 2 and tomato paste to the pot.
7. Mix well then return the pork to the pot.
8. Seal the Instant Pot lid and turn the pressure valve to sealing position.
9. Select Manual mode for 60 minutes at high pressure
10. Once done, release the pressure completely then remove the lid.
11. Switch the Instant pot to sauté mode.
12. Cook the mixture for 15 minutes until reduced.
13. Adjust seasoning with salt and pepper. Shred the pork using forks.
14. Serve warm with buns, sauce, and coleslaw.

Nutrition Calories per serving: 427 Carbohydrate: 6.8g Protein: 27.4g Fat: 23g Sugar: 2.3g Sodium: 536mg

Sauces and Dressings Recipes

Keto Hollandaise

Serves: 4/Prep Time: 15 mins
Ingredients

- 2 tablespoons fresh lemon juice
- Dash hot sauce
- 4 egg yolks

- ½ cup butter, melted
- 1 pinch sea salt and cayenne pepper

Directions
1. Whisk together egg yolks and lemon juice in a bowl thoroughly.
2. Boil water in a saucepan and place the bowl of eggs mixture over top of the saucepan above water.
3. Whisk in the melted butter slowly and remove from heat.
4. Stir in the hot sauce, sea salt, and cayenne pepper to serve.

Nutrition
Calories: 262 Carbs: 1.3g Fats: 27.6g Proteins: 3g Sodium: 177mg Sugar: 0.3g

Chipotle Mayonnaise

Serves: 4/Prep Time: 10 mins
Ingredients

- ½ tablespoon chipotle powder
- 1 cup mayonnaise

- 1 tablespoon tomato paste

Directions

1. Mix together the tomato paste, mayonnaise, and chipotle powder in a small bowl.
2. Refrigerate for about 30 minutes and serve with your favorite snacks.

Nutrition Calories: 234 Carbs: 14.8g Fats: 19.7g Proteins: 0.9g Sodium: 430mg Sugar: 4.3g

Keto Ranch Sauce

Serves: 8/Prep Time: 10 mins

Ingredients
- ½ cup crème fraiche
- 1 cup mayonnaise
- 2 tablespoons ranch seasoning

Directions
1. Mix together crème fraiche, mayonnaise. and ranch seasoning in a bowl.
2. Serve with your favorite snacks or as a dressing on a salad.

Nutrition Calories: 173 Carbs: 7.4g Fats: 14.9g Proteins: 1.4g Sodium: 420mg Sugar: 1.9g

Homemade Mayonnaise

Serves: 4/Prep Time: 10 mins

Ingredients
- 1 tablespoon Dijon mustard
- 2 teaspoons white wine vinegar
- 1 egg yolk
- 1 cup avocado oil
- Salt and black pepper, to taste

Directions
1. Whisk together egg yolk and mustard with a stick blender in a bowl.
2. Slowly add avocado oil and white wine vinegar.
3. Season with salt and black pepper and mix well.
4. Refrigerate for about 30 minutes and serve.

Nutrition
Calories: 91 Carbs: 3.5g Fats: 8.4g Proteins: 1.5g Sodium: 49mg Sugar: 0.2g

Poppy Seed Salad Dressing

Serves: 8/Prep Time: 15 mins

Ingredients
- 2 tablespoons Swerve
- ¾ cup mayonnaise
- 2 tablespoons apple cider vinegar
- ½ teaspoon sea salt
- 1 tablespoon poppy seeds

Directions
1. Mix together poppy seeds with rest of the ingredients in a small bowl.
2. Refrigerate for about 30 minutes and use it as a dressing for your salad.

Nutrition Calories: 94 Carbs: 6.1g Fats: 7.9g Proteins: 0.4g Sodium: 274mg Sugar: 1.6g

Blue Cheese Dressing

Serves: 16/Prep Time: 5 mins

Ingredients
- ½ cup sour cream
- Garlic salt and black pepper, to taste
- 1 cup blue cheese, crumbled
- ½ cup mayonnaise
- ½ teaspoon lemon juice

Directions
1. Mix together all the ingredients except half of blue cheese.
2. Put the mixture into an immersion blender and blend well.
3. Stir in rest of the blue cheese and use it as a dressing for your salad.

Nutrition Calories: 74 Carbs: 2.3g Fats: 6.4g Proteins: 2.1g Sodium: 174mg Sugar: 0.5g

Honey Mustard Dressing

Serves: 8/Prep Time: 5 mins

Ingredients
- ¼ cup water
- ½ cup full fat sour cream
- ¼ cup Dijon mustard
- 1 tablespoon honey
- 1 tablespoon apple cider vinegar

Directions
1. Whisk together honey and mustard with all the other ingredients in a bowl.
2. Refrigerate for about 30 minutes and use it as a dressing for your salad.

Nutrition
Calories: 44 Carbs: 3.2g Fats: 3.3g Proteins: 0.8g Sodium: 96mg Sugar: 2.3g

Creamy Garlic Salad Dressing

Serves: 10
Prep Time: 5 mins
Ingredients
- 2/3 cup mayo
- 10 garlic cloves, chopped
- 1 can coconut cream
- ½ teaspoon salt
- 1 tablespoon tomato paste

Directions
1. Mix together all the ingredients in a bowl.
2. Refrigerate for about 30 minutes and use it as a dressing for your salad

Nutrition Calories: 156 Carbs: 2g Fats: 16g Proteins: 6.5g Sodium: 204mg Sugar: 0.1g

Eggs and Dairy Recipes

Scrambled Eggs

Serves: 2
Prep Time: 15 mins
Ingredients
- 1 tablespoon butter
- Salt and black pepper, to taste
- 4 eggs, whisked
- 1 tablespoon milk

Directions
1) Combine milk, eggs, salt, and black pepper in a medium bowl.
2) Put butter in a pan over medium-low heat and add the whisked eggs mixture slowly.
3) Stir continuously for about 4 minutes and dish onto a serving plate.

Nutrition Calories: 151 Carbs: 0.7g Fats: 11.6g Proteins: 11.1g Sodium: 144mg Sugar: 0.7g

Pepperoni Omelet

Serves: 8
Prep Time: 15 mins
Ingredients
- 30 pepperoni slices
- 8 tablespoons cream
- 4 tablespoons butter
- 12 eggs
- Salt and freshly ground black pepper, to taste

Directions
1) Whisk together the eggs in a bowl and add the remaining ingredients.
2) Put butter in a pan and add the egg mixture.
3) Cook for about 2 minutes and flip the sides.
4) Cook for another 2 minutes and dish out in a serving plate.

Nutrition Calories: 141 Carbs: 0.6g Fats: 11.3g Proteins: 8.9g Sodium: 334mg Sugar: 0.5g

Eggs Stuffed with Avocado and Watercress

Serves: 3
Prep Time: 15 mins
Ingredients
- ½ medium ripe avocado, peeled, pitted and chopped
- ¼ tablespoon fresh lemon juice
- 3 organic eggs, boiled, peeled and cut in half lengthwise
- ¼ cup fresh watercress, trimmed
- Salt, to taste

Directions
1) Place a steamer basket at the bottom of the pot and pour water.
2) Put the watercress on the trivet and pour water in the pressure cooker.
3) Place the trivet in the cooker and lock the lid.
4) Cook for about 3 minutes at high pressure and then release the pressure quickly.
5) Drain the watercress completely and keep aside.
6) Remove the egg yolks and transfer into a bowl.
7) Mash watercress, lemon juice, avocado and salt completely with a fork.
8) Place the egg whites in a plate and stuff the egg whites with the watercress mixture.
9) Serve immediately.

Nutrition
Calories: 132 Carbs: 3.3g Fats: 10.9g Proteins: 6.3g Sodium: 65mg Sugar: 0.5g

Cheesy Mini Frittatas

Serves: 3/Prep Time: 25 mins
Ingredients
- 4 tablespoons cheddar cheese, shredded
- ¼ cup unsweetened almond milk
- 3 organic eggs
- 1 scallion, chopped
- ¼ teaspoon lemon pepper seasoning
- 2 cooked bacon slices, crumbled
- Salt and black pepper, to taste
- 1 medium zucchini, finely chopped

Directions
1) Preheat the oven to 400 degrees F and grease the silicone moulds.
2) Whisk together eggs and stir in the remaining ingredients, mixing well.
3) Pour the eggs mixture into the silicone moulds and transfer the moulds in the oven.
4) Bake for about 15 minutes and remove from the oven to serve.

Nutrition Calories: 185 Carbs: 3.5g Fats: 13.2g Proteins: 13.6g Sodium: 435mg Sugar: 1.6g

Keto Coconut Pancakes

Serves: 4/Prep Time: 15 mins
Ingredients
For Pancakes
- 4 eggs
- ¼ cup full-fat coconut milk
- ¼ cup melted ghee or butter
- ½ tablespoon salt
- ½ tablespoon baking powder
- ¼ cup coconut flour

For Keto Caramel Sauce
- ¼ cup grass-fed butter
- ¼ cup full-fat coconut milk
- ½ tablespoon pure vanilla extract
- 1 pinch salt

Directions
For Pancakes
1) Take a non-stick skillet and heat butter or ghee in it at a low flame.
2) Now take a bowl and add butter, salt, milk, vanilla, and eggs to it.
3) Whisk and add coconut flour and baking powder. Keep whisking until a smooth mixture is formed.
4) Pour the batter to heated skillet and cook until the edges rise.
5) Flip and cook from the other side for a minute.
6) Add a bit of butter in between the batches to make the edges crispy.
7) Serve after topping with your favorite ones.

For Keto Caramel Sauce
1) Melt the butter in a small saucepan until it turns brown and bubbly in appearance.
2) Add coconut milk and keep stirring until you achieve the thickness you desire.
3) Remove when it is boiled and add vanilla and salt to it.
4) Drizzle it over the pancakes to serve.
5) This sauce is in its best flavor, if used the same day.

Nutrition Calories: 267 Carbs: 7.4g Fats: 24g Proteins: 7g Sodium: 943mg Sugar: 1.1g

Nut Porridge

Serves: 4/Prep Time: 25 mins
Ingredients
- 4 teaspoons coconut oil, melted
- 1 cup pecan, halved
- 1 cup water
- 1 cup coconut milk
- 2 tablespoons stevia
- 1 cup cashew nuts, raw and unsalted

Directions
1) Place the cashew nuts and pecans in the food processor and pulse until chunked.
2) Put the chunked nuts into the pot and stir in coconut oil, stevia and water.
3) Cook for about 5 minutes on high heat and reduce the heat to low.
4) Simmer for about 10 minutes and dish out to serve.

Nutrition Calories: 260 Carbs: 12.7g Fats: 22.9g Proteins: 5.6g Sodium: 9mg Sugar: 1.8g

Lemon Mousse

Serves: 4/Prep Time: 25 mins
Ingredients
- 1 cup heavy cream
- ¼ cup fresh lemon juice
- 1 teaspoon lemon liquid stevia
- 8-ounce cream cheese, softened
- ¼ teaspoon salt

Directions
1) Preheat the oven to 360 degrees and grease 4 ramekins.
2) Mix together lemon liquid stevia, cream cheese, lemon juice, heavy cream, and salt in a bowl.
3) Pour the mixture into the ramekins and transfer the ramekins into the oven.

4) Bake for about 12 minutes and pour into the serving glasses.
5) Refrigerate for at least 2 hours and serve chilled.

Nutrition Calories: 305 Carbs: 2.7g Fats: 31g Proteins: 5g Sodium: 299mg Sugar: 0.5g

Vanilla Yogurt

Serves: 12/Prep Time: 13 hours
Ingredients
- ½ tablespoon pure vanilla extract
- 2 scoops stevia
- ½ cup full-fat milk
- ¼ cup yogurt starter
- 1 cup heavy cream

Directions
1) Pour milk into the slow cooker and set it on low for about 2 hours.
2) Whisk vanilla extract, stevia and heavy cream in the slow cooker.
3) Allow the yogurt to sit and set the slow cooker on LOW to cook for about 3 hours.
4) Mix the yogurt starter with full-fat milk and return this mixture to the slow cooker.
5) Lock the lid of the slow cooker again and wrap it in two small towels.
6) Let the wrapped slow cooker to sit for about 8 hours and allow the yogurt to culture.
7) Dish out in a serving bowl or alternatively, store it by refrigerating.

Nutrition Calories: 292 Carbs: 8.2g Fats: 26.2g Proteins: 5.2g Sodium: 86mg Sugar: 6.6g

Appetizer Recipes

Cheesy Cauliflower Breadsticks

Serves: 2/Prep Time: 40 mins
Ingredients
- ½ cup Monterey jack cheese, freshly grated
- 1/8 teaspoon ground sage
- 1/8 teaspoon ground mustard
- ½ cup cauliflower, riced
- 1 small egg, beaten
- 1/8 teaspoon ground oregano
- 1/8 teaspoon dried thyme
- Salt and black pepper, to taste
- Fresh parsley, minced

Directions
1. Put the cauliflower in a toaster oven and cook for about 8 minutes.
2. Dish out the cauliflower in a mixing bowl and season with sage, oregano, thyme and mustard.
3. Add egg and ½ of cheese to the seasoned cauliflower and sprinkle with salt and black pepper.
4. Preheat the oven to 450 degrees F and grease a baking sheet.
5. Place cauliflower in the baking sheet and transfer into the oven.
6. Bake for about 8 minutes and top with rest of the cheese.
7. Bake for 5 more minutes and dish out to serve with garnished parsley.

Nutrition Calories: 142 Carbs: 2.2g Fats: 10.5g Proteins: 10g Sodium: 188mg Sugar: 0.9g

Low Carb Broccoli and Cheese Fritters

Serves: 2/Prep Time: 15 mins
Ingredients
The Fritters
- 2 tablespoons + 1 tablespoon flaxseed meal
- 4 tablespoons almond flour
- 1-ounce fresh broccoli
- 1 small egg
- Salt and black pepper, to taste
- 1-ounce mozzarella cheese
- ¼ teaspoon baking powder

The Sauce
- 4 tablespoons fresh chopped dill
- 4 tablespoons mayonnaise
- ½ teaspoon lemon juice
- Salt and black pepper, to taste

Directions
1. Put broccoli into a food processor and process until completely chopped.
2. Place the broccoli in a bowl and add mozzarella cheese, egg, 2 tablespoons flaxseed meal, baking powder, almond flour, salt and black pepper.
3. Mix well and roll the batter into balls.
4. Coat the balls in 1 tablespoon flaxseed meal and keep aside.
5. Heat a deep fat fryer to 375 degrees F and drop the balls in the basket.
6. Fry the fritters for about 5 minutes until golden brown and dish out in a platter.
7. Mix together all the ingredients for the sauce and make a dip to serve with fritters.

Nutrition Calories: 428 Carbs: 11.4g Fats: 38.6g Proteins: 12.9g Sodium: 367mg Sugar: 0.6g

Sun Dried Tomato Pesto Mug Cake

Serves: 2/Prep Time: 15 mins
Ingredients
Base
- 4 tablespoons butter
- 2 large eggs

Flavor
- 10 teaspoons sun dried tomato pesto
- 2 pinches salt

- 4 tablespoons almond flour
- 1 teaspoon baking powder

- 2 tablespoons almond flour

Directions
1. Mix together all the ingredients in a mug and transfer into a microwave oven.
2. Microwave on high for 70 seconds.
3. Take the mug cake out and top with extra tomato pesto to serve.

Nutrition Calories: 404 Carbs: 6.1g Fats: 38g Proteins: 11.1g Sodium: 400mg Sugar: 0.4g

Low Carb Cauliflower Hummus

Serves: 2/Prep Time: 15 mins
Ingredients
- ¾ tablespoon water
- ¼ teaspoon salt
- ½ tablespoon Tahini paste
- ¾ tablespoon extra-virgin olive oil
- 1 cup raw cauliflower florets

- ¾ tablespoon avocado oil
- 2 whole garlic cloves
- ¾ tablespoon lemon juice
- 1/3 tsp kosher salt
- ¼ teaspoon smoked paprika

Directions
1. Mix together cauliflower, water, 1 garlic clove and half of salt, avocado oil and olive oil in a microwave safe dish.
2. Microwave for about 15 minutes and transfer the mixture into a food processor.
3. Add tahini paste, lemon juice and rest of the garlic clove, avocado oil, olive oil and kosher salt to the blender and blend until smooth.
4. Dish out the hummus in a bowl and sprinkle with paprika to serve.

Nutrition Calories: 93 Carbs: 5g Fats: 8.1g Proteins: 2g Sodium: 312mg Sugar: 1.4g

Spicy Keto Roasted Nuts

Serves: 2/Prep Time: 13 mins
Ingredients
- 1/3 teaspoon salt
- 2 oz. pecans, almonds and walnuts
- 1/3 tablespoon olive oil

- 1/3 teaspoon paprika powder or chili powder
- 1/3 teaspoon ground cumin

Directions
1. Mix together all the ingredients and transfer in a medium frying pan.
2. Cook for about 5 minutes on medium heat until the nuts are completely warmed.
3. Allow to cool and serve immediately.

Nutrition Calories: 220 Carbs: 4.4g Fats: 22.7g Proteins: 3.2g Sodium: 393mg Sugar: 1.1g

Bread Baking for Beginners Recipes

Keto Bread

Serves: 6
Prep Time: 5 hours 10 mins
Ingredients
- 6 large eggs, separated
- ¼ teaspoon cream of tartar
- 6 drops liquid stevia
- 1½ cups almond flour

- ¼ cup butter, melted
- 3 teaspoons baking powder
- 1 pinch pink salt

Directions
1. Preheat oven to 365 degrees F and grease a loaf pan.
2. Whisk together egg whites with cream of tartar.
3. Put 1/3 of the beaten egg whites, egg yolks, butter, baking powder, liquid stevia, salt, and almond flour in a food processor and process until combined.
4. Stir in the remaining 2/3 of the egg whites and process until completely incorporated.

5. Pour mixture into the loaf pan and transfer in the oven.
6. Bake for about 30 minutes and dish out to serve hot.

Nutrition
Calories: 310 Carbs: 7.7g Fats: 26g Proteins: 12.4g Sodium: 207mg Sugar: 0.4g

Macadamia Nut Bread

Serves: 5
Prep Time: 40 mins
Ingredients
- 5 large eggs
- 5 oz macadamia nuts
- ¼ cup coconut flour
- ½ teaspoon apple cider vinegar
- ½ teaspoon baking soda

Directions
1. Preheat oven to 350 degrees F and grease a standard-size bread pan.
2. Put macadamia nuts and eggs in a food processor and pulse until combined.
3. Add coconut flour, apple cider vinegar, and baking soda and pulse until incorporated.
4. Pour this mixture in the bread pan and transfer in the oven.
5. Bake for about 40 minutes and dish out to serve.

Nutrition
Calories: 299 Carbs: 8.3g Fats: 27.1g Proteins: 9.3g Sodium: 197mg Sugar: 1.7g

Cauliflower Bread with Garlic & Herbs

Serves: 18
Prep Time: 1 hour
Ingredients
- 10 large eggs, separated
- 1¼ cups coconut flour
- 3 cups cauliflower, finely chopped
- ¼ teaspoon cream of tartar
- 1½ tablespoons gluten-free baking powder
- 1 teaspoon sea salt
- 6 cloves garlic, minced
- 1 tablespoon fresh parsley, chopped
- 6 tablespoons butter, melted
- 1 tablespoon fresh rosemary, chopped

Directions
1. Preheat the oven to 350 degrees F and line a loaf pan with parchment paper.
2. Steam the riced cauliflower and keep aside to dry out completely.
3. Whisk together egg whites, and cream of tartar in a bowl and keep aside.
4. Place the baking powder, coconut flour, sea salt, egg yolks, butter, garlic, whipped egg whites and cauliflower in a food processor.
5. Process until combined and add in the parsley and rosemary.
6. Transfer the batter into the loaf pan and transfer in the oven.
7. Bake for about 50 minutes and slice to serve.

Nutrition
Calories: 115 Carbs: 7.4g Fats: 7.5g Proteins: 5.1g Sodium: 372mg Sugar: 0.6g

Fluffy Keto Buns

Serves: 4 Prep Time: 45 mins
Ingredients
- 2 tablespoons ground psyllium husks
- 2 egg yolks
- ½ tablespoon apple cider vinegar
- Salt and black pepper, to taste
- ¼ cup coconut flour
- 4 egg whites
- 1 teaspoon gluten free baking powder
- 1 cup water
- 1 teaspoon dried thyme
- 1 teaspoon dried oregano

Directions
1. Preheat the oven to 350 degrees and grease a baking sheet.
2. Whisk together eggs in a bowl and keep aside.
3. Mix together rest of the ingredients in another bowl and add whisked egg whites.
4. Form four rolls of equal size from the dough and arrange on the baking sheet.
5. Transfer in the oven and bake for about 40 minutes.
6. Remove from your oven and serve warm.

Nutrition
Calories: 86 Carbs: 8.7g Fats: 3.1g Proteins: 6g Sodium: 237mg Sugar: 0.3g

Garlic and Herb Focaccia Bread

Serves: 8
Prep Time: 30 mins
Ingredients

Wet Ingredients
- 1 tablespoon lemon juice
- 2 eggs

- 2 teaspoons olive oil + 2 tablespoons olive oil, to drizzle

Dry Ingredients
- 1 teaspoon flaky salt
- ½ teaspoon xanthan gum
- ¼ cup coconut flour
- 1 cup almond flour

- 1 teaspoon garlic powder
- ½ teaspoon baking soda
- ½ teaspoon baking powder

Directions
1. Preheat the oven to 350 degrees F and line a baking tray with parchment.
2. Mix together the dry ingredients in a bowl and keep aside.
3. Whisk together the wet ingredients until combined and mix with the dry ingredients.
4. Make a dough and flatten it with a spatula.
5. Arrange the focaccia on the baking tray and transfer in the oven.
6. Cover and bake for about 10 minutes.
7. Drizzle with olive oil and bake uncovered for about 15 more minutes.
8. Remove from the oven and serve warm.

Nutrition Calories: 162 Carbs: 7g Fats: 13.4g Proteins: 5g Sodium: 425mg Sugar: 0.2g

Coconut Bread

Serves: 5
Prep Time: 1 hour
Ingredients
- ¼ teaspoon salt
- ½ cup coconut flour
- ¼ teaspoon baking soda

- 6 eggs
- ¼ cup unsweetened almond milk
- ¼ cup coconut oil, melted

Directions
1. Preheat the oven to 350 degrees F and grease a loaf pan.
2. Mix together the coconut flour, baking soda and salt in a bowl.
3. Combine the eggs, milk, and coconut oil in another bowl.
4. Slowly add the wet ingredients into the dry ingredients and mix until combined.
5. Pour the mixture into the prepared loaf pan and transfer in the oven.
6. Bake for about 50 minutes and dish out to serve.

Nutrition Calories: 219 Carbs: 8.5g Fats: 17.5g Proteins: 8.3g Sodium: 262mg Sugar: 0.4g

Keto Mug Bread

Serves: 2 Prep Time: 15 mins
Ingredients
- ¼ cup almond flour
- 1 egg
- 1 tablespoon coconut flour

- 1 tablespoon coconut oil
- ¼ teaspoon baking powder

Directions
1. Preheat the oven to 350 degrees and grease a mug.
2. Put all ingredients into a mug and mix with a fork until combined.
3. Transfer the mug in the oven and bake for about 8 minutes.
4. Serve immediately.

Nutrition
Calories: 190 Carbs: 6g Fats: 16g Proteins: 6.3g Sodium: 36mg Sugar: 0.2g

Simple Cakes Recipes

Italian Pecan Cake

Serves: 8 Prep Time: 1 hour
Ingredients
Cake
- 1 cup Swerve
- 1 teaspoon vanilla essence
- ½ cup coconut, shredded
- ½ cup butter, softened
- 4 large eggs, separated
- ½ cup heavy cream

- ½ cup pecans, chopped
- 2 teaspoons baking powder
- 1½ cups almond flour
- ¼ teaspoon tartar cream
- ¼ cup coconut flour
- ½ teaspoon salt

Frosting
- ½ cup heavy whipping cream
- 1 teaspoon vanilla essence
- 8 ounces cream cheese, softened
- ½ cup butter, softened
- 1 cup powdered Swerve

Garnish
- 2 tablespoons pecans, chopped and lightly toasted
- 2 tablespoons coconut, shredded and lightly toasted

Directions
1. **Cake:** Preheat the oven to 330 degrees F and grease 2 baking pans of 8 inches each.
2. Whisk together egg yolks, butter, cream, Swerve, and vanilla essence in a bowl.
3. Combine almond flour, coconut flour, chopped pecans, baking powder, salt, and coconut.
4. Add the flour mixture to the egg yolk mixture and combine well.
5. Whisk together egg whites in a bowl until foamy and add this to the flour mixture.
6. Divide the mixture into the baking pans and transfer in the oven.
7. Bake for about 45 minutes and remove from the oven.
8. **Frosting:** Put all ingredients for frosting in a mixer and process until frothy.
9. Top the icing mixture over 1 cake and place the other cake over it.
10. Spread the rest of the icing on the top of the upper cake.
11. Garnish it with pecans and coconut.
12. Dish out to slice and serve.

Nutrition Calories: 267 Carbs: 8.4g Fats: 44.5g Proteins: 3.1g Sodium: 217mg Sugar: 2.3g

Citrus Cream Cake

Serves: 4/Prep Time: 1 hour 15 mins
Ingredients
For Cake
- 4 whole eggs
- 1¼ cups almond flour
- ¼ teaspoon lemon essence
- ¾ teaspoons baking powder
- ¾ teaspoons vanilla essence
- ¼ cup butter, unsalted softened
- ¾ cup erythritol
- ¼ teaspoon salt
- 4 ounces cream cheese

For Cream Frosting
- 1½ tablespoons heavy whipping cream
- 1/8 cup erythritol
- ¼ teaspoon vanilla essence

Directions
1. Preheat the oven to 350 degrees and grease a baking pan.
2. Mix together butter, Erythritol, and cream cheese in a bowl.
3. Stir in eggs, vanilla essence, and lemon essence and mix well.
4. Whisk in baking powder, almond flour, and salt.
5. Pour the mixture into a baking pan and transfer in the oven.
6. Bake for about 1 hour and remove from the oven.
7. Mix together all ingredients for cream frosting in a bowl and spread on the cake.
8. Refrigerate the cake for about 1 hour and serve chilled.

Nutrition Calories: 255 Carbs: 2.5g Fats: 23.4g Proteins: 7.9g Sodium: 112mg Sugar: 12.5g

Layered Cream Cake

Serves: 8/Prep Time: 45 mins
Ingredients
For Cream Cheese Icing:
- ½ cup butter, softened
- 2 tablespoons heavy cream
- 8 oz. cream cheese softened
- ½ cup powdered Swerve
- 1 teaspoon vanilla essence

For Carrot Cake Layers:
- ¾ cup Erythritol
- 14 tablespoons butter, melted
- ½ cup coconut flour
- 2 teaspoons baking powder
- 1¼ cups carrots, shredded
- 5 eggs large
- 2 teaspoons vanilla essence
- ¼ teaspoon unsweetened coconut, shredded
- ¼ teaspoon salt
- 1¾ cups almond flour
- 1½ teaspoons cinnamon, ground

Directions
1. **For Cream Cheese Icing:** Mix together all ingredients for the cream cheese icing until foamy and keep aside.
2. **For Carrot Cake Layers:** Preheat the oven to 350 degrees and grease 2 baking pans.
3. Whisk together eggs with Erythritol in a bowl and keep aside.
4. Mix together almond flour, coconut flour, salt, cinnamon, and baking powder in another bowl.

5. Combine the two mixtures and stir in coconut, butter and carrots.
6. Divide the cake mixture into 2 baking pans and transfer in the oven.
7. Bake for about 30 minutes and remove from the oven to cool.
8. Top the icing mixture over 1 cake and place the other cake over it.
9. Spread the rest of the icing on the top of the upper cake.
10. Dish out to slice and serve.

Nutrition Calories: 307 Carbs: 7g Fats: 29g Proteins: 6g Sodium: 122mg Sugar: 1g

Chunky Carrot Cake

Serves: 8/Prep Time: 45 mins
Ingredients
- ¾ cup butter
- ½ teaspoon pineapple extract
- 2½ cups almond flour
- ½ teaspoon sea salt
- 1 cup pecans, chopped
- ¾ cup Erythritol
- 1 teaspoon vanilla essence
- 4 large eggs
- 2 teaspoons gluten-free baking powder
- 2 teaspoons cinnamon
- 2½ cups carrots, grated

Directions
1. Preheat the oven at 350 degrees and grease two 9-inch baking dishes.
2. Mix Erythritol, cream, vanilla essence, and pineapple extract in a bowl.
3. Whisk in eggs one by one, then add cinnamon, baking powder, salt and flour to mix well.
4. Stir in pecans and carrots and divide the entire batter in the two pans.
5. Transfer in the oven and bake for about 30 minutes.
6. Remove the cakes from the pans and allow them to cool slightly.
7. Dish out to slice and serve.

Nutrition Calories: 359 Carbs: 8.5g Fats: 34g Proteins: 7.5g Sodium: 92mg Sugar: 2g

Zesty Lemon Cake

Serves: 8/Prep Time: 1 hour
Ingredients
For Cake
- 5 eggs
- ½ cup coconut flour
- ¼ cup Swerve
- Juice from ½ lemon
- ½ teaspoon lemon zest
- ½ teaspoon salt
- ½ cup butter, melted
- ½ teaspoon xanthan gum

For Icing
- 3 tablespoons swerve
- ½ teaspoon lemon zest
- 1 cup cream cheese
- 1 teaspoon vanilla essence

Directions
1. Preheat the oven at 340 degrees and grease a loaf pan.
2. Whisk egg whites using an electric mixer until it forms stiff peaks.
3. Mix together the remaining ingredients in another bowl and combine with egg whites.
4. Pour the batter to the loaf pan and transfer in the oven.
5. Bake for about 45 minutes and dish out.
6. Meanwhile, prepare the topping by beating icing ingredients in the electric mixer.
7. Place the baked cake on the wire rack and allow it to cool.
8. Layer the cream cheese icing over the cake and evenly spread it.
9. Refrigerate for about 30 minutes and cut into slices to enjoy.

Nutrition Calories: 251 Carbs: 4.3g Fats: 24.5g Proteins: 5.9g Sodium: 142mg Sugar: 0.5g

Perfect Cookies Recipes

Chocolate Chip Butter Cookies

Serves: 8/Prep Time: 25 mins
Ingredients
- ⅓ cup butter, unsalted
- 2 large eggs
- ⅛ teaspoon salt
- ¼ cup coconut flour
- 3 tablespoons Swerve
- 3 tablespoons sugar-free chocolate chips
- ¼ teaspoon vanilla essence

Directions
1. Preheat the oven at 350 degrees and grease a cookie sheet.
2. Mix salt, Swerve and coconut flour in a bowl.
3. Beat the vanilla essence, butter, and eggs in a mixer.

4. Stir in the flour mixture to the eggs mixture to combine.
5. Add chocolate chips and spoon this mixture on a cookie sheet.
6. Bake the cookies in the oven for 15 minutes and allow it to cool before serving.

Nutrition Calories: 198 Carbs: 4.5g Fats: 19.2g Proteins: 3.4g Sodium: 142mg Sugar: 3.3g

Buttery Energy Cookies

Serves: 8/Prep Time: 15 mins
Ingredients
- 3 tablespoons butter
- 1 cup almond flour
- 2 tablespoons erythritol
- Pinch of salt
- 1 teaspoon vanilla essence

Directions
1. Preheat the oven at 350 degrees and grease a cookie sheet.
2. Put all ingredients in a bowl and whisk until well combined.
3. Divide the cookie dough into small cookies and arrange on the cookie sheet.
4. Transfer the cookie sheet in the oven and bake for about 12 minutes.
5. Refrigerate to chill for about 1 hour and serve.

Nutrition Calories: 114 Carbs: 3.1g Fats: 9.6g Proteins: 3.5g Sodium: 155mg Sugar: 1.4g

Cream Dipped Cookies

Serves: 8/Prep Time: 40 mins
Ingredients
- ½ cup cacao nibs
- ½ cup almond butter
- 2 large eggs
- ¼ teaspoon salt
- 1 cup almond flour
- ½ cup coconut flakes, unsweetened
- 1/3 cup Erythritol
- ¼ cup butter, melted
- Stevia, to taste

Glaze:
- 1/8 teaspoon xanthan gum
- ½ teaspoon vanilla essence
- ¼ cup heavy whipping cream
- Stevia, to taste

Directions
1. Preheat the oven at 350 degrees and grease a cookie sheet.
2. Combine all the dry ingredients in a bowl.
3. Beat eggs, Stevia almond butter, butter, and vanilla essence in another bowl.
4. Stir in the almond flour mixture and mix well.
5. Make cookies on a cookie sheet by dropping the batter with spoon.
6. Press each cookie to flatten it and transfer in the oven.
7. Bake for about 25 minutes and keep aside.
8. Combine the glaze ingredients in a saucepan and cook until the sauce thickens.
9. Once the cookies are done, pour this cooked glaze over the cookies equally.
10. Allow this glaze to set for about 15 minutes and enjoy.

Nutrition Calories: 192 Carbs: 2.2g Fats: 17.4g Proteins: 4.7g Sodium: 135mg Sugar: 1.4g

Keto Coconut Cookies

Serves: 18/Prep Time: 35 mins
Ingredients
- ½ cup butter
- ½ tablespoon heavy cream
- 6 tablespoons coconut flour
- 1 teaspoon baking powder
- ½ teaspoon salt
- ¾ cup Splenda
- 3 eggs
- 1 teaspoon almond milk
- ½ cup unsweetened coconut flakes
- ¼ cup almond flour
- 1 teaspoon baking soda

Directions
1. Preheat the oven to 350 degrees and grease lightly a baking sheet.
2. Mix together Splenda, butter, heavy cream, eggs, and almond milk in a bowl until smooth.
3. Combine coconut flakes, coconut flour, almond flour, baking powder, baking soda, and salt in another bowl.
4. Combine both mixtures until dough comes together.
5. Drop spoonful of cookie dough onto the baking sheet and transfer to the oven.
6. Bake for about 18 minutes and cool to serve.

Nutrition
Calories: 98 Carbs: 3.3g Fats: 8.9g Proteins: 2g Sodium: 211mg Sugar: 0g

Vanilla Cream Cheese Cookies

Serves: 8/Prep Time: 30 mins
Ingredients
- 2 oz. plain cream cheese
- 2 teaspoons vanilla essence
- ¼ teaspoon sea salt
- ¼ cup butter
- ½ cup erythritol
- 1 large egg white
- 3 cups almond flour

Directions
1. Preheat the oven to 350 degrees and grease lightly a cookie sheet.
2. Put butter, cream cheese, egg white, and vanilla essence in a blender and blend until smooth.
3. Add Erythritol, flour, and salt, and mix well until smooth.
4. Divide the dough into small cookies on the cookie sheet and transfer in the oven.
5. Bake for about 15 minutes and allow the cookies to cool to serve.

Nutrition Calories: 195 Carbs: 4.5g Fats: 14.3g Proteins: 3.2g Sodium: 125mg Sugar: 0.5g

Peanut Butter Cookies

Serves: 6/Prep Time: 1 hour
Ingredients
- ½ cup Swerve
- ½ cup peanut butter
- 1 egg

Directions
1. Preheat the oven to 350 degrees and grease a baking sheet.
2. Mix together all ingredients in a bowl until thoroughly combined.
3. Scoop out dough with a cookie scoop and form balls.
4. Arrange on the baking sheet and press with a fork.
5. Transfer in the oven and bake for about 15 minutes.
6. Allow the cookies to cool for about 10 minutes.

Nutrition Calories: 82 Carbs: 2.5g Fats: 6g Proteins: 3g Sodium: 65mg Sugar: 1g

Coconut Vanilla Cookies

Serves: 4/Prep Time: 20 mins
Ingredients
- ¾ teaspoon baking powder
- 1/6 cup coconut oil
- 2 large eggs
- ½ teaspoon vanilla essence
- 6 tablespoons coconut flour
- 1/8 teaspoon salt
- 3 tablespoons butter
- 6 tablespoons Swerve
- ½ tablespoon coconut milk

Directions
1. Preheat the oven to 375 degrees and grease a cookie sheet.
2. Put all the wet ingredients in a food processor and process.
3. Stir in the remaining ingredients and mix well.
4. Divide the dough into small cookies and arrange on the cookie sheet.
5. Transfer in the oven and bake for about 10 minutes.
6. Allow the cookies to cool and serve.

Nutrition Calories: 151 Carbs: 1.5g Fats: 14.7g Proteins: 0.8g Sodium: 53mg Sugar: 0.3g

Cinnamon Snickerdoodle Cookies

Serves: 8/Prep Time: 25 mins
Ingredients
Cookies:
- 2 teaspoons vanilla essence
- ½ cup almond milk
- 2 eggs
- 1 cup almond butter
- ¼ cup coconut oil, solid, at
- 1½ cups monk fruit sweetener
- 1 cup coconut flour
- 2 teaspoons tartar cream
- 1 teaspoon cinnamon
- 1¾ cups almond flour
- 1 teaspoon baking soda
- 1/8 teaspoon pink Himalayan salt

Topping:
- 1 tablespoon cinnamon
- 3 tablespoons monk fruit sweetener

Directions
1. Preheat the oven to 350 degrees and grease a cookie sheet.
2. Add the wet ingredients of the cookies to a blender and beat well.
3. Stir in the dry mixture and combine well.
4. Place this batter in the refrigerator for 20 minutes to set.
5. Make small balls from this mixture.

6. Mix cinnamon and monk fruit in a shallow plate.
7. Roll these balls into this cinnamon mixture to coat well.
8. Place these balls on a baking sheet and transfer in the oven.
9. Bake for about 12 minutes and dish out to serve.
Nutrition Calories: 252 Carbs: 7.2g Fats: 17.3g Proteins: 5.2g Sodium: 153mg Sugar: 0.3g

Nutmeg Gingersnap Cookies

Serves: 8/Prep Time: 25 mins
Ingredients
- ¼ cup butter, unsalted
- 1 teaspoon vanilla essence
- 2 cups almond flour
- 1 cup Erythritol
- 1 large egg
- ¼ teaspoon salt
- ¼ teaspoon nutmeg, ground
- ½ teaspoon cinnamon, ground
- 2 teaspoons ginger, ground
- ¼ teaspoon cloves, ground

Directions
1. Preheat the oven to 350 degrees F and grease a cookie sheet.
2. Beat the wet ingredients in an electric mixer.
3. Stir in the leftover ingredients and mix until smooth.
4. Divide the dough into small cookies and arrange on the cookie sheet spoon by spoon.
5. Transfer in the oven and bake for about 12 minutes.
6. Dish out to serve and enjoy.
Nutrition Calories: 78 Carbs: 5.4g Fats: 7.1g Proteins: 2.3g Sodium: 15mg Sugar: 0.2g

Vanilla Shortbread Cookies

Serves: 6/Prep Time: 25 mins
Ingredients
- 6 tablespoons butter
- 1 teaspoon vanilla essence
- 2½ cups almond flour
- ½ cup erythritol

Directions
1. Preheat the oven to 350 degrees and grease a cookie sheet.
2. Beat Erythritol with butter until frothy.
3. Stir in flour and vanilla essence while beating the mixture.
4. Divide this batter and arrange on a cookie sheet in small cookies.
5. Transfer in the oven and bake for about 15 minutes.
6. Dish out to serve and enjoy.
Nutrition Calories: 288 Carbs: 9.6g Fats: 25.3g Proteins: 7.6g Sodium: 74mg Sugar: 0.1g

Easy Tarts and Bars Recipes

Mixed Berries Tart

Serves: 8/Prep Time: 25 mins
Ingredients
Tart crust:
- ¼ cup Erythritol, powdered
- ¼ teaspoon sea salt
- 2¼ cups almond flour
- 5 tablespoons butter, melted

Filling:
- 2 tablespoons erythritol
- 6 oz. mascarpone cheese
- 1/3 cup heavy cream
- ¼ teaspoon lemon zest
- 1 teaspoon vanilla essence

To garnish:
- 6 blueberries
- 6 raspberries
- 6 blackberries

Directions
1. **Crust:** Preheat the oven to 350 degrees and grease 8 small tart pans with butter.
2. Put butter, almond flour, Erythritol, and salt in a food processor and process until coarse.
3. Divide this mixture into the tart pans and press firmly.
4. Transfer in the oven and bake for about 10 minutes.
5. **Filling:** Put the erythritol and cream in an electric mixer and beat for about 2 minutes.
6. Stir in the cream, lemon zest, and vanilla essence slowly and continue beating until the mixture thickens.
7. Fill this mixture in the baked crust of each tart pan and garnish with the berries.
8. Chill for 10 minutes in the refrigerator to serve and enjoy.
Nutrition Calories: 237 Carbs: 5g Fats: 22g Proteins: 5g Sodium: 118mg Sugar: 1g

Creamy Chocolate Tart

Serves: 8 Prep Time: 40 mins
Ingredients
Crust
- 2 tablespoons Erythritol
- 6 tablespoons coconut flour
- 4 tablespoons butter, melted

- 1 large egg
- 2 (4-inch) tart pans

Filling
- ½ cup heavy whipping cream
- 2 oz. sugar-free chocolate
- ¼ cup Erythritol, powdered

- 1 large egg
- Liquid Stevia, to taste
- 1 oz. cream cheese

Directions
1. Preheat the oven to 350 degrees and grease 2 (4 inches) tart pans with butter.
2. Put all the ingredients for the crust in a food processor and process until coarse.
3. Divide this mixture into each tart pan and press firmly.
4. Pierce few holes in the crusts with a fork and transfer in the oven.
5. Bake both the crusts for about 12 minutes.
6. Meanwhile, heat cream in a saucepan on medium heat and add chocolate.
7. Cook until it melts and transfer in an immersion blender.
8. Puree this mixture and add egg, cream cheese, Erythritol, and Stevia.
9. Divide this filling into each crust and return both the pans to the oven.
10. Bake for about 15 minutes and allow to cool.
11. Transfer to the refrigerator for about 3 hours to serve chilled.

Nutrition Calories: 190 Carbs: 5.5g Fats: 17.2g Proteins: 3g Sodium: 28mg Sugar: 2.8g

Strawberry Vanilla Tart

Serves: 3/Prep Time: 25 mins
Ingredients
Coconut crust:
- ¾ cup coconut flour
- ½ cup coconut oil
- 2 eggs

- 1 teaspoon powdered sweetener
- 1 teaspoon vanilla essence

Cream Filling:
- 2 eggs, separated
- 1 cup strawberries
- 1 cup mascarpone

- 1 teaspoon vanilla essence
- 2 tablespoons Stevia, powdered

Directions
1. **Crust:**
2. Preheat the oven to 350 degrees and grease a baking pan.
3. Whisk together eggs in a bowl and add rest of the ingredients.
4. Spread this dough in between two sheets of parchment paper.
5. Place this dough sheet in a greased pan and pierce holes in it with a fork.
6. Transfer in the oven and bake for about 10 minutes.
7. **Cream Filling:**
8. Whisk the egg whites in an electric mixer until frothy.
9. Stir in mascarpone cream, egg yolks, sweetener, and vanilla and beat for about 3 minutes.
10. Spread this filling evenly in the baked crust and top with Stevia and strawberries.
11. Place the pie in the refrigerator for about 30 minutes and serve hot.

Nutrition Calories: 236 Carbs: 7.6g Fats: 21.5g Proteins: 4.3g Sodium: 21mg Sugar: 1.4g

Peanut Butter Bars

Serves: 8/Prep Time: 15 mins
Ingredients
Bars
- 2 oz. butter
- ¾ cup almond flour
- ¼ cup Swerve

- ½ teaspoon vanilla extract
- ½ cup peanut butter

Topping
- ½ cup sugar-free chocolate chips

Directions
1. Preheat the oven to 300 degrees and grease a baking pan.
2. Put all the ingredients for the bars in a bowl and mix well.
3. Spread this mixture in the pan and top with chocolate chips.
4. Transfer in the oven and bake for about 15 minutes.

5. Remove from the oven and transfer the pan in the refrigerator for about 1 hour.
6. Remove the base from pan and slice to serve.
Nutrition Calories: 214 Carbs: 6.5g Fats: 19g Proteins: 6.5g Sodium: 123mg Sugar: 1.9g

Cheesecake Jam Tarts

Serves: 6
Prep Time: 45 mins
Ingredients
Crust
- ½ cup almond flour
- 1½ tablespoons butter, melted

Filling
- 1 small egg
- ½ teaspoon vanilla essence
- 1/8 teaspoon salt
- 6 oz. cream cheese
- 1/8 cup Erythritol
- ½ tablespoon fresh lemon juice

Toppings
- 1/8 cup strawberry jam, sugar-free
- 1/8 cup blueberries

Directions
1. Preheat the oven to 340 degrees and grease muffin tins.
2. Mix butter and almond flour in a bowl and pour this mixture into the muffin tin.
3. Transfer in the oven and bake for about 8 minutes.
4. Meanwhile, beat cream cheese in an electric mixture along with an egg.
5. Stir in Erythritol, vanilla essence, salt, and lemon juice and combine well.
6. Divide this filling into the muffin crust and transfer in the oven.
7. Bake the tarts for 20 minutes and allow it to cool after removing from oven.
8. Top with jam and blueberries and refrigerate overnight to serve.
Nutrition Calories: 175 Carbs: 2.8g Fats: 16g Proteins: 9g Sodium: 8mg Sugar: 1.8g

Tasty Pies Recipes

Pumpkin Almond Pie

Serves: 8/Prep Time: 1 hour 15 mins
Ingredients
Almond Flour Pie Crust
- 4 tablespoons butter, melted
- 2 cups almond flour
- 1 teaspoon vanilla
- ½ teaspoon cinnamon
- 1 egg yolk

Pumpkin Spice Filling
- 1 cup heavy cream
- 2 teaspoons pumpkin pie spice
- ⅔ cups Swerve
- 8 ounces cream cheese
- 4 eggs
- 1 teaspoon vanilla
- ¼ teaspoon salt

Directions
1. Preheat the oven to 400 degrees and grease a pie pan.
2. Mix together all the ingredients for the crust in a bowl and transfer into the pie pan.
3. Press this mixture and transfer into the oven.
4. Bake this crust for about 12 minutes and keep aside.
5. **Filling:** Whisk together eggs and cream cheese until it turns frothy.
6. Add rest of the ingredients and stir well to combine.
7. Spread this filling evenly into the baked crust and return the stuffed pie to the oven.
8. Bake for another 45 minutes and allow to cool for 10 minutes.
9. Slice and enjoy.
Nutrition Calories: 285 Carbs: 3.5g Fats: 27.3g Proteins: 7.2g Sodium: 165mg Sugar: 0.4g

Meringue Pie

Serves: 10/Prep Time: 1 hour
Ingredients
- 2 tablespoons coconut flour
- 1 tablespoon granulated Swerve
- ¼ teaspoon salt
- 4 tablespoons ice water
- 1¼ cups almond flour
- 2 tablespoons arrowroot starch
- 1 teaspoon xanthan gum
- 5 tablespoons chilled butter, cut into small pieces

For Filling:
- 1½ cups plus 2 tablespoons water, divided
- ¼ teaspoon salt
- 3 tablespoons butter
- 1 tablespoon grass-fed gelatin
- 4 large organic egg yolks
- 1 cup granulated Swerve
- 2 teaspoons fresh lemon zest, grated
- 1/3 cup fresh lemon juice
- ½ teaspoon xanthan gum

For Meringue Topping:
- ¼ teaspoon cream of tartar
- ¼ cup powdered Swerve
- ½ teaspoon organic vanilla extract
- 4 large organic egg whites
- Pinch of salt
- ¼ cup granulated Swerve

Directions
1. Preheat the oven to 335 degrees and grease a pie pan.
2. **For crust:** Put the flours, butter, arrowroot starch, Swerve, xanthan gum, and salt in a food processor until combined.
3. Add ice water slowly to form a dough and transfer into a pie pan.
4. Press gently and pierce holes in the crust with a fork.
5. Transfer in the oven and bake for about 12 minutes.
6. Remove from the oven and keep aside to cool completely.
7. Reheat the oven to 300 degrees F.

For filling: Whisk together egg yolks in a bowl and slowly add ½ cup of water, beating until well combined.
8. Boil Swerve, salt and lemon zest in 1 cup of the water in a pan.
9. Whisk in the egg yolks mixture slowly into the pan, beating continuously.
10. Lower the heat and cook for about 1 minute, stirring continuously.
11. Remove from the heat and stir in the butter and lemon juice until smooth.
12. Top with xanthan gum and beat vigorously with a wire whisk until well combined.
13. Meanwhile, dissolve the gelatin into remaining 2 tablespoons of water in a small bowl.
14. Keep aside for about 2 minutes and add the gelatin mixture into hot lemon mixture.
15. Beat until well combined and cover the pan to keep aside.

For topping: Whisk together the egg whites, cream of tartar, and salt in a large bowl and beat until frothy.
16. Add the powdered Swerve, granulated Swerve, and vanilla extract slowly until stiff peaks form.
17. Pour the warm filling evenly over the crust and top with meringue.
18. Transfer in the oven and bake for about 20 minutes.
19. Remove from the oven and keep aside to cool.
20. Refrigerate for at least 3 hours and serve chilled.

Nutrition
Calories: 215 Carbs: 7.2g Fats: 18.5g Proteins: 6.7g Sodium: 159mg Sugar: 1.1g

Chayote Squash Mock Apple Pie

Serves: 16
Prep Time: 1 hour
Ingredients
Crust
- 1½ cups almond flour
- ½ teaspoon salt
- ½ cup butter, melted
- ¾ cup coconut flour
- 4 eggs
- 1 tablespoon whole psyllium husks

Filling
- ¾ cup stevia
- ¼ teaspoon ginger
- 1 tablespoon lemon juice
- 1/3 cup butter cut in small pieces
- 5 medium chayote squash, peeled and sliced
- 1½ teaspoons cinnamon
- 1/8 teaspoon nutmeg
- 1 tablespoon xanthan gum
- 2 teaspoons apple extract

Topping
- 1 tablespoon Stevia
- 1 egg

Directions
1. Preheat the oven to 375 degrees and grease a 9-inch pie pan.
2. Mix together crust ingredients to form a dough ball.
3. Transfer the dough ball into the pie dish and press firmly.
4. **Filling:** Boil sliced chayote and drain completely.
5. Add Stevia, apple extract, lemon juice, and xanthan gum to cooked chayote squash.
6. Pour chayote mixture into pie pan and top with butter.
7. **Topping:** Brush egg on pie top and sprinkle with Stevia.
8. Bake for about 35 minutes and dish out to serve.

Nutrition
Calories: 187 Carbs: 6.6g Fats: 16.7g Proteins: 2g Sodium: 204mg Sugar: 0.5g

Brownie Truffle Pie

Serves: 10/Prep Time: 55 mins
Ingredients
Crust:
- 3 tablespoons coconut flour
- 5 tablespoons butter, cut into small pieces
- 1¼ cups almond flour

- 1 tablespoon granulated Swerve
- ¼ teaspoon salt
- 4 tablespoons ice water

Filling:
- 6 tablespoons cocoa powder
- 1 teaspoon baking powder
- ¼ cup melted butter
- ½ cup almond flour
- 6 tablespoons Swerve Sweetener

- 2 large eggs
- 5 tablespoons water
- 1 tablespoon Sukrin Fiber Syrup
- 3 tablespoons sugar-free chocolate chips
- ½ teaspoon vanilla extract

Topping:
- 2 tablespoons Swerve Sweetener
- ½ ounce sugar-free dark chocolate

- 1 cup whipping cream
- ¼ teaspoon vanilla extract

Directions
1. **Crust:** Preheat the oven to 325 degrees and grease a pie pan.
2. Mix together almond flour, coconut flour, water, Swerve, butter, and salt in a bowl to form a dough.
3. Press evenly into the pie pan and transfer in the oven.
4. Bake for about 12 minutes and remove from the oven.
5. **Filling:** Whisk together the cocoa powder, almond flour, Swerve, and baking powder in a bowl.
6. Add water, eggs, butter, chocolate chips, and vanilla extract until well combined.
7. Pour this batter into the pie crust and transfer in the oven.
8. Bake for about 30 minutes and allow to cool.
9. **Topping:** Mix together cream, vanilla extract, and Swerve in a large bowl.
10. Beat until stiff peaks form and layer over cooled filling.
11. Top with dark chocolate and chill until completely set.

Nutrition Calories: 374 Carbs: 5.7g Fats: 33.9g Proteins: 8.5g Sodium: 280mg Sugar: 0.8g

Delicious Pizza Recipes

Mini Pizza Crusts

Serves: 4 Prep Time: 20 mins
Ingredients
- 1 cup coconut flour, sifted
- 8 large eggs, 5 whole eggs and 3 egg whites
- ½ teaspoon baking powder

- Italian spices, to taste
- Salt and black pepper, to taste

For the pizza sauce
- 2 garlic cloves, crushed
- 1 teaspoon dried basil

- ½ cup tomato sauce
- ¼ teaspoon sea salt

Directions
1. Preheat the oven to 350 degrees and grease a baking tray.
2. Whisk together eggs and egg whites in a large bowl and stir in the coconut flour, baking powder, Italian spices, salt, and black pepper.
3. Make small dough balls from this mixture and press on the baking tray.
4. Transfer in the oven and bake for about 20 minutes.
5. Allow pizza bases to cool and keep aside.
6. Combine all ingredients for the pizza sauce together and sit at room temperature for half an hour.
7. Spread this pizza sauce over the pizza crusts and serve.

Nutrition Calories: 170 Carbs: 5.7g Fats: 10.5g Proteins: 13.6g Sodium: 461mg Sugar: 2.3g

Keto Pepperoni Pizza

Serves: 4 Prep Time: 40 mins
Ingredients
Crust
- 6 oz. mozzarella cheese, shredded

- 4 eggs

Topping
- 1 teaspoon dried oregano
- 1½ oz. pepperoni
- 3 tablespoons tomato paste

- 5 oz. mozzarella cheese, shredded
- Olives

Directions
1. Preheat the oven to 400 degrees and grease a baking sheet.

2. Whisk together eggs and cheese in a bowl and spread on a baking sheet.
3. Transfer in the oven and bake for about 15 minutes until golden.
4. Remove from the oven and allow it to cool.
5. Increase the oven temperature to 450 degrees.
6. Spread the tomato paste on the crust and top with oregano, pepperoni, cheese, and olives on top.
7. Bake for another 10 minutes and serve hot.

Nutrition

Calories: 356 Carbs: 6.1g Fats: 23.8g Proteins: 30.6g Sodium: 790mg Sugar: 1.8g

BBQ Chicken Pizza

Serves: 4
Prep Time: 30 mins
Ingredients
Dairy Free Pizza Crust
- 6 tablespoons Parmesan cheese
- 6 large eggs
- 3 tablespoons psyllium husk powder
- Salt and black pepper, to taste
- 1½ teaspoons Italian seasoning

Toppings
- 6 oz. rotisserie chicken, shredded
- 4 oz. cheddar cheese
- 1 tablespoon mayonnaise
- 4 tablespoons tomato sauce
- 4 tablespoons BBQ sauce

Directions
1. Preheat the oven to 400 degrees and grease a baking dish.
2. Place all Pizza Crust ingredients in an immersion blender and blend until smooth.
3. Spread dough mixture onto the baking dish and transfer in the oven.
4. Bake for about 10 minutes and top with favorite toppings.
5. Bake for about 3 minutes and dish out.

Nutrition

Calories: 356 Carbs: 2.9g Fats: 24.5g Proteins: 24.5g Sodium: 396mg Sugar: 0.6g

Buffalo Chicken Crust Pizza

Serves: 6
Prep Time: 25 mins
Ingredients
- 1 cup whole milk mozzarella, shredded
- 1 teaspoon dried oregano
- 2 tablespoons butter
- 1-pound chicken thighs, boneless and skinless
- 1 large egg
- ¼ teaspoon black pepper
- ¼ teaspoon salt
- 1 stalk celery
- 3 tablespoons Franks Red Hot Original
- 1 stalk green onion
- 1 tablespoon sour cream
- 1-ounce bleu cheese, crumbled

Directions
1. Preheat the oven to 400 degrees and grease a baking dish.
2. Process chicken thighs in a food processor until smooth.
3. Transfer to a large bowl and add egg, ½ cup of shredded mozzarella, oregano, black pepper, and salt to form a dough.
4. Spread the chicken dough in the baking dish and transfer in the oven
5. Bake for about 25 minutes and keep aside.
6. Meanwhile, heat butter and add celery, and cook for about 4 minutes.
7. Mix Franks Red Hot Original with the sour cream in a small bowl.
8. Spread the sauce mixture over the crust, layer with the cooked celery and remaining ½ cup of mozzarella and the bleu cheese.
9. Bake for another 10 minutes, until the cheese is melted

Nutrition Calories: 172 Carbs: 1g Fats: 12.9g Proteins: 13.8g Sodium: 172mg Sugar: 0.2g

Fresh Bell Pepper Basil Pizza

Serves: 3/Prep Time: 25 mins
Ingredients
Pizza Base
- ½ cup almond flour
- 1 teaspoon Italian seasoning
- ½ teaspoon black pepper
- 6 ounces mozzarella cheese
- 2 tablespoons psyllium husk
- 2 tablespoons cream cheese
- 2 tablespoons fresh Parmesan cheese
- 1 large egg
- ½ teaspoon salt

Toppings
- 4 ounces cheddar cheese, shredded
- ¼ cup Marinara sauce
- 2/3 medium bell pepper
- 1 medium vine tomato
- 3 tablespoons basil, fresh chopped

Directions
1. Preheat the oven to 400 degrees and grease a baking dish.
2. Microwave mozzarella cheese for about 30 seconds and top with the remaining pizza crust.
3. Add the remaining pizza ingredients to the cheese and mix together.
4. Flatten the dough and transfer in the oven.
5. Bake for about 10 minutes and remove pizza from the oven.
6. Top the pizza with the toppings and bake for another 10 minutes.
7. Remove pizza from the oven and allow to cool.

Nutrition Calories: 411 Carbs: 6.4g Fats: 31.3g Proteins: 22.2g Sodium: 152mg Sugar: 2.8g

Keto Thai Chicken Flatbread Pizza

Serves: 12/Prep Time: 25 mins

Ingredients

Peanut Sauce
- 2 tablespoons rice wine vinegar
- 4 tablespoons reduced sugar ketchup
- 4 tablespoons pbfit
- 4 tablespoons soy sauce
- 4 tablespoons coconut oil
- ½ lime, juiced
- 1 teaspoon fish sauce

Pizza Base
- ¾ cup almond flour
- 3 tablespoons cream cheese
- ½ teaspoon garlic powder
- 8 oz. mozzarella cheese
- 1 tablespoon psyllium husk powder
- 1 large egg
- ½ teaspoon onion powder
- ½ teaspoon ginger
- ½ teaspoon black pepper
- ½ teaspoon salt

Toppings
- 3 oz. mung bean sprouts
- 2 medium green onions
- 2 tablespoons peanuts
- 2 chicken thighs
- 6 oz. mozzarella cheese
- 1½ oz. carrots, shredded

Directions
1. Preheat oven to 400 degrees and grease a baking tray.
2. Mix together all peanut sauce ingredients and set aside.
3. Microwave cream cheese and mozzarella cheese for the pizza base for 1 minute.
4. Add eggs, then mix together with all dry ingredients.
5. Arrange dough onto a baking tray and bake for about 15 minutes.
6. Flip pizza and top with sauce, chopped chicken, shredded carrots, and mozzarella.
7. Bake again for 10 minutes, or until cheese has melted.
8. Top with bean sprouts, spring onion, peanuts, and cilantro.

Nutrition Calories: 268 Carbs: 3.2g Fats: 21g Proteins: 15g Sodium: 94mg Sugar: 0.2g

Apple and Ham Flatbread Pizza

Serves: 8/Prep Time: 15 mins

Ingredients

For the crust:
- ¾ cup almond flour
- ½ teaspoon sea salt
- 2 cups mozzarella cheese, shredded
- 2 tablespoons cream cheese
- 1/8 teaspoon dried thyme

For the topping:
- ½ small red onion, cut into thin slices
- 4 ounces low carbohydrate ham, cut into chunks
- Salt and black pepper, to taste
- 1 cup Mexican blend cheese, grated
- ¼ medium apple, sliced
- 1/8 teaspoon dried thyme

Directions
1. Preheat the oven to 425 degrees and grease a 12-inch pizza pan.
2. Boil water and steam cream cheese, mozzarella cheese, almond flour, thyme, and salt.
3. When the cheese melts enough, knead for a few minutes to thoroughly mix dough.
4. Make a ball out of the dough and arrange in the pizza pan.
5. Poke holes all over the dough with a fork and transfer in the oven.
6. Bake for about 8 minutes until golden brown and reset the oven setting to 350 degrees.
7. Sprinkle ¼ cup of the Mexican blend cheese over the flatbread and top with onions, apples, and ham.
8. Cover with the remaining ¾ cup of the Mexican blend cheese and sprinkle with the thyme, salt, and black pepper.

9. Bake for about 7 minutes until cheese is melted and crust is golden brown.
10. Remove the flatbread from the oven and allow to cool before cutting.
11. Slice into desired pieces and serve.

Nutrition

Calories: 179 Carbs: 5.3g Fats: 13.6g Proteins: 10.4g Sodium: 539mg Sugar: 2.1g

The Fat Bomb Recipes

Savory sesame fat bombs

Yield: 6 Servings/Total Time: 33 Minutes /Prep Time: 10 Minutes /Cook Time: 8 Minutes

Ingredients

- 2 teaspoons toasted sesame seeds
- 1/4 teaspoon chili flakes
- 2 tablespoons sesame oil
- 1/4 cup butter
- 1 teaspoon sea salt

Directions

1. In a pan set over medium-low heat, roast sesame seeds until golden brown; transfer to a plate and set aside.
2. In a bowl, mix together chili flakes, sesame oil, butter and salt until well blended; refrigerate for at least 15 minutes. Form about 12 balls from the mixture; roll the balls in the toasted sesame seeds and serve.

Nutritional info per Serving:

Calories: 182; Total Fat: 20.4 g; Carbs: 0.2 g; Dietary Fiber: 0.1 g; Sugars: 0 g; Protein: 0.4 g; Cholesterol: 41 mg; Sodium: 513 mg

Cheesy Sausage Fat Bombs

Yield: 6 Servings/Total Time: 28 Minutes /Prep Time: 10 Minutes /Cook Time: 18 Minutes

Ingredients

- 2 tablespoons sour cream
- 4 1/2 tablespoons melted butter
- 1/3 cup coconut flour
- 1 lb. breakfast sausage, browned
- 4 eggs
- 1/4 teaspoon baking powder
- 2 cups shredded cheddar cheese
- 1/4 teaspoon salt

Directions

1. Preheat oven to 375 degrees. Lightly grease cookie sheets and set aside.
2. In a bowl, whisk together sour cream, melted butter, eggs and salt until well blended. Whisk in coconut flour and baking powder and then fold in sausage until well combined. Stir in cheese and drop the batter by spoonful on the prepared sheet. Bake for about 18 minutes or until browned. Serve warm.

Nutritional info per Serving: *Calories: 89; Total Fat: 7.4 g; Carbs: 0.6 g; Dietary Fiber: 0.3 g; Sugars: 0 g; Protein: 4 g; Cholesterol: 65 mg; Sodium: 291 mg*

Healthy Keto Coconut & Blackberry Fat Bombs

Yield: 16 Fat Bombs/Total Time: 1 Hour 15 Minutes /Prep Time: 10 Minutes /Cook Time: 5 Minutes

Ingredients
- 1/2 cup frozen blackberries
- 1 cup coconut oil
- 1 cup coconut butter
- 1 tablespoon lemon juice
- 1/2 teaspoon vanilla extract
- 1/2 teaspoon Stevia drops

Directions
1. In a pot, heat together blackberries, coconut oil and coconut butter until well combined; transfer to a blender along with the remaining ingredients and blend until very smooth. Spread the mixture on a baking pan lined with paper and refrigerate for at least 1 hour or until firm. Cut into squares and serve.

Nutritional info per Serving:
Calories: 170; Total Fat: 18.7 g; Carbs: 3 g; Dietary Fiber: 2.3 g; Sugars: 0.7 g; Protein: 1.1 g; Cholesterol: 0 mg; Sodium: 233 mg

Savory Dill & Salmon Fat Bombs

Yield: 6 Servings/Total Time: 1 Hour 10 Minutes /Prep Time: 10 Minutes

Ingredients
- 1/2 package smoked salmon
- 1/3 cup butter
- 1/2 cup cream cheese
- Pinch salt
- 2 tablespoons chopped dill
- 1 tablespoon fresh lemon juice

Directions
1. In a food processor, process together smoked salmon, butter, cream cheese, dill, salt and fresh lemon juice until very smooth.
2. Form small balls from the mixture and place them on a tray lined with paper; refrigerate for at least 1 hour before serving.

Nutritional info per Serving: *Calories: 147; Total Fat: 15.7 g; Carbs: 0. 8g; Dietary Fiber: 0.1 g; Sugars: 0.6 g; Protein: 3.2 g; Cholesterol: 91 mg; Sodium: 143 mg*

Healthy Mocha Ice Bombs

Yield: 20 Fat Bombs/Total Time: 1 Hour 10 Minutes /Prep Time: 10 Minutes

Ingredients
- 240 g cream cheese
- 60 ml strong coffee chilled
- 2 tablespoons cocoa powder
- 4 tablespoons powdered sweetener

Chocolate coating
- 28 g cocoa butter melted
- 70 g dark chocolate melted

Directions
1. In a bowl, whisk together melted cocoa butter and chocolate until well blended; set aside.
2. In a food processor, pulse together cocoa powder, cream cheese, coffee and sweetener until very smooth; roll the mixture into bite sized balls and then dip them in the cocoa butter mixture and arrange on a baking tray lined with baking paper. Refrigerate for at least 1 hour before serving.

Nutritional info per Serving:
Calories: 127; Total Fat: 12.9 g; Carbs: 2.2 g; Dietary Fiber: 0.7 g; Sugars: 1.1 g; Protein: 1.9 g; Cholesterol: 22 mg; Sodium: 94 mg

Keto Almond Fudge Fat Bomb

Yield: 24 Fat Bombs/Total Time: 1 Hour 10 Minutes /Prep Time: 10 Minutes

Ingredients
- 2 tablespoons coconut oil
- 1/4 cup butter
- 1/2 cup almond butter
- 1 tablespoon sugar-free maple syrup

Directions
1. Melt coconut oil, butter and almond butter for about 2 minutes in the microwave; whisk until smooth and well combined. Whisk in maple syrup and then pour the mixture into muffin cups.
2. Freeze for at least 1 hour or until firm. Enjoy!

Nutritional info per Serving:
Calories: 60; Total Fat: 5 g; Carbs: 1 g; Dietary Fiber: 0 g; Sugars: 0.4 g; Protein: 1 g; Cholesterol: 5 mg; Sodium: 18 mg

Macadamia Chocolate Fat Bomb

Yield: 6 bars/Total Time: 40 Minutes/Prep Time: 20 Minutes

Ingredients
- 1/3 cup coconut oil
- 2 tbsp unsweetened cocoa powder
- 1 tsp vanilla extract
- 2 tbsp sweetener
- 12 macadamia nuts
- Pinch salt

Directions
1. Prepare a small container by lining with parchment paper; set aside.
2. In a bowl, whisk together coconut oil, cocoa powder, vanilla and sweetener until well combined. Pour the mixture into the container, spreading it evenly; add the macadamia nuts into the chocolate mixture and sprinkle with a pinch of salt; freeze for at least 20 minutes or until firm.
3. Remove from the freezer and cut into 6 squares. Enjoy!

Nutritional info per Serving:
Calories: 115; Total Fat: 9.8 g; Carbs: 7 g; Dietary Fiber: 0 g; Sugars: 1. 7 g; Protein: 4 g; Cholesterol: 10 mg; Sodium: 11 mg

Low Carb Butter Burger Fat Bombs

Yield: 12 Fat Bombs/Total Time: 20 Minutes /Prep Time: 10 Minutes /Cook Time: 10 Minutes

Ingredients
- 1 lb. ground beef
- 1/4 cup cheese
- 3 tablespoons butter
- 1 teaspoon garlic powder
- 1 teaspoon onion powder
- pepper & salt

Directions
1. Preheat your oven to 375 degrees.
2. Combine ground beef with onion powder, garlic powder, salt and pepper until well combined.
3. Press tablespoonfuls of the meat mixture into greased muffin cups and top each with a pat of butter and a piece of cheese. Add another layer of beef mixture and press to flatten. Bake for about 10 minutes.
4. Remove from oven and serve.

Nutritional info per Serving:
Calories: 331; Total Fat: 18 g; Carbs: 9 g; Dietary Fiber: 0 g; Sugars: 1.1 g; Protein: 12 g; Cholesterol: 66 mg; Sodium: 220 mg

Minty Matcha Fat Bombs

Yield: 10 Fat Bombs/Total Time: 35 Minutes /Prep Time: 10 Minutes /Cook Time: 10 Minutes

Ingredients:
- 1 tablespoon organic coconut oil
- ½ cup coconut butter
- 1 1/2 teaspoons matcha powder
- 2 teaspoons pure maple syrup
- 2 teaspoons peppermint extract

Directions
1. In a double boiler, melt coconut oil and coconut butter; stir in matcha powder, peppermint extract and maple syrup. Pour the mixture into molds and freeze for at least 15 minutes or until set. Pop the bombs out and enjoy!

Nutritional info per Serving: *Calories: 82; Total Fat: 5 g; Carbs: 6 g; Dietary Fiber: 0 g Sugars: 4.8 g; Protein: 8 g; Cholesterol: 4 mg; Sodium: 62 mg*

Bacon Onion Butter

Yield: 12 Fat Bombs/Total Time: 20 Minutes /Prep Time: 10 Minutes /Cook Time: 10 Minutes

Ingredients
- 4 strips bacon sliced into small strips
- 9 tablespoons butter
- 90 g onion, diced
- 1/2 teaspoon pepper
- 2 teaspoons spicy brown mustard

Directions
1. Melt butter in a pan over medium heat; cook in bacon for about 2 minutes. Add in onions and cook until bacon is crispy.
2. Remove from heat and let cool for at least 5 minutes; add in pepper and mustard until well blended. Divide the mixture among muffin cups and refrigerate until firm.

Nutritional info per Serving: *Calories: 92; Total Fat: 10 g; Carbs: 1 g; Dietary Fiber: 0 g; Sugars: 0 g; Protein: 1 g; Cholesterol: 23 mg; Sodium: 151 mg*

Cashew Butter Fat Bombs

Yield: 12 Fat Bombs/Total Time: 25 Minutes/Prep Time: 25 Minutes

Ingredients
- 6 tablespoons cashew butter
- 6 tablespoons grass-fed butter
- ½ teaspoon liquid Stevia
- 1 teaspoon vanilla extract
- 1 pinch sea salt

Directions
1. Prepare mini muffin tin by lining with liners; set aside.
2. In a microwave safe bowl, mix grass-fed butter and cashew butter then microwave for 1 minute or until melted. Stir in the remaining ingredients until well blended. Spoon the mixture into the prepared muffin tin and freeze for at least 10 minute or until firm. Enjoy!

Nutritional info per Serving:
Calories: 121; Total Fat: 13 g; Carbs: 6.2 g; Dietary Fiber: 0 g; Sugars: 0.8 g; Protein: 8 g; Cholesterol: 9 mg; Sodium: 211 mg

Jalapeno Popper Fat Bombs

Yield: 10 Fat Bombs/Total Time: 20 Minutes/Prep Time: 15 Minutes/Cook Time: 5 Minutes

Ingredients
- 3 slices bacon
- 2 jalapeno peppers, deseeded, diced
- ½ cup chopped scallions
- 3 ounces cream cheese
- ¼ teaspoon garlic powder
- ¼ teaspoon onion powder
- ½ teaspoon dried parsley
- Salt & pepper

Directions
1. In a skillet, fry bacon for about 5 minutes or until crisp; transfer to paper towel to drain. Save bacon grease.
2. In a bowl, mix together spices, scallions, bacon fat and cream cheese; season with salt and pepper and form balls from the mixture and set aside.
3. Crumble the bacon and place in a bowl. Roll the balls in the crumbled bacon and serve.

Nutritional info per Serving:
Calories: 208; Total Fat: 20.1 g; Carbs: 1.2 g; Dietary Fiber: 0 g; Sugars: 1.1 g; Protein: 4 g; Cholesterol: 53 mg; Sodium: 230 mg

Piña Colada Keto Fat Bombs

Yield: 15 Servings/Total Time: 25 Minutes/Prep Time: 25 Minutes

Ingredients
- 8 tbsp coconut butter
- 8 drops Piña Colada flavoring drops
- 1/8 tsp Stevia
- 4 tbsp unsweetened coconut flakes

Directions
1. Insert a jar of coconut butter into a bowl of boiling water for about 20 minutes or until melted; transfer to a bowl and stir in the remaining ingredients. Pour the mixture into fat bomb molds and freeze for about 30 minutes or until firm. Enjoy!

Nutritional info per Serving:
Calories: 74; Total Fat: 6 g; Carbs: 6.3 g; Dietary Fiber: 0 g; Sugars: 4 g; Protein: 8 g; Cholesterol: 8.6 mg; Sodium: 14 mg

Keto Avocado & Prosciutto Fat Bombs

Yield: 12 Fat Bombs/Total Time: 10 Minutes /Prep Time: 10 Minutes

Ingredients
- 12 slices prosciutto
- 1 avocado, diced into 12 slices
- 1/2 cup freshly squeezed lemon juice

Directions
1. Add avocado slices to a large bowl; drizzle with fresh lemon juice. Lay the prosciutto slices on a flat work surface and top each with an avocado slice. Drizzle with more fresh lemon juice and roll each prosciutto up to form wraps. Enjoy!

Nutritional info per Serving:
Calories: 90; Total Fat: 6.9 g; Carbs: 1 g; Dietary Fiber: 1 g; Sugars: 0 g; Protein: 8 g; Cholesterol: 12 mg; Sodium: 102 mg

Low Carb Crab Fat Bombs

Yield: 24 Fat Bombs/Total Time: 15 Minutes /Prep Time: 15 Minutes

Ingredients
- 10 slices bacon
- 3/4 cup shredded mozzarella cheese
- 170 g canned crab
- 1 cup cream cheese
- 1 teaspoon onion powder
- 1 teaspoon garlic powder
- 1 teaspoon minced garlic
- dash of salt and pepper

Directions
1. In a bowl, mix together shredded mozzarella, cream cheese, canned crab meat, garlic, onion powder, garlic powder, salt and pepper until well combined. Refrigerate for about 30 minutes.
2. In a pan over medium-low heat, cook bacon until crispy; chop into small pieces.
3. Roll the crab-cheese mixture into small balls and then roll them in chopped bacon pieces. Enjoy!

Nutritional info per Serving:
Calories: 134; Total Fat: 11.2 g; Carbs: 2.9 g; Dietary Fiber: 0.3 g; Sugars: 1.6 g; Protein: 10.5 g; Cholesterol: 51 mg; Sodium: 113 mg

Keto Pecan Fudge Fat Bombs

Yield: 10 Fudge fat bombs/Total Time: 4 Hours 20 Minutes/Prep Time: 20 Minutes

Ingredients
- 1/2 cup coconut oil
- 4 oz food-grade cocoa butter
- 4 tablespoons unsweetened cocoa powder
- 1/3 cup heavy cream
- 1/2 cup pecans, roughly chopped
- 4 tablespoons Erythritol/Swerve

Directions
1. Melt coconut oil and cocoa butter in a double boiler; whisk in cocoa powder until very smooth and then transfer the mixture to a blender. Add in the sweetener and blend until very smooth. Add in cream and continue blending for about 5 minutes.
2. Arrange molds onto a sheet pan and fill each half with the pecans; top each with the chocolate mixture and freeze for about 4 hours or until firm.

Nutritional info per Serving:
Calories: 56; Total Fat: 6 g; Carbs: 1 g; Dietary Fiber: 0 g; Sugars: 0.4 g; Protein: 1 g; Cholesterol: 5 mg; Sodium: 18 mg

Peanut Butter Fat Bombs

Yield: 12 peanut butter cups/Total Time: 1 Hour 5 Minutes/Prep Time: 10 Minutes/Cook Time: 5 Minutes

Ingredients
Chocolate layers
- 5 tbsp coconut oil
- 10 oz unsweetened dark chocolate
- 1/2 tsp vanilla extract

Peanut butter layer
- 2 tsp coconut oil
- 3 1/2 tbsp creamy peanut butter
- 1 1/2 tsp peanut flour
- 1/8 tsp vanilla extract
- 4 tsp powdered sweetener
- 1 pinch sea salt

Directions
1. Prepare muffin cups by lining with paper liners; set aside.
2. In a double boiler, melt half of the coconut oil and half of the chocolate; stir in half of vanilla until well blended. Spread the mixture into the bottom of the cups and freeze for about 10 minutes or until firm.
3. In the meantime, prepare the peanut butter layer; in a double boiler, heat coconut oil and peanut butter and then stir in vanilla, peanut flour, sweetener and salt until well combined; spoon the mixture over the chocolate into the center of each cup. Freeze for another 10 minutes or until firm.
4. Heat the remaining coconut oil and chocolate and stir in the remaining vanilla; pour the mixture over the peanut butter layer and freeze for about 25 minutes or until completely firm. Enjoy!

Nutritional info per Serving:
Calories: 212; Total Fat: 16.2 g; Carbs: 5.8 g; Dietary Fiber: 0 g; Sugars: 2.4 g; Protein: 13 g; Cholesterol: 9 mg; Sodium: 289 mg

Healthy Mediterranean Fat Bombs

Yield: 5 Servings/Total Time: 10 Minutes/Prep Time: 10 Minutes

Ingredients
- 1/4 cup butter, softened
- 1/2 cup cream cheese
- 4 kalamata olives
- 4 pieces sun-dried tomatoes
- 2 cloves garlic, crushed
- 5 tablespoons grated parmesan cheese
- 1/4 teaspoon salt
- 3 tablespoons chopped herbs
- 1/4 teaspoon pepper

Directions
1. In a bowl, mash together cream cheese and butter until well combined; stir in olives and sun-dried tomatoes, herbs, garlic, salt and pepper until well combined.
2. Roll the mixture into balls and then roll each ball into the grated parmesan cheese. Enjoy!

Nutritional info per Serving: *Calories: 164; Total Fat: 17.1 g; Carbs: 1.7 g; Dietary Fiber: 0.4 g; Sugars: 0.7 g; Protein: 3.4 g; Cholesterol: 13 mg; Sodium: 280 mg*

Low Carb Guacamole Bombs

Yield: 6 Servings/Total Time: 25 Minutes/Prep Time: 15 Minutes/Cook Time: 10 Minutes

Ingredients
For the guacamole
- 2 ripe avocados
- 1 teaspoon lime juice
- 2 tablespoons chopped cilantro
- ¼ cup salsa
- 1/2 teaspoon ground cumin
- 1/2 teaspoon onion powder
- salt & pepper

For the coating
- 2 tablespoons oil
- ½ cup seasoned breadcrumbs
- 1 egg beaten

Directions
1. In a bowl, mash together all guacamole ingredients until well combined; season with salt and pepper. Make 12 balls from the guacamole mixture and arrange them on a baking tray lined with paper. Cover and freeze for at least 2 hours.
2. In a bowl, blend together breadcrumbs and egg; dip the balls into the mixture and then fry them over a medium heat until browned on both sides. Enjoy!

Nutritional info per Serving: *Calories: 191; Total Fat: 16.1 g; Carbs: 8 g; Dietary Fiber: 6 g; Sugars: 0 g; Protein: 5 g; Cholesterol: 28 mg; Sodium: 159 mg*

Key-Lime Cashew Fat-Bombs

Yield: 30 Fat Bombs/Total Time: 1 Hour/Prep Time: 10 Minutes

Ingredients
- 3/4 cup key lime juice
- 2 cups raw cashews, soaked for at least 2 hours
- 1/2 cup coconut butter
- 1 cup coconut oil, melted
- 1/4 tsp powdered stevia

Directions
1. Mix together all the ingredients in a food processor; process until very smooth; transfer the mixture to a bowl and freeze for about 30 minutes or until firm.
2. Remove from the freezer and cut into balls. Return the balls to the freezer to harden further. Enjoy!

Nutritional info per Serving: *Calories: 367; Total Fat: 35.3 g; Carbs: 11.1 g; Dietary Fiber: 1.1 g ;Sugars: 2.2 g; Protein: 6.2 g; Cholesterol: 16 mg; Sodium: 53 mg*

Almond Butter Fat Bombs

Yield: 6 Fat Bombs/Total Time: 5 Minutes/Prep Time: 5 Minutes

Ingredients
- 1/4 cup coconut oil
- 1/4 cup almond butter
- 2 tbsp. cacao powder
- 1/4 cup Erythritol

Directions
1. Combine coconut oil and almond butter in a microwave safe bowl and microwave for about 30 seconds.
2. Stir in cacao powder and sweetener until smooth and then pour into the silicone molds. Freeze until firm.

Nutritional info per Serving: *Calories: 94; Total Fat: 12 g; Carbs: 3 g; Dietary Fiber: 0 g; Sugars: 0.9 g; Protein: 9.5 g; Cholesterol: 0 mg; Sodium: 116 mg*

Savory Bacon Fat Bombs

Yield: 6 Fat Bombs/Total Time: 40 Minutes/Prep Time: 10 Minutes /Cook Time: 20 Minutes

Ingredients
- 1 tablespoon mayonnaise
- 4 tablespoons butter
- 1/4 avocado
- 1 hardboiled egg
- 1 tablespoon cilantro, chopped
- 1 serrano pepper, diced
- kosher salt & pepper
- juice of 1/4 lime
- 6 cooked bacon slices
- 2 tablespoons bacon grease

Directions
1. In a bowl, add butter, avocado, hardboiled egg, cilantro, serrano pepper and mayonnaise; mash until smooth. Season with salt and pepper.
2. Fry bacon until crispy; drizzle the avocado mixture with bacon grease and stir to combine well. Refrigerate the mixture until firm and then form balls from the mixture. Roll them into the crumbled bacon and serve right away.

Nutritional info per Serving: *Calories: 183; Total Fat: 18 g; Carbs: 1 g; Dietary Fiber: 0 g; Sugars: 0.5 g; Protein: 5 g; Cholesterol: 70 mg; Sodium: 273 mg*

Keto Savory Fat Bombs

Yield: 6 Fat Bombs/Total Time: 30 Minutes/Prep Time: 30 Minutes

Ingredients
- 6 olives chopped
- 1 teaspoon garlic minced
- 150 g cream cheese
- 1/4 teaspoon salt
- 2 tablespoons parmesan cheese

Directions
1. In a bowl, mix together chopped olives, garlic, cream cheese and salt until well combined; form 6 balls from the mixture and roll them into parmesan cheese. Enjoy!

Nutritional info per Serving: *Calories: 75; Total Fat: 7 g; Carbs: 1 g; Dietary Fiber: 0.2 g; Sugars: 0.4 g; Protein: 2 g; Cholesterol: 41 mg; Sodium: 81 mg*

Lemon Macadamia Fat Bombs

Yield: 30 Servings/Total Time: 45 Minutes/Prep Time: 20 Minutes/Cook Time: 5 Minutes

Ingredients
- 2 ounces organic coconut cream concentrate
- 1 ounce cocoa butter
- Cacao powder
- 6 ounces organic coconut oil
- ¼ cup freshly squeezed lemon juice
- 2 tablespoons fresh lemon zest
- 3 tablespoons coconut flour
- 3 tablespoons almond flour
- 1 splash organic vanilla extract
- 1 pinch sea salt
- Liquid Stevia
- ½ cups macadamia nuts
- ½ cup unsweetened shredded coconut

Directions
1. Melt cocoa butter, coconut cream concentrate, and coconut oil over low heat; transfer to a blender and stir in lemon juice, cocoa powder, lemon zest, vanilla, flours and Stevia. Bend until well combined then add in macadamia nuts and shredded coconut; pulse to chop the nuts and press the mixture into molds. Freeze until firm and serve.

Nutritional info per Serving: *Calories: 165; Total Fat: 7 g; Carbs: 3.1 g; Dietary Fiber: 0 g; Sugars: 1.3g; Protein: 7 g; Cholesterol: 16mg; Sodium: 74mg*

Ginger Fat Bombs

Yield: 10 Servings/Total Time: 5 Minutes/Prep Time: 5 Minutes

Ingredients
- 75 g softened coconut oil
- 75 g softened coconut butter
- 25 g shredded unsweetened coconut
- 1 tsp ginger powder
- 1 tsp granulated sweetener

Directions
1. In a pouring jug, stir together all ingredients until sweetener is completely dissolved. Pour the mixture into molds and freeze for about 10 minutes or until firm.

Nutritional info per Serving: *Calories: 84; Total Fat: 10.2 g; Carbs: 5 g; Dietary Fiber: 1 g; Sugars: 0.6 g; Protein: 6 g; Cholesterol: 11 mg; Sodium: 213 mg*

Lemon Cheesecake Fat Bombs

Yield: 12 Servings/Total Time: 4 Hours 10 Minutes/Prep Time: 10 Minutes

Ingredients

- 1/4 cup melted coconut oil
- 4 tbsp softened unsalted butter
- 4 oz softened cream cheese
- 1 tsp fresh lemon juice
- 1 tbsp fresh lemon zest
- Stevia
- lemon extract

Directions

1. Combine all ingredients in a bowl with a hand mixer; blend until smooth and then pour into cupcake liners or molds. Freeze for at least 4 hours or until firm. Sprinkle with fresh lemon zest and serve.

Nutritional info per Serving:

Calories: 239; Total Fat: 15.3 g; Carbs: 7.7 g; Dietary Fiber: 0 g; Sugars: 2.1 g; Protein: 9 g; Cholesterol: 12 mg; Sodium: 196 mg

Hard-Boiled Egg & Bacon Egg Fat Bombs

Yield: 12 Fat Bombs/Total Time: 10 Minutes/Prep Time: 10 Minutes

Ingredients

- 2 hard-boiled eggs
- 4 bacon slices, cooked and chopped
- 1/4 cup butter
- 2 tablespoons mayonnaise
- 1 tablespoon minced chives
- 1 tablespoon nutritional yeast

Directions

1. In a mixing bowl, chop the boiled eggs then stir in the remaining ingredients until well blended; form 12 balls from the mixture and freeze for at least 15 minutes. Enjoy!

Nutritional info per Serving:

Calories: 190; Total Fat: 17.9 g; Carbs: 3 g; Dietary Fiber: 1.8 g; Sugars: 1.2 g; Protein: 6.9 g; Cholesterol: 39 mg; Sodium: 193 mg

Cheese and Garlic Mushroom Fat Bombs

Yield: 20 Fat Bombs/Total Time: 40 Minutes/Prep Time: 25 Minutes /Cook Time: 15 Minutes

Ingredients

- 20 button mushrooms, cleaned and stems removed
- 2 tablespoons unsalted butter
- 1 cup grated cheddar cheese
- 1/8 cup chopped parsley
- 5 garlic cloves, minced
- salt & black pepper

Directions

1. In a bowl, mix together butter, cheese, parsley, garlic and pepper until well combined.
2. Season each mushroom cap with salt and pepper and stuff with the garlic mixture; arrange them on a baking tray and bake for about 15 minutes at 375 degrees. Serve warm.

Nutritional info per Serving:

Calories: 38; Total Fat: 3.4 g; Carbs: 0.2 g; Dietary Fiber: 0 g; Sugars: 0 g; Protein: 2 g; Cholesterol: 8 mg; Sodium: 36 mg

Guacamole Bacon Fat Bombs

Yield: 10 Servings/Total Time: 10 Minutes /Prep Time: 10 Minutes

Ingredients

- 2 avocados, pitted, peeled, and mashed
- 1 cup cream cheese, softened
- 1/2 red onion, minced
- 1 garlic clove, minced
- 1/2 cup fresh lime juice
- 2 tablespoons chopped cilantro
- 1 small jalapeno, chopped
- 1/2 teaspoon cumin
- 1/2 teaspoon chili powder
- Kosher salt & pepper
- 12 slices bacon, cooked and crumbled

Directions

1. In a large bowl, mix together diced avocado, red onion, garlic, lime juice, cream cheese, cilantro, jalapeno, and spices until well combined. Refrigerate for at least 30 minutes.
2. Place crumbled bacon on a large plate; scoop out guacamole mix and roll in bacon; repeat with the remaining guacamole mix and bacon. Refrigerate for a few minutes before serving.

Nutritional info per Serving:

Calories: 289; Total Fat: 15.1 g; Carbs: 6.4 g; Dietary Fiber: 0 g; Sugars: 3.7g; Protein: 11.3 g; Cholesterol: 4 mg; Sodium: 116 mg

Sugar-Free Peanut Butter Fat Bombs

Yield: 12 Servings/Total Time: 7 Minutes/Prep Time: 5 Minutes/Cook Time: 2 Minutes

Ingredients
- 1/4 cup vanilla almond milk
- 1 cup coconut oil
- 1 cup peanut butter

Optional Topping:
- 2 tablespoons melted coconut oil
- 1/4 cup unsweetened cocoa powder
- 2 tablespoons Swerve

Directions
1. Melt coconut oil and peanut butter over low heat; transfer to a blender along with the remaining ingredients and blend until very smooth.
2. Pour the mixture into a loaf pan lined with parchment paper. Whisk the topping ingredients in a bowl and drizzle over the fudge. Freeze until firm and serve.

Nutritional Information per Serving:
Calories: 287; Total Fat: 29.7 g; Carbs: 4 g; Dietary Fiber: 1.7 g; Sugars: 0.7 g; Protein: 5.4 g; Cholesterol: 0 mg; Sodium: 4 mg

Healthy Hazelnut Fat Bombs

Yield: 12 Servings/Total Time: 27 minutes /Prep Time: 15 minutes /Cook Time: 12 minutes

Ingredients
- 1/3 cup heavy cream
- 2 (8oz) bars milk chocolate, melted
- 2-3 drops vanilla
- 1/4 tsp hazelnut extract
- 1/4 cup toasted hazelnuts, crushed

Directions
1. In a bowl, whisk together heavy cream and melted chocolate until well combined; stir in hazelnut and vanilla flavoring and refrigerate overnight. Form the mixture into balls and roll them in the crushed toasted hazelnuts. Serve.

Nutritional Information per Serving:
Calories: 70; Total Fat: 7 g; Carbs: 3 g; Dietary Fiber: 2 g; Sugars: 0.5 g; Protein: 1 g; Cholesterol: 0 mg; Sodium: 10 mg

Low Carb Matcha Fudge Fat Bombs

Yield: 24 Fat Bombs/Total Time: 2 Hours 15 Minutes /Prep Time: 10 Minutes /Cook Time: 5 Minutes

Ingredients
- 1/2 cup cocoa butter
- 1/3 cup heavy cream
- 2 scoops matcha powder
- 3 tablespoons coconut oil
- 1/2 cup coconut butter
- 2 teaspoons vanilla essence
- 1/2 cup sugar free maple syrup

Directions
1. In a saucepan, mix all ingredients over low heat until cocoa butter is melted; stir to combine well then transfer to a square baking pan. Refrigerate for at least 3 hours or until firm. Slice into 24 squares and enjoy!

Nutritional info per Serving:
Calories: 94; Total Fat: 6 g; Carbs: 0 g; Dietary Fiber: 0 g Sugars: 0 g; Protein: 0.9 g; Cholesterol: 4 mg; Sodium: 11 mg

Low Carb Pina Colada Fat Bombs

Yield: 16 Fat Bombs/Total Time: 1 Hour 11 Minutes /Prep Time: 10 Minutes /Cook Time: 1 Minute

Ingredients
- 1/2 cup Coconut Cream
- 2 teaspoons pineapple essence
- 3 teaspoons Erythritol
- 2 scoops MCT Powder
- 1/2 cup boiling water
- 2 tablespoons gelatin
- 1 teaspoon rum extract

Directions
1. Dissolve Erythritol and gelatin in a jug of boiling water; stir in pineapple essence and let cool for at least 5 minutes. Stir in rum extract and coconut cream and pour into silicon molds. Freeze for at least 1 hour. Enjoy!

Nutritional info per Serving: *Calories: 23; Total Fat: 2.5 g; Carbs: 0.4 g; Dietary Fiber: 0.1 g Sugars: 0.2 g; Protein: 2 g; Cholesterol: 0 mg; Sodium: 5 mg*

Creamy Raspberry Fat Bombs

Yield: 10 Fat Bombs/Total Time: 1 Hour 11 Minutes /Prep Time: 10 Minutes /Cook Time: 1 Minutes

Ingredients
- 1/2 cup heavy cream
- 15 g gelatin powder
- 1 packet raspberry sugar-free Jell-O
- 1/2 cup water boiling

Directions
1. Dissolve Jell-O and gelatin in a jug of boiling water; whisk in cream and then pour the mixture into candy molds. Chill for at least 1 hour or until firm. Enjoy!

Nutritional info per Serving:
Calories: 21; Total Fat: 2 g; Carbs: 0.1 g; Dietary Fiber: 0 g; Sugars: 0.01 g; Protein: 0.4 g; Cholesterol: 6 mg; Sodium: 3 mg

Lemony Poppy Seed Fat Bombs

Yield: 18 Fat Bombs/Total Time: 1 Hour 10 Minutes /Prep Time: 10 Minutes

Ingredients
- 2 tablespoons lemon juice
- 4 tablespoons sour cream
- 1 cup cream cheese softened
- 1 lemon zest only
- 1 tablespoon poppy seeds
- 3 tablespoons Erythritol

Directions
1. Mix together all ingredients with a hand mixer until well combined; spoon the mixture into cupcake cases and refrigerate for at least 1 hour. Enjoy!

Nutritional info per Serving:
Calories: 60; Total Fat: 5 g; Carbs: 1 g; Dietary Fiber: 0.1 g; Sugars: 1 g; Protein: 1 g; Cholesterol: 7 mg; Sodium: 54 mg

Creamy Strawberry Fat Bombs

Yield: 10 Fat Bombs/Total Time: 3 Hours 30 Minutes /Prep Time: 30 Minutes /Cook Time: 15 Minutes

Ingredients
- 3 tablespoons coconut oil
- 3/4 cup double cream
- 1 cup cream cheese softened
- 1 oz vanilla collagen protein powder
- 1 teaspoon strawberry essence
- 2 teaspoon coconut oil for rolling the batter into balls

Directions
1. In a bowl, beat together all ingredients with a hand mixer until well blended. Refrigerate the mixture for at least 1 hour. Remove from the fridge and roll the mixture into bite sized balls. Freeze until firm before serving.

Nutritional info per Serving:
Calories: 179; Total Fat: 17 g; Carbs: 0.5 g; Dietary Fiber: 0.1 g Sugars: 1 g; Protein: 3 g; Cholesterol: 8 mg; Sodium: 80 mg

Dark Chocolate Fat Bombs

Yield: 24 Fat Bombs/Total Time: 3 Hours 20 Minutes /Prep Time: 20 Minutes

Ingredients
- 1 cup heavy cream
- 1 cup cream cheese softened
- 1 teaspoon vanilla essence
- 1/2 cup dark chocolate
- 2 ounces Stevia icing mix

Directions
1. In a heatproof bowl, melt chocolate over boiling water.
2. Meanwhile, beat together the remaining ingredients until the mixture is fluffy; gradually beat in the melted chocolate until well combined and then divide the mixture among muffin cups. Refrigerate for about 3 hours or until firm. Enjoy!

Nutritional info per Serving:
Calories: 97; Total Fat: 5 g; Carbs: 1 g; Dietary Fiber: 0 g; Sugars: 0 g; Protein: 1 g; Cholesterol: 21 mg; Sodium: 33 mg

Low Carb Creamy Red Velvet Fat Bombs

Yield: 24 Fat Bombs/Total Time: 55 Minutes /Prep Time: 10 Minutes /Cook Time: 5 Minutes

Ingredients
- 1/3 cup heavy cream whipped
- 100 g butter
- 125 g cream cheese
- 100 g dark chocolate
- 4 drops red food coloring
- 1 tsp vanilla extract
- 3 tablespoons Stevia

Directions
1. In a heatproof bowl, melt chocolate over boiling water.
2. Meanwhile, beat together the remaining ingredients until the mixture is fluffy; gradually beat in the melted chocolate until well combined and then divide the mixture among muffin cups. Refrigerate for about 40 minutes or until firm. Enjoy!

Nutritional info per Serving:
Calories: 59; Total Fat: 3.8 g; Carbs: 0.1 g; Dietary Fiber: 0 g; Sugars: 0 g; Protein: 0.9 g; Cholesterol: 19 mg; Sodium: 47 mg

Low Carb Maple Pecan Fat Bombs

Yield: 30 Fat Bombs/Total Time: 2 Hours 15 Minutes /Prep Time: 5 Minutes /Cook Time: 10 Minutes

Ingredients
- 9 pecan nuts
- 2 ounces pecan butter
- 4 ounces unsalted butter
- 2 tablespoons sugar-free maple syrup
- 1 scoop vanilla collagen powder

Directions
1. In a saucepan set over low heat, whisk together all ingredients except pecans. Remove from heat and let cool for at least 5 minutes and then pour into a pan lined with baking paper. Refrigerate for at least 2 hours.
2. Cut into small squares and serve.

Nutritional info per Serving:
Calories: 147; Total Fat: 15 g; Carbs: 1 g; Dietary Fiber: 1 gg; Sugars: 01 g; Protein: 3.4 g; Cholesterol: 27 mg; Sodium: 2 mg

Vanilla Cream Cheese Fat Bombs

Yield: 18 Fat Bombs/Total Time: 1 Hour 10 Minutes /Prep Time: 10 Minutes

Ingredients
- 1 cup heavy cream
- 1 cup cream cheese softened
- 2 tablespoons Erythritol
- 2 teaspoons vanilla extract

Directions
1. With a hand mixer, beat together cream cheese, vanilla and sweetener until smooth; beat in half of the heavy cream and let sit for at least 3 minutes or until the sweetener is dissolved.
2. Beat in the remaining heavy cream until the mixture is thick and then divide among the muffin cups lined with liners. Chill for at least 1 hour before serving.

Nutritional info per Serving:
Calories: 88; Total Fat: 9 g; Carbs: 1 g; Dietary Fiber: 0 g Sugars: 1 g; Protein: 1 g; Cholesterol: 21 mg; Sodium: 56 mg

Chocolate Chip Keto Fat Bombs

Yield: 30 Fat Bombs/Total Time: 1 Hour 5 Minutes /Prep Time: 5 Minutes

Ingredients
- 2 cup almond flour
- 8 tablespoons butter, softened
- 1/2 teaspoon pure vanilla extract
- 1/3 cup Swerve
- 2/3 cup dark chocolate chips
- 1/2 teaspoon kosher salt

Directions
1. Beat butter with a hand mixer until fluffy; beat in vanilla extract, sweetener and salt until well blended. Gradually beat in almond flour until smooth then fold in chocolate chips. Cover and refrigerate for at least 20 minutes.
2. With a cookie scoop, scoop out the dough into bite sized balls and arrange them on a baking sheet. Chill for at least 30 minutes before serving.

Nutritional info per Serving: *Calories: 278; Total Fat: 17 g; Carbs: 9.3 g; Dietary Fiber: 0 g; Sugars: 3.8 g; Protein: 14.2 g; Cholesterol: 58 mg; Sodium: 359 mg*

Chocolate & Raspberry Fat Bombs

Yield: 12 Fat Bombs/Total Time: 1 Hour 5 Minutes/Prep Time: 5 Minutes

Ingredients
- 1/2 cup dried raspberries
- 2 ounces cacao butter
- 1/2 cup coconut oil
- 1/4 cup powdered sweetener

Directions
1. Prepare muffin pan by lining it with paper liners; set aside.
2. In a saucepan, melt coconut oil and then remove from heat. Stir in cocoa butter.
3. In a food processor, grind the raspberries and add to the pan along with sweetener. Divide the raspberry mixture among the prepared muffin cups and chill for at least 1 hour or until firm. Enjoy!

Nutritional info per Serving:
Calories: 153; Total Fat: 16.6 g; Carbs: 1.2 g; Dietary Fiber: 0.4 g Sugars: 0.2 g; Protein: 1.2 g; Cholesterol: 0 mg; Sodium: 33 mg

Bagel Keto Fat Bombs

Yield: 36 Servings/Total Time: 15 Minutes/Prep Time: 15 Minutes

Ingredients
- 1 cup cream cheese
- 2 scallions, sliced
- 4 ounces wild caught smoked salmon

Bagel Seasoning
- 1 tablespoon dried minced onion
- 1 tablespoon dried minced garlic
- 1 tablespoon black sesame seeds
- 1 tablespoon white sesame seeds
- 2 tablespoons poppy seeds
- 2 teaspoons flaked sea salt

Directions
1. In a bowl, mix together all the seasoning ingredients until well combined. Set aside.
2. Beat cream cheese with a hand mixer until light and fluffy; add in sliced scallions and chopped smoked salmon and beat until well blended. Form the mixture into bite-sized balls and roll each in the bagel seasoning. Refrigerate the balls for at least 2 hours before serving.

Nutritional info per Serving:
Calories: 125; Total Fat: 2.9 g; Carbs: 0.5 g; Dietary Fiber: 0.02 g; Sugars: 0.4 g; Protein: 1 g; Cholesterol: 8 mg; Sodium: 50 mg

Healthy Pecan Pie Fat Bombs

Yield: 18 Fat Bombs/Total Time: 15 Minutes/Prep Time: 15 Minutes

Ingredients
- 2 tablespoons pecan butter
- ¼ cup coconut butter
- ½ cup shredded coconut
- 1½ cups pecans
- 1 teaspoon coconut oil
- 2 tablespoons hemp seeds
- 2 tablespoons flax meal
- 2 tablespoons chia seeds
- ½ teaspoon vanilla extract
- 1½ teaspoons cinnamon
- ¼ teaspoon kosher salt

Directions
1. Combine all ingredients in a food processor and pulse the mixture into powder. Continue pulsing until the mixture forms a smooth batter. Roll 18 balls from the mixture and arrange them onto a baking sheet. Refrigerate for at least 30 minutes before serving. Freeze the rest.

Nutritional info per Serving:
Calories: 121; Total Fat: 12 g; Carbs: 3.8 g; Dietary Fiber: 2.9 g; Sugars: 0.2 g; Protein: 2 g; Cholesterol: 0 mg; Sodium: 102 mg

Keto Dill Pickle Fat Bombs

Yield: 15 Fat Bombs/Total Time: 5 Minutes/Prep Time: 5 Minutes

Ingredients
- 2 cups chopped cheddar cheese
- 18 oz cream cheese
- 6 dill pickles, chopped fine, drained

Directions
1. In a bowl, mix all ingredients until well combined; from balls from the mixture and serve right away.

Nutritional info per Serving:
Calories: 121; Total Fat: 11 g; Carbs: 0.2 g; Dietary Fiber: 0 g; Sugars: 1 g; Protein: 5 g; Cholesterol: 31 mg; Sodium: 267 mg

Cheesy Meat Fat Bombs

Yield: 3 Servings /Total Time: 20 Minutes /Prep Time: 10 Minutes /Cook Time: 10 Minutes

Ingredients
- 500 g ground beef
- 1 teaspoon garlic powder
- 1/2 teaspoon salt
- 1/2 teaspoon pepper
- 3 tablespoons parmesan cheese, diced
- 100 g cheese mozzarella

Directions
1. In a bowl, mix together minced meat, garlic powder, salt and pepper; fold in cheese and form meat balls from the mixture; pan fry the meat balls until lightly browned. Enjoy!

Nutritional info per Serving:
Calories: 444; Total Fat: 28 g; Carbs: 2 g; Dietary Fiber: 0.6 g Sugars: 1 g; Protein: 46 g; Cholesterol: 212 mg; Sodium: 678 mg

Savory Chorizo & Chive Deviled Eggs

Yield: 8 Servings/Total Time: 27 Minutes /Prep Time: 15 Minutes /Cook Time: 2 Minutes

Ingredients
- 4 oz Spanish chorizo
- 2 tablespoons olive oil
- 1 tablespoon lemon juice
- 8 hard-boiled eggs
- 1/4 cup Greek yogurt
- 1 teaspoon lemon zest
- 1/2 garlic powder
- 1/2 teaspoon chili powder
- 1 tablespoon chives chopped
- 1/2 teaspoon kosher salt

Directions
1. Heat oil in a skillet over medium high heat and cook chorizo until crispy; drain chorizo on paper and reserve 1 tablespoon of cooking oil.
2. Half each boiled egg and scoop out yolks.
3. In a bowl, whisk together the reserved oil, yolks, lemon juice, zest, yogurt, garlic powder, chili powder and salt until creamy.
4. Press the yolk mixture inside each egg white. Top each with chives and chorizo and serve. Enjoy!

Nutritional info per Serving:
Calories: 144; Total Fat: 11 g; Carbs: 1.8 g; Dietary Fiber: 0.1 g; Sugars: 0.8 g; Protein: 9.2 g; Cholesterol: 162 mg; Sodium: 353 mg

Ginger Coconut Fat Bombs

Yield: 4 Servings/Total Time: 5 Minutes/Prep Time: 5 Minutes

Ingredients
- 1 teaspoon ginger powder
- 25 g shredded coconut
- 75 g coconut oil
- 75 g coconut butter
- 1 teaspoon granulated sweetener

Directions
1. In a bowl, mix together all ingredients then pour the mixture into molds; refrigerate for at least 10 minutes before serving. Enjoy!

Nutritional info per Serving:
Calories: 120; Total Fat: 12.8 g; Carbs: 2.2 g; Dietary Fiber: 1.4 g; Sugars: 0.1 g; Protein: 0.5 g; Cholesterol: 0 mg; Sodium: 221 mg

Swiss Chocolate Fat Bombs

Yield: 18 Fat Bombs/Total Time: 20 Minutes/Prep Time: 20 Minutes

Ingredients
- 1/3 cup unsweetened coconut flakes
- ½ cup cashews
- ½ cup macadamias
- 2 tablespoons organic coconut cream
- 2 tablespoons unsweetened cocoa powder
- 1 tablespoon coconut oil

Directions
1. Combine all the ingredients in food processor and pulse until creamy.
2. Roll into small balls and line them up on a baking tray and chill in the fridge. Yum!

Nutritional info per Serving:
Calories: 203; Total Fat: 19 g; Carbs: 7.8 g; Dietary Fiber: 3.8 g; Sugars: 1.7 g; Protein: 3 g; Cholesterol: 0 mg; Sodium: 4 mg

Buttery Raspberry Fat Bombs

Yield: 18 Fat Bombs/Total Time: 20 Minutes /Prep Time: 20 Minutes
Ingredients
- ¼ cup coconut butter
- ¼ cup organic almond butter
- 2 tablespoons chopped walnuts
- 2 tablespoons chopped almonds
- 2 drops Stevia
- 1 tablespoon raw cocoa powder
- 1/3 cup frozen raspberries, thawed

Directions
1. Combine the butters, Stevia and cocoa powder in a large bowl and mix well. Fold in the nuts and raspberries then spread this on a large tray. Put in the freezer for an hour then break it up into chunks.En joy!

Nutritional info per Serving:
Calories: 82; Total Fat: 7.3 g; Carbs: 3.2 g; Dietary Fiber: 1.7 g; Sugars: 0.86 g; Protein: 3.1 g; Cholesterol: 0 mg; Sodium: 19 mg

KETO MEDITERRANEAN RECIPES

Morning Olive Guacamole

Yield: 4 Servings/Total Time: 10 Minutes/Prep Time: 10 Minutes
Ingredients
- 2 Hass avocadoes
- 1 tbsp chopped sun-dried tomatoes
- 4 cherry tomatoes, halved
- 2 tbs. freshly squeezed lemon juice
- 3 kalamata olives, pitted and roughly chopped
- 3 tbsp sliced red onion
- ½ cup freshly chopped parsley
- 1 tsp semi-fresh oregano, chopped
- Pink sea salt and freshly ground black pepper to taste

Directions
1. Cut the avocadoes in half and remove seeds. Scoop out the flesh into a large bowl and use a fork to mash to desired consistency.
2. Sprinkle the lemon juice on the mashed avocado and mix until well combined. Add in all the remaining ingredients and until well incorporated.
3. Adjust the salt, pepper and herbs to taste. If you like your guacamole tangier, squeeze in more lemon juice and for a more tomatoey flavor, add the sun-dried tomatoes.
4. Serve immediately with whole multi-grain bread or veggies such as carrot and celery sticks. Enjoy!

Nutritional Information per Serving:
Calories: 167; Total Fat: 23 g; Carbs: 5.7 g; Dietary Fiber: 3.8 g; Protein: 11 g; Cholesterol: 0.9 mg; Sodium: 54 mg

Crunchy Breakfast Smoothie

Yield: 3 Servings/Total Time: 10 Minutes/Prep Time: 10 Minutes
Ingredients
- 2 tbsp raw almond butter
- 1 ½ cups vanilla flavored unsweetened almond milk
- 2 tbsp. roughly chopped almonds, for topping
- ½ frozen banana
- ½ cup mixed berries
- 1 tbsp raw honey, if desired
- ½ - 1 cup ice cubes

Directions
1. Combine all the ingredients, apart from the chopped almonds, in your blender and pulse until you achieve your desired consistency.
2. Serve in a tall glass and top with the chopped almonds. Enjoy!

Nutritional Information per Serving:
Calories: 213; Total Fat: 12 g; Carbs: 11.7 g; Dietary Fiber: 6 g; Protein: 6 g; Cholesterol: 0 mg; Sodium: 173 mg

Simple Egg Veggie Sandwich

Yield: 2 Servings/Total Time: 13 Minutes/Prep Time: 8 Minutes/Cook Time: 5 Minutes

Ingredients
- 4 wide butter lettuce leaves
- 8 asparagus spears, steamed
- 1 medium avocado, roughly mashed
- 2 hard-boiled eggs, sliced
- 2 tbsp Dijon mustard
- Pink sea salt and freshly cracked black pepper
- 1 tsp extra virgin olive oil

Directions
1. Start by spreading the leaves with mustard and set aside. Next, spread two of the leaves with the mashed avocado. Top with the steamed asparagus and egg.
2. Season with salt and pepper and top with the olive oil. Top the sandwich with the two lettuce leaves that had been set aside. Enjoy!

Nutritional Information per Serving: Calories: 279; Total Fat: 24 g; Carbs: 10.6 g; Dietary Fiber: 9 g; Protein: 12 g; Cholesterol: 93mg; Sodium: 411 mg

Egg White Scramble w/Veggies

Yield: 3 Servings/Total Time: 15 Minutes/Prep Time: 5 Minutes/Cook Time: 10 Minutes

Ingredients
- 9 egg whites
- ½ cup light cream
- 2 cups baby spinach
- 1 tbsp extra virgin olive oil
- ¼ cup shredded parmesan cheese
- 1 cup cherry tomatoes, cut in half
- 1 tsp minced garlic
- Sea salt and freshly ground black pepper, to taste

Directions
1. In a large bowl, whisk the egg whites, light cream, salt and pepper then set aside.
2. Place a large non-stick pan over medium to high heat and add the olive oil and garlic then cook for about half a minute until lightly browned. Don't let the garlic burn. Stir in the tomatoes and spinach and cook for a minute, stirring often, until the spinach wilts.
3. Transfer the veggies to a hot plate.
4. Use the same pan to cook the egg white mixture. Lower the heat to medium and don't stir the eggs until it starts setting on the bottom. Use a rubber spatula to gently fold the cooked edges so the uncooked egg whites flow to the bottom. Keep doing this for about 2 minutes or until glossy and cooked to preference.
5. Serve hot with the veggies and top with shredded parmesan.

Nutritional Information per Serving: Calories: 142; Total Fat: 11 g; Carbs: 7 g; Dietary Fiber: 2 g; Protein: 15 g; Cholesterol: 6 mg; Sodium: 581 mg

Overnight Ginger Spiced Bulgur w/Wild Berries

Yield: 2 Servings/Total Time: 8Minutes/Prep Time: 8 Minutes

Ingredients
- ¼ cup bulgur
- 2 tbsp raw honey
- 2/3 cup plain Greek yogurt
- 1 tbsp crystallized ginger
- 3 tbsp chilled coconut milk
- 1/3 cup fresh wild blackberries

Directions
1. In a medium bowl, combine the bulgur, yogurt, honey, coconut milk and ginger. Cover with cling wrap and chill overnight.
2. Divide into two portions and top with the fresh blackberries. Enjoy!

Nutritional Information per Serving: Calories: 215; Total Fat: 4 g; Carbs: 7 g; Dietary Fiber: 3 g; Protein: 8 g; Cholesterol: 0 mg; Sodium: 74 mg

Decadent Berrylicious Pancakes

Yield: 2 Servings/Total Time: 30 Minutes/Prep Time: 10 Minutes/Cook Time: 20 Minutes

Ingredients
- ¾ cup almond flour
- ¼ cup mixed berries (blueberries, raspberries, strawberries, blackberries)
- ¼ cups sour/butter milk
- 1 egg
- ½ tsp baking powder
- ¼ tsp baking soda
- A pinch of salt
- 3 tbsp olive oil
- Mixed berries and raw honey for topping

Directions
1. Combine the flour, baking powder, baking soda, and salt in a large bowl and whisk together.

2. Lightly beat the egg in a medium bowl and combine with the milk and oil. Add the wet mixture to the flour mixture and whisk until well combined but slightly lumpy. Fold in the mixed berries and let stand for 5 minutes.
3. Lightly grease your griddle iron over medium heat and use a ladle to pour the batter on the griddle. Cook each side for about 2 minutes or until bubbles form on top and the bottom turns golden. Turn the pancake and cook the other side. Repeat the process for the remaining batter.
4. Serve hot and top with berries and raw honey. Yum!

Nutritional Information per Serving: Calories: 285; Total Fat: 10 g; Carbs: 12.3 g; Dietary Fiber: 6 g; Protein: 11 g; Cholesterol: 0 mg; Sodium: 133 mg

Nutty Acai Breakfast Bowl

Yield: 2 Servings/Total Time: 40 Minutes/Prep Time: 15 Minutes/Cook Time: 25 Minutes

Ingredients
- 1 ½ cups acai puree, unsweetened and frozen
- 1 banana, sliced and frozen
- ½ cup mixed berries, frozen
- ¼ cup coarse coconut flakes, unsweetened
- ¼ cup pumpkin seeds
- ¼ cup sliced almonds
- ½ tsp. grated ginger
- 1 egg white
- 1 tbsp ground flaxseed
- ½ tbsp honey
- ¼ tsp kosher salt
- ¼ cup plain Greek yogurt
- ¼ cup unsweetened almond milk
- Fruit of choice for topping (kiwi, peach, mango slices, pineapple)

Directions
1. Start by setting your oven to 325 degrees. Line a baking pan with parchment paper and set aside. Combine the egg white, salt and honey in a bowl, toss in the almond and pumpkin seeds, ground flaxseed and coconut flakes. Spread the mixture on the prepared baking pan and bake for 20-30 minutes or until golden (stirring the nut mixture halfway through cook time). Remove from oven and let cool.
2. Next, combine the banana slices, berries, acai puree, yogurt, almond milk and ginger in a blender and pulse until smooth. Divide the puree into 4 bowls and top with desired fruit and baked nut mix. Enjoy!

Nutritional Information per Serving: Calories: 251; Total Fat: 11 g; Carbs: 11.7 g; Dietary Fiber: 7 g; Protein: 10 g; Cholesterol: 4 mg; Sodium: 85 mg

Keto Coconut Porridge w/Healthy Toppings

Yield: 2 Servings/Total Time: 10 Minutes/Prep Time: 5 Minutes/Cook Time: 5 Minutes

Ingredients
Porridge
- 1 cup almond milk
- 1/4 cup coconut flour
- 1/4 cup ground flaxseed
- 10 drops liquid Stevia
- 1 tsp vanilla extract
- 1 tsp cinnamon
- 1 pinch salt

Toppings
- 1 tablespoon shaved coconut
- 2 tablespoon pumpkin seeds
- 60 g blueberries
- 2 tablespoons peanut butter

Directions
1. Add almond milk to a saucepan over low heat; stir in coconut flour, flaxseed, cinnamon and salt until well blended. Heat until thick and bubbly and stir in vanilla extract and Stevia. Remove from heat and serve topped with shaved coconut, blueberries, pumpkin seeds and peanut butter.

Nutritional Info per Serving: *Calories: 405; Total Fat: 34 g; Carbs: 8 g; Dietary Fiber: 3.5 g; Sugars: 3.7 g; Protein: 10 g; Cholesterol: 0 mg; Sodium: 159 mg*

Healthy Keto PB & Berry Pancakes

Yield: 2 Servings/Total Time: 10 Minutes/Prep Time: 5 Minutes/Cook Time: 5 Minutes

Ingredients
- 1/2 cup almond flour
- 2 tsp coconut flour
- 5 drops Stevia
- 1/4 tsp cinnamon
- 1/4 tsp baking powder
- 1 pinch salt
- 2 eggs
- 1 tbsp coconut oil
- 1 ½ tbsp natural peanut butter
- 2 tbsp almond milk
- 60 g Strawberries

Directions

1. In a blender, blend together all dry ingredients, except strawberries, until well blended; add in wet ingredients until very smooth and then fold in strawberries.
2. Heat coconut oil in a pan and then pour in half of the batter; cook for a minute and then flip to cook the other side for about 30 seconds. Repeat with the remaining batter and then serve the pancakes with a glass of freshly squeezed lemon juice.
3. Heat until thick and bubbly and then stir in vanilla extract and Stevia. Remove from heat and serve topped with shaved coconut, strawberries, pumpkin seeds and peanut butter.

Nutritional Info per Serving:
Calories: 326; Total Fat: 27.9 g; Carbs: 10.2 g; Dietary Fiber: 4.6 g; Sugars: 4.4 g; Protein: 11.6 g; Cholesterol: 164 mg; Sodium: 144 mg

Yummy Almond Butter Smoothie w/Acai

Yield: 1 Serving/Total Time: 5 Minutes/Prep Time: 5 Minutes
Ingredients
- 3/4 cup almond milk
- 1-100 g pack organic acai puree
- 1 tablespoon almond butter
- 1 tablespoon coconut oil
- 3 tablespoons protein powder
- 1/4 of an avocado
- 1/2 tsp vanilla extract
- 2 drops liquid Stevia

Directions
1. Blend together all ingredients until very smooth. Enjoy!

Nutritional Info per Serving:
Calories: 345; Total Fat: 20 g; Carbs: 8.1 g; Dietary Fiber: 2 g; Sugars: 2.1 g; Protein: 15 g; Cholesterol: 0 mg; Sodium: 14 mg

Vanilla-Infused Hemp Seed Porridge

Yield: 2 Servings/Prep Time 5 minutes/Cook Time 4 minutes/Total Time 9 minutes
Ingredients
- 1/3 cup coconut milk
- 1/2 cup water
- 1 tablespoon coconut flour
- 1/4 cup hemp seeds
- 1/2 cup shredded coconut
- 2 teaspoons liquid Stevia
- 1 teaspoon vanilla
- 1/2 tablespoon ground cinnamon

Directions
1. In a saucepan, combine milk, hemp seeds, coconut and water; bring to a gentle boil and then simmer for about 2 minutes or until thickened. Stir in Stevia, cinnamon and vanilla and serve hot with more milk and topped with nuts. Enjoy!

Nutritional Info per Serving:
Calories: 374; Total Fat: 33 g; Carbs: 9 g; Dietary Fiber: 5 g; Sugars: 1 g; Protein: 11 g; Cholesterol: 0 mg; Sodium: 211 mg

Meaty Frittata w/ Green Onion

Yield: 4 Servings/Total Time: 20 Minutes/Prep Time: 10 Minutes/Cook Time: 10 Minutes
Ingredients
- 3 tablespoons olive oil
- 1 red sweet bell pepper
- 1 cup chopped green onion
- 1/4 cup shredded parmesan cheese
- 150 g bacon
- 1/4 tsp salt
- 1 tsp pepper
- 6 large eggs
- 2 tablespoons parmesan cheese, grated

Directions
1. Heat olive oil in a skillet and cook bacon, onion and bell pepper until bacon is crispy; season with salt and pepper.
2. In a bowl, whisk together eggs and parmesan cheese until well blended; pour the mixture over the bacon mixture and cook until the egg is almost set. Sprinkle with the remaining cheese and grill for 4 minutes or until browned. Remove from the oven and slice to serve.

Nutritional Info per Serving:
Calories: 494; Total Fat: 40 g; Carbs: 3.5 g; Dietary Fiber: 0.1 g; Sugars: 1 g; Protein: 27 g; Cholesterol: 382 mg; Sodium: 1424 mg

Mint-Flavored Green Smoothie

Yield: 1 Serving/Total Time: 5 Minutes/Prep Time: 5 Minutes

Ingredients:
- 1 cup fresh spinach
- 1/2 cup coconut milk
- 1 tablespoon fresh mint
- 1/2 cup cucumber
- 1 cup filtered water
- 1 scoop whey protein
- 3-4 ice cubes

Directions:
1. Blend together all ingredients until very smooth. Enjoy!

Nutritional Info per Serving: Calories: 360; Total Fat: 24 g; Carbs: 10 g; Dietary Fiber: 6.6 g; Sugars: 1.1 g; Protein: 27 g; Cholesterol: 0 mg; Sodium: 53 mg

Chocolate -for-Breakfast Pudding

Yield: 2 Servings/Total Time: 2 Hours 25 Minutes/Prep Time: 10 minutes/Cook Time: 15 Minutes

Ingredients
- 1 cup unsweetened almond milk
- 1 cup heavy cream
- 1 teaspoon vanilla extract
- 1 teaspoon xanthan gum
- 1 extra large egg
- 1/4 cup unsweetened cacao powder
- 1/4 cup liquid Stevia

Directions
1. In a saucepan, whisk together almond milk, heavy cream, cocoa powder, egg, Stevia and xanthan gum until well combined. Cook on medium low heat, whisking frequently until the pudding is thickened. Remove from heat and whisk in vanilla. Transfer to a container and refrigerate, covered, for at least 2 hours. Serve the pudding topped with whipping cream and toasted walnuts.

Nutritional Info per Serving: Calories: 247; Total Fat: 24.3 g; Carbs: 5.1 g; Dietary Fiber: 2.1 g; Sugars: 1 g; Protein: 3 g; Cholesterol: 122 mg; Sodium: 142 mg

Low Carb Green Frittata

Yield: 4 Servings/Total Time: 40 Minutes/Prep Time: 10 Minutes/Cook Time: 30 Minutes

Ingredients
- 1 cup (packed) baby spinach
- 2 tablespoons butter
- ½ cup heavy whipping cream
- 8 eggs
- 1/2 cup shredded cheddar cheese
- A pinch of salt & pepper

Directions
1. Preheat your oven to 350 degrees and grease a square baking dish; set aside.
2. In a pan, fry bacon on medium heat until crispy; stir in spinach and salt for about 2 minutes or until just wilted; transfer to a plate and set aside.
3. In a bowl, whisk together cream, eggs, salt and pepper until well blended; pour into the baking dish and top with the bacon-spinach mixture; bake for about 30 minutes or until the egg is set. Serve with fresh lime juice.

Nutritional Info per Serving: Calories: 661; Total Fat: 59 g; Carbs: 9.4 g; Dietary Fiber: 3.1 g; Sugars: 1 g; Protein: 27 g; Cholesterol: 129 mg; Sodium: 243 mg

Creamy & Zingy Berry Parfaits

Yield: 2 Servings/Total Time: 6 Minutes/Prep Time: 6 minutes

Ingredients

For Granola Nut Topping:
- 1 tablespoon shredded coconut
- 10 toasted almonds
- ¼ tsp cinnamon
- 1 tsp sweetener

For Fruit Compote:
- 1 tablespoon lemon juice
- 2/3 cup blueberries fresh
- 1 tablespoon berry jam
- 1 teaspoon vanilla extract
- ½ tablespoon sweetener

For Cream:
- 4 tablespoons whipped cream
- A few drops liquid Stevia

Directions
1. In a blender, blend together all nut topping ingredients until chopped up; set aside.
2. Mix together all fruit compote ingredients until well blended.

3. To make the parfaits, add a layer of whipped cream to the bottom of the glasses and layer with fruit compote; top with nutty topping and repeat the layers to fill the glasses. Enjoy!
Nutritional Info per Serving: Calories: 275; Total Fat: 11.1 g; Carbs: 11.8 g; Dietary Fiber: 7 g; Sugars: 7 g; Protein: 2.1 g; Cholesterol: 0 mg; Sodium: 92 mg

Tasty Seafood Omelet

Yield: 2 Servings/Total Time: 15 Minutes /Prep Time: 10 Minutes /Cook Time: 5 Minutes
Ingredients
- 6 fresh asparagus, trimmed
- 180 g crabmeat, drained
- 2 tablespoons butter
- 1/2 cup plum tomatoes, diced
- 4 large eggs
- 1/2 cup shredded cheese
- Dash salt & pepper

Directions
1. Steam asparagus in a steamer basket for about 5 minutes; set aside.
2. Whisk together eggs, tomatoes, salt and pepper.
3. Melt butter in a skillet set over medium heat; add in half of the egg mixture and cook for about 30 seconds or until set underneath. Spoon half of asparagus, crab meat and cheese on one side of the omelet and fold over the filling; cook for about 2 minutes or until cheese is melted. Repeat with the remaining ingredients and then serve.

Nutritional Info per Serving:
Calories: 407; Total Fat: 27 g; Carbs: 6 g; Dietary Fiber: 1 g; Sugars: 4 g; Protein: 35 g; Cholesterol: 541 mg; Sodium: 733 mg

Delicious Keto 'Oatmeal'

Yield: 1 Serving/Total Time: 10 Minutes/Prep Time: 5 Minutes/Cook Time: 5 Minutes
Ingredients
- 3/4 cup coconut milk
- 1 tablespoon sunflower seeds
- 1 tablespoon chia seeds
- 1 tablespoon flaxseed, whole

Directions
1. Combine all ingredients in a pan and bring to a gentle boil. Lower heat and simmer for a few minutes or until thick. Serve topped with nuts, and berries of choice.

Nutritional Info per Serving:
Calories: 554; Total Fat: 53.1 g; Carbs: 12.4 g; Dietary Fiber: 11.8 g; Sugars: 6.3 g; Protein: 9.8 g; Cholesterol: 0 mg; Sodium: 188 mg

Classic Tuna Salad w/Fennel

Yield: 4 Servings /Total Time: 10 Minutes /Prep Time: 10 Minutes
Ingredients
For the salad:
- 150 g canned tuna, drained
- 1sShallot, thinly sliced (in rounds)
- 2 small fennel bulbs, thinly sliced
- ½ yellow pepper, thinly sliced
- ½ red pepper, thinly sliced

- 12 mixed olives
- 1 tbsp capers
- 2 hard-boiled eggs, cut into quarters
- 8 radishes
- Sweet rice vinegar, as required

For the Dressing
- 1 tbsp freshly squeezed lemon juice
- Zest of 1 lemon
- 1 tsp fennel greens, finely chopped

- 4 tbsp extra virgin olive oil
- Sea salt and freshly ground pepper, to taste
- Vinegar, for marinating the onions

Directions
1. Start by making the dressing by combining all the dressing ingredients in a small bowl and whisking until well combined.
2. For the salad, sprinkle 2-3 tablespoons of vinegar on the sliced onions and toss well to combine. Let stand for five minutes tossing them twice in between.
3. On a large platter, arrange the peppers followed by the fennel. Arrange the olives and radishes on the edges then top the fennel with the boiled egg and the tuna in the middle. Drain the marinated onions and spread them on the salad followed by the capers.
4. Drizzle the salad dressing over the salad and season lightly with salt and pepper. Enjoy!

Nutritional Information per Serving:
Calories: 276; Total Fat: 21 g; Carbs: 9 g; Dietary Fiber: 2 g; Protein: 15 g; Cholesterol: 8 mg; Sodium: 505 mg

Roast Chicken Breast with Nutty Yogurt Dip

Yield: 3 Servings/Total Time: 2 Hours 10 Minutes/Prep Time: 2 Hours/Cook Time: 10 Minutes

Ingredients

For the Roast Chicken:
- 3 boneless chicken breast halves, skinned
- 1 clove garlic, minced
- Juice of ½ lemon
- 1 tbsp extra virgin olive oil
- 1 tsp dried oregano
- ½ tsp dried thyme
- Salt and freshly ground black pepper, to taste

For the yogurt dip:
- 1 cup plain Greek yogurt
- 1 clove garlic, minced
- 1 tsp fresh dill, minced
- ½ cup cucumber, very thinly sliced or shredded
- ½ cup pistachios, shelled and chopped, (divide in two)

Directions

1. Use a sharp knife to gently slice through the thickest part of the chicken breast without cutting all the way through so you can open it up like a book. Do this for the other two breasts. Marinate the chicken with the remaining chicken ingredients in a large bowl. Cover with cling wrap and set in the fridge for 1 ½ to 2 hours.
2. Preheat your grill to medium-high heat. Take out the chicken from the marinade. Lightly grease your grill rack then place the breasts on top. Cook for about 3 minutes on each side or until done.
3. Meanwhile, combine all the yogurt ingredients in a medium bowl. Remember to set aside one half of the pistachios.
4. Serve each breast on a large plate. Place a dollop of the nutty yogurt on the side and top the chicken with the remaining pistachios. Yum!

Nutritional Information per Serving:
Calories: 318; Total Fat: 13 g; Carbs: 8 g; Dietary Fiber: 4 g; Protein: 37 g; Cholesterol: 38 mg; Sodium: 468 mg

Traditional Mediterranean Salad

Yield: 2 Servings/Total Time: 10 Minutes/Prep Time: 10 Minutes

Ingredients
- 2, ripe but firm tomatoes, sliced
- ½ green pepper, sliced
- 1 shallot, sliced
- 8 kalamata olives, pitted and sliced
- ½ cucumber, peeled and sliced
- 100 g feta cheese, crumbled
- 2 tbs. capers
- 2 tbsp extra virgin olive oil
- ½ tsp dried oregano
- Salt and freshly ground black pepper to taste

Directions
1. Combine all the vegetables in a large bowl and toss well for even distribution.
2. Next, add the capers, salt, pepper and oregano and toss well to combine.
3. Divide the salad into four bowls. Top each bowl with the crumbled cheese and drizzle each bowl with a tablespoon of olive oil. Enjoy!

Nutritional Information per Serving:
Calories: 11.3; Total Fat: 26 g; Carbs: 9 g; Dietary Fiber: 3.1 g; Protein: 9 g; Cholesterol: 0.8 mg; Sodium: 77 mg

Simple Avocado Salad Wraps

Yield: 4 Servings/Prep Time: 10 minutes/Total Time: 10 minutes

Ingredients
- 4 eggs, hard-boiled, sliced
- 1 Hass avocado, diced
- 2 teaspoons fresh lemon juice
- 3 tablespoons high quality mayonnaise
- 2 tablespoons chives finely chopped
- 1/2 teaspoons salt
- 1/4 teaspoon pepper
- 8 leaves butter lettuce or romaine

Directions
1. In a bowl, combine sliced eggs and avocado.
2. In a small bowl, whisk together mayonnaise, lemon juice, chives, salt and pepper until well blended; pour over the avocado egg mixture and toss to coat well.
3. Add a quarter cup of the avocado mixture onto each lettuce leaf and fold to wrap. Enjoy!

Nutritional Information per Serving:
Calories: 136; Total Fat: 12 g; Carbs: 3.7 g; Dietary Fiber: 0.6 g; Sugars: 0 g; Protein: 5 g; Cholesterol: 168 mg; Sodium: 419 mg

Tasty Avocado & Massaged Collard Salad

Yield: 4 Servings/Total Time: 25 Minutes/Prep Time: 5 Minutes/Cook Time: 20 Minutes

Ingredients

For Salad:
- 4 cups Collard greens, stem removes and roughly sliced
- 1 tablespoon avocado oil
- 1 tablespoon fresh lemon juice
- ¼ tsp sea salt

For Dressing:
- 1 avocado, mashed
- 1 tablespoon avocado oil
- 1 tablespoon fresh lemon juice
- 1 tsp nutritional yeast
- 1/4 tsp sea salt
- 1/4 teaspoon pepper
- 3 tablespoons pumpkin seeds

Directions
1. Place collards to a large bowl and add in lemon juice, avocado oil and salt; massage the greens for about 2 minutes or until greener in color.
2. In a small bowl, whisk together lemon juice, avocado oil, avocado, salt, nutritional yeast and pepper until very smooth and creamy.
3. Pour the dressing over the massaged kale and serve garnished with toasted pumpkin seeds. Enjoy!

Nutritional Info per Serving:
Calories: 187; Total Fat: 17.3 g; Carbs: 7.6 g; Dietary Fiber: 4.5 g; Sugars: 1.1 g; Protein: 4.7 g; Cholesterol: 0 mg; Sodium: 359 mg

Crunchy Triple A Salad

Yield: 2 Servings/Total Time: 25 Minutes/Prep Time: 5 Minutes/Cook Time: 20 Minutes

Ingredients
- 20 stalks asparagus, rinsed, trimmed and sliced
- 1 cup micro greens
- 2 cups fresh arugula
- 1 tablespoon olive oil
- salt & pepper
- 2 tablespoons toasted sunflower seeds
- 2 hard-boiled eggs, sliced
- 1/2 avocado

Lemon Vinaigrette
- 1/2 teaspoon shallot, diced
- 3 tsp lemon juice
- 1/4 teaspoon Dijon mustard
- 2 tablespoons olive oil
- salt & pepper

Directions
1. Heat oil in a skillet over medium high heat and stir in asparagus, salt and pepper; cook for about 4 minutes; remove from heat and set aside.
2. In a small bowl, whisk together dressing ingredients until well blended; set aside.
3. Divide micro greens and arugula between two serving bowls; add sunflower seeds and asparagus. Add avocado and sliced eggs and then drizzle with the vinaigrette. Enjoy!

Nutritional Information per Serving:
Calories: 433; Total Fat: 38 g; Carbs: 12.7 g; Dietary Fiber: 8.1 g; Sugars: 3.7 g; Protein: 15 g; Cholesterol: 163 mg; Sodium: 84 mg

Tropical Fish Curry w/Spinach

Yield: 2 Servings/Total Time: 25 Minutes/Prep Time: 5 Minutes/Cook Time: 20 Minutes

Ingredients
- 300 g halibut or other firm white fish, cubed
- 450 g spinach, roughly chopped and blanched with excess water squeezed off
- 100 g coconut cream
- 2 ½ tbsp Thai curry paste
- 2 tbsp coconut oil
- 100 ml water
- Kosher salt and pepper, to taste

Directions
1. Add the oil to a large saucepan over medium heat. Stir in the curry paste and cook for 3 minutes to bring the spices to life.
2. Pour in the coconut cream and water. Increase the temperature to high, to bring the sauce to a boil.
3. Add in the fish cubes and lower the heat to medium-low and simmer for 15 minutes.
4. Gently stir in the blanched spinach and cook for 2 minutes.
5. Serve hot!

Nutritional Information Per Serving: *Calories: 550; Total Fat: 37.5 g; Carbs: 9.9 g; Dietary Fiber: 7.1 g; Sugars: 1.6 g; Protein: 19 g; Cholesterol: 24 mg; Sodium: 223 mg*

Crunchy Fish Salad

Yield: 2 Servings/Total Time: 20 Minutes/Prep Time: 10 Minutes/Cook Time: 10 Minutes

Ingredients

- 250 g fish, your favorite
- 1/4 cup tamari soy sauce
- 1 tablespoon avocado oil
- 1 tablespoon olive oil
- 1/2 tablespoon lemon juice
- 4 radishes, sliced
- 6 cherry tomatoes, halved
- 1/2 red bell pepper, sliced
- 2 cups salad greens
- ¼ teaspoon salt
- 1 tablespoon toasted almonds, chopped

Directions

1. Pour tamari sauce in a large bowl; add in fish and toss to coat well; cover and let marinate for a few hours before cooking.
2. In another bowl, combine green salad, radishes, tomatoes, bell peppers, lemon juice, olive oil and salt; toss to coat well and set aside.
3. Heat avocado oil in a skillet over medium-high heat; cook the fish for 3-5 minutes per side or until cooked through and browned on the outside. Remove from heat and let cool for a minute before slicing to serve. Divide the salad between two plates and top each with fish slices and almonds.

Nutritional Information per Serving:

Calories: 500; Total Fat: 37 g; Carbs: 7 g; Dietary Fiber: 2 g; Sugars: 1 g; Protein: 33 g; Cholesterol: 105 mg; Sodium: 928 mg

Pork Salad with Spicy Avocado Dressing

Yield: 2 Servings/Total Time: 10 Minutes/Prep Time: 10 Minutes

Ingredients

Salad:

- 3/4 pound grilled pork, sliced
- 1 cup salad greens
- 1/2 cup sliced cucumber

Dressing:

- 1 avocado
- 2 tablespoons avocado oil
- 2 tablespoons balsamic vinegar
- 2 tablespoons lime juice
- ½ cup sliced black olives
- 1 avocado
- 1/2 cup grape tomatoes, halved
- 1/4 teaspoon red pepper flakes
- 1 cup fresh cilantro
- 1 clove garlic minced
- 1/2 teaspoon sea salt

Directions

1. In a bowl, mix all salad ingredients and set aside.
2. In a blender, blend together all dressing ingredients until very smooth; pour over the salad and toss to coat well. Divide between serving bowls and enjoy!

Nutritional Information per Serving:

Calories: 644; Total Fat: 53 g; Carbs: 6 g; Dietary Fiber: 3.2 g; Sugars: 1.7 g; Protein: 3 6g; Cholesterol: 105 mg; Sodium: 698 mg

Simple Mediterranean Avo-Shrimp Salad

Yield: 4 Servings Total Time: 8 Minutes/Prep Time: 8 Minutes

Ingredients

- 250 g cooked shrimp, cut in half lengthwise

For the dressing:

- 1 small and ripe avocado, roughly chopped
- 2 tbsp fresh cilantro, chopped
- 1 tbsp extra virgin olive oil
- 1 small cucumber, peeled and diced
- 1 tbsp freshly squeezed lemon juice
- 2 tbsp low-fat, plain Greek yogurt
- Lemon slices, optional

Directions

1. Divide the cooked shrimp in four serving bowls and top with the diced cucumbers.
2. For the dressing, combine all the dressing ingredients, apart from the lemon slices, in a blender and pulse until desired consistency is achieved.
3. Spoon the dressing over the salads in the different bowls. Top with a slice of lemon, if desired. Enjoy!

Nutritional Information per Serving:

Calories: 186; Total Fat: 8.2 g; Carbs: 9 g; Dietary Fiber 6 g; Protein: 4.3 g; Cholesterol: 0 mg; Sodium: 172 mg

Spicy Lamb Chops with Kale

Yield: 2-3 Servings/Total Time: 30 Minutes/Prep Time: 10 Minutes/Cook Time: 20 Minutes

Ingredients
- 6 lean lamb chops, fat trimmed
- 400 g kale, stems removed, and leaves torn
- ¼ cup dates, pitted and chopped

For the spice rub:
- 2 tsp caraway seeds
- ¾ tsp crushed red chili

- 1 shallot, chopped
- 5 tsp extra virgin olive oil
- ¼ cup toasted pine nuts

- 3 tsp ground cumin
- ½ tsp freshly cracked black pepper

Directions
1. Combine the spice rub ingredients in a small bowl and mix well to combine. Rub the spice rub on the lamb chops and let stand for 5 minutes.
2. Toast the pine nuts in a small-medium skillet over low heat, tossing constantly for about 4 minutes or until browned and fragrant. Remove from heat and transfer to a bowl.
3. Add half the olive oil to a skillet over medium heat and add the chops to the hot pan. Cook for roughly 23 minutes per side or until well browned and slightly crisp. Lower the heat and cook for 5 more minutes on each side or until done. Remove from heat and transfer to a large platter and cover with foil to keep warm.
4. Add the remaining olive oil to the same pan over medium heat and stir in chopped shallots and dates. Cook for a minute, stirring until soft. Add in the torn kale and cook for 2 minutes until wilted. Season with salt and add in the toasted pine nuts.
5. Serve hot and top with the lamb chops. Enjoy!

Nutritional Information per Serving: Calories: 319; Total Fat: 21 g; Carbs: 8.5 g; Dietary Fiber 6 g; Protein: 29 g; Cholesterol: 79 mg; Sodium: 553 mg

Delicious Rosemary-Infused Tuna Salad

Yield: 4 Servings/Total Time: 10 Minutes/Prep Time: 10 Minutes

Ingredients
- 2 cans water-packed tuna, drained and flaked using a fork
- 1/3 can chickpeas, rinsed
- 1 Vidalia onion, finely diced
- 1 red pepper, finely diced
- 1 tsp fresh rosemary, finely chopped

- 6 packed cups of mixed salad greens
- ½ cup finely chopped parsley
- 4 tbsp extra virgin olive oil, divided into two
- ½ cup freshly squeezed lemon juice
- 4 tsp capers
- Sea salt and freshly ground black pepper

Directions
1. In a medium bowl, combine the tuna, drained chickpeas, capers, onion, peppers, rosemary, half the lemon juice and half the olive oil.
2. In a large bowl, combine the remaining olive oil and lemon juice with salt and pepper. Toss in the salad greens until they are evenly coated then divide among four large plates.
3. Top with the tuna-chickpea salad and serve immediately. Enjoy!

Nutritional Information per Serving: Calories: 302; Total Fat: 16 g; Carbs: 13.2 g; Dietary Fiber 7 g; Protein: 14 g; Cholesterol: 15 mg; Sodium: 628 mg

Zesty Whole Roasted Sea Bass

Yield: 4 Servings/Total Time: 35 Minutes/Prep Time: 15 Minutes/Cook Time: 20 Minutes

Ingredients
- 2 medium-sized whole sea bass
- 1 tbsp extra virgin olive oil
- 2 garlic cloves, finely chopped
- ½ tsp dried oregano

- 2 tsp freshly squeezed lemon juice
- Kosher salt and freshly ground pepper, to taste
- 2 lemons, thinly sliced

Directions
1. Start by preheating your broiler or grill to medium-high heat. Lightly grease the rack with olive oil cooking spray.
2. Combine the lemon juice, olive oil, salt, pepper and oregano in a bowl and let stand. Use a sharp knife to make 3 horizontal slits on each side of the fish and rub with some kosher salt. Use a brush to rub the lemon-herb mixture in the slits.
3. Cook the fish in the preheated broiler/grill for about 15-20 minutes, turning twice during cook time and baste with the lemon-oregano mixture. Grill until the flesh turns opaque or until desired doneness is achieved.
4. Let the sea bass rest for 5-10 minutes before serving. Serve with steamed veggies or a salad. Enjoy!

Rainbow-Colored Veggie Stew

Yield: 6 Servings/Total Time: 55 Minutes/Prep Time: 15 Minutes/Cook Time: 40 Minutes

Ingredients
- 2 zucchinis, sliced thickly
- ¼ can organic chickpeas, rinsed
- 1 medium-small red pepper, cut into strips
- 1 medium-small yellow pepper, cut into strips
- ½ cup tomato chunks
- 1 onion, cut into large chunks
- 1 cup egg plant, cut into large cubes and sprinkled with salt
- 1 small bunch fresh parsley, chopped
- 1 small bunch fresh cilantro, chopped
- 2 cloves garlic, minced
- 2 tbsp. tomato paste
- 6 tbsp extra virgin olive oil
- ½ tsp turmeric
- 1 tsp. sweet paprika
- Salt and freshly ground pepper, to taste
- Harissa, optional, for serving

Directions
1. Rinse the eggplant sprinkled with salt and pat dry using a kitchen towel.
2. Add 4 tablespoons of the olive oil in a large skillet over medium to high heat until it almost starts smoking. Stir in the eggplant then lower the heat and cook for 10 minutes, turning constantly then transfer to a plate.
3. Add the remaining olive oil to a Dutch oven set over medium heat. Stir in the onion chunks, zucchini and pepper strips and cook for 8 minutes. Add in the turmeric, garlic and paprika and cook for 30 seconds, turning constantly to avoid burning the garlic. Add a tablespoon or two of water then stir in the tomato paste.
4. Next, pour in the drained chickpeas and cooked eggplant and stir well to combine. Add about 1 cup of water and season with salt and pepper. Lower the heat and allow to simmer for 20 minutes, stirring twice.
5. Check the food for seasoning and stir in the harissa, parsley and cilantro. Enjoy!

Nutritional Information per Serving: Calories: 289; Total Fat: 16 g; Carbs: 12 g; Dietary Fiber 10 g; Protein: 7 g; Cholesterol: 0 mg; Sodium: 723 mg

Weight Loss Tomato & Cucumber Salad

Yield: 4 Servings/Total Time: 5 Minutes/Prep Time: 5 Minutes

Ingredients
- 2 cups heirloom tomatoes, diced
- 1 large English cucumber, peeled, halved, and thinly sliced
- 5 large basil leaves, thinly sliced
- 3 tablespoons olive oil
- 1 1/2 tablespoons balsamic vinegar
- 1 teaspoon raw honey
- 1/2 teaspoon kosher salt
- 1/4 teaspoon freshly ground black pepper

Directions
1. In a large bowl, combine all ingredients until well coated; refrigerate for at least 30 minutes before serving. Enjoy!

Nutritional Info per Serving: *Calories: 132; Total Fat: 11.8 g; Carbs: 9.2 g; Dietary Fiber: 2.9 g; Sugars: 5.9 g; Protein: 1.6 g; Cholesterol: 0 mg; Sodium: 309 mg*

Gooey Veg Risotto

Yield: 4 Servings /Total Time: 35 Minutes/Prep Time: 30 Minutes/Cook Time: 5 Minutes

Ingredients
- 50 g dried mushrooms
- 120 g sliced fresh button mushrooms
- 3 cloves garlic, minced
- 2 shallots, finely chopped
- 2 cups riced cauliflower
- 2 tsp dried sage
- 2 tsp extra virgin olive oil
- ½ cup freshly grated parmesan cheese
- Salt and freshly ground black pepper to taste

Directions
1. In a medium bowl, soak the dried mushrooms with the boiling-hot water and let stand for 20 minutes.
2. Drain the mushrooms and rinse thoroughly until all the grit is removed and slice the mushrooms.
3. Place a saucepan over medium heat and pour in the beef stock.
4. Add the olive oil to a Dutch oven and place on medium heat then stir in the onion, button mushrooms, garlic and the chopped dried mushrooms. Cook for about 3 minutes, stirring constantly so the garlic doesn't burn.

5. Stir in the salt, pepper, sage, and cauliflower rice and cook for another 1 minute.
6. Stir in the parmesan cheese and serve hot. Enjoy!

Nutritional Information per Serving:
Calories: 196; Total Fat: 5 g; Carbs: 9.7 g; Dietary Fiber 7 g; Protein: 8.6 g; Cholesterol: 0 mg; Sodium: 399 mg

Italian Shrimp w/Tomato Gazpacho

Yield: 4 Servings/Total Time: 2 Hour 40 Minutes/Prep Time: 2 hours 10 Minutes/Cook Time: 30 Minutes

Ingredients
- 350 g cooked shrimp, chilled
- 6 large ripe but firm tomatoes, cut into quarters with seeds removed
- 1 red onion, wedged
- 1 red pepper, cut into quarters with core removed
- 2 small cucumbers, chopped
- 2 cloves garlic, peeled and cut into four
- ½ cup Ezekiel bread (crusty) cut into chunks
- 1 tsp fresh tarragon, chopped
- 2 tbsp red-wine vinegar
- 3 tbsp extra virgin olive oil
- Sea salt and freshly ground pepper to taste
- Freshly chopped parsley, to serve
- ½ cup water

Directions
1. Start by setting your oven to 375 degrees. arrange the peppers, onions and tomatoes in a large baking pan. You can use 2 pans if they don't fit in one. Lightly season with salt and pepper and drizzle with 2 tablespoons of olive oil and roast the veggies for half an hour or until they are brown at the edges.
2. Transfer the veggies and any residual juices to your food processor. Add the bread chunks and process until your desired consistency is achieved and transfer to a large bowl.
3. Stir in the vinegar, cucumber and tarragon. If the gazpacho is too thick, stir in some water. Check for seasoning and adjust the salt and pepper as desired. Cover the bowl with cling wrap and chill for a minimum of 2 hours or overnight, for best results.
4. Serve the gazpacho in bowls and top with the shrimp. Drizzle the remaining olive oil in the bowls and garnish with the chopped parsley. Enjoy!

Nutritional Information per Serving:
Calories: 237; Total Fat: 8 g; Carbs: 11.9 g; Dietary Fiber 3 g; Protein: 16 g; Cholesterol: 110 mg; Sodium: 695 mg

Walnut Crusted Salmon

Yield: 4 Servings/Total Time: 20 Minutes/Prep Time: 10 Minutes/Cook Time: 10 Minutes

Ingredients
- 450 g salmon fillets, with skin removed
- 3 tbsp walnuts, finely chopped
- 1 ½ tsp extra virgin olive oil
- 2 ½ tbsp panko breadcrumbs
- ½ tsp raw honey
- 1 tsp fresh rosemary, chopped
- 1 tsp freshly squeezed lemon juice
- ¼- ½ tsp. fresh lemon zest
- 1 clove garlic, minced
- ¼ tsp crushed red pepper
- 2 tsp Dijon mustard
- Sea salt and freshly ground black pepper, to taste

Directions
1. Set your oven to 425 degrees. Line a large baking sheet with parchment paper.
2. In a small bowl, combine the lemon juice, lemon zest, mustard, honey, rosemary, crushed pepper, garlic, salt and pepper.
3. In a separate bowl, combine the walnuts, breadcrumbs and olive oil.
4. Place the salmon fillets on the baking sheet and evenly spread the rosemary mixture on both sides, pressing on it gently. Next sprinkle with the nutty mixture and lightly coat with olive oil cooking spray.
5. Bake for about 10 minutes, or until it flakes easily with a fork. Enjoy!

Nutritional Information per Serving:
Calories: 223; Total Fat: 12 g; Carbs: 4 g; Dietary Fiber 0.8 g; Protein: 16 g; Cholesterol: 62 mg; Sodium: 256 mg

Mediterranean Chicken Keto Style!

Yield: 4 Servings/Total Time: 35 Minutes/Prep Time: 15 Minutes/Cook Time: 20 Minutes

Ingredients

For the Chicken:
- 2 medium boneless chicken breasts
- ½ cup finely chopped almonds
- ¼ cup mayonnaise
- 3 tbsp freshly grated parmesan cheese
- 6 cloves garlic, minced
- 2 cups asparagus, cut into 1 inch pieces
- 1 ½ cups cherry tomatoes, cut in half

For the vinaigrette:
- 1 tbsp extra virgin olive oil
- ½ tsp honey
- 1 tbsp freshly squeezed lemon juice

- 1 ½ cup freshly sliced cremini mushrooms
- 1 tbsp extra virgin olive oil
- Kosher salt and freshly ground black pepper to taste
- Olive oil cooking spray
- A small bunch of fresh dill

- ½ tsp fresh lemon zest
- 1 tbsp feta cheese, crumbled

Directions
1. Start with the vinaigrette by whisking all the ingredients in a small bowl and setting aside.
2. Preheat your oven to 475 degrees and place a large baking pan in the oven.
3. Cut the chicken breasts lengthwise without going all the way through so it looks like a book. Place the chicken breasts, one at a time, between two sheets of plastic wrap and flatten using a mallet until ½ inch thick.
4. Place the flattened chicken pieces in a large bowl and add in two garlic cloves and mayonnaise. Toss well until evenly coated.
5. In another dish combine the cheese, chopped almonds, salt and pepper, then dip the chicken pieces in the cheese until well coated. Shake off any excess coating and arrange on one side of the hot baking pan and spray with olive oil.
6. Mix the remaining veggies and garlic in a large bowl. Season with salt and pepper then spread on the remaining part of the hot pan and lightly spray with olive oil.
7. Roast for 20 minutes or until desired doneness is achieved.
8. Remove from oven and serve on individual plates. Drizzle the chicken and roast veggies with the vinaigrette and garnish with dill. Enjoy!

Nutritional Information per Serving: Calories: 306; Total Fat: 15 g; Carbs: 9.4 g; Dietary Fiber 3 g; Protein: 28 g; Cholesterol: 90 mg; Sodium: 431mg

Creamy Pepper & Cucumber Salad

Yield: 4 Servings/Total Time: 5 Minutes/Prep Time: 5 Minutes

Ingredients
- 1 red onion, sliced
- 3 cucumbers, sliced
- 1 large red pepper, sliced
- 2 tablespoons fresh chopped chives

- 2 tablespoons mayonnaise
- 1/2 cup sour cream
- Salt & black pepper

Directions
1. In a bowl, combine red onion, red pepper and cucumber.
2. In a small bowl, whisk together mayonnaise, sour cream, chives and pepper until well blended; stir into the cucumber salad until well coated; sprinkle with salt and serve.

Nutritional Info per Serving: *Calories: 190; Total Fat: 11.1 g; Carbs: 10.5 g; Dietary Fiber: 0.8 g; Sugars: 2.5 g; Protein: 3.5 g; Cholesterol: 20 mg; Sodium: 251 mg*

Tropical Salad w/Spicy Peanut Sauce

Yield: 2 Servings/Total Time: 5 Minutes/Prep Time: 5 Minutes

Ingredients
Thai sauce
- 1/3 cup natural peanut butter, whipped
- 1 clove garlic, minced
- 1 red pepper flakes

- 1/4 cup low sodium soy sauce
- 1 teaspoon liquid stevia

Salad
- 1 red bell pepper
- 1 red onion
- 1 cucumber
- 1 medium tomato

- 1 avocado
- 1 tablespoon chopped cilantro
- Salt & pepper

Directions
1. In a small bowl, whisk together all sauce ingredients until well blended; cover and refrigerate until ready to serve. Combine all salad ingredients in a bowl; drizzle with sauce and serve topped with cilantro.

Italian Chicken Salad

Yield: 4 Servings/Total Time: 15 Minutes/Prep Time: 15 Minutes
Ingredients
For the Dressing:
- 2 tablespoons red wine vinegar
- ¼ cup olive oil
- 2 teaspoons dried oregano
- 1 teaspoon minced garlic
- 1/4 teaspoon salt

For the Salad:
- 400 g grilled chicken, diced
- 1 Hass avocado, diced
- ½ red onion, sliced
- 1 green pepper, sliced
- 4 tomatoes, diced
- 1 large cucumber, sliced
- ½ cup pitted Kalamata olives
- 200g feta cheese, cubed

Directions
1. In a jar, shake together dressing ingredients until well blended.
2. In a large bowl, mix salad ingredients; pour in the dressing. Toss to coat well and season with salt. Serve with grilled chicken and sprinkled with oregano.

Nutritional Information per Serving:
Calories: 305; Total Fat: 27 g; Carbs: 12 g; Dietary Fiber: 5.4 g; Sugars: 5.8 g; Protein: 10 g; Cholesterol: 44 mg; Sodium: 975 mg

Healthy Island Cabbage Salad

Yield: 2 Servings/Total Time: 15 Minutes/Prep Time: 15 Minutes
Ingredients
- 1/2 head green cabbage, shredded
- 1/3 cup shredded coconut
- 2 tablespoons fresh lemon juice
- 1/4 cup tamari sauce
- 1/4 cup coconut oil
- 3 teaspoons sesame seeds
- 1/2 teaspoon cumin
- 1/2 teaspoon curry powder
- 1/2 teaspoon ginger, dried

Directions
1. In a large bowl, toss together all ingredients; chill for at least 1 hour before serving.

Nutritional Information per Serving:
Calories: 309; Total Fat: 29 g; Carbs: 12 g; Dietary Fiber: 6 g; Sugars: 3 g; Protein: 5 g; Cholesterol: 74 mg; Sodium: 425 mg

Tasty Shrimp & Avocado Salad

Yield: 2 Servings/Total Time: 15 Minutes/Prep Time: 10 Minutes/Cook Time: 5 Minutes
Ingredients
- 2 tablespoons salted butter, melted
- 225 g raw shrimp, peeled & deveined
- 1 large avocado, diced
- 1/2 red onion, minced
- 1 cup diced cherry tomatoes
- 1 tablespoon olive oil
- 1 tablespoon lemon juice
- Handful chopped cilantro
- Pink sea salt & pepper, to taste

Directions
1. In a large bowl, toss together shrimp and melted butter until well coated.
2. Set a large skillet over medium high heat; add the shrimp and cook for about 2 minutes or until seared; transfer to a plate to cool. In a large bowl, mix together the remaining ingredients until well combined; stir in shrimp, salt and pepper and serve.

Nutritional Info per Serving:
Calories: 415; Total Fat: 30.7 g; Carbs: 9.2 g; Dietary Fiber: 7.3 g; Sugars: 2.3 g; Protein: 25.5 g; Cholesterol: 304 mg; Sodium: 1049 mg

Mozzarella & Peach Skewers

Serving Total: 2 servings/Total Time: 5 Minutes/Prep Time: 5 Minutes

Ingredients
- 2 peaches, halved then sliced
- ½ cup mozzarella balls
- 1 cup cherry tomatoes
- 6 fresh basil leaves

Directions
1. Thread the ingredients onto 2 wooden skewers in an alternating fashion. Enjoy!

Nutritional Information per Serving:
Calories: 143; Total Fat: 6 g; Carbs: 12.5 g; Dietary Fiber 3 g; Protein: 0 g; Cholesterol: 20 mg; Sodium: 90 mg

Grilled Beef Salad w/Nutty Dressing

Yield: 3 Servings/Total Time: 15 Minutes/Prep Time: 10 Minutes/Cook Time: 5 Minutes

Ingredients
For the Dressing
- 2 tbsp freshly squeezed orange juice
- 2 tbsp freshly squeezed lemon juice
- 3 tbsp extra-virgin olive oil
- 1/2 tsp Stevia
- 1 tsp. raw apple-cider vinegar
- 4 fresh sliced basil leaves, plus more for garnish
- 1 1/2 tbsp chopped fresh parsley, plus more for garnish
- 1 1/2 tbs. chopped fresh dill, plus sprigs for garnish
- 1/4 cup toasted and chopped macadamia nuts
- Coarse salt

For the Salad
- 300 g grilled beef, sliced/diced
- 1 cup asparagus, trimmed
- 1/2 cup baby carrots, scrubbed
- 1/4 pound green beans, trimmed
- 1/2 large fennel bulb, cut into 1/2-inch slices
- ½ tsp. coarse salt

Directions
1. In a bowl, whisk together the dressing ingredients and season with salt; set aside.
2. Steam veggies in steamer set over a saucepan of boiling water for about 5 minutes or until crisp and tender. Halve the steamed carrots and asparagus spears lengthwise.
3. Arrange the veggies on a serving platter and sprinkle with salt; drizzle with the dressing and garnish with herbs. Top with the grilled beef.

Nutritional Information Per Serving:
Calories: 515; Fat: 35.8 g (61%); Carbs: 13.8 g (9%); Protein: 39.3 g (30%)

Creamy Fish Salad w/Avocado Dressing

Yield: 6 Servings/Prep Time: 10 minutes/Total Time: 10 minutes

Ingredients
Salad:
- 400 g firm white fish fillet
- 200 g spinach
- 80 g cherry tomatoes
- 1 cucumber, sliced
- 1 yellow bell pepper, sliced
- 1 avocado sliced
- 2 to 3 tbsp lemon juice
- 3 tablespoons butter
- 1/2 teaspoon paprika
- 1/2 teaspoon onion powder
- 6 cloves garlic, chopped
- salt & pepper

Dressing:
- 2 tablespoons lemon juice
- 1/3 cup yogurt
- 1 avocado
- 1/8 teaspoon ground sage
- 1/8 teaspoon dried basil
- Stevia

Directions
1. Sprinkle tilapia fillets with onion powder, paprika, salt and pepper; set aside. Arrange the fish fillet in a greased baking pan and top with yellow bell pepper and cherry tomatoes; brush with melted butter and sprinkle with garlic. Bake for about 12 minutes at 400 degrees.
2. In a blender, blend together dried basil, avocado, yogurt, lemon juice and sage until very smooth.
3. Lay spinach on a serving plate and top with tilapia, roasted yellow bell pepper, and cucumber, avocado and roasted cherry tomatoes. Drizzle the salad with fresh lemon juice followed by the dressing. Enjoy!

Nutritional Information per Serving:
Calories: 348; Total Fat: 22 g; Carbs: 12 g; Dietary Fiber: 9 g; Sugars: 3 g; Protein: 23 g; Cholesterol: 74 mg; Sodium: 505 mg

Buffalo Chicken Fingers & Kale Salad

Yield: 4 Servings/Total Time: 25 Minutes/Prep Time: 10 Minutes/Cook Time: 15 Minutes

Ingredients
- 400 g chicken, sliced into strips
- 2 tablespoons fresh lemon juice
- 2 tablespoons hot sauce

- 1 tbsp. crushed almonds
- Pinch of salt & black pepper

Salad
- 4 tablespoons extra virgin olive oil
- 1 pound Lacinato kale, sliced into thin strips
- 1/2 cup roasted almonds

- Pinch of sea salt
- Pinch of pepper

Directions:
1. Prepare salad: Place kale in a bowl and add olive oil; massage olive oil into kale until kale is tender; sprinkle with salt and pepper and toss with toasted almonds.
2. Marinate chicken in fresh lemon juice and salt for a few hours and then coat with crushed almonds; fry in a pan until cooked through and browned. Toss with black pepper and hot sauce and serve with kale salad.

Nutritional Information Per Serving: *Calories: 414; Fat: 26.7 g (60%); Carbs: 11.7 g (10%); Protein: 32.2 g (30%)*

Turkey Meatloaf w/Mushrooms

Yield: 2 Servings/Total Time: 40 Minutes/Prep Time: 15 Minutes/Cook Time: 25 Minutes

Ingredients
- 2 eggs
- 400 g ground turkey
- 1/2 cup chopped onion
- 1/4 cup chopped yellow bell pepper
- 1/4 cup chopped red bell pepper
- 1/2 cup salsa

- 1/4 cup crushed almonds
- A pinch of lemon pepper
- 1 cup button mushrooms, sliced
- 1 tablespoon olive oil
- 1 red onion

Directions
1. Preheat your oven to 350 degrees.
2. In a bowl, mix together bell peppers, crushed almonds, salsa, egg, turkey, onion and lemon pepper until well blended. Roll the mixture to form a loaf and place on a baking sheet lined with foil. Bake for 25 minutes or until the meat loaf is golden brown on the outside.
3. Meanwhile, heat olive oil in a skillet; sauté red onion until fragrant; stir in button mushrooms and cook until tender. Serve the meatloaf topped with sautéed mushrooms for a healthy satisfying meal.

Nutritional Information per Serving: *Calories: 112; Total Fat: 15.1 g; Carbs: 6.1 g; Dietary Fiber: 2.1 g; Sugars: 1.2 g; Protein: 10.3 g; Cholesterol: 73 mg; Sodium: 174 mg*

Chicken Chili w/Avocado and Green Onions

Yields: 8 servings/Prep Time: 10 Minutes /Total Time: 45 Minutes

Ingredients
- 600 g ground chicken
- 3 slices bacon, cut into thin strips
- ½ yellow onion, chopped
- 2 cloves garlic, minced
- 1 green bell pepper, chopped
- 2 celery stalks, chopped
- 1/2 cup sliced baby Bella mushrooms
- 2 tbs. smoked paprika
- 2 tsp dried oregano

- 2 tsp ground cumin
- 2 tbsp chili powder
- 2 cup low-sodium beef broth
- 2 avocados, sliced
- 2 cups sliced green onions
- 1 cup shredded cheddar
- 1 cup sour cream
- A pinch of salt
- A pinch of pepper

Directions
1. Cook bacon in a pot over medium heat until bacon is crisp; remove bacon from the pot and add in onion, mushrooms, celery and pepper. Cook for about 6 minutes and then stir in garlic for about 1 minute. Push the veggies to the side and add in ground chicken. Cook until it is no longer pink. Stir in paprika, oregano, cumin, chili powder, salt and pepper.
2. Cook for about 2 minutes and then stir in broth; simmer for about 15 minutes or until the liquid is evaporated.
3. Ladle the chili into serving bowls and top each serving with reserved bacon, cheese, sour cream avocado and green onions.

Delicious Grilled Tilapia w/Arugula

Yield: 3 Servings/Total Time: 20 Minutes/Prep Time: 10 Minutes/Cook Time: 10 Minutes

Ingredients

- 2 Tilapia fillets
- 4 tbsp extra virgin olive oil, and extra for drizzling
- 2 tbsp. fresh lemon juice
- 2 ounces shaved Parmesan
- 4 ounces caper berries, halved if large
- 1 red chili, thinly sliced
- ¼ medium red onion, thinly sliced
- 1 bunch arugula, tough stems removed
- Kosher salt and pepper
- 1 cup parsley

Directions

1. Preheat your grill on medium high heat.
2. Sprinkle fish with salt and pepper and grill, turning often, for 5-8 minutes or until the fish flakes easily with a fork; transfer to a platter and let rest for at least 10 minutes.
3. In a medium bowl, toss together caper berries, chili, onion, arugula, parsley and parmesan cheese; drizzle with lemon juice and toss to coat well. Season to taste.
4. Drizzle the grilled fish with extra virgin olive oil and season with more salt and pepper. Serve with arugula salad.

Nutritional Information Per Serving: *Calories: 376; Total Fat: 29.1 g; Carbs: 9.8 g; Dietary Fiber: 6.7 g; Sugars: 3.2 g; Protein: 21.5 g; Cholesterol: 0 mg; Sodium: 509 mg*

Baked Mahi Mahi w/Caramelized Onions

Yield: 3 servings/Total Time: 1 Hour/Prep Time: 45 Minutes/Cook Time: 15 Minutes

Ingredients

- 3 Mahi Mahi fillets
- ¼ cup olive oil
- 1 tbsp Dijon mustard
- ¼ cup aged balsamic vinegar
- 2 cups medium sliced white onions
- 100 g goat cheese or your favorite cheese, crumbled
- 2 tbsp butter
- 1 tsp Stevia
- 2 tsp dried rosemary
- Cracked black pepper
- Seasoned salt

Directions

1. Generously season the fillets with the cracked black pepper and seasoned salt then place them in a baking dish in a single layer.
2. In a medium bowl, combine the vinegar, olive oil, rosemary and mustard until well incorporated. Pour this over the filets and coat both sides. Cover the baking dish with cling wrap and transfer to your fridge to marinate for 30 minutes.
3. Meanwhile, melt the butter in a heavy bottomed skillet over medium to low heat and cook the onion slices for 5-10 minutes until soft. Stir in the Stevia and keep cooking until the onions become beautifully caramelized then remove from heat and keep warm.
4. Preheat your grill to medium on one side and high on the other side and oil the grate.
5. Put marinated fish on the high-heat side of the grill and cook for about 8 minutes, flipping once. Move the steaks to the medium-heat side for the remaining 3 minutes and top each fillet with the crumbled cheese and caramelized onions. Close the lid until the cheese becomes gooey.
6. Serve hot. Enjoy!

Nutritional Information Per Serving: *Calories: 476; Total Fat: 36.8 g; Carbs: 9.6 g; Dietary Fiber: 2.1 g; Sugars: 3.8 g; Protein: 32.9 g; Cholesterol: 23 mg; Sodium: 488 mg*

Tangy Chili Steak Lettuce Fajitas

Yield: 4 Servings/Total Time: 25 Minutes/Prep Time: 10 Minutes/Cook Time: 15 Minutes

Ingredients

- 8 lettuce leaves
- 1 large yellow pepper, seeded, sliced
- 1 large red pepper, seeded, sliced
- 1 large red onion, halved, sliced
- 1 tbsp pickled jalapeno chilies, drained, chopped
- 1 tbsp. chopped fresh coriander
- 1/3 cup sour cream
- 500 g lean mutton steak
- ¼ cup freshly squeezed lime juice
- 3 tsp chili powder
- Fresh coriander
- 4 cups freshly squeezed lemonade

Directions

1. In a bowl, combine 2 tablespoons of lime juice, chili, and salt; add steak and toss until well coated. Marinade, covered, for about 10 minutes.
2. In a separate bowl, combine chili, chopped coriander, and sour cream; season and set aside.
3. Place a nonstick frying pan over high heat and spray with canola oil; add steak and cook for about 4 minutes per side or until cooked through. Transfer the cooked steak to a plate and keep warm.
4. In the meantime, preheat chargrill on high.
5. Add onion to a small bowl and spray with oil; toss until well coated and cook, turning occasionally, for about 7 minutes or until charred. Transfer the onions to a bowl and set aside.
6. Spray capsicum with oil and cook, turning occasionally, for about 7 minutes or until charred; add to the bowl with onions.
7. Slice the steak into thin slices and divide the lettuce leaves among serving plates; top with steak, sour cream mixture, onion-capsicum mixture, and sprinkle with chopped coriander. Wrap the lettuce leaves to form rolls and enjoy!

Nutritional Information Per Serving:
Calories: 378; Total Fat: 26.8 g; Carbs: 10.3 g; Dietary Fiber: 9.7 g; Sugars: 3.2 g; Protein: 27.5 g; Cholesterol: 56 mg; Sodium: 447 mg

Keto Turkey Ratatouille

Yield: 4 Servings/Total Time: 35 Minutes/Prep Time: 15 Minutes/Cook Time: 20 Minutes

Ingredients

- 4 tablespoons extra-virgin olive oil
- 450 g boneless turkey cutlet
- 1 cup sliced mushrooms
- 1 sweet red pepper
- 1 medium zucchini
- 1 eggplant
- 1/2 cup tomato puree
- 1 tsp garlic
- 1 tsp leaf basil
- 1/8 tsp salt
- 1/2 teaspoon sweetener
- 1/8 tsp black pepper

Directions

1. Heat a tablespoon of oil in a skillet over medium heat; sprinkle the meat with salt and pepper and sauté for about 3 minutes per side; transfer to a plate and add the remaining oil to the skillet. Sauté red pepper, zucchini and eggplant for about 5 minutes. Stir in garlic, mushrooms, basil, tomato puree, and sweetener. Bring the mixture to a boil and simmer for 5 minutes. Stir in salt and pepper and then stir in the turkey. Cook for about 3 minutes or until the turkey is heated through. Serve hot.

Nutritional Information Per Serving:
Calories: 346; Total Fat: 21.1 g; Carbs: 9.4 g; Dietary Fiber: 8.2 g; Sugars: 3 g; Protein: 17 g; Cholesterol: 87 mg; Sodium: 367 mg

Turkey Roast w/Capers & Creamy Dip

Yield: 4 Servings/Total Time: 55 Minutes/Prep Time: 15 Minutes/Cook Time: 40 Minutes

Ingredients

- 450 g turkey breast
- ¼ cup small capers
- ½ cup cream cheese
- 1 cup sour cream
- 2 tbsp butter
- 1 tbsp tamari sauce
- A pinch of sea salt
- A pinch of pepper

Directions

1. Preheat your oven to 350 degrees.
2. Heat half of the butter in a skillet over medium heat until melted; season turkey with salt and pepper and fry until golden brown. Transfer the turkey to the oven and cook for about 20 minutes or until the internal temperature is 165 degrees. Transfer to a foil and let rest.
3. In a large saucepan, mix the turkey drippings, cream cheese and sour cream; bring to a gentle boil and then simmer until the sauce is thick. Season the sauce with tamari, salt and pepper and remove from heat.
4. Melt the remaining butter in a pan and sauté the capers over high heat until crispy.
5. Serve the turkey meat with the fried capers and creamy sauce. Enjoy!

Nutritional Information Per Serving:
Calories: 498; Total Fat: 34.1 g; Carbs: 7.9 g; Dietary Fiber: 4.7 g; Sugars: 4.3 g; Protein: 39 g; Cholesterol: 134 mg; Sodium: 409 mg

Cheesy Pork Chops w/Chili Verde Dip

Yield: 4 Servings/Total Time: 20 Minutes/Prep Time: 10 minutes/Cook Time: 10 minutes

Ingredients
- 4 pork chops
- 3 tbsp oil (divided)
- 1/4 tsp chili powder
- 1/4 tsp powdered cumin

Chile Verde Sauce
- 1 tbsp oil
- 1/2 tsp. chicken base
- 1/2 cup salsa verde

- 1/4 tsp salt
- 1/8 tsp black pepper
- ½ cup crumbled cheese
- ½ cup chopped cilantro

- 1 clove garlic, minced
- 1/4 cup chopped onion

Directions
1. In a bowl, mix together chopped cilantro, minced garlic and chopped onion; crumble in cheese and set aside.
2. Rub the pork chops with a teaspoon of olive oil and sprinkle with seasoning.
3. Add a tablespoon of oil to a skillet set over medium heat; add in the pork chops and cook for about 3 minutes; flip over to cook the other sides for another 3 minutes.
4. Add the remaining oil to another skillet and sauté garlic and onion for about 1 minute or until fragrant; stir in the chicken base and cook for about 1 minute. Stir in salsa verde along with the pork juices, scraping up the browned bits into the pan. Simmer until the sauce is thickened.
5. To serve, divide the pork chops among serving plates and top with the chili verde sauce. Serve garnished with cilantro and more crumbled cheese. Enjoy!

Nutritional information per Serving: *Calories: 232; Total Fat: 17 g; Carbs: 8 g; Dietary Fiber: 3 g; Sugars: 5 g; Protein: 15 g; Cholesterol: 78 g; Sodium: 352 mg*

Peppered Steak Salad

Yield: 4 Servings/Total Time: 25 Minutes/Prep Time: 10 Minutes/Cook Time: 10 Minutes

Ingredients
- 4 sirloin steaks, trimmed
- 2 tbsp extra virgin olive oil
- 2 tbsp freshly cracked black pepper
- 1 bunch rocket, trimmed

- 2 cups cherry tomatoes
- 4 cups green salad
- olive oil cooking spray

Directions
1. Brush the steak with oil. Place the pepper on a large plate and press the steaks into the pepper until well coated.
2. Preheat the chargrill or barbecue grill on medium high and barbecue the steaks for about 5 minutes per side or until cooked well.
3. Transfer the cooked steaks to a plate and keep warm.
4. In the meantime, brush the tomatoes with oil and barbecue them, turning occasionally, for about 5 minutes or until tender.
5. Arrange the rocket on serving plates and add steaks and tomatoes; serve with green salad.

Nutritional Info per Serving: *Calories: 237; Total Fat: 11.1 g; Carbs: 10.7 g; Dietary Fiber: 8.1 g; Sugars: 2.1 g; Protein: 14.8 g; Cholesterol: 45 mg; Sodium: 35 mg*

Keto Leek Burgers w Butter Green Beans

Yield: 4 Servings/Total Time: 45 Minutes/Prep Time: 15 Minutes/Cook Time: 30 Minutes

Ingredients
For the lamb burgers:
- 600 g minced lamb
- 1/2 cup leeks, finely chopped
- 2 garlic cloves, minced

For the French beans:
- 350 g green beans, trimmed
- 2 garlic cloves, minced
- 1 tbsp shredded parmesan cheese

For the lemon cream:
- Juice of 1 lemon
- 1/2 tsp freshly grated lemon zest

- 2 tbsp coconut oil, divided
- Sea salt and freshly ground pepper, to taste

- 1 tbsp extra virgin olive oil
- Salt and pepper, to taste

- 1/2 cup organic coconut cream

Directions

1. For the cream, use a fork or mini-blender to combine the lemon juice, zest and coconut cream. Serve in a small bowl.
2. For the burgers, add 1 tablespoon of coconut oil to a pan over medium heat and add in the leeks. Cook for about 3 minutes until soft. Transfer the leeks to a bowl and let cool.
3. In a separate bowl, combine the minced lamb, garlic, salt and pepper. Mix in the cooled leeks until well combined. Form 4 patties and set aside.
4. Add the other tablespoon of coconut oil to another skillet over medium-low heat and cook the patties for about 5 minutes on each side, or until done and transfer to a hot plate.
5. For the French beans, start by filling a large bowl with ice and water. This will be used for blanching.
6. Bring water to a boil in a saucepan then add the green beans. Allow to steam for about 5 minutes. Drain and immediately put them in the prepared water bath. As the beans are cooling, melt the butter in a skillet. Stir in the garlic and olive oil.
7. Toss in the green beans and season with salt and pepper. Sprinkle with parmesan and mix well to combine. Serve hot with the burgers and cream. Enjoy!

Nutritional Information Per Serving:
Calories: 620; Total Fat: 46 g; Carbs: 11.7 g; Dietary Fiber: 11 g; Sugars: 7.1 g; Protein: 44.1 g; Cholesterol: 233 mg; Sodium: 368 mg

Lemon Baked Tilapia w/Broccoli

Yield: 2 Servings/Total Time: 20 Minutes/Prep Time: 10 Minutes/Cook Time: 10 Minutes

Ingredients

- 2 medium tilapia fillets
- 3 tbsp butter, melted
- Juice of 1 lemon
- Zest of 1 lemon
- 1 large garlic clove, minced
- 2 tbsp freshly chopped parsley
- Sea salt and freshly cracked black pepper
- 2 cups steamed broccoli

Directions

1. Set your oven to 425 degrees and lightly coat a baking pan with cooking spray then set aside.
2. Combine the melted butter, lemon juice and zest and garlic in a bowl using a fork and set aside.
3. Season the fish fillets generously with salt and pepper and gently place on the prepared baking pan. Brush with the butter mixture and bake for about 10 minutes, or until it easily flakes with a fork.
4. Serve hot with steamed broccoli. Enjoy!

Nutritional Information Per Serving:
Calories: 272; Total Fat: 19.3 g; Carbs: 5.2 g; Dietary Fiber: 8.6 g; Sugars: 2.7 g; Protein: 21.9 g; Cholesterol: 118 mg; Sodium: 417 mg

Turkey Patties w/Garlic Tahini Sauce

Yield: 8 Servings/Total Time: 26 Minutes/Prep Time: 10 Minutes/Cook Time: 16 Minutes

Ingredients

- 450 g ground turkey
- 1/4 teaspoon cayenne pepper
- 3/4 teaspoon ground ginger
- 1 teaspoon dried sage

- 1 1/2 teaspoons salt
- 1 1/2 teaspoons pepper
- 4 cups of green salad for serving

Low Carb Lemon Tahini Sauce

- 4 tablespoons lemon juice
- ½ cup organic tahini
- 1 tablespoon olive oil

- 2 cloves garlic
- ⅓ cup water
- A pinch sea & pepper

Directions

1. Prepare Tahini: in a blender, blend together all ingredients until very smooth. Refrigerate until ready to use.
2. Mix together ground turkey, cayenne pepper, sage, ginger, salt and pepper in a bowl until well blended. Form patties from the mixture and place on a plate.
3. Heat olive oil in a skillet over medium high heat and fry the patties for about 8 minutes per side or until browned on the outside and no longer pink in the middle. Serve the turkey patties with green salad drizzled with lemon tahini.

Nutritional Information per Serving:
Calories: 169; Total Fat: 18.6 g; Carbs: 4.5 g; Dietary Fiber: Sugars: Protein: 22.5 g; Cholesterol: 84 mg; Sodium: 500 mg

Scrumptious Shrimp & Cabbage Stir-Fry

Yield: 4 Servings/Total Time: 30 Minutes/Prep Time: 10 Minutes/Cook Time: 20 Minutes

Ingredients
- 500 g shrimp, diced
- 5 tablespoons olive oil
- 1 cup vegetable broth
- 4 clove garlic, minced
- 2 cups shredded cabbage

- Dash of Chinese 5 Spice
- dash of onion powder
- ½ packet Stevia
- Pinch of salt & pepper
- 2 avocados, diced

Directions:
1. Add olive oil to a pan and sauté garlic; stir in cabbage and broth. Cook over medium heat for a few minutes; transfer cabbage to a plate while still crunchy and stir the remaining ingredients in the pan; stir fry and return cabbage. Cook for about 1-2 minutes. Serve topped with avocado slices.

Nutritional Information per Serving:
Calories: 478; Total Fat: 32.7 g; Carbs: 13.1 g; Dietary Fiber:7.4 ;g Sugars: 5.2 g; Protein: 37.5 g; Cholesterol: 110 mg; Sodium: 430 mg

Lemon Grilled Cod w/Steamed Veggies

Yields: 4 Servings/Total Time: 35 Minutes/Prep Time: 15 Minutes/Cook Time: 20 Minutes

Ingredients
- 450 g cod filets
- 5 tablespoons extra-virgin olive oil
- 2 minced garlic cloves
- 1/8 teaspoon cayenne pepper
- 3 tablespoons fresh lime juice

- 1 ½ teaspoon fresh lemon juice
- ¼ cup freshly squeezed orange juice
- 1/3 cup water
- 1 tablespoon chopped fresh thyme
- 2 tablespoon chopped fresh chives

Healthy Steamed Veggies
- 1 head broccoli
- 2 red bell peppers, sliced into bite-sized lengths

- ¼ cup zucchini, sliced into rounds
- 2 baby carrots, sliced into rounds

Direction
1. Add water in a pot, up to 1 ½ inches from the bottom; set the steamer inside the pot and heat over medium high heat or until the water boils. Add the veggies into the steamer and season with salt and garlic powder. Cover and cook until the veggies are tender.
2. In a bowl, mix together lemon, lime juice, orange, cayenne pepper, extra virgin olive oil, garlic and water. Place fish in a dish and add the marinade, reserving ¼ cup; marinate in the refrigerator for at least 30 minutes. Broil or grill the marinated fish for about 4 minutes per side, basting regularly with the marinade. Serve the grilled fish on a plate with steamed veggies topped with chives, thyme and the reserved marinade.

Nutritional Information per Serving:
Calories: 254; Total Fat: 17.6 g; Carbs: 6.2 g; Dietary Fiber: 9.1 g; Sugars: 3.7 ;g Protein: 18.4 g; Cholesterol:221 mg; Sodium: 335 mg

Whole Turkey Roast w/Avocado Relish

Yield: 8 Servings/Total Time: 1 Hour 40 Minutes/Prep Time: 10 Minutes/Cook Time: 1 Hour 30 Minutes

Ingredients:
- 5 tablespoons extra-virgin olive oil
- 1/4 cup apple cider vinegar
- 2 cloves garlic, minced
- 2 tablespoons minced ginger
- Whole turkey

- 1 cup chopped carrots
- Handful of rosemary
- Pinch of sea salt
- Pinch of pepper

Avocado Relish
- 4 avocados, diced
- 1 seedless grapefruit, cut into segments and discarding the membranes
- 1 small Vidalia onion, minced

- 1 tsp red wine vinegar
- 1 tbsp fresh cilantro, chopped
- 1 tsp liquid Stevia

Directions:
1. Preheat oven to 400 degrees. Place turkey in a baking dish. In a bowl, whisk together olive oil, apple cider vinegar, garlic, and ginger until well combined; pour over the turkey and top with carrots and rosemary. Sprinkle with salt and pepper and Stevia for about 1 ½ hours or until turkey is cooked through.

2. **Prepare Relish:** Combine the avocado, grapefruit segments, onion, honey, vinegar and cilantro and toss well to combine. Next, combine all the spices for the turkey in a shallow bowl then dredge the cutlets in the spice mix. Add the oil to a pan over medium heat and sear the turkey until cooked to desired doneness for about 3-5 minutes on each side.
3. Serve turkey with the avocado relish.

Nutritional Information per Serving:
Calories: 377; Total Fat: 25.4 g; Carbs: 11.6 g; Dietary Fiber: Sugars: 5.9 g; Protein: 28 g; Cholesterol: 108 mg; Sodium: 395 mg

Roast Leg of Lamb w/Olive Salsa

Yield: 8 Servings/Total Time: 1 Hour 45 Minutes/Prep Time: 15 Minutes/Cook Time: 1 Hour 30 Minutes

Ingredients
- 1 kg leg of lamb
- 2 tbsp balsamic vinegar
- 1 red onions, each cut into 6 wedges
- 3 garlic cloves, sliced
- 3 cups hot lamb stock
- 2 tbsp fresh lemon zest
- 8 good sprigs thyme
- ½ cup red wine
- 5 tbsp extra-virgin olive oil

Chili Olive Salsa
- 2 large tomatoes, finely chopped
- 4 avocados, diced
- 1 cup olives, finely chopped
- 1 bird's eye chili, finely chopped
- Juice of 1 lemon
- ½ cup parsley, finely chopped

Directions
1. **Make salsa:** mix chopped tomato, avocado, olives, chili, lemon juice, and parsley in a large bowl.
2. With a knife, make slits all over lamb and push a garlic slice into each.
3. Mix lemon zest, wine, 3 tablespoons of olive oil, thyme and pepper in a freezer bag and add in the lamb, seal and refrigerate for about 4 hours or overnight.
4. Preheat oven to 450 degrees; place the remaining thyme in the bottom of the roasting tin. Remove lamb from the marinade and place it over thyme in the tin; roast for about 20 minutes, turn over and roast for 15 minutes more or until cooked through.
5. In the meantime, strain the marinade through a fine mesh into a pan and cook for about 20 minutes or until stock is reduced by two thirds; set aside.
6. Transfer lamb to a cutting board and wrap in foil. Place onions in a bowl and set aside.
7. Place the roasting pan over low heat and add in balsamic vinegar and a splash of stock; cook, scraping all the bits from the base and add to the jug with gravy.

Nutritional Information per Serving:
Calories: 459; Total Fat: 31.8 g; Carbs: 15. 1 g; Dietary Fiber: Sugars: Protein: 30 g; Cholesterol: 97 mg; Sodium: 467 mg

Broiled Scallops w/Coconut Spinach

Yield: 4 Servings/Prep Time: 11 Minutes

Ingredients
- 800 g pounds scallops
- 3 tablespoons melted butter
- 2 tablespoons lemon juice
- 1 tablespoon garlic salt

Garlic Creamed Sautéed Spinach
- 2 tablespoons melted butter
- 4 cloves garlic, thinly sliced
- 4 cups fresh spinach, rinsed
- 1 cup coconut cream
- 1 teaspoon lemon juice
- Sea salt & pepper

Directions
1. Prepare spinach: Melt butter in a skillet and sauté garlic until fragrant. Stir in spinach, lemon juice and coconut cream and cook for about 3 minutes. Stir in salt and pepper and remove from heat.
2. Preheat your broiler. Place scallops in a baking pan and drizzle with melted butter, lime juice and garlic salt. Broil for about 8 minutes or until golden. Serve hot with extra melted butter.

Nutritional Information per Serving:
Calories: 537; Total Fat: 36.8 g; Carbs: 13.4 g; Dietary Fiber: 7.3 g; Sugars: 5.9 g; Protein: 37.7 g; Cholesterol: 122 mg; Sodium: 432 mg

Keto Turkey w/Veggies & Cream Sauce

Yield: 6 Servings/Total Time: 55 Minutes/Prep Time: 15 Minutes/Cook Time: 40 Minutes

Ingredients
- 500 g turkey breast
- ½ cup sliced zucchini
- ½ cup sliced carrots
- ½ cup sliced red pepper
- 1 cup cream cheese
- 2 cups sour cream
- 2 tbsp butter
- 1 tbsp tamari sauce
- A pinch of sea salt
- A pinch of pepper

Directions
1. Preheat your oven to 350 degrees.
2. Heat half of the butter in a skillet over medium heat until melted; season turkey with salt and pepper and fry until golden brown. Transfer the turkey to the oven and cook for about 20 minutes together with the veggies or until the internal temperature of the turkey is 165 degrees. Transfer to foil and let rest.
3. In a large saucepan, mix the turkey drippings, cream cheese and sour cream; bring to a gentle boil and then simmer until the sauce is thick. Season the sauce with tamari, salt and pepper and remove from heat.
4. Serve the turkey meat with the roast veggies and creamy sauce. Enjoy!

Nutritional Information per Serving:
Calories: 498; Total Fat: 34. 1g; Carbs: 7.9 g; Dietary Fiber: 8 g; Sugars:3 g; Protein: 39 g; Cholesterol: 187 mg; Sodium: 364 mg

Baked Halibut w/Green Salad

Yield: 12 Servings/Prep Time: 12 Minutes

Ingredients
- 800 g skinless halibut fillet
- 1 cup chopped green onions
- 4 tablespoons lemon juice
- 3 tablespoons mayonnaise
- 1 tablespoon butter, softened
- 2 tablespoons parmesan cheese
- 1 dash hot pepper sauce
- 1/4 teaspoon salt
- 2 cups chopped romaine lettuce
- 2 carrots, diced
- 2 cucumbers, diced
- 6 cups baby spinach
- 1 tablespoon olive oil
- 1 tablespoon balsamic vinegar

Directions
1. Make the salad: in a large bowl, mix together cucumbers, lettuce, carrots, spinach, olive oil, vinegar, salt and pepper; toss to coat well and chill until ready to serve.
2. Preheat your oven broiler and grease baking dish with oil.
3. In a large bowl, mix together green onions, lemon juice, mayonnaise, butter, parmesan cheese, hot pepper sauce and salt until well combined.
4. Place the halibut fillet in the baking dish and broil for 8 minutes or until it flakes easily with fork. Remove from oven and spread with the butter mixture. Return to oven and broil for 2 minutes more. Serve with salad.

Nutritional Information per Serving:
Calories: 401; Total Fat: 28.9 g; Carbs: 6.5 g; Dietary Fiber: 9.3 g; Sugars: Protein: 28.3 g; Cholesterol: 211 mg; Sodium: 312 mg

Mexican Turkey Wraps

Yield: 6 Servings/Total Time: 25 Minutes/Prep Time: 5 Minutes/Cook Time: 20 Minutes

Ingredients
- 450 g ground turkey
- 1 red bell pepper, diced
- 3/4 cup Mexican blend cheese, shredded
- 1 tsp sweet paprika
- 1 tsp dried oregano
- 1 tbsp olive oil
- 1 tsp onion powder
- 1 tsp ground cumin
- 6 butter lettuce leaves
- 1 cup sour cream
- Handful chopped cilantro

Directions
1. Heat oil in a skillet until hot, but not smoky; sauté onion for about a minute and then add ground turkey; cook until browned. Stir in paprika, red bell pepper, oregano and cumin and cook until the peppers are tender. Stir in shredded cheese and cook until melted. Remove the pan from heat and then stir in cilantro.

2. Divide the turkey mixture among lettuce leaves and roll to form wraps. Serve the wraps with sour cream.

Nutritional Information per Serving:

Calories: 242; Total Fat: 16.3 g; Carbs: 9.3 g; Dietary Fiber: 5 g; Sugars: 3.8 g; Protein: 19.9 g; Cholesterol: 215 mg; Sodium: 439 mg

Fried Salmon w/Creamy Mushrooms

Yield: 6 Servings/Prep Time: 10 Minutes

Ingredients

- ¼ teaspoon dried oregano
- ¼ teaspoon finely chopped basil
- ¼ teaspoon dried thyme
- ¼ teaspoon ground white pepper
- 2 teaspoons sea salt
- ¼ teaspoon onion powder
- ¼ teaspoon ground cayenne pepper
- ¼ teaspoon ground sweet paprika
- 1 1/2 pounds tilapia fillet, skin and bones removed
- 2 tablespoons extra virgin olive oil
- 4 cups sliced white mushrooms
- 4 tablespoons butter
- 2 red onions, chopped
- 1 cup cream cheese

Directions

1. Combine oregano, basil, thyme, white pepper, salt, onion powder, cayenne pepper, and paprika in a small bowl.
2. Brush fish with half of oil and sprinkle with the spice mixture. Drizzle with the remaining oil and cook fish in a skillet set over high heat until blackened and flakes easily with a fork. Add butter to a skillet over medium heat and sauté red onion until fragrant; stir in mushrooms and fry for about 5 minutes or until browned. Stir in cream cheese and then season with salt and pepper. Cook for about 10 minutes or until liquid is reduced to half.
3. Serve fish with creamed mushrooms.

Nutritional Information per Serving:

Calories: 365; Total Fat: 25.8 g; Carbs: 7.2 g; Dietary Fiber: 4 g; Sugars: 3 g; Protein: 28.1 g; Cholesterol: 191 mg; Sodium: 269 mg

Teriyaki Fish w/Fried Zucchini

Yield: 2 Serving/Prep Time: 15 Minutes

Ingredients

- 350 g salmon fillet
- 2 tablespoons teriyaki sauce (low-sodium)
- 2 tablespoon sesame seeds
- 2 tablespoons canola oil
- 4 scallions, chopped
- 2 small zucchinis, thinly sliced

Directions

1. Mix fish with 5 tablespoons of teriyaki sauce in a zip-lock bag and marinate for at least 20 minutes.
2. In a skillet set over medium heat, toast sesame seeds; set aside. Drain the marinated fish and discard the marinade.
3. Add fish to the skillet and cook for about 5 minutes; remove fish from skillet and keep warm.
4. Add oil, scallions and zucchini to the skillet and sauté for about 4 minutes or until browned.
5. Stir in the remaining teriyaki sauce and sprinkle with toasted sesame seeds; serve with fish.

Nutritional Information per Serving:

Calories: 582; Total Fat: 35.7 g; Carbs: 11.6 g; Dietary Fiber: 6.1 g; Sugars: 4.2 g; Protein: 35.3 g; Cholesterol: 90 mg; Sodium: 398 mg

Steamed Spring Veggies w/Grilled Chicken

Yield: 8 Servings/Total Time: 1 Hour 40 Minutes/Prep Time: 10 Minutes/Cook Time: 1 Hour 30 Minutes

Ingredients

- Whole chicken
- 5 tablespoons olive oil
- 3 heads garlic, cut in half across
- 3 brown onions, cut into wedges
- 1 cup cauliflower
- 4 cups broccoli
- 1 cup green beans
- 1 pouch cheese sauce
- 2 tbsp. chicken seasoning blend: Mix together ½ tsp each of crushed dried rosemary, paprika, dry mustard powder, garlic powder, ground dried thyme, ground black pepper, 1 tsp dried basil, 1 ½ tsp sea salt, ¼ tsp celery seeds, ¼ tsp dried parsley, 1/8 tsp each of cayenne pepper, ground cumin, and chicken bouillon granules.

Directions

1. Preheat your oven to 350 degrees.
2. In an ovenproof roasting pan, combine garlic and onion; sprinkle with olive oil.
3. Rub the chicken seasoning blend into the chicken and place it on top of a bed of garlic and onion; bake for about 90 minutes or until cooked through.
4. Place the beans in a steamer and add cauliflower and broccoli; steam for about 10 minutes or until tender.
5. Serve the chicken and steamed veggies on a plate; heat the cheese sauce and pour over the veggies. Enjoy!

Nutritional Information per Serving:
Calories: 665; Total Fat: 46.6 g; Carbs: 12.4 g; Dietary Fiber: 8.5 g; Sugars:5 g; Protein: 34.7 g; Cholesterol: 254 mg; Sodium: 578 mg

BBQ Salmon Salad

Yield: 4 Servings/Prep Time: 15 Minutes
Ingredients

- 500 g Atlantic salmon fillets, with skin on
- 2 tablespoons extra-virgin olive oil
- 1 bunch roughly chopped lemon thyme
- 1/2 cup finely chopped dill leaves
- 2 tbsp drained and chopped capers
- 2 fresh lemons, juiced
- 2 garlic cloves, finely chopped
- A pinch of sea salt
- 1 cup baby spinach
- 1 cup diced lettuce
- 1 cup diced carrots
- 1 cup diced cucumbers
- 2 tablespoons lemon juice
- 1 tablespoon olive oil

Directions

1. In a bowl, mix lettuce, spinach, cucumber, carrots, red onions, olive oil, lemon juice, salt and pepper; toss to mix well and refrigerate until ready to serve.
2. In a large jug, mix together lemon thyme, dill, capers, 1/3 cup lemon juice, garlic, extra virgin olive oil, sea salt and pepper.
3. Arrange salmon fillets, in a single layer, in a ceramic dish and pour half the marinade over fillets. Turn over and pour over the remaining marinade. Refrigerate, covered, overnight.
4. Remove the fish from the refrigerator at least 30 minutes before cooking.
5. Grease barbecue plate and heat on medium high. Barbecue the marinated fish, skin side down, for about 3 minutes. Turn and continue barbecuing, basting occasionally with the marinade, for 6 minutes more or until cooked through.
6. Serve fish with spinach salad garnished with lemon wedges.

Nutritional Information per Serving:
Calories: 432; Total Fat: 26.8 g; Carbs: 13.2 g; Dietary Fiber:6.8 g; Sugars: 3.2 g; Protein: 37 g; Cholesterol: 23 mg; Sodium: 443 mg

Minty Baked Salmon Salad

Yield: 2 Serving/Total Time: 35 Minutes/Prep Time: 15 Minutes/Cook Time: 20 Minutes
Ingredients

- 300 g salmon fillet
- 2 tablespoon olive oil
- 2 red onions, thinly sliced
- 1 cucumber, sliced
- 2 radishes, thinly sliced
- ½ cup baby spinach
- 1 cup mixed salad leaves
- ½ cup chopped parsley

The dressing:

- 1 tbsp rice vinegar
- 1 tablespoon olive oil
- 1 tbsp natural yogurt
- 1 tsp mayonnaise
- 1 tbsp finely chopped mint leaves
- salt and black pepper

Directions

1. Preheat your oven to 400 degrees.
2. Place the fillet on a baking tray and drizzle with olive oil; bake in the preheated oven for about 15 minutes or until cooked through; remove from oven and keep warm.
3. In a bowl, mix together rice wine vinegar, yogurt, oil, mayonnaise, mint, salt and pepper; let stand for at least 5 minutes for flavors to blend.
4. Arrange salad leaves and spinach on a plate and top with red onions, cucumber, radishes, and parsley. Flake the fish and place onto the salad; drizzle with the mint dressing and serve.

Nutritional Information per Serving:
Calories: 258; Total Fat: 23.9 g; Carbs: 11.9 g; Dietary Fiber: 8.6 g; Sugars: 4 g; Protein: 31 g; Cholesterol: 12 mg; Sodium: 367 mg

Chicken Curry Salad w/Avocado

Yield: 2 Servings/Total Time: 10 Minutes/Prep Time: 10 Minutes

Ingredients
- 1/2 cup mashed garlic and avocado, at room temperature
- 1 tsp apple-cider vinegar
- ½ lemon, juiced
- 2 tsp powdered turmeric
- 1 tsp powdered ginger
- ¼ tsp sea salt
- 2 cups chicken curry leftovers
- 2 tablespoons olive oil
- ¼ cup chopped red onion
- 2 tbsp chopped parsley
- 2 tbsp golden raisins

Directions
1. In a bowl, mix together lemon juice, half of olive oil, apple cider vinegar, avocado mash, ginger, turmeric and sea salt until well blended.
2. Add chicken breasts, raisins, and red onion; stir to mix well.
3. Garnish with chopped parsley and serve.

Nutritional Information per Serving:
Calories: 595; Total Fat: 21.3 g; Carbs: 10.5 g; Dietary Fiber: 8 g; Sugars: 9.1 g; Protein: 22.7 g; Cholesterol: 0 mg; Sodium: 340 mg

Grilled Snapper w/Fried Cabbage

Yield: 4 Servings/Total Time: 35 Minutes/Prep Time: 20 Minutes/Cook Time: 15 Minutes

Ingredients
- 4 (150 g each) snapper fillets, skin removed
- 3 tablespoons olive oil
- 1 garlic clove, crushed
- 2 cm piece fresh ginger, peeled, grated
- 2 tbsp reduced-salt soy sauce
- 1 tbsp sweet chili sauce
- 2 tbsp sweet rice wine
- 1 lemon, sliced
- 2 green onions, thinly sliced
- 4 cups shredded cabbage
- 1 tablespoon butter
- 1 cup cream cheese

Directions
1. Preheat your oven to 450 degrees.
2. In a small bowl, combine olive oil, garlic, ginger, soy sauce, sweet chili sauce, and rice wine; whisk to mix well.
3. Cut 4-40 cm lengths of the foil and place one fillet in the center of each foil; spoon over the marinade and top with the lemon slices and onions.
4. Fold the foil edges and seal to form parcels; place them on a baking tray and bake for about 20 minutes or until the fish is cooked through.
5. In the meantime, heat butter in a skillet; sauté onion and garlic. Stir in cabbage and sauté for about 3 minutes. Stir in creamed cheese and season with salt and pepper.
6. Transfer the fish to serving bowls and drizzle with any cooking juices; serve with creamed fried cabbage.

Nutritional Information per Serving:
Calories: 508; Total Fat: 35.1 g; Carbs: 9.5 g; Dietary Fiber: 6 g; Sugars: 3 g; Protein: 32.4 g; Cholesterol: 120 mg; Sodium: 512 mg

Keto Ground Chicken Tacos with Salsa

Yield: 4 Serving/Total Time: 35 Minutes/Prep Time: 10 Minutes/Cook Time: 25 Minutes

Ingredients
- 500 grams ground chicken
- 5 tablespoons olive oil
- 2 clove garlic, minced
- 2 red onions, minced
- 8 butter lettuce leaves
- A pinch of cayenne pepper
- Fresh chopped cilantro
- Pinch of dried oregano
- Dash of onion powder
- Dash of garlic powder
- Pinch of salt & pepper

Directions:
1. Fry chicken in olive oil until browned; add garlic, onion and spices, and water and simmer for about 5-10 minutes. Season with salt and serve taco style in butter lettuce or with a side of salsa.

Nutritional Information per Serving:
Calories: 294; Total Fat: 26.3 g; Carbs: 2.8 g; Dietary Fiber: 5 g; Sugars:1.9 g; Protein: 20.6 g; Cholesterol: 0 mg; Sodium: 230 mg

Tasty Citrus Chicken w/Butter Mushrooms

Yield: 4 Servings/Total Time: 40 Minutes/Prep Time: 10 Minutes/Cook Time: 30 Minutes

Ingredients

- 500 g chicken breast
- 1 red onion, minced
- Juice of ½ lemon
- Pinch of lemon zest
- Pinch of saffron
- Pinch of ground coriander
- Pinch of ginger
- Pinch of salt & pepper
- Lemon slices
- 2 cups sliced white mushrooms
- 4 tablespoons butter
- 2 red onion, chopped

Directions:

1. Soak saffron in fresh lemon juice; crush into paste and then add dry spices.
2. Dip in chicken and rub remaining spices into chicken; sprinkle with salt and pepper and wrap in foil; place in baking dish and cover with lemon slices and saffron . Bake in a 350 degrees oven for about 20-30 minutes or until chicken is cooked through.
3. Add butter to a skillet over medium heat and sauté red onion until fragrant; stir in mushrooms and cook for about 6 minutes or until tender. Season with salt and pepper. Serve the fish over the mushrooms.

Nutritional Information per Serving: *Calories: 222; Total Fat: 21.6 g; Carbs: 7.6 g; Dietary Fiber: 5 g; Sugars:4.7 g; Protein: 21.4 g; Cholesterol: 35 mg; Sodium: 403 mg*

Grilled Pork w/Caraway Cabbage

Yield: 4 Servings/Total Time: 25 Minutes/Prep Time: 15 Minutes/Cook Time: 8 Minutes

Ingredients

- 100g leftover grilled pork
- 1 1/4 tbsp butter
- 1 cup green cabbage, chopped
- 1/2 tsp celery seeds
- 1 tsp caraway seeds
- A pinch of salt & black pepper

Directions

1. Cook cabbage in boiling water for 90 seconds and then drain; return to heat and add butter, celery, caraway seed and salt. Cook until butter is melted; stir in salt and pepper. Serve hot with pork.

Nutritional Information Per Serving: *Calories: 375; Total Fat: 26.2 g; Carbs: 8.1 g; Dietary Fiber: 7 g; Sugars: 2 g; Protein: 27.6 g; Cholesterol: 67 mg; Sodium: 380 mg*

Yummy Caramelized Onion Pork Chops

Yield: 6 Servings/Total Time: 45 Minutes/Prep Time: 5 Minutes/Cook Time: 40 Minutes

Ingredients

- 4 tablespoon vegetable oil
- 2 cups sliced sweet onions
- 2 lb. pork loin chops
- 3 teaspoons seasoning salt
- 2 teaspoons ground black pepper
- 1 onion, cut into strips
- 1 cup water
- 2 cups chopped green beans, steamed
- 3 avocados, diced

Directions

1. Season the chops with salt and pepper; heat oil in a skillet over medium heat and brown the chops for about 5 minutes per side. Stir in onions and water and simmer, covered, for about 20 minutes.
2. Stir and continue cooking for 10 minutes or until the liquid is reduced.
3. Meanwhile, add the remaining oil to another skillet set over medium-low heat; add in onions and cook, stirring, for about 10 minutes or until caramelized.
4. Serve the chops with caramelized onions and steamed green beans topped with avocado slices. Enjoy!

Nutritional Information Per Serving: *Calories: 387; Total Fat: 18.6 g; Carbs: 10.4 g; Dietary Fiber: 4.3 g; Sugars:3 g; Protein: 17.9 g; Cholesterol: 88 mg; Sodium: 398 mg*

Keto Salmon Burger w/Fried Cabbage & Creamy Sauce

Yield: 6 Servings/Total Time: 40 Minutes/Prep Time: 10 Minutes/Cook Time: 30 Minutes

Ingredients

Burger patties

- 1 tbsp butter
- 1 tbsp olive oil
- 3 lb. ground salmon
- 100g feta cheese, crumbled
- 1 egg
- Handful chopped parsley
- 1 tsp salt
- ¼ tsp black pepper

Sauce
- 2 tbsp tomato paste
- ¾ cup heavy whipping cream

Fried green cabbage
- 2 tablespoons butter
- 4 cups shredded green cabbage

- Handful chopped parsley
- salt and pepper

- salt and pepper

Directions
1. In a large bowl, mix burger ingredients until well blended; form eight patties from the mixture.
2. Heat olive oil and butter in a pan and fry the patties for about 10 minutes per side or until golden browned. Stir the whipping cream and tomato sauce in the patties and simmer for about 5 minutes. Stir in salt and pepper and sprinkle with chopped parsley.
3. Prepare cabbage: Heat butter in a skillet over medium heat; sauté the cabbage for about 15 minutes or until golden brown on the edges. Season with salt and pepper. Serve cabbage in serving bowls and top each with burgers and the sauce. Enjoy!

Nutritional Information Per Serving:
Calories: 436; Total Fat: 31 g; Carbs: 7.8 g; Dietary Fiber: 5.5 g; Sugars: 8 g; Protein: 24.4 g; Cholesterol: 58 mg; Sodium: 393 mg

Turkey Patties w/Pesto

Yield: 4 Servings/Total Time: 20 Minutes/Prep Time: 10 Minutes/Cook Time: 10 Minutes

Ingredients
- 500 g ground turkey
- 1/2 cup crushed almonds
- 1 teaspoon minced onion

Low Carb Lemon Pesto
- 1 tablespoon fresh lemon juice
- 2 tablespoons lemon zest, chopped
- 1/2 cup grated parmesan cheese
- 5 cloves garlic, chopped

- 1 tablespoon red pepper flakes
- 1 tablespoon garlic powder
- 2 eggs

- 1/4 cup pine nuts
- 1/4 cup extra virgin olive oil
- 2 cups basil leaves, packed
- Pinch of salt & pepper

Directions
1. Prepare pesto: blend together all ingredients in a blender until very smooth; refrigerate until ready to use.
2. Preheat your grill to high.
3. In a bowl, mix together all ingredients until well combined; form four large patties from the mixture and cook on the grill for about 5 minutes per side until cooked through.

Nutritional Information Per Serving:
Calories: 297; Total Fat: 17 g; Carbs: 8 g; Dietary Fiber: 2 g; Sugars:1.7 g; Protein: 16.3 g; Cholesterol: 0 mg; Sodium: 523 mg

Pork Roast w/Steamed Asparagus & Avocado

Yield: 8 Servings Total Time: 1 Hour 30 Minutes/Prep Time: 15 Minutes /Cook Time: 1 Hour 5 Minutes

Ingredients
- 1 pork loin roast, boneless, trimmed and tied with kitchen string
- 6 tbsp olive oil
- 2 tbsp chopped garlic
- 2 tsp salt

- 1 tsp pepper
- 1 tbsp chopped fresh thyme
- 1 tbsp chopped fresh rosemary
- 500 g asparagus, steamed
- 2 medium avocados, diced

Directions
1. In a small bowl, stir together thyme, rosemary, garlic, salt and pepper and rub the mixture over the pork.
2. Light one side of your grill and heat to 400 degrees, leaving the other side unlit; place the pork on the lit side and cover; grill for about 10 minutes per side or until browned.
3. Transfer the pork to the unlit side and cover; grill for about 45 minutes or until internal temperature reads 150 degrees. Remove from heat and let stand for about 10 minutes before slicing. Serve pork hot with avocado slices and steamed asparagus.

Nutritional Information Per Serving:
Calories: 541; Total Fat: 37.5 g; Carbs: 12.2 g; Dietary Fiber: 9 g; Sugars 0.7 g; Protein: 27.5 g; Cholesterol: 68 mg; Sodium: 388 mg

Grilled Tuna w/Tomato Salad

Yields: 4 Servings/Total Time: 19 Minutes/Prep Time: 15 Minutes/Cook Time: 4 Minutes

Ingredients
- 4 tablespoons extra-virgin olive oil
- 3 scallions, thinly sliced
- 1 tablespoon fresh lemon juice
- 1/4 cup fresh tarragon leaves
- 2 avocados, diced
- 2 cups heirloom tomatoes, cored, diced
- Sea salt
- 4 (8 ounce) tuna steaks

Directions
1. In a bowl, mix together three-quarters of the oil, scallions, lemon juice, tarragon, tomatoes, avocado, and salt; set aside.
2. Lightly grease the grill grates with oil and heat to medium. Drizzle tuna with the remaining oil and then season with salt and grill for about 4 minutes or until cooked through. Serve tuna with bean salad.

Nutritional Information Per Serving:
Calories: 427; Total Fat: 29 g; Carbs: 12.3 g; Dietary Fiber: 4.5 g; Sugars:1.8 g; Protein: 31.2 g; Cholesterol: 0 mg; Sodium: 290 mg

Simple Spiced Pork Chops w/Steamed Veggies

Yield: 4 Servings/Prep Time: 5 minutes/Cook Time: 10 minutes/Total Time: 15 minutes

Ingredients

Pork Chops
- 4 (100 g each) boneless pork chops
- ½ tsp garlic paste
- 1 tsp lemon juice
- 1 tbsp Worcestershire sauce
- 4 tbsp olive oil
- ½ tsp ground cumin
- ½ tsp onion powder
- 1 tsp paprika
- A pinch of salt
- A pinch of pepper

Steamed Veggies
- 1 head broccoli, cut into florets
- 1 head cauliflower, cut into florets
- 2 zucchinis, halved and sliced
- 5 ginger-lemongrass tea bass
- A two inch ginger root, chopped roughly
- Freshly ground pepper to taste

Directions
1. **Prepare the Veggies:** Add the water to the bottom of a pot or steamer and add the chopped ginger. Cover and bring to a boil. Once the water boils add the tea bags together with the pepper and a pinch of salt. Turn off the heat, cover the pot and let the tea steep for 5 minutes. Turn on the heat again and bring to a boil. In the steamer basket or colander, place the broccoli and cauliflower at the bottom. Season with salt and pepper and top with zucchini. Cover and steam for 10 minutes until tender but not mushy.
2. For the Pork Chops: Combine all ingredients in a bag; add in the pork chops and massage the marinade around the meat. Remove the meat and discard the remaining marinade; season the meat with salt and pepper. Cook the pork on a preheated grill for about 5 minutes per side or until cooked through.
3. Serve the pork chops with the steamed veggies. Enjoy!

Nutritional Information Per Serving:
Calories: 275; Total Fat: 17.3 g; Carbs: 5.9 g; Dietary Fiber: 11 g; Sugars:3.7 g; Protein: 24.1 g; Cholesterol: 11 mg; Sodium: 299 mg

Steamed Bass w/Spring Veggies

Yields: 2 Servings/Total Time: 30 Minutes/Prep Time: 15 Minutes/Cook Time: 15 Minutes

Ingredients
- 2 fillets of striped bass
- 2 tablespoons extra-virgin olive oil
- 1/2 lemon, juiced
- 1 fennel bulb, sliced
- 1/4 medium onion, sliced
- 1/4 cup chopped parsley
- 1 tablespoon capers, rinsed
- 1/2 teaspoon sea salt
- Chopped parsley and olive oil, for garnish

Directions
1. Add lemon juice, fennel and onion to a pan and cover with 1-inch water; bring the mixture to a gentle boil. Lower heat and simmer for about 5 minutes.
2. Add seasoned fish and sprinkle with parsley and capers; cover and simmer for about 10 minutes.
3. Transfer to a serving bowl and drizzle with extra-virgin olive oil and top with more parsley to serve.

Nutritional Information Per Serving:
Calories: 325; Total Fat: 14.6 g; Carbs: 10.1 g; Dietary Fiber: 5 g; Sugars:2 g; Protein: 20.9 g; Cholesterol: 0 mg; Sodium: 201 mg

Sesame Crusted Salmon with Cucumber Salad

Yield: 3 Servings/Total Time: 30 Minutes + Chilling Time/Prep Time: 5 Minutes/Cook Time: 25 Minutes

Ingredients

- 1 teaspoon dried chili flakes
- 1 teaspoon minced ginger root
- 2 tablespoon rice vinegar
- 2 tablespoons olive oil
- 2 tablespoons soy sauce
- 1 large clove garlic, minced
- 3 skinless wild salmon fillets
- 3 tablespoons white sesame seeds
- Handful chopped lettuce
- 2 carrots, chopped
- 2 cucumbers, diced
- 6 plum tomatoes
- 2 red onions, chopped
- 2 tablespoons olive oil
- 1 tablespoon vinegar
- Salt and pepper

Directions

1. In a zip-lock bag, mix chili flakes, ginger, oil, rice vinegar, soy sauce, and garlic; add salmon filets in the bag and refrigerate for at least 1 hour.
2. Preheat oven to 375 degrees.
3. Sprinkle sesame seeds onto a plate into a single layer; arrange the filets, face down, in the sesame seeds and transfer the fish onto a baking sheet lined with baking paper; sprinkle with more sesame seeds and bake for about 20 minutes. Switch the oven to broil and cook the fish for about 5 minutes or until sesame seeds are toasted. In a bowl, toss together lettuce, carrots, cucumbers, onion, tomatoes, oil, vinegar, salt and pepper until well coated. Serve fish with salad.

Nutritional Information Per Serving:

Calories: 248; Total Fat: 21.8 g; Carbs: 6.5 g; Dietary Fiber: 10.1 g; Sugars: 3 g; Protein: 35.2 g; Cholesterol: 100 mg; Sodium: 520 mg

Crock Pot Shrimp Curry with Sweet & Sour Kale

Yield: 8 Servings/Total Time: 2 Hours 5 Minutes/Prep Time: 5 Minutes/Cook Time: 2 Hours

Ingredients

- 900 g shrimp, with shells
- 2 cups water
- 3 cups light coconut milk
- ½ cup Thai red curry sauce
- ¼ cup cilantro
- 2½ teaspoon lemon garlic seasoning

Sweet & Sour Steamed Kale

- 10 cups fresh kale leaves & stems – chopped into bite sized pieces
- 2 tbsp apple cider vinegar
- 4 tbsp sesame oil
- 1 tbsp minced fresh ginger
- 4 drops liquid Stevia extract
- sea salt

Directions

1. In a slow cooker, combine water, coconut milk, red curry paste, cilantro, and lemon garlic seasoning; stir to mix well and cook on high for about 2 hours. Add shrimp and continue cooking for another 30 minutes or until shrimp is cooked through.
2. **Prepare Kale:** In a small skillet set over medium low heat, heat 1 tablespoon sesame oil; add ginger and cook for about 1 minute. Remove the pan from heat and let cool slightly. When cool, add Stevia, apple cider vinegar, and salt; stir to mix well and transfer to a small dish. Set aside. In a steamer set over a large saucepan of boiling water, steam kale leaves and stems for about 4 minutes or until tender. In a mixing bowl, combine the steamed kale, ginger mixture and the remaining sesame oil; toss well. Adjust seasoning and serve warm.
3. Serve shrimp over steamed kale.

Nutritional Information Per Serving:

Calories: 501; Total Fat: 26.4 g; Carbs: 11.4 g; Dietary Fiber: 8 g; Sugars:8 g; Protein: 25 g; Cholesterol: 0 mg; Sodium: 393 mg

Beef Stir Fry w/Cabbage

Yield: 4 Servings/Total Time: 20 Minutes/Prep Time: 10 Minutes/Cook Time: 10 Minutes

Ingredients:

- 550 g grass-fed flank steak, thinly sliced strips
- 1 tablespoon rice wine
- 2 teaspoons balsamic vinegar
- Pinch of sea salt
- pinch of pepper
- 4 tablespoons extra-virgin olive oil
- 1 large yellow onion, thinly chopped
- 1/2 red bell pepper, thinly sliced
- 1/2 green bell pepper, thinly sliced
- 1 tablespoon toasted sesame seeds
- 1 teaspoon crushed red pepper flakes
- 3 cups cabbage
- 1 avocado, diced

Directions:
1. Place meat in a bowl; stir in rice wine and vinegar, sea salt and pepper. Toss to coat well.
2. Heat a tablespoon of olive oil in a pan set over medium high heat; add meat and cook for about 2 minutes or until meat is browned; stir for another 2 minutes and then remove from heat. Heat the remaining oil in the pan and sauté onions for about 2 minutes or until caramelized; stir in pepper and cook for 2 minutes more. Stir in cabbage and cook for 2 minutes; return meat to pan and stir in sesame seeds and red pepper flakes. Serve hot topped with diced avocado!

Nutritional Information Per Serving: *Calories: 459; Total Fat: 30 g; Carbs: 12.6 g; Dietary Fiber: 10 g; Sugars:8 g; Protein: 35.3 g; Cholesterol: 224 mg; Sodium: 550 mg*

Ginger Spiced Chicken w/Veggies

Yields: 4 Servings/Total Time: 15 Minutes/Prep Time: 10 Minutes/Cook Time: 5 Minutes

Ingredients
- 2 cup skinless, boneless, and cooked chicken breast meat, diced
- ¼ cup extra-virgin olive and canola oil mixture
- 1 teaspoon powdered ginger
- ½ red onion, sliced
- 2 cloves garlic, minced
- ½ bell pepper, sliced
- 1 cup thinly sliced carrots
- ½ cup finely chopped celery
- 1 cup chicken broth (not salted)

Directions
1. Add the oil mixture to a skillet set over medium heat; sauté onion and garlic until translucent. Stir in the remaining ingredients and simmer for a few minutes or until the veggies are tender.

Nutritional Information Per Serving: *Calories: 425; Total Fat: 21.1 g; Carbs: 6.5 g; Dietary Fiber: 7 g; Sugars:2.9 g; Protein: 32.8 g; Cholesterol: 0 mg; Sodium: 295 mg*

Coconut Crusted Cod with Salsa

Yield: 4 Servings/Total Time: 25 Minutes/Prep Time: 15 Minutes/Cook Time: 10 Minutes

Ingredients
- 600 g cod fillet, sliced into small strips
- 2 tbsp coconut oil
- 1/2 cup finely shredded coconut
- ½ cup coconut milk
- 2 tablespoons coconut flour
- ¼ tsp sea salt
- 1 ½ tsp. ginger powder

For the salsa
- 1 large tomato, finely chopped
- 1 tablespoon capers, finely chopped
- 1 bird's eye chili, finely chopped
- Juice of ¼ lemon
- ½ cup parsley, finely chopped

Directions
1. Make salsa: mix chopped tomato, capers, chili, lemon juice, and parsley in a large bowl.
2. Rinse and debone the fish fillets.
3. In a bowl, combine ginger powder, coconut flour and sea salt; set aside.
4. Add coconut milk to another bowl and set aside.
5. Add shredded coconut to another bowl and set aside.
6. Dip the fillets into coconut milk, then into the flour mixture, back into the milk, and finally into shredded coconut.
7. Add coconut oil to a skillet set over high heat; when melted and hot, add the fish fillets and cook for about 5 minutes per side or until cooked through.
8. Serve the cooked cod fillets with salsa.

Nutritional Information Per Serving: *Calories: 364; Total Fat: 25.7 g; Carbs: 7.3 g; Dietary Fiber: 6 g; Sugars:4.3 g; Protein: 27.9 g; Cholesterol: 24 mg; Sodium: 370 mg*

Sesame Salmon Burgers with Creamy Keto Pesto

Yield: 6 Servings/Total Time: 30 Minutes/Prep Time: 15 Minutes /Cook Time: 15 Minutes

Ingredients
- 100 g salmon, skin removed
- 1 tbsp coconut flour
- 4 large eggs
- ¼ cup toasted sesame seeds
- ¼ cup finely chopped scallions (only green and white parts)
- 1 tsp. fresh ginger, peeled and minced
- 1 clove garlic, pressed
- 1 tbsp vinegar
- 4 tbsp toasted sesame oil
- 1 tbsp coconut oil, for frying

Creamy Low Carb Pesto

- 4 cups fresh basil
- 2 1/2 tablespoons olive oil
- 2 tablespoons butter
- ½ cup grated parmesan cheese
- 1/3 cup cashews
- 1/3 cup walnuts
- 5 large cloves garlic, chopped
- Pinch of salt & black pepper

Directions

1. **Prepare Pesto:** Combine all pesto ingredients in a food processor and process until very smooth. Rinse the fish and pat dry with paper towel; cut into ¼-inch cubes.
2. Mix together eggs, sesame seeds, scallions, ginger, garlic, vinegar, oil, and salmon in a large bowl.
3. Stir in the coconut flour and form small patties.
4. Add coconut oil to a skillet set over medium high heat to melt. Add the patties and cook for about 6 minutes per side or until golden brown.
5. Place the cooked patties onto a plate lined with paper towels to drain. Serve with the creamy low carb pesto. Enjoy!

Nutritional Information Per Serving:
Calories: 636; Total Fat: 33.7 g; Carbs: 11.3 g; Dietary Fiber: 7.8 g; Sugars:6 g; Protein: 40.6 g; Cholesterol: 115 mg; Sodium: 556 mg

Minty Cucumber Metabolism Booster

Serving Total: 16 servings/Total Time: 5 Minutes/Prep Time: 5 Minutes/Cook Time: 0 Minutes

Ingredients

- 1 cucumber, thinly sliced
- A handful fresh mint leaves
- 2 quarts drinking water
- 1 Scoop protein powder

Directions

1. Place the mint leaves at the bottom of your water pitcher and gently mash up by pressing down on them using a wooden spoon.
2. Pour in the water and stir in the cucumber slices and protein powder.
3. Chill in the fridge for a minimum of one hour. Enjoy!

Nutritional Information per Serving:
Calories: 100; Total Fat: 3 g; Carbs: 0 g; Dietary Fiber 2.7 g; Protein: 11 g; Cholesterol: 0 mg; Sodium: 6 mg

Decadent Date-Prosciutto Wraps

Serving Total: 6-8 servings/Total Time: 10 Minutes/Prep Time: 10 Minutes/Cook Time: 0 Minutes

Ingredients

- 8 dates, pitted
- 8 thin prosciutto slices
- Pink Sea salt and freshly ground black pepper, to taste

Directions

1. Wrap the thin prosciutto slices around the dates, one at a time. Sprinkle with sea salt and pepper and serve on a large platter. Enjoy!

Nutritional Information per Serving:
Calories: 35; Total Fat: 1 g; Carbs: 6 g; Dietary Fiber 1 g; Protein: 2 g; Cholesterol: 6 mg; Sodium: 190 mg

Tangerine-Almond Ricotta

Serving Total: 2 servings/Total Time: 5 Minutes/Prep Time: 5 Minutes

Ingredients

- 1 tangerine, peeled and cut into segments
- 2/3 cup ricotta, preferably part-skim
- 2 tsp almonds, toasted and chopped

Directions

1. Add the yogurt to a bowl and stir in the figs.
2. Divide the ricotta between two bowls and top with the chopped nuts and the tangerines. Enjoy!

Nutritional Information per Serving:
Calories: 166; Total Fat: 8.2 g; Carbs: 11 g; Dietary Fiber 4 g; Protein: 13 g; Cholesterol: 19 mg; Sodium: 83 mg

Figs n' Yogurt

Serving Total: 4 servings/Total Time: 3 Minutes/Prep Time: 3 Minutes

Ingredients
- 12 dried figs, thinly sliced
- 2 cups plain Greek yogurt
- 4 tsp raw honey

Directions
1. Add the yogurt to a bowl and stir in the figs.
2. Gently drizzle the honey using the narrow end of a spoon to create a swirl. Enjoy!

Nutritional Information per Serving:
Calories: 207 Total Fat: 3 g; Carbs: 38.5 g; Dietary Fiber 2 g; Protein: 2 g; Cholesterol: 10 mg; Sodium: 116 mg

Clementine-Berry Smoothie

Serving Total: 3 servings/Total Time: 5Minutes/Prep Time: 5 Minutes

Ingredients
- 1 clementine, peeled
- 1 cup strawberries
- ¼ cup grape tomatoes
- 1 small bunch fresh basil leaves, stems removed
- 1 tbsp chia seeds
- 2 tbsp goji berries
- 1 cup crushed ice
- 1 cup water

Directions
1. Combine all the ingredients in your blender and pulse until desired consistency is achieved. Enjoy!

Nutritional Information per Serving:
Calories: 118 Total Fat: 4 g; Carbs: 11 g; Dietary Fiber 3.5 g; Protein: 4 g; Cholesterol: 0 mg; Sodium: 12 mg

Chocolate Trail Mix

Serving Total: 10 servings/Total Time: 1 Hour 35 Minutes/Prep Time: 5 Minutes/Cook Time: 1 Hour 30 Minutes

Ingredients
- 1 cup cashew nuts, halved
- 2 cups walnuts, halved
- 1/3 cup coconut sugar
- 1 cup large coconut flakes, unsweetened
- 2 tbsp extra virgin coconut oil
- 120 g dried banana slices, unsweetened
- ½ cup dark chocolate chips
- 1 tsp pure vanilla extract

Directions
1. Combine all the ingredients apart from the chocolate and banana slices in a crockpot and set the heat to high for 1 hour. Stir a couple of times to ensure nothing burns. 45 minutes into cook time, lower the heat to medium.
2. After one hour, cook on low for about 30 minutes or until well browned.
3. Transfer the trail mix to a parchment paper lined tray and spread out to cool.
4. Transfer to a tin and toss in the chocolate chips and banana slices. Cover with an airtight lid.
5. Enjoy!

Nutritional Information per Serving:
Calories: 250 Total Fat: 16; Carbs: 18.6 g; Dietary Fiber 3.5 g; Protein: 4 g; Cholesterol: 22 mg; Sodium: 185 mg

Spiced Pineapple Detox Smoothie

Serving Total: 3 servings/Total Time: 5 Minutes/Prep Time: 5 Minutes

Ingredients
- 1 cup organic pineapple chunks
- 1 small yellow squash, chopped
- ½ inch fresh ginger root, sliced
- 1 tbsp hemp seeds
- 15 g kumquats
- 350 ml Maple water
- 1 cup crushed ice

Directions
1. Combine all the ingredients in your blender and pulse until smooth.
2. Serve in a tall glass. Enjoy!

Nutritional Information per Serving:
Calories: 92; Total Fat: 2 g; Carbs: 12.5 g; Dietary Fiber 2 g; Protein: 4 g; Cholesterol: 0 mg; Sodium: 12 mg

Almond-Blueberry Smoothie

Serving Total: 3 servings/Total Time: 5 Minutes/Prep Time: 5 Minutes

Ingredients

- 1 cup blueberries
- 1 cup unsweetened almond milk
- 2 tablespoons almond butter
- ½ inch fresh ginger root, sliced
- 1 scoop protein powder

Directions

1. Combine all the ingredients in your blender and pulse until smooth.
2. Serve in a tall glass. Enjoy!

Nutritional Information per Serving:

Calories: 215; Total Fat: 9 g; Carbs: 7 g; Dietary Fiber 3 g; Protein: 23 g; Cholesterol: 9 mg; Sodium: 182 mg

Healthy Green Smoothie

Serving Total: 3 servings/Total Time: 5 Minutes/Prep Time: 5 Minutes

Ingredients

- 1 cup spinach
- ½ cup kale
- 1 ½ cups almond milk
- 2 tablespoons pumpkin seeds
- 1 mango
- 1 cup crushed ice

Directions

1. Combine all the ingredients in your blender and pulse until smooth.
2. Serve in a tall glass. Enjoy!

Nutritional Information per Serving:

Calories: 187; Total Fat: 8 g; Carbs: 9.6 g; Dietary Fiber 8 g; Protein: 7 g; Cholesterol: 0 mg; Sodium: 180 mg

Mixed Berry Heaven

Serving Total: 3 servings/Total Time: 5 Minutes/Prep Time: 5 Minutes

Ingredients

- 2 cups frozen mixed berries
- 1 tablespoon coconut cream
- 1 ½ cups coconut milk
- 2 tablespoon chia seeds
- 1 cup crushed ice

Directions

1. Combine all the ingredients in your blender and pulse until smooth.
2. Serve in a tall glass. Enjoy!

Nutritional Information per Serving:

Calories: 256; Total Fat: 16 g; Carbs: 8.4 g; Dietary Fiber 4 g; Protein: 11 g; Cholesterol: 16 mg; Sodium: 129 mg

Filling 'Salad' Smoothie

Serving Total: 3 servings/Total Time: 5 Minutes/Prep Time: 5 Minutes

Ingredients

- ½ cup sliced cucumber
- ½ cup avocado
- ¼ cup celery
- 1 teaspoon chia seeds
- 1 cup spinach
- 1 tablespoon almond butter
- 1 ½ cup almond milk
- 1 cup crushed ice

Directions

1. Combine all the ingredients in your blender and pulse until smooth.
2. Serve in a tall glass. Enjoy!

Nutritional Information per Serving:

Calories: 365; Total Fat: 25 g; Carbs: 5 g; Dietary Fiber 6 g; Protein: 21 g; Cholesterol: 0 mg; Sodium: 113 mg

Keto Air Fryer

Ham, Spinach & Egg in a Cup

Serves: 8/Prep Time: 35 mins
Ingredients
- 2 tablespoons olive oil
- 2 tablespoons unsalted butter, melted
- 2 pounds fresh baby spinach
- 8 eggs
- 8 teaspoons milk
- 14-ounce ham, sliced
- Salt and black pepper, to taste

Directions
1. Preheat the Air fryer to 360 degrees and grease 8 ramekins with butter.
2. Heat oil in a skillet on medium heat and add spinach.
3. Cook for about 3 minutes and drain the liquid completely from the spinach.
4. Divide the spinach into prepared ramekins and layer with ham slices.
5. Crack 1 egg over ham slices into each ramekin and drizzle evenly with milk.
6. Sprinkle with salt and black pepper and bake for about 20 minutes.

Nutrition: Calories: 228 Carbs: 6.6g Fats: 15.6g Proteins: 17.2g Sodium: 821mg Sugar: 1.1g

Eggs with Sausage & Bacon

Serves: 2/Prep Time: 25 mins
Ingredients
- 4 chicken sausages
- 4 bacon slices
- 2 eggs
- Salt and freshly ground black pepper, to taste

Directions
1. Preheat the Air fryer to 330 degrees and place sausages and bacon slices in an Air fryer basket.
2. Cook for about 10 minutes and lightly grease 2 ramekins.
3. Crack 1 egg in each prepared ramekin and season with salt and black pepper.
4. Cook for about 10 minutes and divide sausages and bacon slices in serving plates.

Nutrition Calories: 245 Carbs: 5.7g Fats: 15.8g Proteins: 17.8g Sodium: 480mg Sugar: 0.7g

Eggless Spinach & Bacon Quiche

Serves: 8/Prep Time: 20 mins
Ingredients
- 1 cup fresh spinach, chopped
- 4 slices of bacon, cooked and chopped
- ½ cup mozzarella cheese, shredded
- 4 tablespoons milk
- 4 dashes Tabasco sauce
- 1 cup Parmesan cheese, shredded
- Salt and freshly ground black pepper, to taste

Directions
1. Preheat the Air fryer to 325 degrees and grease a baking dish.
2. Put all the ingredients in a bowl and mix well.
3. Transfer the mixture into prepared baking dish and cook for about 8 minutes.
4. Dish out and serve.

Nutrition Calories: 72 Carbs: 0.9g Fats: 5.2g Proteins: 5.5g Sodium: 271mg Sugar: 0.4g

Pumpkin Pancakes

Serves: 8/Prep Time: 20 mins
Ingredients
- 2 squares puff pastry
- 6 tablespoons pumpkin filling
- 2 small eggs, beaten
- ¼ teaspoon cinnamon

Directions
1. Preheat the Air fryer to 360 degrees and roll out a square of puff pastry.
2. Layer it with pumpkin pie filling, leaving about ¼-inch space around the edges.
3. Cut it up into equal sized square pieces and cover the gaps with beaten egg.
4. Arrange the squares into a baking dish and cook for about 12 minutes.
5. Sprinkle some cinnamon and serve.

Nutrition Calories: 51 Carbs: 5g Fats: 2.5g Proteins: 2.4g Sodium: 48mg Sugar: 0.5g

Herbed Duck Legs

Serves: 4/Prep Time: 40 mins
Ingredients
- 1 tablespoon fresh thyme, chopped
- 2 garlic cloves, minced
- 1 tablespoon fresh parsley, chopped
- 2 teaspoons five spice powder
- 4 duck legs
- Salt and freshly ground black pepper, to taste

Directions
1. Preheat the Air fryer to 345 degrees.
2. Mix together herbs, garlic, five spice powder, salt and black pepper in a bowl.
3. Rub the duck legs generously with garlic mixture.
4. Cook the duck legs in Air fryer for about 25 minutes.
5. Reset the Air fryer to 390 degrees and cook for about 5 more minutes.

Nutrition Calories: 138 Carbs: 1g Fats: 4.5g Proteins: 22g Sodium: 82mg Sugar: 0g

Spicy Green Crusted Chicken

Serves: 6/Prep Time: 40 mins
Ingredients
- 6 teaspoons oregano
- 6 eggs, beaten
- 6 teaspoons parsley
- 4 teaspoons thyme
- Salt and freshly ground black pepper, to taste
- 4 teaspoons paprika
- 1-pound chicken pieces

Directions
1. Preheat the air fryer to 360 degrees and grease Air fryer basket.
2. Place eggs in a bowl and mix together remaining ingredients in another bowl except chicken pieces.
3. Dip the chicken in eggs and then coat with the dry mixture.
4. Arrange half of the chicken pieces in Air fryer basket and cook for about 20 minutes.
5. Repeat with the remaining mixture and serve.

Nutrition Calories: 218 Carbs: 2.6g Fats: 10.4g Proteins: 27.9g Sodium: 128mg Sugar: 0.6g

Creamy Chicken Tenders

Serves: 8/Prep Time: 20 mins
Ingredients
- 2 pounds chicken tenders
- 4 tablespoons olive oil
- 1 cup cream
- Salt and freshly ground black pepper, to taste
- 1 cup feta cheese

Directions
1. Season chicken tenders with salt and black pepper in a bowl.
2. Preheat the air fryer to 340 degrees.
3. Put the chicken tenderloins and oil in Air fryer basket.
4. Top with feta cheese and cream and cook for about 15 minutes.
5. Reset the Air fryer to 390 degrees and cook for about 5 more minutes.

Nutrition Calories: 344 Carbs: 1.7g Fats: 21.1g Proteins: 35.7g Sodium: 317mg Sugar: 1.4g

Mirin Coated Chicken Kebabs

Serves: 8/Prep Time: 15 mins
Ingredients
- 2 tablespoons mirin
- ½ cup light soy sauce
- 2 teaspoons garlic salt
- 8 (4-ounce) skinless, boneless chicken thighs, cubed into 1-inch size
- 2 teaspoons sugar
- 10 scallions, cut into 1-inch pieces lengthwise

Directions
1. Mix together mirin, soy sauce, garlic salt and sugar in a large baking dish.
2. Thread green onions and chicken onto pre-soaked wooden skewers.
3. Place the skewers into the baking dish and coat with marinade generously.
4. Cover and refrigerate for about 1 hour.
5. Preheat the air fryer to 355 degrees and place the skewers in a fryer basket.
6. Cook for about 12 minutes and dish out.

Nutrition: Calories: 161 Carbs: 5.6g Fats: 4.1g Proteins: 26g Sodium: 370mg Sugar: 3.2g

Honey Glazed Chicken Drumsticks

Serves: 8/Prep Time: 22 mins

Ingredients

- 2 tablespoons honey
- 2 tablespoons fresh thyme, minced
- 8 chicken drumsticks
- ½ cup Dijon mustard
- 4 tablespoons olive oil
- 1 tablespoon fresh rosemary, minced
- Salt and freshly ground black pepper, to taste

Directions

1. Put all the ingredients in a bowl except the drumsticks and mix well.
2. Add drumsticks and coat generously with the mixture.
3. Cover and refrigerate to marinate for overnight.
4. Preheat the Air fryer at 325 degrees and place the drumsticks in air fryer basket.
5. Cook for about 12 minutes and reset the air fryer to 355 degrees.
6. Cook for about 10 minutes and serve.

Nutrition Calories: 301 Carbs: 6g Fats: 19.7g Proteins: 4.5g Sodium: 316mg Sugar: 4.5g

Honey Mustard Cheesy Meatballs

Serves: 8/Prep Time: 15 mins

Ingredients

- 2 onions, chopped
- 1-pound ground beef
- 2 teaspoons garlic paste
- 4 tablespoons fresh basil, chopped
- 2 teaspoons honey
- Salt and freshly ground black pepper, to taste
- 2 teaspoons mustard
- 2 tablespoons cheddar cheese, grated

Directions

1. Preheat the Air fryer to 385 degrees.
2. Put all the ingredients in a bowl and mix until well combined.
3. Make equal-sized balls from the mixture and arrange the balls in an Air fryer basket.
4. Cook for about 15 minutes and serve with fresh greens.

Nutrition Calories: 134 Carbs: 4.6g Fats: 4.4g Proteins: 18.2g Sodium: 50mg Sugar: 2.7

Spicy Lamb Kebabs

Serves: 6/Prep Time: 30 mins

Ingredients

- 4 eggs, beaten
- 1 cup pistachios, chopped
- 2 teaspoons chili flakes
- 1-pound ground lamb
- 4 garlic cloves, minced
- 2 tablespoons fresh lemon juice
- 4 tablespoons plain flour
- 2 teaspoons cumin seeds
- 1 teaspoon fennel seeds
- 2 teaspoons dried mint
- 2 teaspoons salt
- Olive oil
- 1 teaspoon coriander seeds
- 4 tablespoons chopped flat-leaf parsley
- 1 teaspoon freshly ground black pepper

Directions

1. Mix together lamb, pistachios, eggs, lemon juice, chili flakes, flour, cumin seeds, fennel seeds, coriander seeds, mint, parsley, salt and pepper in a bowl.
2. Mold handfuls of the lamb mixture to form sausages around skewers.
3. Grease lamb skewers with olive oil.
4. Preheat the air fryer to 355 degrees F and place the lamb skewer in air fryer basket.
5. Cook for about 8 minutes on each side and dish out.

Nutrition Calories: 284 Carbs: 8.4g Fats: 15.8g Proteins: 27.9g Sodium: 932mg Sugar: 1.1g

Simple Beef Burgers

Serves: 6/Prep Time: 25 mins

Ingredients

- 2 pounds ground beef
- 12 cheddar cheese slices
- 6 tablespoons tomato ketchup
- Salt and freshly ground black pepper, to taste
- 12 dinner rolls

Directions

1. Preheat the Air fryer to 390 degrees F and grease an Air fryer pan.
2. Mix together beef, salt and black pepper in a bowl and make small patties from mixture.
3. Place half of patties onto the prepared pan and cook for about 12 minutes.
4. Top each patty with 1 cheese slice and arrange patties between rolls.
5. Top with ketchup and repeat with the remaining batch.

Nutrition Calories: 537 Carbs: 7.6g Fats: 28.3g Proteins: 60.6g Sodium: 636mg Sugar: 4.2g

Garlicy Lamb Chops

Serves: 8/Prep Time: 45 mins

Ingredients
- 2 bulbs garlic
- 2 tablespoons fresh thyme, chopped
- Salt and freshly ground black pepper, to taste
- 16 (4-ounce) lamb chops

- ½ cup olive oil, divided
- 2 tablespoons fresh oregano, chopped

Directions
1. Preheat the Air fryer to 385 degrees and coat the garlic bulbs with olive oil.
2. Place the garlic bulb in an Air fryer basket and cook for about 12 minutes.
3. Mix together remaining oil, herbs, salt and black pepper in a large bowl.
4. Coat the chops with about 2 tablespoons of the herb mixture.
5. Place 4 chops in Air fryer basket with 1 garlic bulb.
6. Cook for about 5 minutes and repeat with the remaining lamb chops.
7. Squeeze the garlic bulb in remaining herb mixture and mix until well combined.
8. Serve lamb chops with herb mixture.

Nutrition: Calories: 433 Carbs: 1.9g Fats: 25.2g Proteins: 47.9g Sodium: 130mg Sugar: 0.1g

Simple Steak

Serves: 4/Prep Time: 15 mins
Ingredients
- 1-pound quality cut steaks
- Salt and freshly ground black pepper, to taste

Directions
1. Preheat the Air fryer to 385 degrees and rub the steaks evenly with salt and pepper.
2. Place the steak in air fryer basket and cook for about 15 minutes until crispy.

Nutrition Calories: 301 Carbs: 0g Fats: 25.1g Proteins: 19.1g Sodium: 65mg Sugar: 0g

Almond Crusted Rack of Lamb

Serves: 3/Prep Time: 50 mins
Ingredients
- 1 garlic clove, minced
- 1-pound rack of lamb
- ½ tablespoon olive oil
- Salt and freshly ground black pepper, to taste

- 1 egg
- 3-ounce almonds, finely chopped
- 1 tablespoon breadcrumbs
- ½ tablespoon fresh rosemary, chopped

Directions
1. Mix together oil, garlic, salt and black pepper in a bowl.
2. Coat the rack of lamb evenly with oil mixture.
3. Beat the egg in a shallow dish and mix together breadcrumbs, almonds and rosemary in another shallow dish.
4. Dip the rack of lamb in egg and coat with almond mixture.
5. Preheat the Air fryer to 230 degrees and place the rack of lamb in an Air fryer basket.
6. Cook for about 30 minutes and reset the Air fryer to 390 degrees.
7. Cook for about 5 more minutes and dish out.

Nutrition: Calories: 471 Carbs: 8.5g Fats: 31.6g Proteins: 39g Sodium: 145mg Sugar: 1.5g

Leg of Lamb

Serves: 6/Prep Time: 1 hour 15 mins
Ingredients
- 2 tablespoons olive oil
- 2 pounds leg of lamb
- Salt and freshly ground black pepper, to taste

- 3 fresh thyme sprigs
- 3 fresh rosemary sprigs

Directions
1. Preheat the Air fryer to 310 degrees.
2. Coat the leg of lamb with olive oil and season with salt and black pepper.
3. Cover the leg of lamb with herb sprigs and place the chops in an Air fryer basket.
4. Cook for about 1 hour 15 minutes and dish out.

Nutrition Calories: 325 Carbs: 0.7g Fats: 15.9g Proteins: 42.5g Sodium: 115mg Sugar: 0g

Buttered Scallops

Serves: 4/Prep Time: 15 mins
Ingredients
- 2 tablespoons butter, melted
- 1½ pounds sea scallops

- 1 tablespoon fresh thyme, minced
- Salt and freshly ground black pepper, to taste

Directions
1. Preheat the Air fryer to 385 degrees and grease Air fryer basket.

2. Put all the ingredients in a large bowl and toss to coat well.
3. Arrange half of the scallops in an Air fryer basket and cook for about 5 minutes.
4. Repeat with the remaining scallops and serve.
Nutrition Calories: 202 Carbs: 4.4g Fats: 7.1g Proteins: 28.7g Sodium: 315mg Sugar: 0g

Spicy Shrimp

Serves: 4/Prep Time: 15 mins
Ingredients
- 2 tablespoons olive oil
- 1 pound tiger shrimp
- 1 teaspoon old bay seasoning
- ½ teaspoon cayenne pepper
- ½ teaspoon smoked paprika
- Salt, to taste

Directions
1. Preheat the Air fryer to 390 degrees and grease an Air fryer basket.
2. Put all the ingredients in a large bowl and mix until well combined.
3. Place the shrimp in an Air fryer basket and cook for about 5 minutes.
Nutrition Calories: 174 Carbs: 0.3g Fats: 8.3g Proteins: 23.8g Sodium: 414mg Sugar: 0.1g

Bacon Wrapped Shrimp

Serves: 8/Prep Time: 20 mins
Ingredients
- 2 pounds bacon
- 2½ pounds tiger shrimp, peeled and deveined

Directions
1. Wrap each shrimp with a slice of bacon and refrigerate for about 20 minutes.
2. Preheat the Air fryer to 385 degrees and arrange half of the shrimps in Air fryer basket.
3. Cook for about 7 minutes and repeat with the remaining shrimps.
Nutrition Calories: 492 Carbs: 7.2g Fats: 35g Proteins: 41.8g Sodium: 1979mg Sugar: 0g

Cajun Spiced Salmon

Serves: 4/Prep Time: 15 mins
Ingredients
- 4 tablespoons Cajun seasoning
- 4 salmon steaks

Directions
1. Rub the salmon evenly with the Cajun seasoning and keep aside for about 10 minutes.
2. Preheat the Air fryer to 385 degrees and arrange the salmon steaks on the grill pan.
3. Cook for about 8 minutes, flipping once in the middle way.
Nutrition Calories: 225 Carbs: 0g Fats: 10.5g Proteins: 33.1g Sodium: 225mg Sugar: 0g

Tangy Salmon

Serves: 4/Prep Time: 15 mins
Ingredients
- 2 tablespoons Cajun seasoning
- 4 (7-ounce) (¾-inch thick) salmon fillets
- 2 tablespoons fresh lemon juice

Directions
1. Preheat the air fryer to 360 degrees and season evenly with Cajun seasoning.
2. Place the fish in an Air fryer, grill pan, skin-side up and cook for about 7 minutes.
3. Drizzle with lemon juice and serve
Nutrition Calories: 264 Carbs: 0.2g Fats: 12.3g Proteins: 38.6g Sodium: 164mg Sugar: 0.2g

Haddock with Cheese Sauce

Serves: 4/Prep Time: 15 mins
Ingredients
- 2 tablespoons olive oil
- 4 (6-ounce) haddock fillets
- Salt and freshly ground black pepper, to taste
- 6 tablespoons fresh basil, chopped
- 4 tablespoons pine nuts
- 2 tablespoons Parmesan cheese, grated

Directions
1. Preheat the Air fryer at 360 degrees.
2. Coat the haddock fillets evenly with oil and season with salt and black pepper.
3. Place the fish fillets in an Air fryer basket and cook for about 8 minutes.
4. Meanwhile, add remaining ingredients in a food processor and pulse until smooth.
5. Transfer the fish fillets in serving plates and top with cheese sauce to serve.
Nutrition Calories: 354 Carbs: 1.7g Fats: 17.5g Proteins: 47g Sodium: 278mg Sugar: 0.3g

Fudge Brownies Muffins

Serves: 6/Prep Time: 20 mins
Ingredients
- 1/8 cup walnuts, chopped
- ½ package Betty Crocker fudge brownie mix
- 1 egg
- 1 teaspoon water
- ¼ cup vegetable oil

Directions
1. Preheat the Air fryer to 300 degrees F and grease 6 muffin tins.
2. Mix together all the ingredients in a bowl and transfer the mixture into prepared muffin molds.
3. Cook for about 10 minutes and remove the muffin molds from Air fryer.
4. Keep on wire rack to cool for about 10 minutes.

Nutrition Calories: 115 Carbs: 2.2g Fats: 11.4g Proteins: 1.6g Sodium: 18mg Sugar: 1.3g

Keto Mushroom Frittata

Yield: 2 servings/Total Time: 20 minutes/Prep time: 8 minutes/Cook time: 12 minutes
Ingredients
- 4 egg whites
- 1/3 cup mushrooms, sliced
- 1 large tomato, sliced
- ¼ cup finely chopped chives
- 2 tbsp. milk
- 2 tbsp. coconut oil
- Salt and freshly ground black pepper to taste

Directions
1. Start by setting your air fryer to 320° F.
2. Beat the egg whites and milk in a large bowl. Add in the fresh ingredients and mix until well combined then set the bowl aside.
3. Grease your air fryer's frying pan with coconut oil and transfer the egg mixture into the pan.
4. Cook in the fryer for about 10 -12 minutes until done.

Nutritional Information per Serving:
Calories: 360; Total Fat: 28.6 g; Carbs: 10.8 g; Dietary Fiber: 2.7 g; Sugars: 7.7 g; Protein: 4.6 g; Cholesterol: 0 mg; Sodium: 177 mg

Keto Spinach Scramble

Yield: 1 serving/Total Time: 38 minutes/Prep time: 8 minutes/Cook time: 30 minutes
Ingredients
- 3 egg whites
- 1 cup (packed) spinach
- 1 onion, chopped
- 2 tbsp. extra virgin olive oil
- ½ tsp. onion powder
- ½ tsp. garlic powder
- 1 tsp. turmeric powder
- Ground pepper to taste

Directions
1. Preheat your air fryer to 350° F.
2. Beat the egg whites and oil in a large bowl, add in the fresh ingredients and mix until well combined, then set the bowl aside.
3. Lightly grease your air fryer's frying pan and transfer the egg mixture into the pan.
4. Cook in the fryer for about 10 minutes or until done.
5. Serve hot.

Nutritional Information per Serving:
Calories: 285; Total Fat: 21.6 g; Carbs: 12.3 g; Dietary Fiber: 3 g; Sugars: 4.9 g; Protein: 13 g; Cholesterol: 0 mg; Sodium: 189 mg

Ham and Cheese Sandwich

Yield: 2 servings/Total Time: 35 minutes/Prep time: 15 minutes/Cook time: 20 minutes
Ingredients
- 2 eggs
- 4 kale leaves
- 1 cup chopped turkey
- 4 slices ham
- 6 tbsp. half and half cream
- 2 tsp. melted butter
- 50 g Swiss cheese
- ¼ tsp. pure vanilla extract
- Raspberries, for serving

Directions
1. Mix the eggs, vanilla and cream in a bowl and set aside.

2. Make a sandwich with the kale, cheese slice, turkey, ham, cheese slice and the top kale leaf to make two sandwiches, folding the sides. Set your air fryer to 350° F.
3. Spread out aluminum foil and cut them about the same size as each sandwich and spread the melted butter on the surface of the foil.
4. Dip the sandwich in the egg mixture and let it soak for about 20 seconds on each side. Repeat this for the other sandwich. Place the soaked sandwiches on the prepared foil sheets then place in the basket in your fryer.
5. Cook for 12 minutes then flip the sandwiches and brush with the remaining butter and cook for another 5 minutes or until well browned.
6. Place the cooked sandwiched on a plate and serve with raspberries
7. Enjoy!

Nutritional Information per Serving:
Calories: 735; Total Fat: 47.9 g; Carbs: 13.4 g; Dietary Fiber: 2.8 g; Sugars: 2.4 g; Protein: 40.8 g; Cholesterol: 0 mg; Sodium: 479 mg

Simple Fried Catfish

Yield: 3 servings/Total Time: 50 minutes/Prep time: 10 minutes/Cook time: 40 minutes
Ingredients
- 3 medium catfish fillets
- 1 tbsp. extra virgin olive oil
- ¼ cup fish fry seasoning of choice
- 2 tbsp. finely chopped fresh parsley for serving

Directions
1. Start by setting your air fryer to 400° F.
2. Rinse the fillets under tap water and pat dry using a kitchen towel.
3. In a large Ziploc bag, pour in the fish fry seasoning and add in one fish fillet and shake well to ensure it's coated on all sides then place it on a plate. Do this for the remaining fillets.
4. Gently brush olive on all the seasoned fillets and arrange them on your air fryer's basket. (Cook in batches if they don't all fit)
5. Cook for 10 minutes then turn the fillets and cook for an additional 10 minutes or until golden brown.
6. You can cook for another 3-5 minutes for a crispier crust.
7. Serve hot and sprinkle with the Parsley. Enjoy!

Nutritional Information per Serving:
Calories: 423; Total Fat: 38.4 g; Carbs: 14.5 g; Dietary Fiber: 2.3 g; Sugars: 0.1 g; Protein: 30 g; Cholesterol: 0 mg; Sodium: 594 mg

Coconut Coated Shrimp with Spicy Dip

Yield: 2 servings/Total Time: 50 minutes/Prep time: 30 minutes/Cook time: 20 minutes
Ingredients
For the coconut coated shrimp:
- 6 jumbo shrimp, shelled, deveined and thoroughly cleaned
- 150 ml coconut milk
- ¼ cup finely chopped almonds

For the spicy dip:
- ½ cup orange marmalade
- 1 tsp. mustard

- ½ cup sweetened grated coconut
- ¼ tsp. freshly ground pepper, divided
- ½ tsp. cayenne pepper, divided
- ½ tsp. sea salt, divided

- 1 tbsp. pure honey
- ¼ tsp. tabasco or hot sauce of choice

Directions
1. Mix the coconut milk with part of the cayenne, salt and ground pepper in a medium bowl until well blended and set aside.
2. Next, combine the shredded coconut, chopped almond and the remaining salt, cayenne and ground pepper.
3. Dunk the jumbo shrimp, one at a time, roll in the almond mix then gently place in the basket of your air fryer. Repeat this process for all your shrimp.
4. Set your air fryer to 350° F and cook for 20 minutes, turning the shrimp halfway though.
5. Meanwhile, combine all the spicy dip ingredients in a small bowl.
6. Serve hot with the marmalade dip.
7. Enjoy!

Nutritional Information per Serving:

Calories: 326; Total Fat: 24.7 g; Carbs: 13.3 g; Dietary Fiber: 4 g; Sugars: 5 g; Protein: 17 g; Cholesterol: 0 mg; Sodium: 288 mg

Crunchy Caramelized Salmon

Yield: 2 servings/Total Time: 2 hours 30 minutes/Prep time: 2 hours 10 minutes/Cook time: 20 minutes

Ingredients

- 2 salmon fillets
- 3 tsp. sweet rice wine vinegar
- 2 tbsp. pure honey
- 6 tbsp. low sodium soy sauce
- 2 tsp. water

Directions

1. Combine the soy sauce, vinegar, honey and water in a small bowl and divide into two portions, setting one portion aside.
2. Pour one portion of the marinade in a Ziploc bag and add in the salmon fillets. Shake well and let marinate in the fridge for a minimum of 2 hours.
3. Set your air fryer to 350° F and bake the fillets for 8 minutes, turning the fish halfway through cook time,
4. Use the leftover marinade to baste the salmon for 3-5 minutes, turning frequently until you get a beautiful and crunchy caramelized exterior.
5. For the sauce, place a pan on low-medium heat and simmer the remaining sauce portion for a minute or two and serve with the salmon.
6. Enjoy!

Nutritional Information per Serving:
Calories: 326; Total Fat: 24.7 g; Carbs: 13.3 g; Dietary Fiber: 4 g; Sugars: 5 g; Protein: 17 g; Cholesterol: 0 mg; Sodium: 288 mg

Tasty Salmon Fish Cakes

Yield: 6 servings/Total Time: 1 hours 10 minutes/Prep time: 1 hour/Cook time: 10 minutes

Ingredients

- 2 large pink salmon fillets
- 2 eggs
- 2 tbsp. almond flour
- 1 yellow onion, minced
- 1 medium carrot, thinly grated
- 3 tbsp. mayonnaise
- 1 ½ tbsp. minced chives
- 2 tsp. fresh lemon juice
- 2 tsp. Italian seasoning
- ¼-1/2 tsp. freshly ground black pepper
- 1 tsp. sea salt

Directions

1. Start by squeezing out excess water from the minced onion and grated carrot and combine with the salmon in a large bowl.
2. Add in the cornmeal, mayonnaise, eggs, Italian seasoning, salt, chives, salt and lemon juice. Mix well until evenly combined.
3. Make patties on your palm, to the size you desire. Cover with cling wrap and place in the fridge for half an hour and for the flavors to marry.
4. Arrange the patties in your air fryer's basket in a single layer (you may have to do several batches). Spray the patties with olive oil cooking spray and cook for about 6 minutes at about 400° F. Turn the patties , lightly spray the top side and cook for 4-5 minutes or until golden brown.
5. Serve hot with your favorite dip.

Nutritional Information per Serving:
Calories: 398; Total Fat: 28.2 g; Carbs: 11.7 g; Dietary Fiber: 2.1 g; Sugars: 3 g; Protein: 21 g; Cholesterol: 0 mg; Sodium: 317 mg

Crunchy Keto Shrimp

Yield: 3-4 servings/Total Time: 18 minutes/Prep time: 10 minutes/Cook time: 8 minutes

Ingredients

For the shrimp:

- 450 g shrimp, peeled, deveined and cleaned
- ¾ cup finely chopped almonds
- ½ cup coconut flour
- 1 large egg white
- 1 tsp. sweet paprika
- Sea salt and freshly ground pepper to taste
- Chicken seasoning to taste

For the hot and sweet sauce:
- ¼ cup sweet chili sauce
- 1/3 cup plain yogurt
- 2 tbsp. sriracha
- Olive oil cooking spray

Directions
1. Start by setting your air fryer to 400° F.
2. Place the egg white in a shallow bowl and beat slightly. Place the chopped almonds and the flour in two separate bowls.
3. Season the shrimp with the paprika, salt, pepper and chicken seasoning then dip in the flour followed by the egg white and coat with almonds.
   Note: Don't dunk the shrimp in the egg white, rather, lightly coat the floured shrimp with the egg white so most of the flour adheres to the shrimp for a crunchier finish.
4. Lightly spray the coated shrimp with cooking spray and gently arrange on the basket of your air fryer. Cook each side for 4 minutes or until golden and crispy.
5. For the hot and sweet sauce, mix all the ingredients in a small bowl. You can either toss the cooked shrimp in the sauce or serve the sauce as a dip. Enjoy!

Nutritional Information per Serving:
Calories: 302; Total Fat: 24.9 g; Carbs: 13.7 g; Dietary Fiber: 3.2 g; Sugars: 6 g; Protein: 19 g; Cholesterol: 0 mg; Sodium: 195 mg

Tasty Collard Tacos with Hot Slaw

Yield: 2-3 servings/Total Time: 50 minutes/Prep time: 30 minutes/Cook time: 20 minutes

Ingredients

For the collard tacos:
- 6 collard leaves
- ½ cup coconut flour
- ¼ cup milk
- 1 egg, lightly beaten
- 3 snapper or mahi mahi fillets
- 1 cup finely chopped almonds
- ½ tsp. baking powder
- 1/2 tsp. ground cumin
- 1 tsp. red chili powder
- Freshly ground black pepper to taste
- 1 tsp. kosher salt
- 1 tbsp. vegetable oil
- 1 lemon, cut into wedges/slices

For the Hot Slaw:
- 4 cups shredded green cabbage
- 2 scallions, chopped
- ¼ cup grated carrots
- 2 tbsp. sweet rice vinegar
- ½ cup mayonnaise
- 2 tbsp. sriracha sauce
- ½-1 tsp. sugar
- Kosher salt and freshly ground pepper to taste

Directions
1. Start with the slaw. Mix the vinegar, mayonnaise, sriracha and sugar in a bowl until well blended. Toss in the carrots, cabbage and scallions. Keep tossing until the veggies are evenly coated with the dressing. Sprinkle the slaw with salt and pepper. Cover the bowl with cling wrap and put in the fridge.
2. Next mix the flour, cumin, chili, baking powder, salt and pepper in a bowl. Add in the milk and egg and whisk until you get a smooth batter.
3. Place the chopped almonds in a bowl. Next cut the fillets into strips, approximately 1 inch in width. Dip the slices in the batter, shake off the excess batter and gently roll them in the almonds then place on a plate.
4. Set your air fryer to 400° F.
5. Lightly brush the coated fish slices with oil and arrange them in the basket of your air fryer.
6. Cook for 3 minutes then flip the fish slices and cook for 2-3 minutes or until golden brown.
7. To make the tacos, place the fish slices on each collard leaf and top with the spicy slaw. Squeeze the lemon slice/ wedge over the slaw and enjoy!

Nutritional Information per Serving:
Calories: 287; Total Fat: 27.5 g; Carbs: 11.9 g; Dietary Fiber: 9 g; Sugars: 4 g; Protein: 18.7 g; Cholesterol: 0 mg; Sodium: 332 mg

Classic Shrimp Scampi

Yield: 2 servings/Total Time: 18 minutes/Prep time: 10 minutes/Cook time: 8 minutes

Ingredients

- 300 g shrimp, peeled, deveined and cleaned
- 4 tbsp. butter
- 2 tbsp. white wine
- 1 tbsp. freshly squeezed lemon juice
- 2 tsp. red pepper flakes
- 1 ½ tbsp. minced basil, divided
- 1 tbsp. chopped chives
- 1 tbsp. minced garlic

Directions

1. Set our air fryer fitted with a pan to 330° F.
2. Add the butter, pepper flakes and garlic to the hot pan and let cook for 2 minutes, stirring twice until the butter melts completely.
3. Add the remaining ingredients to the pan, gently stirring all the while.
4. Cook the shrimp for 5 minutes and remove the pan. Let it stand for a minute so the shrimp can cook slightly more without risking overcooking them in the air fryer as this would give them a rubbery texture.
5. Stir in the remaining minced basil and serve.
6. Enjoy!

Nutritional Information per Serving:

Calories: 279; Total Fat: 21.3 g; Carbs: 9.7 g; Dietary Fiber: 3 g; Sugars: 3.1 g; Protein: 17.5 g; Cholesterol: 0 mg; Sodium: 196 mg

Crisp-Skinned Keto Cod

Yield: 4 servings/Total Time: 18 minutes/Prep time: 10 minutes/Cook time: 8 minutes

Ingredients

- 2 pieces cod fish
- 5 tbsp. light soy sauce
- 1 tsp. dark soy sauce
- 3 tiny pieces of rock sugar
- 3 tbsp. vegetable oil
- 1 dash of sesame oil
- ½-inch ginger, thinly sliced
- 1 cup water
- Raw honey to taste
- Salt to taste
- 3 scallions, sliced (white and green parts sliced separately)
- Chopped coriander for garnishing

Directions

1. Thoroughly clean the cod then pat dry using a clean kitchen towel.
2. Season well with honey, salt and 1 dash of sesame oil in a bowl and let stand for 15 minutes.
3. Set your air fryer to 350° F and cook the fish for 12 minutes.
4. Meanwhile, pour the cup of water in a pan and over medium-high heat and bring to a boil, add the rock sugar, soy sauces and stir well until all the sugar dissolves.
5. Heat the oil in a pan and cook the white part of the scallions and ginger slices until they start browning.
6. Take out the cod and place on a serving dish. Garnish and pour the hot ginger oil over the fish and spoon the cooked sauce over it.
7. Enjoy!

Nutritional Information per Serving:

Calories: 318; Total Fat: 20.6 g; Carbs: 10.1 g; Dietary Fiber: 1.9 g; Sugars: 7 g; Protein: 16.9 g; Cholesterol: 0 mg; Sodium: 226 mg

Tilapia Roast in Garlic and Olive Oil

Yields: 4 Servings/Total Time: 25 Minutes/Prep Time: 15 Minutes/Cook Time: 8 Minutes

Ingredients

- 4 tilapia fillets
- 4 cloves crushed garlic
- 2 tablespoon extra-virgin olive oil
- 1 white onion, chopped
- Salt, to taste

Directions

1. Rub the tilapia fillets with garlic and arrange them on a large plate. Drizzle the fish with olive oil until well coated and top with onion. Refrigerate the fish, covered, for at least 8 hours or overnight to soak in the marinade.
2. When ready, preheat your air fryer to 350° F. Transfer the fish fillets to the basket of your air fryer; Reserve the marinade for basting. Bake for 8 minutes, four minutes per side, and baste with the marinade halfway through cook time.
3. Enjoy!

Nutritional Information per Serving:

Calories: 269; Total Fat: 17.8 g; Carbs: 6.4 g; Dietary Fiber: 1.6 g; Sugars: 2 g; Protein: 14 g; Cholesterol: 0 mg; Sodium: 166 mg

Red Snapper in Spicy Veggie Sauce

Yields: 4 Servings/Total Time: 30 Minutes/Prep Time: 15 Minutes/Cook Time: 15 Minutes
Ingredients
- 400 g red snapper fillets
- 2 tbsp. canola or extra virgin olive oil
- ½ red bell pepper, chopped
- ½ green bell pepper, chopped
- 4 scallions, thinly sliced
- 2 tomatoes, diced
- 2 cloves garlic
- 2 tablespoon fresh lemon juice
- ½ cup freshly squeezed lime juice
- 1 teaspoon cayenne pepper
- 1 teaspoon pepper
- Cilantro for garnish

Directions
1. Add extra virgin olive oil to the pan of your air fryer and sauté garlic for about 2 minutes on your cooker, careful not to burn the garlic. Place fish in the oil and drizzle with lemon and lime juice. Sprinkle with black pepper and cayenne pepper and top with green and red bell peppers, scallions, and tomatoes.
2. Put the pan in your air fryer and cook for about 10 minutes or until the fish flakes easily with fork.
3. To serve, garnish with cilantro.

Nutritional Information per Serving:
Calories: 312; Total Fat: 26.4 g; Carbs: 10.9 g; Dietary Fiber: 6.6 g; Sugars: 4 g; Protein: 17.9 g; Cholesterol: 0 mg; Sodium: 233 mg

Keto Salmon with Fennel & Fresh Herbs

Yield: 4 Servings/Total Time: 21 Minutes/Prep Time: 15 Minutes/Cook Time: 6 Minutes
Ingredients
- 1 tablespoon extra-virgin olive oil
- 6 ounces wild salmon fillets, skinless
- Fennel fronds
- 1 tablespoon chopped parsley
- 1 tablespoon chopped dill
- 1 tablespoon chopped chives
- 1 tablespoon chopped tarragon
- 1 tablespoon chopped basil
- 1 tablespoon chopped shallot
- 1 tablespoon lemon juice

Directions
1. Lightly oil the basket of your air fryer with olive oil; add salmon and fennel wedges and cook for about 6 minutes at 350° F.
2. In a bowl, combine the chopped herbs, extra virgin olive oil, shallots and lemon juice; stir until well combined. Use spoon to spread over cooked fish.
3. Serve with steamed rice or mashed potatoes.
4. Enjoy!

Nutritional Information per Serving:
Calories: 251; Total Fat: 19.4 g; Carbs: 8.7 g; Dietary Fiber: 6.2 g; Sugars: 1.8 g; Protein: 17.3 g; Cholesterol: 0 mg; Sodium: 184 mg

Delicious Cranberry Crusted Salmon

Yield: 4 Servings/Total Time: 30 Minutes/Prep Time: 15 Minutes/Cook Time: 15 Minutes
Ingredients
- Olive oil cooking spray
- 4 salmon filets
- Salt & pepper to taste
- 2 tablespoons extra virgin olive oil
- ¼ cup dried cranberries, chopped
- ½ cup walnuts, chopped
- 1 teaspoon orange zest
- 1 tablespoon Dijon mustard
- 2 tablespoons parsley, chopped

Directions
1. Preheat your air fryer to 370°F. Lightly coat the basket of your air fryer with olive oil cooking spray. Generously season the fish filets with sea salt and pepper and arrange them on the baking sheet.
2. Mix the remaining ingredients in a small bowl until well blended; press onto the filets and bake in the preheated fryer for about 15 minutes or until the topping is lightly browned.
3. Remove from air fryer and serve.

Nutritional Information per Serving:
Calories: 327; Total Fat: 22.8 g; Carbs: 12.9 g; Dietary Fiber: 5.4 g; Sugars: 4 g; Protein: 18.1 g; Cholesterol: 0 mg; Sodium: 337 mg

Authentic Jamaican Jerk Pork Roast

Yield: 10 Servings/Total Time: 1 Hour 20 Minutes/Prep Time: 10 Minutes /Cook Time: 1 Hour 10 Minutes

Ingredients
- 1200 g pork shoulder
- 1 tbsp. olive oil
- 1/4 cup Jamaican Jerk spice blend
- 1/2 cup beef broth

Directions
1. Rub the roast with oil and dust with spice blend; set your air fryer to 400° F and brown roast on both sides for 4 minutes on each side in a large pan.
2. Stir in broth and lock lid. Lower the temperature to 350° F and bake for 1 hour then remove from fryer.
3. Shred and serve.

Nutritional Information per Serving:
Calories: 298; Total Fat: 21.3 g; Carbs: 7.4 g; Dietary Fiber: 1.4 g; Sugars: 2 g; Protein: 19.6 g; Cholesterol: 0 mg; Sodium: 455 mg

Green Salmon Salad with Toasted Walnuts

Yield: 6 Servings/Total Time: 25 Minutes/Prep Time: 15 Minutes/Cook Time: 10 Minutes

Ingredients
- 1 tablespoon extra-virgin olive oil
- 8 cups mixed greens (arugula, baby spinach, romaine lettuce)
- ¼ cup chopped toasted walnuts
- 2 teaspoons balsamic vinegar
- 1 teaspoon walnut oil
- ¼ teaspoon sea salt
- 300 g salmon fillet
- Honey Mustard salad spray

Directions
1. In a skillet set over medium heat, toast walnuts for about 1 minute and transfer to a plate. Add half of the extra virgin olive oil to the same skillet and sauté half of the greens for about 1 minute; transfer to a salad bowl and repeat with the remaining oil and greens.
2. Add balsamic vinegar, walnut oil and salt to the salad and toss until well combined.
3. Lightly brush the basket of your air fryer with oil and place the salmon, skin side down and spray with salad spray. Cook at 350° for 10 minutes or until cooked through. Remove the fish from the fryer and cut into 4 pieces; divide the green salad among four serving bowls and top each with one piece of fish. Enjoy!

Nutritional Information per Serving:
Calories: 415; Total Fat: 36.7 g; Carbs: 12.2 g; Dietary Fiber: 9 g; Sugars: 6 g; Protein: 21.5 g; Cholesterol: 0 mg; Sodium: 297 mg

Hot Tangy Tilapia with Asparagus

Yield: 6 Servings/Total Time: 2 Hours 15 Minutes/Prep Time: 15 Minutes/Cook Time: 2 Hours

Ingredients
- 6 tilapia filets
- 1 bundle of asparagus
- ½ cup freshly squeezed lemon juice
- Lemon pepper seasoning
- 3 tbsp. melted coconut oil

Directions
1. Divide asparagus into equal amounts per each fillet.
2. Place each fillet in the center of a piece of foil and sprinkle with about 1 tsp. lemon pepper seasoning; drizzle with about 2 tbsp. lemon juice and about ½ tbsp. melted coconut oil. Top each filet with the asparagus and fold the foil to form a packet. Repeat with the remaining ingredients and then place the packets in the basket of your air fryer
3. Set the air fryer to 350° F and cook for 15 minutes.
4. Enjoy!

Nutritional Information per Serving:
Calories: 374; Total Fat: 28.2 g; Carbs: 9.4 g; Dietary Fiber: 8.1 g; Sugars: 1.9 g; Protein: 19.3 g; Cholesterol: 0 mg; Sodium: 224 mg

Spicy Stuffed Peppers

Yield: 4 servings/Total Time: 40 minutes/Prep time: 20 minutes/Cook time: 20 minutes

Ingredients
- 4 green peppers, seeds and stems removed

- 150 g lean minced meat
- 80 g grated cheddar cheese, divided
- ½ cup tomato sauce, divided
- ½ tsp. dried mango powder
- ½ tsp. chili powder
- ½ tsp. turmeric powder
- 1 tsp. Worcestershire sauce
- 1 tsp. coriander powder
- 1 onion, minced
- 1 clove garlic, minced
- 2 tsp., minced coriander leaves
- 1 tsp. vegetable oil

Directions
1. Start by setting your air fryer to 390° F.
2. Cook the peppers in boiling water with salt for 3 minutes then transfer to a plate
3. Add the oil to a small pan over medium-low heat and sauté the onion and garlic for 1-2 minutes then remove from heat.
4. Combine all the ingredients in a large bowl apart from half the cheese and tomato sauce.
5. Stuff the peppers with the meat mixture and top with the remaining cheese and tomato sauce.
6. Lightly grease the basket of your air fryer and arrange the 4 stuffed peppers.
7. Cook for 15 – 20 minutes or until done.
8. Enjoy!

Nutritional Information per Serving:
Calories: 338; Total Fat: 24 g; Carbs: 11.7 g; Dietary Fiber: 9 g; Sugars: 3 g; Protein: 16.8 g; Cholesterol: 0 mg; Sodium: 335 mg

Beef and Veggie Stir Fry

Yield: 4 servings/Total Time: 1 hour/Prep time: 45 minutes/Cook time: 15 minutes

Ingredients
- 450 g beef sirloin, cut into strips
- 1 yellow pepper, sliced
- 1 red pepper, sliced
- 1 green pepper, sliced

For the marinade:
- 2 tsp. minced garlic
- 1 tbsp. low sodium soy sauce
- ¼ cup hoisin sauce

- 1 broccoli, cut into florets
- 1 large red onion, sliced
- 1 large white onion, sliced
- 1 tsp. sesame oil

- ¼ cup water
- 1 tsp. sesame oil
- 1 tsp. ground ginger

Directions
1. Start by whisking all the marinade ingredients in a large bowl. Add in the beef strips and toss well until all the pieces are evenly coated. Cover using cling wrap and let it sit in the fridge for 30 minutes.
2. Combine all the veggies with the sesame oil and put in the basket of your air fryer at 200° F. Cook for 5 minutes.
3. Transfer the veggies to a bowl and put the meat in the basket of your air fryer. Make sure you drain all the marinade. Increase the temperature to 360° F and cook for 5 minutes. Shake the meat and cook for 3 more minutes or until done.
4. Add in the veggies and cook for 2 more minutes.
5. Enjoy!

Nutritional Information per Serving:
Calories: 367; Total Fat: 31.9 g; Carbs: 12.7 g; Dietary Fiber: 9.6 g; Sugars: 4 g; Protein: 28.6 g; Cholesterol: 0 mg; Sodium: 442 mg

Keto Chili Beef with Toasted Cashews

Yields: 4 Servings/Total Time: 35 Minutes/Prep Time: 10 Minutes/Cook Time: 25 Minutes

Ingredients
- ½ tablespoon extra-virgin olive oil or canola oil
- 450 g sliced lean beef
- 2 teaspoon red curry paste
- 1 teaspoon liquid Stevia, optional
- 2 tablespoons fresh lime juice

- 2 teaspoon fish sauce
- 1 cup green capsicum, diced
- ½ cup water
- 20 toasted cashews
- 1 teaspoon arrowroot starch

Directions
1. Set your air fryer to 375° F. Add beef and olive oil and fry until it's no longer pink inside-for about 15 minutes, turning twice. Stir in red curry paste and cook for a few more minutes.

2. Transfer to a large pot and stir in Stevia, lime juice, fish sauce, capsicum and water; simmer for about 10 minutes.
3. Mix cooked arrowroot with water to make a paste; stir the paste into the sauce to thicken.
4. Remove the pan from heat and add the fried cashews. Serve.

Nutritional Information per Serving:
Calories: 366; Total Fat: 35 g; Carbs: 13.8 g; Dietary Fiber: 7.9 g; Sugars: 4 g; Protein: 27.9 g; Cholesterol: 0 mg; Sodium: 459 mg

Beef Stir Fry w/ Red Onions & Peppers

Yield: 4 Servings/Total Time: 20 Minutes/Prep Time: 10 Minutes/Cook Time: 10 Minutes
Ingredients:
- 450 g grass-fed flank steak, thinly sliced strips
- 1 tablespoon rice wine
- 2 teaspoons balsamic vinegar
- Pinch of sea salt
- Pinch of pepper
- 3 teaspoons extra-virgin olive oil
- 1 large yellow onion, thinly chopped
- 1/2 red bell pepper, thinly sliced
- 1/2 green bell pepper, thinly sliced
- 1 tablespoon toasted sesame seeds
- 1 teaspoon crushed red pepper flakes

Directions:
1. Place meat in a bowl; stir in rice wine and vinegar, sea salt and pepper. Toss to coat well.
2. Set your air fryer to 375° F. Add the meat and 1 tsp. olive oil and cook for about 3-5 minute or until meat is browned.
3. Heat the remaining oil on a stove top pan and sauté onions for about 2 minutes or until caramelized; stir in pepper and cook for 2 minutes.
4. Add the caramelized onions to the air fryer and stir in sesame seeds and red pepper flakes and cook for 1-2 minutes
5. Serve hot!

Nutritional Information per Serving:
Calories: 315; Total Fat: 29 g; Carbs: 10.7 g; Dietary Fiber: 6 g; Sugars: 3 g; Protein: 22 g; Cholesterol: 0 mg; Sodium: 279 mg

Italian Keto Beef

Yield: 8 Servings/Total Time: 1 Hours 40 Minutes/Prep Time: 10 Minutes/Cook Time: 1 Hour 30 Minutes
Ingredients
- 1000 g grass-fed chuck roast
- 6 cloves garlic
- 1 tsp. marjoram
- 1 tsp. basil
- 1 tsp. oregano
- 1/2 tsp. ground ginger
- 1 tsp. onion powder
- 2 tsp. garlic powder
- 1 tsp. salt
- 1/4 cup apple cider vinegar
- 1 cup beef broth

Directions
1. Cut slits in the roast with a sharp knife and then stuff with garlic cloves.
2. In a bowl, whisk together marjoram, basil, oregano, ground ginger, onion powder, garlic powder, and salt until well blended; rub the seasoning all over the roast and place in a large air fryer pan.
3. Add vinegar and broth and lock lid; Cook at 400° F for 90 minutes. Take the roast out and then shred meat with a fork.
4. Serve along with cooking juices.

Nutritional Information per Serving:
Calories: 392; Total Fat: 21.8 g; Carbs: 9.3 g; Dietary Fiber: 3 g; Sugars: 1.6 g; Protein: 20.5 g; Cholesterol: 0 mg; Sodium: 342 mg

Healthy Cauliflower Rice Bowl with Grilled Steak & Veggies

Yield: 4 Servings/Total Time: 30 Minutes/Prep Time: 10 Minutes/Cook Time: 20 Minutes
Ingredients
- 2 cups cauliflower rice
- 16 ounces steak, cut into bite-size pieces
- 1 cup baby arugula
- 1 cup red pepper, chopped

- 1 cup scallions, chopped
- 1/2 cup toasted salted pipits
- 2 tsp. fresh cilantro leaves
- 2 cups micro greens
- 2 tbsp. tomato sauce
- 2 tbsp. extra-virgin olive oil
- Kosher salt
- Black pepper
- 1 tbsp. fresh lime juice

Directions
1. Cook cauliflower in your instant pot, to desire.
2. Meanwhile, grill steak to medium rare for about 15 minutes at 350° F in your air fryer. Grill scallions, red pepper, and sweet potatoes along with the steak until tender.
3. Place cooked cauliflower rice in a bowl; top with grilled steak, scallions, veggies, pepitas, cilantro, and micro greens.
4. In a small bowl, whisk together oil, tomato sauce, salt, and pepper until well blended; drizzle over the steak mixture and serve drizzled with lime juice.

Nutritional Information per Serving:
Calories: 433; Total Fat: 37.5 g; Carbs: 12.7 g; Dietary Fiber: 9 g; Sugars: 5 g; Protein: 26.9 g; Cholesterol: 0 mg; Sodium: 244 mg

Veggie Turkey Wraps

Yields: 4 Servings/Total Time: 25 Minutes/Prep Time: 15 Minutes/Cook Time: 10 Minutes
Ingredients
- 250 g ground turkey
- 1/2 small onion, finely chopped
- 1 garlic clove, minced
- 2 tablespoons extra virgin olive oil
- 1 head lettuce
- 1 teaspoon cumin
- 1/2 tablespoon fresh ginger, sliced
- 2 tablespoons apple cider vinegar
- 2 tablespoons freshly chopped cilantro
- 1 teaspoon freshly ground black pepper
- 1 teaspoon sea salt

Directions
1. Sauté garlic and onion in extra virgin olive oil until fragrant and translucent in your air fryer pan at 350° F.
2. Add turkey and cook well for 5-8 minutes or until done.
3. Add in the remaining ingredients and continue cooking for 5 minutes.
4. To serve, ladle a spoonful of turkey mixture onto a lettuce leaf and wrap. Enjoy!

Nutritional Information per Serving:
Calories: 197; Total Fat: 17.9 g; Carbs: 8.4 g; Dietary Fiber: 9 g; Sugars: 5 g; Protein: 13.4 g; Cholesterol: 0 mg; Sodium: 356 mg

Crunchy Almond & Kale Salad with Roasted Chicken

Yield: 1 Serving/Total Time: 30 Minutes/Prep Time: 10 Minutes/Cook Time: 20 Minutes
Ingredients:
Salad
- 1 teaspoon extra virgin olive oil
- 100 g Lacinato kale, sliced into thin strips
- 1/4 cup roasted almonds
- Pinch of sea salt
- Pinch of pepper

Roasted Chicken
- 100 g chicken breast
- Pinch of sea salt
- Pinch of pepper
- 1 teaspoon apple cider vinegar
- 1/2 teaspoon extra-virgin olive oil
- 1 tablespoon rosemary
- 1 tablespoon cup sage

Directions:
1. Place kale in a bowl and add olive oil; massage olive oil with hands into kale until kale is tender; sprinkle with salt and pepper and toss with toasted almonds.
2. Preheat your air fryer to 360°F. Sprinkle chicken with salt and pepper; add vinegar and olive oil and season with rosemary and sage. Roast in the basket of your air fryer for about 20 minutes, turning the chicken halfway through cook time or until chicken is cooked through. Serve chicken with kale and almond salad.

Nutritional Information per Serving:
Calories: 293; Total Fat: 16.4 g; Carbs: 10 g; Dietary Fiber: 9.7 g; Sugars: 3 g; Protein: 14 g; Cholesterol: 0 mg; Sodium: 204 mg

Spinach & Chicken Soup

Yield: 1 Serving/Total Time: 40 Minutes/Prep Time: 10 Minutes/Cook Time: 30 Minutes
Ingredients
- 1 teaspoon extra-virgin olive oil
- 100 g chicken
- 1 clove garlic, minced
- 1 tablespoon chopped red onion
- ½ lemon with rind
- 1 stalk lemongrass

- ¼ teaspoon thyme
- Pinch of cayenne pepper
- Pinch of salt & pepper
- 2 cups chicken broth
- ¼ cup fresh lemon juice
- 2 cups chopped spinach

Directions
1. In your air fryer, brown chicken in olive oil for 6 minutes at 350° F, turning the chicken halfway through cook time. Transfer to a saucepan and stir in garlic, onion, herbs, spices, broth, lemon juice and lemon rind and simmer for about 25 minutes, adding spinach during the last 5 minutes. Serve hot.

Nutritional Information per Serving:
Calories: 197; Total Fat: 15 g; Carbs: 7.8 g; Dietary Fiber: 6 g; Sugars: 2 g; Protein: 17 g; Cholesterol: 0 mg; Sodium: 188 mg

Collard Wraps with Tasty Dipping Sauce

Yield: 6 Servings/Total Time: 26 Minutes/Prep Time: 10 Minutes/Cook Time: 16 Minutes
Ingredients
Wraps
- 4 large collard leaves, stems removed
- 1 medium avocado, sliced
- ½ cucumber, thinly sliced
- 1 cup diced mango

- 6 large strawberries, thinly sliced
- 6 (200g) grilled chicken breasts, diced
- 24 mint leaves

Dipping Sauce
- 2 tablespoons almond butter
- 2 tablespoons coconut cream
- 1 birds eye chili, finely chopped
- 2 tablespoons unsweetened applesauce
- ¼ cup fresh lime juice
- 1 teaspoon sesame oil

- 1 tablespoon apple cider vinegar
- 1 tablespoon tahini
- 1 clove garlic, crushed
- 1 tablespoon grated fresh ginger
- ⅛ teaspoon sea salt

Directions
For the chicken breasts:
1. Start by setting your air fryer to 350° F. lightly coat the basket of the air fryer with oil. Season the breasts with salt and pepper and arrange on the prepared basket and fry for 8 minutes on each side.
2. Once done, remove from air fryer and set on a platter to cool slightly then dice them up.

For the wraps
1. Divide the veggies and diced chicken breasts equally among the four large collard leaves; fold bottom edges over the filling, and then roll both sides. Roll very tightly up to the end of the leaves; secure with toothpicks and cut each in half.

Make the sauce:
1. Combine all the sauce ingredients in a blender and blend until very smooth. Divide between bowls and serve with the wraps.

Nutritional Information per Serving:
Calories: 389; Total Fat: 38.2 g; Carbs: 11.7 g; Dietary Fiber: 9.3 g; Sugars: 4 g; Protein: 26 g; Cholesterol: 0 mg; Sodium: 448 mg

Crisp Chicken w/ Mustard Vinaigrette

Yield: 1 Serving/Total Time: 15 Minutes/Prep Time: 5 Minutes/Cook Time: 10 Minutes
Ingredients
Salad:
- 250 g chicken breast
- 1 cup shaved Brussels sprouts
- 2 cups baby spinach
- 2 cups mixed greens
- 1/2 avocado sliced

- Segments of one orange
- 1 teaspoon raw pumpkin seeds
- 1 teaspoon toasted almonds
- 1 teaspoon hemp seeds

Dressing:
- 1/2 shallot, chopped
- 1 garlic clove, chopped
- 2 teaspoons balsamic vinegar
- 1 teaspoon extra virgin olive oil
- ½ cup fresh orange juice
- 1 teaspoon Dijon mustard
- 1 teaspoon raw honey
- Fresh ground pepper

Directions
1. In a blender, blend together all dressing ingredients until very smooth; set aside.
2. Set your air fryer to 350° F and brush the basket of the air fryer with oil. Place the chicken breast on the basket and cook for 10 minutes, 5 minutes per side. Take out of the air fryer and transfer to a plate. Let sit for 5 minutes then cut into bite sized chunks.
3. Combine all salad ingredients in a large bowl; drizzle with dressing and toss to coat well before serving.

Nutritional Information per Serving:
Calories: 457; Total Fat: 37 g; Carbs: 13.6 g; Dietary Fiber: 8 g; Sugars: 3.3 g; Protein: 31.8 g; Cholesterol: 0 mg; Sodium: 512 mg

Chicken with Oregano Chimichurri & Green Salad

Yield: 4 Servings/Total Time: 17 Minutes/Prep Time: 5 Minutes/Cook Time: 12 Minutes

Ingredients
- 1 teaspoon finely grated orange zest
- 1 teaspoon dried oregano
- 1 small garlic clove, grated
- 2 teaspoon vinegar (red wine, cider, or white wine)
- 1 tablespoon fresh orange juice
- 1/2 cup chopped fresh flat-leaf parsley leaves
- 700 g chicken breast, cut into 4 pieces
- Sea salt and pepper
- 1/4 cup and 2 teaspoons extra virgin olive oil
- 4 cups arugula
- 2 bulbs fennel, shaved
- 2 tablespoons whole-grain mustard

Directions
1. Make chimichurri: In a medium bowl, combine orange zest, oregano and garlic. Mix in vinegar, orange juice and parsley and then slowly whisk in ¼ cup of olive oil until emulsified. Season with sea salt and pepper.
2. Sprinkle the chicken with salt and pepper and set your air fryer to 350° F. brush the chicken steaks with the remaining olive oil and cook for about 6 minutes per side or until evenly browned. Take out from the fryer and let rest for at least 10 minutes.
3. Toss the cooked chicken, greens, and fennel with mustard in a medium bowl; season with salt and pepper.
4. Serve steak with chimichurri and salad. Enjoy!

Nutritional Information per Serving:
Calories: 312; Total Fat: 33.6 g; Carbs: 12 g; Dietary Fiber: 6 g ; Sugars: 5 g; Protein: 29 g; Cholesterol: 0 mg; Sodium: 660 mg

Keto Chicken w/ Water Chestnuts

Yield: 4 Servings/Total Time: 25 Minutes/Prep Time: 10 Minutes/Cook Time: 15 Minutes

Ingredients
- 2 tablespoons sesame oil
- ¼ cup wheat-free tamari
- 4 small chicken breasts, sliced
- 1 small cabbage, chopped
- 3 garlic cloves, chopped
- 1 teaspoon Chinese five spice powder
- 1 cup dried plums
- 1 cup water chestnuts
- Toasted sesame seeds

Directions
1. Start by preheating your air fryer at 370° F. Heat sesame oil in your air fryer's pan set over medium heat; stir in all the ingredients, except sesame seeds, and transfer to the air fryer. Cook until cabbage and chicken are tender for 15-20 minutes.
2. Serve warm sprinkled with toasted sesame seeds.
3. Enjoy!

Nutritional Information per Serving:
Calories: 404; Total Fat: 29 g; Carbs: 11.3 g; Dietary Fiber: 9 g; Sugars: 4 g; Protein: 22 g; Cholesterol: 0 mg; Sodium: 318 mg

Garden Salad with Tangy Vinaigrette

Yield: 3 Servings/Total Time: 20 Minutes/Prep Time: 10 Minutes/Cook Time: 10 Minutes

Ingredients

Salad

- 1 large chicken breast
- 1/2 avocado, chopped
- 1 cup baby spinach
- 1/3 red onion thinly sliced
- 1/2 cucumber, sliced

- 1 cup beans sprouts
- 1 carrot, grated
- 1 tomato, diced
- 1/2 cup fresh parsley
- 8 almonds, sliced

Dressing:

- 1 tablespoon extra-virgin olive oil
- 2 tablespoons fresh lemon juice
- 1/4 teaspoon sea salt

- 1/4 teaspoon black pepper
- 1 teaspoon dried oregano

Directions

1. Preheat you air fryer to 370° F.
2. Season the chicken breast with salt and pepper. Lightly coat the basket of your air fryer with olive oil and cook the breast for 10 minutes, 5 minutes per side. Take out of the fryer and let sit for 5-10 minutes then slice into bite sized pieces.
3. In a large bowl, mix all salad ingredients until well combined.
4. In a small bowl, whisk together all dressing ingredients until well blended and drizzle over the salad. Toss until well coated and serve.

Nutritional Information per Serving:

Calories: 416; Total Fat: 37 g; Carbs: 14.2 g; Dietary Fiber: 10.1 g; Sugars: 3.9 g; Protein: 36.1 g; Cholesterol: 0 mg; Sodium: 476 mg

Fried Chicken Roast Served with Fruit Compote

Yield: 12 Servings/Total Time: 1 Hour 5 Minutes/Prep Time: 15 Minutes/Cook Time: 50 Minutes

Ingredients

- 1 full chicken, dissected
- 2 tablespoons extra virgin olive oil
- 2 tablespoons chopped garlic
- 2 teaspoons sea salt

- 1 teaspoon pepper
- 1 tablespoon chopped fresh thyme
- 1 tablespoon chopped fresh rosemary

Fruit Compote

- 1/2 cup red grapes, halved, seeds removed
- 12 dried apricots, sliced
- 16 dried figs, coarsely chopped
- 1/2 cup chopped red onion
- 1/2 cup cider vinegar

- 1/2 cup dry white wine
- 2 teaspoons liquid Stevia
- 1/2 teaspoon salt
- 1/2 teaspoon pepper

Directions

1. In a small bowl, stir together thyme, rosemary, garlic, salt and pepper and rub the mixture over the pork.
2. Light your air fryer and set it to 320°F, place the chicken on the basket and cook for 10 minutes. Increase the temperature and cook for another 10 minutes, turning the chicken pieces once. Increase the temperature one more time to 400° F and cook for 5 minutes to get a crispy finish.

Make Fruit Compote:

1. In a saucepan, combine all ingredients and cook over medium heat, stirring, for about 25 minutes or until liquid is reduced to a quarter.
2. Once the chicken is cooked, serve hot with a ladle of fruit compote. Enjoy!

Nutritional Information per Serving:

Calories: 511; Total Fat: 36.8 g; Carbs: 15 g; Dietary Fiber: 7 g; Sugars: 6 g; Protein: 31.5 g; Cholesterol: 0 mg; Sodium: 519 mg

Mango Chicken Stir Fry

Yield: 4 Servings/Total Time: 35 Minutes/Prep Time: 25 Minutes/Cook Time: 10 Minutes

Ingredients

- ½ tablespoon sesame oil
- 1 tablespoon low-sodium soy sauce
- 1 tablespoon almond flour

- 450 g chicken thighs, skinless, boneless, diced
- ½ tablespoon peanut oil
- 1 tablespoon minced fresh ginger
- 1 red onion, chopped
- 2 cups snow peas
- 1 tablespoon chili garlic sauce
- 1 mango, peeled, chopped
- 1/8 teaspoon sea salt
- 1/8 teaspoon black pepper

Directions
1. In a large mixing bowl, combine sesame oil, soy sauce, almond flour and chicken; let sit for at least 20 minutes.
2. In the pan from your air fryer, heat peanut oil and then sauté ginger and onion for about 2 minutes; add snow peas and stir fry for about 1 minute.
3. Add chicken with the marinade and transfer to your air fryer and cook for 5 minutes at 350° F or until chicken is browned. Add chili sauce, mango and pepper and continue stir frying for 1 minute or until chicken is cooked through and mango is tender. Serve hot!

Nutritional Information per Serving:
Calories: 330; Total Fat: 24.1 g; Carbs: 11.8 g; Dietary Fiber: 6 g; Sugars: 3 g; Protein: 26 g; Cholesterol: 0 mg; Sodium: 298 mg

Vegan Cranberry Instant Pot Cake

Yield: 4-6 Servings/Total Time: 50 Minutes/Prep Time: 5 Minutes/Cook Time: 45 Minutes
Ingredients
Dry Ingredients
- 1 1/4 cup coconut
- 1/2 teaspoon baking powder
- 1/2 teaspoon baking soda
- 1/2 teaspoon ground cardamom

Wet Ingredients
- 1/2 cup unsweetened coconut
- 2 tablespoons coconut oil
- 2 tablespoons ground flax seeds
- 1/4 cup agave
- 1 1/2 cups water

Mix-Ins
- 1/2 cup chopped cranberries

Directions
1. Grease a Bundt pan; set aside.
2. In a mixer, mix all dry ingredients together. In another bowl, mix all wet ingredients; whisk the wet ingredients into the dry until smooth. Fold in the add-ins and spread the mixture into the pan; cover with foil.
3. Place pan in your air fryer and add water in the bottom and bake at 370° F for 35 minutes. When done, use a toothpick to check for doneness. If it comes out clean, then the cake is ready, if not, bake for 5-10 more minutes, checking frequently to avoid burning.
4. Remove the cake and let stand for 10 minutes before transferring from the pan.

Nutritional Information per Serving:
Calories: 309; Total Fat: 27 g; Carbs: 14.7 g; Dietary Fiber: 3.8 g; Sugars: 7 g; Protein: 22.6 g; Cholesterol: 0 mg; Sodium: 347 mg

Crunchy Steamed Broccoli

Yield: 2 Servings/Total Time: 8 Minutes/Prep Time: 5 Minutes/Cook Time: 3 Minutes
Ingredients
- 450 g broccoli florets
- 1½ cups water
- Salt and pepper to taste
- 1 tsp. extra virgin olive oil

Directions
1. Add water to the bottom of your air fryer and set the basket on top. Toss the broccoli florets with, salt, pepper and olive oil until evenly combined then transfer to the basket of your air fryer.
2. Cook at 350° for 5 minutes. Remove the basket and serve the broccoli.

Nutritional Information per Serving:
Calories: 160; Total Fat: 12 g; Carbs: 6.1 g; Dietary Fiber: 8 g; Sugars: 0.8 g; Protein: 13 g; Cholesterol: 0 mg; Sodium: 199 mg

Yummy Brussels sprouts

Yield: 4 Servings/Total Time: 20 Minutes/Prep Time: 10 Minutes/Cook Time: 10 Minutes

Ingredients
- 2 pound Brussels sprouts, halved
- 1 tbsp. chopped almonds
- 1 tbsp. rice vinegar
- 2 tbsp. sriracha sauce
- 1/4 cup gluten free soy sauce
- 2 tbsp. sesame oil
- 1/2 tbsp. cayenne pepper
- 1 tbsp. smoked paprika
- 1 tsp. onion powder
- 2 tsp. garlic powder
- 1 tsp. red pepper flakes
- Salt and pepper

Directions
1. Preheat your air fryer to 370° F.
2. Meanwhile place your air fryer's pan on medium heat and cook the almonds for 3 minutes then add in all the remaining ingredients.
3. Place the pan in the air fryer and cook for 8-10 minutes or until done.
4. Serve hot over a bed of steamed rice. Enjoy!

Nutritional Information per Serving:
Calories: 216; Total Fat: 18 g; Carbs: 8.8 g; Dietary Fiber: 9.3 g; Sugars: 1.7 g; Protein: 18 g; Cholesterol: 0 mg; Sodium: 220 mg

Keto Soup

Yield: 5 Servings/Total Time: 1 Hour 10 Minutes/Prep Time: 10 Minutes/Cook Time: 1 Hour

Ingredients
- 2 tablespoons extra virgin olive oil
- 2 red onions, quartered
- 2 red peppers, deseeded, chopped
- 3 tomatoes, halved
- 3 carrots, peeled, diced
- 2 cans light coconut milk
- 1 teaspoon ground cumin
- 1 tablespoon smoked paprika, plus extra for garnish
- 2 inches fresh root ginger, peeled, minced
- 1 bay leaf
- Salt and black pepper
- Chopped coriander to garnish
- Lime wedges

Directions
1. Preheat oven your air fryer to 400°F.
2. In you air fryer's pan, mix all the veggies and oil and roast in the air fryer for about 40 minutes or until cooked. Remove from air fryer.
3. Chop the roasted vegetables and place them in a saucepan; add the remaining ingredients and stir to mix well; season with salt and bring the mixture to a gentle boil in a saucepan and then simmer for about 20 minutes.
4. Divide the soup among six serving bowls and sprinkle each with coriander, black pepper and smoked paprika. Garnish with lime wedges and enjoy!

Nutritional Information per Serving:
Calories: 390; Total Fat: 22 g; Carbs: 11 g; Dietary Fiber: 8.5 g; Sugars: 4 g; Protein: 19 g; Cholesterol: 0 mg; Sodium: 346 mg

Air-fryer Vegetable Sauté

Yield: 4 Servings/Total Time: 25 Minutes/Prep Time: 10 Minutes/Cook Time: 15 Minutes

Ingredients:
- 2 tablespoons extra virgin olive oil
- 1 tablespoon minced garlic
- 1 large shallot, sliced
- 1 cup mushrooms, sliced
- 1 cup broccoli florets
- 1 cup artichoke hearts
- 1 bunch asparagus, sliced into 3-inch pieces
- 1 cup baby peas
- 1 cup cherry tomatoes, halved
- 1/2 teaspoon sea salt

Vinaigrette
- 3 tablespoons white wine vinegar
- 6 tablespoons extra-virgin olive oil
- 1/2 teaspoon sea salt
- 1 teaspoon ground oregano
- handful fresh parsley, chopped

Directions
1. Add oil to the pan of your air fryer set over medium heat. Stir in garlic and shallots and sauté for about 2 minutes.

2. Stir in mushrooms for about 3 minutes or until golden. Stir in broccoli, artichokes, and asparagus and continue cooking for 3 more minutes. Stir in peas, tomatoes and salt and transfer to the air fryer and cook for 5-8 more minutes.
3. Prepare vinaigrette: mix together vinegar, oil, salt, oregano and parsley in a bowl until well combined.
4. Serve vegetable sauté in a serving bowl and drizzle with vinaigrette. Toss to combine and serve.

Nutritional Information per Serving:
Calories: 293; Total Fat: 27 g; Carbs: 14.6 g; Dietary Fiber: 5 g; Sugars: 2 g; Protein: 25 g; Cholesterol: 0 mg; Sodium: 298 mg

Grilled Mixed Mushrooms

Yield: 4 Servings/Total Time: 20 Minutes/Prep Time: 10 Minutes/Cook Time: 10 Minutes

Ingredients
- 2 cups mixed mushrooms
- 1 tablespoon balsamic vinegar
- 1/4 cup extra virgin olive oil
- 1-2 garlic cloves, minced
- A handful of parsley
- 1 teaspoon salt

Directions
1. Rinse the mushrooms and pat dry; put on foil and drizzle with balsamic vinegar and extra virgin olive oil.
2. Sprinkle the mushrooms with garlic, parsley, and salt.
3. Grill for about 10 minutes in your air fryer at 350° F or until tender and cooked through. Serve warm.

Nutritional Information per Serving:
Calories: 260 Total Fat: 19.1 g; Carbs: 11 g; Dietary Fiber: 7 g; Sugars: 1.6 g; Protein: 22 g; Cholesterol: 0 mg; Sodium: 299 mg

Baked Keto Hummus

Yield: 4 Servings/Total Time: 40 Minutes/Prep Time: 15 Minutes/Cook Time: 25 Minutes

Ingredients
- 1 pound carrots, peeled and chopped
- 19 ounces canned chickpeas, drained and rinsed
- 2 cloves garlic
- 4 tablespoons freshly squeezed lemon juice
- ½ teaspoon cumin
- 3 tablespoons tahini
- 2 ½ tablespoons olive oil
- Sea salt to taste

Directions
1. Toss the carrots and ½ a teaspoon olive oil in a roasting pan and bake for 25 minutes at 400° F in your air fryer.
2. Remove from air fryer and let cool slightly then process in a blender or food processor with the remaining ingredients.
3. Enjoy!

Nutritional Information per Serving:
Calories: 181 Total Fat: 16.1 g; Carbs: 9 g; Dietary Fiber: 6 g; Sugars: 3.3 g; Protein: 19 g; Cholesterol: 0 mg; Sodium: 354 mg

Tangy Green Olives

Yields: 12 Servings/Total Time: 35 Minutes/Prep Time: 53 Minutes/Cook Time: 20 Minutes

Ingredients
- 1 teaspoon extra-virgin olive oil
- 1 teaspoon grated lemon peel
- 1 teaspoon crushed red pepper flakes
- 2 sprigs fresh rosemary
- 3 cups green olives
- Lemon twists, optional

Directions
1. Preheat your air fryer to 400° F. Place pepper flakes, rosemary, olives and grated lemon peel onto a large sheet of foil; drizzle with oil and fold the foil. Pinch the edges of the sheet to tightly seal.
2. Bake in the preheated air fryer for about 30 minutes. Remove from the sheet and place the mixture to serving dish. Serve warm garnished with lemon twists.

Nutritional Information per Serving:
Calories: 146 Total Fat: 14.7 g; Carbs: 8.2 g; Dietary Fiber: 5 g; Sugars: 36 g; Protein: 21 g; Cholesterol: 0 mg; Sodium: 224 mg

Coconut-Blueberry Cereal

Yields: 4 Servings/Total Time: 40 Minutes/Prep Time: 20 Minutes/Cook Time: 20 Minutes

Ingredients

- 1/2 cup dried blueberries
- 1/2 cup unsweetened coconut flakes
- 1 cup pumpkin seeds
- 2 cups chopped pecans
- 6 medium dates, pitted
- 1/3 cup coconut oil
- 2 tsp cinnamon
- 1/2 tsp sea salt

Directions

1. Preheat your air fryer to 325°F.
2. Add coconut oil, dates and half the pecans to a food processor; pulse until finely ground. Add pumpkin seeds and the remaining pecans and continue pulsing until roughly chopped.
3. Transfer the mixture to a large bowl and add cinnamon, vanilla and salt; spread on a baking sheet/pan that can fit in your air fryer and bake for about 20 minutes or until browned.
4. Remove from the air fryer and let cool slightly before stirring in blueberries and coconut.
5. Enjoy!

Nutritional Information per Serving:

Calories: 372 Total Fat: 25.2 g; Carbs: 12 g; Dietary Fiber: 9 g; Sugars: 6.3 g; Protein: 20.1 g; Cholesterol: 0 mg; Sodium: 477 mg

Carrot Crunchies

Yields: 2 Servings/Total Time: 35 Minutes/Prep Time: 5 Minutes/Cook Time: 30 Minutes

Ingredients

- 2 large carrots, peeled and cut into julienne strips
- 1 tablespoon extra-virgin olive oil
- Pinch of cayenne pepper
- Pinch of cinnamon

Directions

1. Preheat air fryer to 375° F.
2. Add the carrot strips into a large bowl and drizzle with extra virgin olive oil and sprinkle with cayenne pepper and cinnamon; toss to coat well and then spread evenly onto a cookie sheet that can fit in your air fryer.
3. Bake for about 30 minutes, stirring every 10 minutes, until crispy.
4. Eat as a snack, salad topper, soup topper, or many other side dishes. Enjoy!

Nutritional Information per Serving:

Calories: 110 Total Fat: 13.1 g; Carbs: 4 g; Dietary Fiber: 5 g; Sugars: 2.3 g; Protein: 19 g; Cholesterol: 0 mg; Sodium: 239 mg

Nutty Berry Crumble

Yield: 4 Servings/Total Time: 40 Minutes/Prep Time: 10 Minutes/Cook Time: 30 Minutes

Ingredients:

- 4 cups fresh mixed berries
- 1 cup almond meal
- ½ cup almond butter
- 1 cup oven roasted walnuts, sunflower seeds, pistachios.
- ½ tsp. ground cinnamon

Directions

1. Preheat air fryer to 375° F.
2. Crush the nuts using a mortar and pestle.
3. In a bowl, combine the nut mix, almond meal, cinnamon, and ghee and combine well.
4. In a pie dish, spread half the nut mixture over the bottom of the dish, then top with the berries and finish with the rest of the nut mixture.
5. Bake for 30 minutes and serve warm with natural vanilla yogurt.
6. Yum!

Nutritional Information per Serving:

Calories: 278 Total Fat: 15.7 g; Carbs: 10.3 g; Dietary Fiber: 4 g; Sugars: 7 g; Protein: 13.8 g; Cholesterol: 0 mg; Sodium: 440 mg

Sausage and Cheese Frittata

Ingredients for four servings
- 12 whole eggs
- 1tbsp. butter
- 1 cup sour cream
- 2 red bell peppers, chopped
- ¼ cup shredded cheddar
- 12oz. ground beef sausage

Method and total time: approx. 60 minutes

Preheat your oven to 350°F. In your blender, blitz the eggs, sour cream, salt, and pepper until smooth. Fry the bell peppers in the butter until tender, or around six minutes. Stir in the beef sausage and cook until browned, continuously stirring and breaking up the lumps. Flatten the beef along the bottom of skillet, then top with the bell peppers, followed by the egg mixture. Sprinkle with cheddar cheese, then put the skillet in the oven and bake for thirty minutes.

Per serving: Cal 617; Fat 50g; Net Carbs 5g; Protein 33g

Beef Zucchini Lasagna

Ingredients for four servings
- ½ cup Pecorino Romano cheese
- Salt and pepper, to taste
- 4 yellow zucchini, sliced
- 1tbsp. lard
- 1tsp. garlic powder
- ½lb. ground beef
- 1tsp. onion powder
- 1½ cups grated mozzarella
- 2tbsp. coconut flour
- 2 cups crumbled goat cheese
- 2 cups marinara sauce
- 1 large egg
- 1tbsp. Italian herb seasoning
- ¼ cup fresh basil leaves
- ¼tsp. red chili flakes

Method and total time: approx. 55 minutes

Preheat your oven to 375°F. Cook the beef in the lard for around ten minutes, then reserve. Mix together the garlic powder, coconut flour, onion powder, salt, mozzarella, pepper, goat cheese, half the Pecorino cheese, and egg. Into the marinara sauce, stir in the Italian herb seasoning and chili flakes. In a baking dish, layer the beef, zucchini slices, egg mixture, and marinara sauce until you run out of ingredients. Top with the rest of the Pecorino cheese, and bake for twenty minutes. Serve garnished with basil.

Per serving: Cal 608; Fat 37g; Net Carbs 5.5g; Protein 52g

Tarragon Meatloaf

Ingredients for four servings
- 3tbsp. flaxseed meal
- 2lb. ground beef
- 2 large eggs
- 1 lemon, zested
- 2tbsp. olive oil
- ¼ cup chopped tarragon
- 4 garlic cloves, minced
- ¼ cup chopped oregano

Method and total time: approx. 70 minutes

Preheat your oven to 400°F, and grease a loaf pan. Mix together the beef, pepper, salt, and flaxseed meal, then reserve. Beat the eggs with the olive oil, tarragon, lemon zest, oregano, and garlic. Stir into the beef and combine. Press into your load pan, and bake for an hour. Drain the liquid, and leave to cool. Garnish with lemon slices.

Per serving: Cal 631; Fat 38g; Net Carbs 2.8g; Protein 64g

Cheesy Beef and Broccoli Bake

Ingredients for four servings
- 1 large broccoli head, cut into florets
- 2tbsp. olive oil
- 6 slices pancetta, chopped
- 1lb. ground beef
- 1 cup coconut cream
- 2tbsp. butter
- 2oz. cream cheese, softened
- ¼ cup chopped scallions
- 1¼ cups grated cheddar

Method and total time: approx. 55 minutes

Preheat your oven to 300°F. Blanche the broccoli in boiling water for around two minutes. Drain and reserve. Fry the pancetta for around seven minutes, and reserve. Brown the beef in the olive oil, then reserve. In the same pan, cook the butter, cream cheese, coconut cream, two-thirds of cheddar cheese, salt, and pepper for seven minutes. Put your broccoli florets in a baking dish, top with the cream mixture, then scatter the top with pancetta and scallions. Cover with the rest of the cheddar, and bake for thirty minutes.

Per serving: Cal 854; Fat 69g; Net Carbs 7.3g; Protein 51g

Crock Pot Beef Sliders

Ingredients for four servings
- 3lb. chuck roast, boneless
- 2tsp. garlic powder
- 1tsp. onion powder
- 1tbsp. smoked paprika
- ¼ cup white vinegar
- 2tbsp. tomato paste
- 2tbsp. tamari sauce
- ¼ cup melted butter
- ½ cup bone broth
- Salt and pepper, to taste
- 4 zero-carb hamburger buns, halved
- 4 slices cheddar cheese
- ¼ cup baby spinach

Method and total time: approx. 12 hours 25 minutes
Halve the beef. Mix together the salt, pepper, onion and garlic powders, and paprika, then rub this all over your beef and pop it into the Crock Pot. Combine the tomato paste, tamari sauce, vinegar, broth, and melted butter. Pour over the beef, and cook for six hours on high. Once cooked, shred the meat. Divide the spinach between the buns, add the meat, and top with a cheese slice.
Per serving: Cal 648; Fat 27g; Net Carbs 17.6g; Protein 72g

Beef Stacks and Cabbage

Ingredients for six servings
- 1 head canon cabbage, shredded
- 3tbsp. coconut flour
- 1lb. chuck steak, sliced thinly across the grain
- ¼ cup olive oil
- ½ cup bone broth
- 2tsp. Italian mixed herb blend

Method and total time: approx. 55 minutes
Preheat your oven to 400°F. Combine the salt, coconut flour, and pepper. Add the beef, and coat. On a greased baking sheet, make small mounds of cabbage. Season, and drizzle with two tablespoons of olive oil. Place two to three strips of beef on each mound of cabbage, sprinkle with the herbs, and drizzle with oil again. Bake for thirty minutes, then add the broth and cook for another ten minutes.
Per serving: Cal 222; Fat 14g; Net Carbs 1.5g; Protein 18g

Beef Burgers in a Mushroom Bun

Ingredients for six servings
- 6 large Portobello caps, destemmed and rinsed
- Salt and pepper, to taste
- 1lb. ground beef
- 1tbsp. Worcestershire sauce
- 6 slices Monterey Jack
- 1tbsp. coconut oil
- 6 lettuce leaves
- ¼ cup mayonnaise
- 6 large tomato slices

Method and total time: approx. 30 minutes
Coat the beef in the salt, pepper, and Worcestershire sauce. Shape into six patties, and reserve. Cook the mushroom caps in coconut oil until softened, for around three to four minutes. Reserve. In the same pan, fry the patties for around ten minutes. Top with the cheese, and cook for another minutes, until melted. On each mushroom cap, add a patty, then top with lettuce, tomato, and mayo.
Per serving: Cal 332; Fat 22g; Net Carbs 0.7g; Protein 29g

Enchilada-Stuffed Peppers

Ingredients for six servings
- 6 bell peppers, deseeded
- 3tbsp. butter, softened
- 1½tbsp. olive oil
- ½ white onion, chopped
- 2½lb. ground beef
- 3 cloves garlic, minced
- 3tsp. enchilada seasoning
- ¼ cup grated cheddar cheese
- 1 cup cauliflower rice
- Sour cream, to serve

Method and total time: approx. 70 minutes
Preheat your oven to 400°F. Cook the garlic and onion in the butter for around three minutes. Add the beef, salt, enchilada seasoning, and pepper, and cook for ten minutes. Stir in the cauliflower rice.
Divide between your pepper halves, then top with cheddar and bake for forty minutes. Dollop with sour cream to serve.
Per serving: Cal 409; Fat 21g; Net Carbs 4g; Protein 45g

Hot Beef Lettuce Wraps

Ingredients for four servings
- 3tbsp. ghee, divided
- 1lb. chuck steak, sliced thinly against the grain
- 1 large white onion, chopped
- 1 jalapeño pepper, chopped
- 2 garlic cloves, minced
- 2tsp. red curry powder
- 8 small lettuce leaves
- 1 cup cauliflower rice
- ¼ cup sour cream, to serve

Method and total time: approx. 20 minutes
Season the beef and fry in the ghee for around ten minutes, then reserve. Sauté the onion for three minutes, then add the garlic, pepper, salt, and jalapeño. Cook for a further minute. Add the rest of the ghee, curry powder, and beef. Cook for another five minutes, then stir in the cauliflower rice. Cook until just softened. Season well, then divide between your lettuce leaves. Top with sour cream, and wrap.
Per serving: Cal 298; Fat 18g; Net Carbs 3.3g; Protein 27g

Cheesy Ground Beef Pizza

Ingredients for four servings
- 6oz. shredded cheese
- 1 egg
- ¾ cup almond flour
- 1tsp. plain vinegar
- 8oz. ground beef sausage
- 2tbsp. cream cheese, softened
- 2tbsp. butter
- ¼ cup tomato sauce
- 4½oz. shredded mozzarella
- ½tsp. dried basil

Method and total time: approx. 45 minutes

Preheat your oven to 400°F, line a pizza pan. In a skillet, melt the cream and mozzarella, stirring continuously. Remove from the heat, then add the almond flour, ½ teaspoon salt, egg, and vinegar. Leave to cool, then press into the pizza pan. Prick all over with a fork, then bake for ten to fifteen minutes.

Fry the sausage in the butter for around eight minutes. Once cooked, spread the crust with the tomato sauce, then top with the rest of the ingredients. Bake for a final twelve minutes.

Per serving: Cal 361; Fat 21g; Net Carbs 0.8g; Protein 37g

Spicy Lemon Cheeseburgers

Ingredients for four servings
- 1 large tomato, sliced into 4 pieces and deseeded
- ½ cup chopped cilantro
- 1lb. ground beef
- 1 lemon, zested and juiced
- 1tsp. garlic powder
- Salt and pepper, to taste
- 2tbsp. hot chili puree
- 4tbsp. mayonnaise
- 16 large spinach leaves
- 1 medium red onion, sliced
- 1 avocado, halved, sliced
- ¼ cup grated parmesan

Method and total time: approx. 15 minutes

Preheat your grill to high. Combine the beef, lemon zest, juice, cilantro, salt, garlic powder, pepper, and chili puree. Shape into four patties, then grill for three minutes per side. Lay two spinach leaves side to side, in four portions, on a clean flat surface. On each, add a beef patty, then spread with mayo, top with tomato and onion, and sprinkle with parmesan cheese. Finally, add the avocado, and top with the remaining spinach.

Per serving: Cal 310; Fat 16g; Net Carbs 6.5g; Protein 29g

Meatballs

Ingredients for four servings
- 1 red onion, finely chopped
- 3 garlic cloves, minced
- 2 red bell peppers, chopped
- 2tbsp. melted butter
- 3lb. ground beef
- 2tbsp. tamari sauce
- 1tsp. dried basil
- Salt and pepper, to taste
- 3tbsp. olive oil
- 1tbsp. dried rosemary

Method and total time: approx. 30 minutes

Preheat your oven to 400°F, and grease a baking sheet. Combine the beef, bell peppers, onion, garlic, basil, butter, tamari sauce, pepper, salt, and rosemary. Shape into meatballs, then arrange on your baking sheet. Top with olive oil, then bake for twenty minutes.

Per serving: Cal 618; Fat 33g; Net Carbs 2.5g; Protein 74g

Beef Pad Thai and Zoodles

Ingredients for four servings
- 1tsp. crushed red pepper flakes
- ¼tsp. freshly ground ginger
- ¼tsp. freshly pureed garlic
- Salt and pepper, to taste
- 3 large eggs, lightly beaten
- 2tbsp. peanut oil
- 2½lb. chuck steak, sliced thinly against the grain
- ⅓ cup beef broth
- 2tbsp. tamari sauce
- 3¼tbsp. peanut butter
- 1tbsp. white vinegar
- 2 garlic cloves, minced
- ½ cup chopped green onions
- 4 zucchinis, spiralized
- ½ cup crushed peanuts
- ½ cup bean sprouts

Method and total time: approx. 35 minutes

Mix together the garlic, salt, ginger, and pepper. Coat the beef in this. In a skillet, cook the beef in the peanut oil for twelve minutes, then reserve. Add the eggs to the skillet, and scramble for a minute, then reserve. Reduce the heat, and combine the broth, tamari sauce, green onions, peanut butter, vinegar, minced garlic, and red pepper flakes. Simmer for three minutes, then stir in the beef, bean sprouts, zoodles, and eggs. Cook for a minute, then serve topped with peanuts.

Per serving: Cal 425; Fat 40g; Net Carbs 3.3g; Protein 70g

Tasty Taco pizza

Ingredients for four servings

- 2 cups shredded mozzarella
- 1 egg
- 2tbsp. cream cheese, softened
- ¾ cup almond flour
- 2tsp. taco seasoning
- 1lb. ground beef
- ½ cup cheese sauce
- 1 cup chopped lettuce
- 1 cup grated cheddar cheese
- 1 tomato, diced
- 1 cup sour cream for topping
- ¼ cup sliced black olives

Method and total time: approx. 45 minutes

Preheat your oven to 390°F, and line a pizza pan. Microwave the mozzarella and cream cheese for a minute, then stir in the egg and almond flour. Spread over the pan, and bake for fifteen minutes. Fry the beef for five minutes, then add the taco seasoning and salt and pepper. Spread the cheese sauce on the crust, then top with the meat. Top with the cheddar cheese, tomato, lettuce, and black olives. Bake for another five minutes, then serve with a drizzle of sour cream.

Per serving: Cal 590; Fat 29g; Net Carbs 7.9g; Protein 64g

Ginger and Cumin Beef Kebabs

Ingredients for four servings

- 2 yellow bell peppers, deseeded and cut into squares
- 2 cups cremini mushrooms, halved
- 2lb. tri-tip steak, cubed
- 1tbsp. tamari sauce
- 2tbsp. coconut oil
- 3 limes, juiced
- ½tsp. ground cumin
- 1tbsp. ginger powder

Method and total time: approx. 1 hour 25 minutes

Combine the coconut oil, lime juice, tamari sauce, ginger, pepper, salt, and cumin powder. Stir in the mushrooms, beef, and bell peppers. Leave to marinate for an hour. Preheat your grill to high. Thread the beef, mushrooms, and bell peppers alternately on skewers, then grill for five minutes per side. Garnish with sesame seeds and parsley.

Per serving: Cal 383; Fat 17g; Net Carbs 3.2g; Protein 51g

Beef and Mushroom Stir-Fry

Ingredients for four servings

- 2 sprigs rosemary, leaves extracted
- 1lb. chuck steak
- 1 green bell pepper, chopped
- 2 cups shiitake mushrooms, halved
- 4 slices prosciutto, chopped
- 1tbsp. freshly pureed garlic
- 1tbsp. coconut oil

Method and total time: approx. 30 minutes

Slice the steak across the grain, then season with salt and pepper. Fry the prosciutto until crisp, then reserve. Cook the beef in the coconut oil for around twelve minutes. Reserve. In the same pan, cook the mushrooms and bell pepper for five minutes. Return the prosciutto and beef to the pan, then add the rosemary and garlic. Season, and cook for another four minutes.

Per serving: Cal 231; Fat 12g; Net Carbs 2.1g; Protein 27g

Nutty Beef with Cauliflower Rice

Ingredients for four servings

- 3tbsp. olive oil
- 2 large eggs, beaten
- 1½lb. chuck steak
- 1tbsp. avocado oil
- ½ cup chopped bell peppers
- 1 red onion, finely chopped
- ½ cup green beans, chopped
- 4 cups cauliflower rice
- 3 garlic cloves, minced
- ¼ cup coconut aminos
- 1tbsp. toasted sesame seeds
- 1 cup toasted cashew nuts

Method and total time: approx. 25 minutes

Season your beef, the cook in two tablespoons of the olive oil until tender, then reserve. In the same pan, scramble the eggs for one minute, the reserve. Put the rest of the olive oil and avocado oil in the pan, then cook the onion, green beans, bell peppers, and garlic. Sauté for around three minutes. Stir in the cauliflower rice and coconut aminos, then stir in the beef, eggs, and cashew nuts. Cook for three minutes. Remove from the heat, then serve garnished with sesame seeds.

Per serving: Cal 500; Fat 32; Net Carbs 3.2g; Protein 44g

Creamy Beef and Mushrooms

Ingredients for four servings
- ¼ cup button mushrooms, sliced
- 1 yellow onion, chopped
- 3tbsp. unsalted butter
- 4 rib-eye steaks
- 2tbsp. coconut cream
- ⅓ cup coconut milk
- ½tsp. dried thyme
- 3tbsp. black olives, sliced
- 2tbsp. chopped parsley

Method and total time: approx. 30 minutes
Cook the mushrooms in two tablespoons butter for around four minutes. Add the onions, and cook for another three minutes. Reserve.

Season the beef, then cook in the rest of the butter for around ten minutes. Put the mushrooms and onion back into the skillet, then stir in the milk, thyme, coconut cream, and a tablespoon of parsley. Simmer for two minutes, then stir in the olives and remove from the heat. Serve topped with parsley.

Per serving: Cal 639; Fat 39g; Net Carbs 1.9g; Protein 69g

Sweet Barbecue Steak

Ingredients for four servings
- 2tbsp. avocado oil
- 3tbsp. barbecue dry rub
- 2lb. rib steak, membrane removed
- 3tbsp. maple syrup

Method and total time: approx. 2 hours 40 minutes
Preheat your oven to 300°F, and line a baking sheet with aluminum foil. Combine the maple syrup and avocado oil, and brush onto the meat. Press the rub into it, then put on the baking sheet, and bake until tender with a crisp outer. This should take around two and a half hours.

Per serving: Cal 490; Fat 26g; Net Carbs 1.8g; Protein 49g

Beef Burgers

Ingredients for four servings
- ½tsp. onion powder
- 1lb. ground beef
- ½tsp. garlic powder
- 4 zero-carb burger buns
- 2tbsp. ghee
- 1tsp. Dijon mustard
- ¼ cup mayonnaise
- 4tbsp. slaw
- 1tsp. Sriracha sauce
- Salt and pepper, to taste

Method and total time: approx. 15 minutes
Combine the beef, garlic powder, salt, onion powder, mustard, and pepper. Shape into four patties, then fry in the ghee for three minutes per side. Serve on a bun with mayonnaise, sriracha sauce, and slaw.

Per serving: Cal 664; Fat 55g; Net Carbs 7.9g; Protein 39g

Flank Fajitas

Ingredients for four servings
- 2lb. flank steak, cut in halves
- 2tbsp. olive oil
- 2tbsp. Adobo seasoning
- 2 large white onion, chopped
- 12 zero-carb tortillas
- 1 cup sliced bell peppers

Method and total time: approx. 10 minutes
Season the steak with the adobo, leave to marinate in the fridge for an hour. Grill for six minutes, flipping once. Remove from the heat, wrap in foil, and let rest for ten minutes. Cook the onion and bell peppers in the oil for five minutes. Strip the steak against the grain, and divide between your tortillas along with the rest of the ingredients.

Per serving: Cal 348, Fat 25g, Net Carbs 5g, Protein 18g

Curried Beef in a Garlic and Cream Sauce

Ingredients for four servings
- 2tbsp. ghee
- 2 garlic cloves, minced
- 4 large rib-eye steak
- ½ cup chopped brown onion
- 1 red bell pepper, sliced
- 1 green bell pepper, sliced
- 2 long red chilies, sliced
- 1 cup coconut milk
- 1 cup beef stock
- 1tbsp. Thai green curry paste
- 3tbsp. chopped cilantro
- 1 lime, juiced

Method and total time: approx. 40 minutes
Season the beef, and cook in half the ghee for three minutes per side. Reserve. In the rest of the ghee, cook the garlic and onion for three minutes. Add the red chili and bell peppers until tender. Add the beef stock, curry paste, coconut milk, and lime juice. Simmer for four minutes, then return the beef to the pan and leave to cook for ten minutes. Broil for another five minutes, then top with cilantro.

Per serving: Cal 644; Fat 35g; Net Carbs 2.6g; Protein 72g

Beef with Brussel Sprouts

Ingredients for four servings
- 1½ cups Brussel sprouts, halved
- 1 garlic clove, minced
- 2tbsp. avocado oil
- ½ white onion, chopped
- 1lb. ground beef
- ¼ cup toasted walnuts, chopped
- Salt and pepper, to taste
- 1 bok choy, quartered
- 1tbsp. black sesame seeds
- 2tbsp. chopped scallions

Method and total time: approx. 30 minutes
In a tablespoon of avocado oil, fry the onion and garlic for three minutes. Add the ground beef, and cook until browned and lump-free. Stir in the Brussel sprouts, walnuts, bok choy, and scallions, the season well. Sauté for five minutes.

Per serving: Cal 302; Fat 18g; Net Carbs 3.1g; Protein 29g

Instant Pot Shredded Beef

Ingredients for four servings
- 3tbsp. coconut oil
- 3 garlic cloves, minced
- 1 large white onion, chopped
- 1 cup shredded red cabbage
- 1tsp. dried Italian herb blend
- 1 lemon, zested and juiced
- 1½tbsp. balsamic vinegar
- 2lb. chuck steak
- ½ cup beef broth
- Salt and pepper, to taste

Method and total time: approx. 45 minutes
Using the sauté setting, cook the garlic, onion, and cabbage in the coconut oil for around three minutes. Add the lemon zest, Italian herb blend, lemon juice, balsamic vinegar, salt, and pepper, and cook for two minutes. Add the broth. Season the meat, and add this too. Secure the lid, and cook on manual at high pressure for 25 minutes. Release the pressure, then shred the meat. Reselect Sauté, then cook until the sauce thickens. Spoon over the beef to serve.

Per serving: Cal 652; Fat 49g; Net Carbs 5.8g; Protein 44g

Easy Cheesy Beef Burger Bake

Ingredients for four servings
- 1tbsp. butter
- ¼ cup shredded Monterey Jack cheese
- 1lb. ground beef
- 1 medium red onion, chopped
- 1 garlic clove, minced
- 2 tomatoes
- Salt and pepper, to taste
- 1tbsp. dried basil
- 2 eggs
- 1 cup coconut cream
- 2tbsp. tomato paste

Method and total time: approx. 35 minutes
Preheat your oven to 400°F. Fry the beef in the butter for around ten minutes. Stir in the garlic and onion, and cook for another three minutes. Add the tomatoes, salt, basil, and pepper, and cook until the tomatoes soften. Stir in ⅔ Monterey Jack cheese, and stir until melted. Beat the eggs with the tomato paste, salt, and coconut cream. Transfer the beef to a baking sheet, the top with the eggs. Top with the last of the cheese, and bake for twenty minutes.

Per serving: Cal 469; Fat 34g; Net Carbs 4.5g; Protein 33g

Taco Beef Zucchini Boats

Ingredients for four servings
- 2tbsp. butter
- 1 red bell pepper, chopped
- 1lb. ground beef
- 2 garlic cloves, minced
- 2tbsp. taco seasoning
- 2 zucchinis, halved and flesh scooped out
- 1 shallot, finely chopped
- ½ cup finely chopped parsley
- 1¼ cups shredded cheddar
- 1tbsp. olive oil

Method and total time: approx. 50 minutes
Preheat your oven to 400°F, and grease a baking sheet. Chop up the zucchini flesh, and reserve. Brown the beef in the butter for around ten minutes. Stir in the bell pepper, zucchini flesh, garlic, taco seasoning, and shallot, then cook for five minutes. Divide between your zucchini boats, then top with parsley and a drizzle of oil. Sprinkle with cheddar, and bake for twenty minutes.

Per serving: Cal 423; Fat 29g; Net Carbs 2.9g; Protein 35g

Meatloaf with Pecans

Ingredients for four servings

- 1 white onion, finely chopped
- ½ cup coconut cream
- 1½lb. ground beef
- ½ cup shredded parmesan
- 2tbsp. olive oil
- 1tbsp. dried sage
- 1 egg, lightly beaten
- 4tbsp. toasted pecans, chopped
- 6 bacon slices
- Salt and pepper, to taste

Method and total time: approx. 45 minutes

Preheat your oven to 400°F. Fry the onion in the olive oil for around three minutes. Combine the ground beef, coconut cream, onion, parmesan, sage, eggs, pecans, salt, and pepper. Shape into a loaf, then wrap with bacon slices and secure with toothpicks. Bake for thirty minutes.

Per serving: Cal 617; Fat 43g; Net Carbs 6.6g; Protein 48g

Ground Beef with Blue Cheese and Cabbage

Ingredients for four servings

- 1 canon cabbage, shredded
- 1tsp. garlic powder
- 1tsp. onion powder
- 2tsp. dried oregano
- 1½lb. ground beef
- 3tbsp. butter
- 1tbsp. red wine vinegar
- 1 cup coconut cream
- ½ cup fresh parsley, chopped
- ¼ cup blue cheese

Method and total time: approx. 25 minutes

Sauté the cabbage, onion and garlic powders, salt, oregano, pepper, and vinegar in the butter for around five minutes. Reserve. In the same skillet, brown the beef in two tablespoons of butter, for around ten minutes. Add the coconut cream and blue cheese, and cook until the cheese melts. Return the cabbage, stir in the parsley, and cook for two minutes.

Per serving: Cal 542; Fat 41g; Net Carbs 4.2g; Protein 41g

Beef and Tomato Tart

Ingredients for four servings

- 2tbsp. olive oil
- 1tbsp. Italian mixed herbs
- 2lb. ground beef
- 4tbsp. tomato paste
- ¾ cup almond flour
- 4tbsp. coconut flour
- 4tbsp. flaxseeds
- 1 small brown onion, chopped
- 1 garlic clove, finely chopped
- 3tbsp. coconut oil, melted
- 1tsp. baking powder
- 1 egg
- ¼ cup shredded cheddar
- ¼ cup ricotta, crumbled

Method and total time: approx. 1 hour 30 minutes

Preheat your oven to 350°F, and line a pie dish. Cook the garlic and onion in the olive oil, until tender. Stir in the beef and cook until brown. Season well, and add the herbs. Mix in the tomato paste and a half-cup water. Simmer for twenty minutes, then reserve. In your blender, combine the flours, baking powder, flaxseeds, a pinch of salt, egg, coconut oil, and four tablespoons water. Mix until a dough is formed. Spread in the pie pan, and bake for twelve minutes. Spread the meat filling on top. Combine the ricotta and cheddar cheeses, and sprinkle on top. Bake for 35 minutes.

Per serving: Cal 603; Fat 39g; Net Carbs 2.3g; Protein 57g

Beef Casserole with Goat Cheese

Ingredients for four servings

- 1½lb. ground beef
- 2tbsp. ghee
- Salt and pepper, to taste
- 5oz. goat cheese, crumbled
- 3oz. pitted green olives
- 1 garlic clove, minced
- 1¼ cups coconut cream
- 3oz. basil pesto

Method and total time: approx. 45 minutes

Preheat your oven to 400°F, and grease a casserole dish. Brown the beef in the ghee, then season well. Spread in your casserole dish. Top with goat cheese, olives, and garlic. Combine the pesto and coconut cream, then pour over the beef. Bake for around 25 minutes.

Per serving: Cal 656; Fat 51g; Net Carbs 4g; Protein 47g

Sweet and Spicy Beef

Ingredients for four servings

- 2tsp. maple syrup
- 1bsp. coconut flour
- Salt and pepper, to taste
- ½tsp. xanthan gum
- 1tbsp. coconut oil
- ½ cup olive oil, for frying
- 1tsp. freshly pureed ginger
- 1 red chili, minced
- 1 clove garlic, minced
- 4tbsp. tamari sauce
- 1lb. ribeye steak, sliced into ¼-inch strips
- 1tsp. fish sauce
- 1tsp. sesame oil
- 2tbsp. white wine vinegar
- 1 small bok choy, quartered
- 1tsp. hot sauce
- ½ jalapeño, sliced into rings
- 1 scallion, chopped
- 1tbsp. toasted sesame seeds

Method and total time: approx. 40 minutes

Season the beef, then rub all over with the coconut flour and xanthan gum. Fry in the olive oil until browned all over. Reserve. Sauté the ginger, red chili, garlic, and bok choy in the olive oil for five minutes. Stir in the tamari sauce, fish sauce, hot sauce, sesame oil, vinegar, and maple syrup, and cook for two minutes. Return the beef to the pan, and cook for two minutes. Serve topped with scallion, jalapeños, and sesame seeds.

Per serving: Cal 507; Fat 43g; Net Carbs 2.9g; Protein 25g

Beef-Stuffed Avocado Boats

Ingredients for four servings

- 1lb. ground beef
- 1tsp. onion powder
- Salt and pepper, to taste
- 1tsp. cumin powder
- 2tsp. taco seasoning
- 1tsp. garlic powder
- 2tsp. smoked paprika
- 1tbsp. hemp seeds, hulled
- 1 cup raw pecans, chopped
- 4tbsp. avocado oil
- 7tbsp. shredded Monterey Jack
- 1 medium tomato, sliced
- 2 avocados, halved and pitted
- ¼ cup shredded iceberg lettuce
- 4tbsp. shredded Monterey Jack
- 4tbsp. sour cream

Method and total time: approx. 30 minutes

Cook the beef in the avocado oil for ten minutes. Season with the salt, onion powder, pepper, cumin, taco seasoning, garlic, and paprika. Stir in the pecans and hemp seeds, and stir-fry for another ten minutes. Stir in three tablespoons Monterey Jack cheese, cooking until melted. Divide between your avocados, then add tomato, lettuce, sour cream, and the rest of the cheese.

Per serving: Cal 840; Fat 70g; Net Carbs 4g; Protein 42g

Beef with Tamari Sauce

Ingredients for four servings

- ¼ cup tamari sauce
- 1lb. beef sirloin, cut into strips
- 2tbsp. lemon juice
- 1tbsp. swerve sugar
- 3tsp. garlic powder
- 1 cup coconut oil
- 1lb. cauliflower rice
- 6 garlic cloves, minced
- 2tbsp. olive oil
- 2tbsp. chopped scallions
- 4 large eggs

Method and total time: approx. 35 min + chilling time

Combine the tamari sauce, garlic powder, lemon juice, and swerve. Add the beef, and marinate overnight. In a wok, fry the beef in the coconut oil, until all the liquid evaporates and the meat is cooked through. Reserve. Sauté the garlic for two minutes, then stir in the cauliflower rice until softened. Season well, then reserve. Fry the eggs in olive oil. To serve top the rice with the beef, then topped with the eggs and a sprinkle of scallions.

Per serving: Cal 908; Fat 83g; Net Carbs 5.1g; Protein 34g

Beefy Pizza

Ingredients for four servings

- 1½lb. ground beef
- 1 large egg
- Salt and pepper, to taste
- 1tsp. rosemary
- 3 garlic cloves, minced
- 1tsp. thyme
- 1tsp. basil
- ¾ cup low-carb tomato sauce
- ½tbsp. oregano
- ¼ cup shredded parmesan
- 1 cup shredded mozzarella
- 1 cup shredded Pepper Jack

Method and total time: approx. 30 minutes

Preheat your oven to 350°F, and grease a pizza pan. Mix together your beef, pepper, salt, egg, basil, thyme, rosemary, garlic, and oregano, then flatten onto your pan. Bake for fifteen minutes. Spread with tomato sauce, add the cheeses, and bake for another five minutes.

Per serving: Cal 319; Fat 10g; Net Carbs 3.6g; Protein 49g

Philly Cheesesteak Omelet

Ingredients for two servings

- 2tbsp. almond milk
- 4 large eggs
- 2tbsp. olive oil
- ½ green bell pepper, sliced
- 1 yellow onion, sliced
- ¼lb. beef ribeye shaved steak
- 2oz. provolone cheese, sliced
- Salt and pepper, to taste

Method and total time: approx. 35 minutes

Beat the eggs with the milk. In a skillet, heat half the oil and pour in half the eggs. Fry until cooked, then flip and cook until set. Repeat with the rest of the eggs. Heat the rest of the olive oil, and sauté the onion and bell pepper for five minutes. Reserve. Season the beef, then cook until browned. Return the onion and pepper to the pan and cook for another minute. Lay the omelets with the provolone cheese, then top with the beef mixture. Roll the eggs, return to the skillet, and cook until the cheese is melted.

Per serving: Cal 497; Fat 36g; Net Carbs 3.6g; Protein 34g

Cheesy Beef-Stuffed Mushrooms

Ingredients for four servings

- 2tbsp. olive oil
- 1 shallot, finely chopped
- ½ celery stalk, chopped
- 1lb. ground beef
- 1tsp. Old Bay seasoning
- 2tbsp. mayonnaise
- ½tsp. garlic powder
- ½ cup shredded Pecorino Romano cheese
- 4 caps Portobello mushrooms
- 2 large eggs
- 1tbsp. flaxseed meal
- 1tbsp. chopped parsley
- 2tbsp. shredded parmesan

Method and total time: approx. 55 minutes

Preheat your oven to 350°F. Sauté the celery and shallot in the oil for three minutes. Reserve. Cook the beef for ten minutes. Reserve. Combine the mayo, garlic powder, Old Bay seasoning, Pecorino cheese, and eggs and stir into the reserved beef and vegetables. Stuff the mushrooms with the beef mix. Arrange the mushrooms on a greased baking sheet and fill with the meat mixture. Top with the flaxseed meal and parmesan. Bake for thirty minutes, and serve with parsley.

Per serving: Cal 375; Fat 22g; Net Carbs 3.5g; Protein 37g

Korean Beef and Kelp Noodles

Ingredients for four servings

- 2 x 16oz. packs kelp noodles, thoroughly rinsed
- 2 pieces star anise
- 1 cinnamon stick
- 1tbsp. coconut oil
- 1-inch ginger, grated
- 1 garlic clove, minced
- 3tbsp. coconut aminos
- ¼ cup red wine
- 2tbsp. swerve brown sugar
- 1½lb. sirloin steak, cut into strips
- 4 cups beef broth
- Scallions, thinly sliced
- 1 head napa cabbage, steamed

Method and total time: approx. 2 hours 15 minutes

Sauté the anise, garlic, cinnamon, and ginger in the oil until fragrant. Stir in the beef, season well, and sear for five minutes per side. Mix together the aminos, wine, sugar, and a quarter-cup water. Stir into the pot, cover, and simmer for an hour to an hour and a half. Once the meat is tender, strain and return the liquid to the pot. Discard the cinnamon and anise. Add the broth, and simmer for ten minutes. Cook the kelp noodles in the broth for six minutes. Spoon the noodles and some broth into bowls, then add the beef, and top with cabbage and scallions.

Per serving: Cal 548; Fat 27g; Net Carbs 26.6g; Protein 44g

Pasta and Meatballs

Ingredients for four servings

- 1 egg yolk
- 1 cup shredded mozzarella
- ½ cup olive oil
- 6 garlic cloves, minced
- 2 yellow onions, chopped
- 2tbsp. tomato paste
- ¼tsp. saffron powder
- 2 large tomatoes, chopped
- 2 cinnamon sticks
- Salt and pepper, to taste
- 4½ cups chicken broth
- 2 cups pork rinds
- 1 egg
- 1lb. ground beef
- ¼ cup almond milk
- 1tbsp. smoked paprika
- ¼tsp. nutmeg powder
- 1½tsp. fresh ginger paste
- ½tsp. cayenne pepper
- 1tsp. cumin powder
- ½tsp. cloves powder
- 4tbsp. chopped scallions
- 4tbsp. chopped cilantro
- 4tbsp. chopped parsley
- 1 cup crumbled feta cheese
- ¼ cup almond flour

Method and total time: approx. 1 hour + chilling time

Microwave the mozzarella for two minutes, then stir in the egg yolk. Roll out between two pieces of parchment paper, then cut into spaghetti strands. Leave in the fridge overnight. Cook for one minute in two cups of water. Drain, and leave to cool. Cook the onions and hal the garlic in three tablespoons olive oil, for around three minutes. Stir in the tomato paste, saffron, tomatoes, and cinnamon sticks, and cook for two minutes. Add the chicken broth, season, and simmer for 25 minutes.

Combine the pork rinds, egg, beef, almond milk, salt, remaining garlic, pepper, paprika, nutmeg, ginger, cayenne, cumin, cloves powder, parsley, cilantro, three tablespoons of scallions, and almond flour. Shape into balls, then fry for ten minutes. Put them into the sauce, and cook for another five to ten minutes. Serve over the pasta, then top with scallions and feta cheese.

Per serving: Cal 783; Fats 56g; Net Carbs 6.3g; Protein 55g

Corned Beef Collard Wraps

Ingredients for four servings

- 1tbsp. butter
- 2tsp. Worcestershire sauce
- Salt and pepper, to taste
- 1tsp. Dijon mustard
- ¼tsp. cloves
- 2lb. corned beef
- 1tsp. whole peppercorns
- ¼tsp. allspice
- 1 large bay leaf
- ½tsp. red pepper flakes
- 1 lemon, zested and juiced
- ¼ cup freshly brewed coffee
- ¼ cup white wine
- ⅓tbsp. swerve sugar
- 1 medium red onion, sliced
- 8 large Swiss collard leaves

Method and total time: approx. 70 minutes

Combine the beef, salt, butter, pepper, mustard, Worcestershire sauce, peppercorns, allspice, cloves, flakes, lemon zest, bay leaf, lemon juice, coffee, wine, and swerve in a pan. Cover, and cook for an hour. Ten minutes before it's finished, bring a pot of water to a boil, then cook the collards with a slice of onion for thirty seconds, then blanch in ice for two to three minutes. Pat dry and lay flat. Take the meat out of the pot and slice. Divide between the collard leaves, top with onions, and wrap.

Per serving: Cal 349; Fat 16g; Net Carbs 1.5g; Protein 47g

Steak and Shirataki Fettucine

Ingredients for four servings

- 1lb. thick-cut New York strip steaks, cut into 1-inch cubes
- 4tbsp. butter
- 1 cup freshly grated Pecorino Romano cheese
- 14oz. packs shirataki fettuccine
- Salt and pepper, to taste
- 2tbsp. chopped fresh parsley
- 4 garlic cloves, minced

Method and total time: approx. 30 minutes

Strain and rinse the pasta, then boil in two cups of water for three minutes, then strain again. Stir fry until dry, then reserve. Season the steaks, then cook in the butter for ten minutes. Stir in the garlic and cook another minute. Add the parsley and shirataki, and season well. Serve topped with the Pecorino Romano cheese.

Per serving: Cal 422; Fats 22g; Net Carbs 7.3g; Protein 36g

Cheesy Beef and Zucchini

Ingredients for two servings

- 3tbsp. sour cream
- 4oz. roast beef deli slices, torn apart
- 1 small zucchini, chopped
- 3oz. shredded cheddar cheese
- 2tbsp. chopped green chilies

Method and total time: approx. 10 minutes

Take two wide mugs, and line with beef slices. Top with half the sour cream, followed by the zucchini slices, and season well. Add the green chilies, the rest of the sour cream, and top with cheddar. Microwave for a minute or two, until the cheese melts.

Per serving: Cal 188; Fat 9g; Net Carbs 3.7g; Protein 18g

Balsamic Beef Meatloaf

Ingredients for eight servings

- ½ cup chopped onion
- 2 garlic cloves, minced
- ½ cup almond flour
- 1 cup sliced mushrooms
- 2tbsp. chopped parsley
- 3lbs. ground beef
- 3 eggs
- ¼ cup chopped bell peppers
- 1tsp. balsamic vinegar
- ⅓ cup grated parmesan

Glaze:

- 2 cups balsamic vinegar
- 2tbsp. ketchup
- 1tbsp. sweetener

Method and total time: approx. 1 hour 15 minutes

Preheat your oven to 370°F. Combine the meatloaf ingredients in a large bowl, then press into a loaf pan. Bake for thirty minutes. In a saucepan, mix together the glaze ingredients and simmer for twenty minutes, until thickened. Pour a quarter-cup of the glaze over the meatloaf, then bake for another twenty minutes.

Per serving: Cal 264; Fat 19g; Net Carbs 6g; Protein 23g

Thai Beef Shirataki

Ingredients for four servings
- 1 cup sliced shiitake mushrooms
- 14oz. packs angel hair shirataki
- 2tbsp. olive oil, divided
- 1 white onion, thinly sliced
- 1¼lb. flank steak, sliced
- 1 red bell pepper, sliced
- 1½ cups Thai basil leaves
- 4 garlic cloves, minced
- 2tbsp. toasted sesame seeds
- 1tbsp. chopped scallions
- 1tbsp. chopped peanuts
- 3tbsp. coconut aminos
- 1tbsp. hot sauce
- 2tbsp. fish sauce

Method and total time: approx. 35 minutes

Strain the shirataki pasta and rinse, then cook in two cups of boiling water for three minutes. Stir fry until dry, then reserve.

Season the meat, and cook the beef in the oil until browned all over. Reserve. In the same skillet, cook the onion, garlic, bell pepper, and mushrooms, and cook for five minutes. Return the beef to the pan, and stir in the pasta. Mix together the fish sauce, aminos, and hot sauce. Pour over the beef. Toss with the Thai basil, and cook for another minute or two. Garnish with peanuts, sesame seeds, and scallions.

Per serving: Cal 358; Fats 16g; Net Carbs 7.5g; Protein 30g

Bacon-Wrapped Hot Dogs

Ingredients for four servings
- ½ cup grated Gruyere cheese
- 8 large beef hot dogs
- 16 slices bacon
- 1tsp. garlic powder
- 1tsp. onion powder
- Salt and pepper, to taste

Method and total time: approx. 45 minutes

Preheat your oven to 400°F. Cut a pocket into each hot dog and stuff with the cheese. Wrap each sausage with two bacon slices, and secure with toothpicks. Season with the onion and garlic powders, salt, and pepper. Grill for forty minutes, until the bacon is crisp.

Per serving: Cal 958; Fat 86g; Net Carbs 4.1g; Protein 37g

Beefy Carbonara

Ingredients for four servings
- 1¼ cups grated parmesan
- 1¼ cups heavy cream
- 4 bacon slices, chopped
- ¼ cup mayonnaise
- 1 cup shredded mozzarella
- 2tbsp. parsley, chopped
- 4 egg yolks
- Salt and pepper, to taste

Method and total time: approx. 30 minutes

Microwave the mozzarella for two minutes, then let cool for one minute. Stir in the egg yolk until combined. Roll out between two bits of parchment paper, then slice into spaghetti strands. Refrigerate overnight. Cook for one minute in two cups of water, then drain again. Add the bacon to a skillet and cook until crisp. Reserve. Pour in the heavy cream, and simmer for five minutes. Season the mayo. Cook for one minute. Spoon two tablespoons of the mixture into a bowl, and mix in the rest of the egg yolks. Pour this into the pot and mix. Stir in a cup of parmesan cheese, then fold in the pasta.

Per serving: Cal 470; Fats 35g; Net Carbs 8.9g; Protein 25g

Salisbury Steak

Ingredients for six servings
- 2lbs. ground beef
- ¾ almond flour
- 1tbsp. onion flakes
- ¼ cup beef broth
- 1tbsp. Worcestershire sauce
- 1tbsp. chopped parsley

Method and total time: approx. 25 minutes

Preheat your oven to 375°F. Mix together everything, then shape into patties. Bake for eighteen minutes.

Per serving: Cal 354; Fat 28g; Net Carbs 2.5g; Protein 27g

Beef Alfredo

Ingredients for four servings
- 2tbsp. olive oil
- 2 medium spaghetti squashes, halved
- 2tbsp. butter
- ½tsp. garlic powder
- 1lb. ground beef
- Salt and pepper, to taste
- 1½ cups heavy cream
- 1tsp. arrowroot starch
- A pinch of nutmeg
- ⅓ cup grated mozzarella
- ⅓ cup grated parmesan

Method and total time: approx. 1 hour 20 minutes
Preheat your oven to 375°F. Coat the squash with olive oil, salt, and pepper. Place in a foil-lined dish, and bake for 45 minutes. Cool, then shred into noodles. Cook the beef in the butter, along with the garlic powder, salt, and pepper, for around ten minutes. Stir in the heavy cream, arrowroot starch, and nutmeg. Cook until the sauce thickens. Spoon the sauce into the squash, and top with parmesan and mozzarella. Broil for three minutes.
Per serving: Cal 563; Fats 42g; Net Carbs 4g; Protein 36g

Beef and Asparagus Shirataki

Ingredients for four servings
- 1lb. fresh asparagus, cut into 1-inch pieces
- 16oz. packs angel hair shirataki
- 1lb. ground beef
- 2 shallots, finely chopped
- 3tbsp. olive oil
- 3 garlic cloves, minced
- 1 cup grated parmesan cheese
- Salt and pepper, to taste

Method and total time: approx. 40 minutes
Drain and rinse the pasta, then boil for three minutes in two cups of water. Strain, and stir fry until dry. Fry the beef in the olive oil for ten minutes, then reserve. Stir the shallots and garlic into the same pan, and cook for two minutes. Season well, the add the beef and the shirataki, and toss until combined. Serve with parmesan cheese.
Per serving: Cal 513; Fat 25g; Net Carbs 7.2g; Protein 44g

Beef Ragu

Ingredients for four servings
- 2tbsp. butter
- Salt and pepper, to taste
- 1lb. ground beef
- 8 mixed bell peppers, spiralized
- ¼ cup tomato sauce
- 1 cup grated parmesan cheese
- 1 small red onion, spiralized

Method and total time: approx. 20 minutes
Brown the beef in the butter for around five minutes. Season well, then add the tomato sauce and cook for ten minutes more. Add the bell pepper and onion noodles, and cook for a final minute. Top with parmesan to serve.
Per serving: Cal 451; Fats 25g; Net Carbs 7.2g; Protein 40g

Barbecued Beef Pizza

Ingredients for four servings
- 1½ cups grated Gruyere cheese
- 1 cup grated mozzarella cheese
- 1lb. ground beef
- ¼ cup BBQ sauce
- 2 eggs, beaten
- ¼ cup sliced red onion
- 2tbsp. chopped parsley
- 2 bacon slices, chopped

Method and total time: approx. 40 minutes
Preheat your oven to 390°F, and line a round pizza pan. Combine the beef, mozzarella, eggs, and salt, then spread over the pan and bake for twenty minutes. Cover with the barbecue sauce, then top with Gruyere cheese, onion, and bacon. Cook for another fifteen minutes. Serve with parsley.
Per serving: Cal 538; Fats 32g; Net Carbs 0.4g; Protein 56g

Beef and Poodles

Ingredients for four servings
- 1 cup sun-dried tomatoes in oil, chopped
- 3tbsp. butter
- 1 cup shaved parmesan cheese
- Salt and pepper, to taste
- 1¼ cups heavy cream
- 1lb. beef stew meat, cut into strips
- 4 large parsnips, spiralized into poodles
- 4 garlic cloves, minced
- ¼tsp. dried basil
- 2tbsp. chopped parsley
- ¼tsp. red chili flakes

Method and total time: approx. 35 minutes
Sauté the parsnips in the butter until softened, then reserve. Season the beef, then cook in the same skillet for around eight to ten minutes. Add the sun-dried tomatoes and garlic, and cook for a further minute. Reduce the heat, then add the heavy cream and parmesan. Simmer until the cheese melts, then season with basil and red chili flakes. Fold in the parsnips, and cook for another two minutes. Serve garnished with parsley.
Per serving: Cal 596; Fats 35g; Net Carbs 6.5g; Protein 37g

Grilled Beef and Veggies

Ingredients for four servings

- 1 red and 1 green bell peppers, cut into strips
- 1¼lbs. sirloin steaks
- 4tbsp. olive oil
- Salt and pepper, to taste
- ½lb. asparagus, trimmed
- 3tbsp. balsamic vinegar
- 1 eggplant, sliced
- 1 red onion, sliced
- 2 zucchinis, sliced

Method and total time: approx. 30 minutes

Combine the salt, olive oil, pepper, and balsamic vinegar. Rub half of this over the beef, and pour the other half over the vegetables. Leave to marinate. Preheat a grill pan, then drain the steaks, reserving the marinade. Sear for five minutes per side, then reserve. Pour the vegetables and marinade into the pan, and cook for five minutes, turning occasionally.

Per serving: Cal 459; Fat 31g; Net Carbs 4.5g; Protein 32.8g

Swedish Meatballs

Ingredients for four servings

- 2tsp. garlic powder
- 1½lb. ground beef
- 1tsp. onion powder
- 2tbsp. olive oil
- Salt and pepper, to taste
- 2tbsp. butter
- 1 cup beef broth
- 2tbsp. almond flour
- ½ cup coconut cream
- ¼ cup chopped parsley
- ¼ freshly chopped dill

Method and total time: approx. 30 minutes

Preheat your oven to 400°F. Mix together the beef, onion powder, garlic powder, salt, and pepper. Shape into meatballs, then arrange on a greased baking sheet. Top with olive oil, and bake for ten to fifteen minutes. Stir the almond flour into the melted butter, and stir until smooth. Slowly add the broth, stirring continuously, until thickened. Add the coconut cream and dill, and allow to simmer for one minute, then stir in the meatballs. Garnish with parsley.

Per serving: Cal 459; Fat 32g; Net Carbs 3.2g; Protein 40g

Simple Bolognese Sauce

Ingredients for four servings

- 2 garlic cloves
- 1lb. ground beef
- 1 onion, chopped
- 1tsp. marjoram
- 1tsp. oregano
- 1tsp. rosemary
- 1tbsp. olive oil
- 7oz. canned chopped tomatoes

Method and total time: approx. 35 minutes

Cook the garlic and onion in the oil for three minutes. Add the beef, and cook until browned. Stir in the herbs and tomatoes, then cook for fifteen minutes.

Per serving: Cal 318; Fat 20g; Net Carbs 9g; Protein 26g

Cheese and Tomato Beef Bake

Ingredients for six servings

- 2lb. ground beef
- 1 cup cauliflower rice
- Salt and pepper, to taste
- 2 cups chopped cabbage
- 1 cup shredded gouda cheese
- 14oz. can diced tomatoes

Method and total time: approx. 30 minutes

Preheat your oven to 370°F. Season the beef, then cook for six minutes. Stir in the cauliflower rice, tomatoes, cabbage, and a quarter-cup water. Bring to a boil for five minutes, until thickened. Transfer to a baking dish, top with cheese, and bake for fifteen minutes.

Per serving: Cal 385, Fat 25g, Net Carbs 5g, Protein 20g

Beef and Brussel Sprouts

Ingredients for four servings

- 1½lb. Brussels sprouts, halved
- 1 egg
- 1lb. ground beef
- ½ onion, chopped
- 4oz. butter
- 1tsp. dried thyme
- Salt and pepper, to taste

Method and total time: approx. 30 minutes

Mix together the beef, onion, egg, salt, thyme, and pepper. Shape into patties, then fry in the butter until cooked. Cover with foil, and leave to rest. Fry the sprouts in the rest of the butter, season, then serve with the burgers.

Per serving: Cal: 443, Fat: 25g, Net Carbs: 5g, Protein: 31g

Flank Steak Salad with Mustard Dressing

Ingredients for four servings

- 1lb. flank steak
- 3 green onions, sliced
- ½lb. Brussel sprouts

Salad Dressing:

- 1tsp. xylitol
- 1tbsp. red wine vinegar
- 2tsp. Dijon mustard
- 3tbsp. extra virgin olive oil

- 1 cucumber, sliced
- 9oz. mixed salad greens
- 1 cup green beans, sliced

Method and total time: approx. 40 minutes

Preheat your oven to 400°F. Preheat a grill pan, then season the meat and brown for five minutes per side. Thinly slice, and reserve. Put the Brussel sprouts on a baking sheet, drizzle with olive oil, and bake for 25 minutes. Reserve. Combine the mustard, salt, xylitol, pepper, vinegar, and olive oil. Reserve. In a salad bowl, toss together the green onions, green beans, salad greens, cucumber, cooled Brussel sprouts, and steak slices, then drizzle with the dressing.

Per serving: Cal 244; Fat 11g; Net Carbs 3.3g; Protein 27.4g

Garlic and Lemon Ribs

Ingredients for six servings

- 3lbs. beef ribs
- 3 onions, halved
- 3 heads garlic, cut in half
- 2 lemons, zested
- 4tbsp. olive oil

- 3tbsp. xylitol
- A pinch of mustard powder
- Salt and pepper, to taste
- ¼ cup red wine
- 3tbsp. fresh sage leaves

Method and total time: approx. 55 minutes

Preheat your oven to 410°F. Score your meat all over. Combine the xylitol, sage, mustard powder, salt, pepper, and lemon zest, then rub this all over the meat with your hands. Chuck your garlic heads and onion halves in a baking dish, toss with olive oil, and bake for fifteen minutes. Add the beef, then pour in a quarter-cup of water and the red wine. Cover in aluminum foil, and bake for another fifteen minutes. Remove the foil and bake for ten minutes.

Per serving: Cal 749; Fat 65.6g; Net Carbs 5.5g; Protein 53g

Hot Cheese and Flank Pinwheel

Ingredients for four servings

- 2tbsp. olive oil
- 1 cup cotija cheese, crumbled
- 1lb. flank steak

- 1 cup kale
- 2tbsp. cilantro, chopped
- 1 habanero pepper, chopped

Method and total time: approx. 42 minutes

Preheat your oven to 400°F. Flatten the meat with a mallet, then top with half the cheese, the kale, cilantro, habanero pepper, and the rest of the cheese. Roll the steak up tightly, and secure with toothpicks. Put into a greased baking sheet, and cook for thirty minutes. Cool slightly, then slice into pinwheels.

Per serving: Cal 349; Fat 22.5g; Net Carbs 2.2g; Protein 33g

Cheesy Beef Zucchini Boats

Ingredients for four servings

- 4 zucchinis, halved then the flesh scooped out
- 1½lb. ground beef
- 2tbsp. olive oil

- 1 medium red onion, chopped
- 1 cup Colby cheese, grated
- 2tbsp. chopped pimiento

Method and total time: approx. 45 minutes

Preheat your oven to 350°F. In a skillet, heat the oil, then cook the ground beef, pimiento, red onion, and zucchini flesh for around six minutes. Season well, then divide between the zucchini shells. Top with cheese, and bake for fifteen minutes.

Per serving: Cal 335, Fat 24g, Net Carbs 7g, Protein 18g

Skirt Steak Salad with Feta and Pickled Peppers

Ingredients for four servings

- 1lb. skirt steak, sliced
- 1 dash olive oil
- 1½ cups mixed salad greens
- 4 radishes, sliced

- 3 chopped pickled peppers
- ½ cup feta cheese, crumbled
- 2tbsp. red wine vinaigrette
- Salt and pepper, to taste

Method and total time: approx. 15 minutes
Coat the steak in olive oil, and salt and pepper. Fry for five to six minutes, then leave to rest. In a salad bowl, toss together the salad greens, pickled peppers, radishes, and vinaigrette. Add the beef, and top with cheese.
Per serving: Cal 315, Fat 26g, Net Carbs 2g, Protein 18g

Satay Beef Stir-Fry

Ingredients for four servings
- 1½tbsp. ghee
- Salt and chili pepper, to taste
- 2lb. beef loin, cut into strips
- 2tsp. ginger-garlic paste
- 2 cups mixed vegetables
- 5tbsp. peanut butter
- ¼ cup chicken broth

Method and total time: approx. 30 minutes
Rub the beef all over with chili pepper, salt, and ginger-garlic paste. Pour the beef into a wok with the ghee, and cook for six minutes. Combine the peanut butter with a little broth, then stir it into the beef and cook for two minutes. Pour in the rest of the broth, then cook for four minutes. Stir in the vegetables, then leave to simmer for five minutes.
Per serving: Cal 571, Fat 49g, Net Carbs 1g, Protein 22.5g

Creamed Beef

Ingredients for four servings
- 1tbsp. olive oil
- 2tbsp. rosemary, chopped
- 3tbsp. butter
- 1tbsp. garlic powder
- 1 red onion, chopped
- 4 beef steaks
- ½ cup half-and-half
- 1tbsp. mustard
- ½ cup beef stock
- 2tsp. lemon juice
- A sprig of thyme
- A sprig of sage

Method and total time: approx. 25 minutes
Rub the garlic powder, olive oil, salt, pepper, and chopped rosemary all over the steaks. Fry for three minutes per side in the butter, then reserve. In the same pan, cook the red onion for three minutes. Add the beef stock, half-and-half, thyme sprig, mustard, and sage sprig, and cook for another eight minutes. Stir in the pepper, lemon juice, and salt. Remove the sage and thyme sprigs, then serve.
Per serving: Cal 481; Fat 25g; Net Carbs 7.8g; Protein 51.7g

Simple Steak Carnitas

Ingredients for four servings
- 2tbsp. Cajun seasoning
- 2lb. sirloin steak, cut into strips
- 4oz. guacamole
- 2tbsp. olive oil
- Salt, to taste
- 2 shallots, sliced
- 8 low-carb tortillas
- 1 red bell pepper, sliced

Method and total time: approx. 35 minutes
Preheat your grill to 425°F. Rub the Cajun seasoning over the steaks, then refrigerate for an hour. Grill for six minutes per side. Wrap in foil, and leave to sit for ten minutes. Sauté the shallots and bell pepper in the oil for five minutes. Divide the beef between the tortillas, top with the vegetables and guacamole, and serve.
Per serving: Cal 381; Fat 16.7g; Net Carbs 5g; Protein 47g

Easy Cheeseburgers

Ingredients for four servings
- 1lb. ground beef
- ½tsp. Worcestershire sauce
- 1tsp. dried parsley
- Salt and pepper, to taste
- 4 zero-carb buns, halved
- 1 cup feta cheese, shredded

Method and total time: approx. 20 minutes
Preheat your grill to 400°F, and grease the grate. Combine the beef, Worcestershire sauce, parsley, salt, and pepper. Shape into patties, and grill for seven minutes. Flip, top with the cheese, and cook for another seven minutes. Sandwich in the buns, and serve.
Per serving: Cal 386, Fat 32g, Net Carbs 2g, Protein 21g

Pesto and Beef-Stuffed Tomatoes

Ingredients for six servings
- 1tbsp. olive oil
- Salt and pepper, to taste
- ¼lb. ground beef
- 4 medium tomatoes, halved
- 5tbsp. shredded parmesan
- 4tsp. basil pesto

Method and total time: approx. 30 minutes
Preheat your oven to 400°F. Cook the beef in the oil, along with a little salt and pepper, for eight minutes. Pull the filling out of the tomatoes, then spoon the beef into them. Spoon with pesto and parmesan, then bake for twenty minutes.
Per serving: Cal 122; Fat 4.4g; Net Carbs 2.9g; Protein 7.3g

Spicy Beef and Cauliflower Pilaf

Ingredients for four servings
- 3tbsp. olive oil
- Salt and pepper, to taste
- ½lb. ground beef
- 1 yellow onion, chopped
- 1 habanero pepper, minced
- 3 garlic cloves, minced
- ½tsp. Italian seasoning
- 2tbsp. tomato paste
- 2½ cups cauliflower rice
- ½ cup beef broth
- 1 lemon, sliced
- ¼ cup chopped parsley

Method and total time: approx. 30 minutes
Cook the beef in the oil for eight minutes. Season well, and reserve. In the same skillet, sauté the garlic, onion, and habanero pepper for around two minutes. Stir in the Italian seasoning, followed by the tomato paste, cauliflower rice, and broth. Season, cover, and cook for ten minutes. Return the beef to the pan, cook for another three minutes, then serve with parsley.
Per serving: Cal 216; Fat 14g; Net Carbs 3.8g; Protein 15g

Beef Burger

Ingredients for four servings
- 2 pearl onions, thinly sliced into 8 pieces
- 2 slices cheddar cheese, cut into 4 pieces each
- ½lb. ground beef
- 1tsp. onion powder
- 1tsp. garlic powder
- 8 slices zero-carb bread
- 4 cherry tomatoes, halved
- 2tbsp. ranch dressing

Method and total time: approx. 30 minutes
Preheat your oven to 400°F. Mix together the beef, pepper, salt, and garlic and onion powders. Shape into eight patties, then bake for ten minutes on a greased baking sheet. Leave cool for three minutes. Top your bread with ranch dressing, then top with the patties. Add the cheese, onions, and tomatoes. Top with the other half of the bun.
Per serving: Cal 281; Fat 12g; Net Carbs 2.8g; Protein 20g

Mexican Salsa Pizza

Ingredients for four servings
- 2tbsp. cream cheese, softened
- 2 eggs, beaten
- ¾ cup almond flour
- ¾lb. ground beef
- 2 cups shredded mozzarella
- Salt and pepper, to taste
- 2tsp. taco seasoning mix
- ½ cup chicken broth
- 2 cups Mexican 4-cheese blend
- 1½ cups salsa

Method and total time: approx. 50 minutes
Preheat your oven to 390°F, and line a pizza pan. Microwave two cups of mozzarella and the cream cheese for thirty seconds. Stir in the almond flour and eggs, then press onto your pan and bake for fifteen minutes. Cook the beef for five minutes, then stir in the taco seasoning, pepper, salt, and chicken broth. Cook for three minutes, then stir in the salsa. Spread across the crust, then top with the cheese blend. Bake for another fifteen minutes.
Per serving: Cal 556; Fats 30g; Net Carbs 4.2g; Protein 59g

Beef and Broccoli

Ingredients for four servings
- 3 cups mixed vegetables
- 2 cups cauliflower rice
- 3tbsp. butter
- 4 fresh eggs
- 1lb. sirloin steak, sliced
- Hot sauce, to serve

Method and total time: approx. 25 minutes
Combine the cauliflower rice and mixed vegetables with a little water, then cook in the microwave for a minute. Season the beef, then fry in the butter for five minutes per side, then put on top of the vegetables. In the same skillet, fry the eggs to your taste, then add to the beef and vegetables. Serve with hot sauce.
Per serving: Cal 320, Fat 26g, Net Carbs 4g, Protein 15g

Polish Tripe

Ingredients for six servings
- 4 cups buttermilk
- 1½lb. beef tripe
- Salt and pepper, to taste
- 2tsp. marjoram
- 1 parsnip, chopped
- 3tbsp. butter
- 3 tomatoes, diced
- 2 large onions, sliced

Method and total time: approx. 30 min + cooling time
Cover the tripe in the buttermilk, and put in the fridge for three hours. Drain the buttermilk, then season the meat well. In a skillet, brown the tripe in two tablespoons butter, for three minutes per side. Stir in the rest of the butter, and sauté the onions for three minutes. Add the tomatoes and parsnip, and cook for fifteen minutes.

Per serving: Cal 342, Fat 27g, Net Carbs 1g, Protein 22g

Paprika and Barbecue Ribs

Ingredients for four servings
- 2tbsp. erythritol
- 1tbsp. olive oil
- Salt and pepper, to taste
- 4tbsp. BBQ sauce + extra for serving
- 3tsp. smoked paprika
- 1lb. beef spare ribs
- 1tsp. garlic powder

Method and total time: approx. 35 minutes
Combine the erythritol, smoked paprika, pepper, salt, oil, and garlic powder, then brush this all over the meat side. Wrap in foil, and leave to marinate for thirty minutes.
Preheat your oven to 400°F, then bake, still wrapped, for forty minutes. Remove the foil, brush with BBQ sauce, and broil for ten minutes per side.

Per serving: Cal 395; Fat 33g; Net Carbs 3g; Protein 21g

Simple Beef Curry

Ingredients for six servings
- 1½lb. ground beef
- 1 head broccoli, cut into florets
- 1tbsp. olive oil
- 1tbsp. ginger-garlic paste
- 7oz. can whole tomatoes
- 1tsp. garam masala
- Salt and chili pepper, to taste

Method and total time: approx. 30 minutes
In the oil, fry the ginger-garlic paste, beef, and garam masala. Cook for five minutes, then stir in the tomatoes and broccoli. Season, and cook for six minutes. Add a quarter-cup of water, and bring to a boil. Simmer for ten minutes, then serve.

Per serving: Cal 374, Fat 33g, Net Carbs 2g, Protein 22g

Steak and Mushrooms

Ingredients for four servings
- 4 ribeye steaks
- 2 cups shitake mushrooms, sliced
- 2tsp. olive oil
- 2tbsp. butter
- Salt and pepper, to taste

Method and total time: approx. 25 minutes
Season the steak, then fry in the oil for four minutes per side. Reserve. In the same pan, cook the mushrooms in the butter for four minutes. Pour over the steaks, and serve.

Per serving: Cal 370; Fat 31g; Net Carbs 3g; Protein 33g

Cheeseburgers with Fried Onion

Ingredients for four servings
- 1 medium white onion, sliced
- 4 zero-carb hamburger buns, halved
- 3tbsp. olive oil
- 2tsp. erythritol
- 2tbsp. balsamic vinegar
- 1lb. ground beef
- 4 slices Gruyere cheese
- Salt and pepper, to taste
- Mayonnaise, to serve

Method and total time: approx. 35 minutes
Cook the onion in the skillet with two tablespoon olive oil. Cook for fifteen minutes. Stir in the balsamic vinegar, erythritol, and salt. Cook for three more minutes, then reserve. Shape into four patties, then season. Fry in the rest of the oil, for four minutes per side. Top with the cheese and the fried onion, then serve in the buns with mayonnaise.

Per serving: Cal 487; Fat 32g; Net Carbs 7.8g; Protein 38g

Fried Egg with Pancetta and Tomatoes

Ingredients for four servings
- 5oz. pancetta, chopped
- 8 eggs
- 2tbsp. olive oil
- 1tbsp. butter, softened
- 2tbsp. chopped oregano
- ¼ cup cherry tomatoes, halved

Method and total time: approx. 30 minutes
Fry the pancetta until crisp, then reserve. Fry the eggs in the oil, then reserve. In the butter, fry the tomatoes until brown around the edges, about eight minutes. Garnish with oregano, and serve.
Per serving: Cal 278; Fat 23g; Net Carbs 0.5g; Protein 20g

Chorizo with Cabbage and Pine Nuts

Ingredients for four servings
- 6tbsp. butter
- 1¼ cups coconut cream
- 25oz. chorizo sausages
- 25oz. green canon cabbage, shredded
- ½ cup fresh sage, chopped
- 2tbsp. toasted pine nuts
- ½ lemon, zested

Method and total time: approx. 30 minutes
Fry the chorizo in two tablespoons butter for around ten minutes. Reserve. In the rest of the butter, fry the cabbage for around four minutes. Stir in the coconut cream, and simmer until the cream reduces. Season with salt, sage, pepper, and lemon zest. Serve the cabbage over the chorizos, then top with pine nuts.
Per serving: Cal 914; Fat 76g; Net Carbs 16.9g; Protein 38g

Hawaiian Pork

Ingredients for four servings
- ⅓ cup flaxseed meal
- 1tsp. onion powder
- ½tsp. nutmeg powder
- 5 large egg
- 1½lb. ground pork
- 3tbsp. coconut oil
- 2tbsp. heavy cream
- 1tbsp. salted butter
- 1 cup sliced oyster mushrooms
- 1 shallot, finely chopped
- 1 cup vegetable stock
- 1tsp. tamari sauce
- 1tsp. Worcestershire sauce
- ½tsp. xanthan gum
- 4 large eggs
- 2tbsp. olive oil

Method and total time: approx. 40 minutes
Mix together the pork, nutmeg, flaxseed meal, salt, onion powders, and pepper. Beat one egg with the heavy cream, then stir into the pork mixture. Shape into eight patties.
Fry the patties in the coconut oil until cooked through. Reserve. In the same skillet, cook the mushrooms and shallots in the butter for around seven minutes. Combine the stock, Worcestershire and tamari sauces, salt, and pepper, then pour into the mushrooms and cook for three minutes. Add the xanthan gum, and leave to thicken for one minute. Fry the eggs, the serve the pork topped with the mushroom sauce and fried egg.
Per serving: Cal 655; Fat 46g; Net Carbs 2.2g; Protein 55g

Sausage and Mushroom Omelet

Ingredients for two servings
- 2tbsp. olive oil
- 1 small white onion, chopped
- ¼ cup sliced cremini mushrooms
- 2oz. pork sausage, crumbled
- 2tbsp. butter
- 2oz. shredded cheddar cheese
- 6 eggs

Method and total time: approx. 30 minutes
Fry the pork in the olive oil for ten minutes, then reserve. In the same pan, sauté the onion and mushrooms for eight minutes. Reserve. Beat the eggs with salt and pepper, then cook in the butter in the same skillet. When the omelet starts to set, top one side with the pork, mushroom-onion mixture, and cheese. Flip the other side over, and cook for another two minutes.
Per serving: Cal 534; Fat 43g; Net Carbs 2.7g; Protein 29g

Pork Pie and Broccoli

Ingredients for four servings
- 1 head broccoli, cut into florets
- 1 whole egg
- ½ cup crème fraîche
- ½ celery, finely chopped
- 5oz. shredded Swiss cheese
- 3oz. butter, melted
- 2tbsp. butter, cold
- 2tbsp. tamari sauce
- 2lb. ground pork
- 2tbsp. Worcestershire sauce
- 1tsp. onion powder
- ½tbsp. hot sauce

Method and total time: approx. 55 minutes

Preheat your oven to 400°F. Cook the broccoli in salted water for three to five minutes. Drain, blend until rice-like. Pour the broccoli into a bowl, then stir in the crème fraiche, celery, half the Swiss cheese, egg, butter, salt, and pepper. Fry the pork in the butter for ten minutes. Combine the tamari, hot and Worcestershire sauces, salt, onion powder, and pepper, and cook for three minutes. Spread into a greased baking dish, then top with the broccoli. Top with the rest of the cheese, and bake for twenty minutes.

Per serving: Cal 701; Fat 49g; Net Carbs 3.3g; Protein 60g

Tex-Mex Casserole

Ingredients for four servings
- 1½lb. ground pork
- 2tbsp. butter
- 3tbsp. Tex-Mex seasoning
- ½ cup crushed tomatoes
- 2tbsp. chopped jalapeños
- ½ cup shredded Monterey Jack
- 1 cup sour cream, to serve
- 1 scallion, chopped, to garnish

Method and total time: approx. 40 minutes

Preheat your oven to 330°F, and grease a baking dish. Fry the pork in the butter for around eight minutes. Stir in the jalapeños, Tex-Mex seasoning, and tomatoes, and simmer for five minutes. Season, then pour into the baking dish. Top with the cheese, and bake for twenty minutes. Serve with scallions and sour cream.

Per serving: Cal 431; Fat 24g; Net Carbs 7.8g; Protein 43g

Thyme-Roast Pork and Brussel Sprouts

Ingredients for four servings
- 2lb. pork roast
- 2tsp. dried thyme
- Salt and pepper, to taste
- 1 bay leaf
- 2½ cups beef broth
- 5 black peppercorns
- 2 garlic cloves, minced
- 1tbsp. coconut oil
- 1½oz. fresh ginger, grated
- 1tbsp. smoked paprika
- 1½ cups coconut cream
- ½lb. Brussel sprouts, halved

Method and total time: approx. 2 hours

Preheat your oven to 360°F. Rub the meat all over with salt, thyme, pepper, bay leaf, and peppercorns, then pour the broth over and cover with foil. Bake for ninety minutes. Remove the foil and the meat, then reserve the juices. Mix together the garlic, coconut oil, ginger, and paprika. Rub this over the meat, and return it to the oven for another ten minutes. Thinly slice and reserve. Strain the reserved juices, then bring to a boil until it's reduced to around a cup and a half. Add the sprouts, and cook for eight minutes. Stir in the cream, and simmer for fifteen minutes.

Per serving: Cal 691; Fat 45g; Net Carbs 9.6g; Protein 59g

Pork and Swiss Cheese Quiche

Ingredients for four servings
- 1¼ cups almond flour
- 4tbsp. chia seeds
- 1tbsp. psyllium husk powder
- 2tbsp. melted butter
- 1tbsp. butter
- 6 egg
- ½lb. smoked pork shoulder
- 1tsp. dried thyme
- 1 yellow onion, chopped
- Salt and pepper, to taste
- ¼ cup shredded Swiss cheese
- 1 cup coconut cream

Method and total time: approx. 70 minutes

Preheat your oven to 350°F, and grease and line a springform pan. In your blender, blitz the almond flour, chia seeds, psyllium husk, a half-teaspoon salt, butter, and one egg until a dough forms. Spread along the bottom of your pan, then pop in the fridge. Fry the pork and onion in the butter for around ten to twelve minutes. Mix in the thyme, salt, and pepper, and cook for another two minutes. Pour the pork and onion onto the crust. Beat the coconut cream with half the Swiss cheese and the rest of the eggs. Pour this over the meat filling, then top with the cheese. Bake for around 45 minutes.

Per serving: Cal 498; Fat 42g; Net Carbs 4.6g; Protein 24g

Spicy Pork Meatballs

Ingredients for four servings
- ⅓ cup mayonnaise
- 1tsp. paprika powder
- 3tbsp. softened cream cheese
- 1 pinch cayenne pepper
- 4oz. grated parmesan cheese
- ¼ cup chopped pimientos
- 1tbsp. Dijon mustard
- 1½lb. ground pork
- 2tbsp. olive oil, for frying
- 1 large egg

Method and total time: approx. 30 minutes

Combine the pimientos, cream cheese, mayo, paprika, mustard, cayenne, parmesan, salt, pork, pepper, and egg. Shape into meatballs, then fry in the olive oil for around ten minutes.

Per serving: Cal 485; Fat 30g; Net Carbs 6.8g; Protein 47g

Italian Pork

Ingredients for four servings
- 2tbsp. avocado oil
- ¼ cup sliced Kalamata olives
- 1½lb. ground pork
- ½ cup cottage cheese, crumbled
- 2 garlic cloves, minced
- 1¼ cups heavy cream
- ½ cup marinara sauce

Method and total time: approx. 40 minutes

Preheat your oven to 400°F, and grease a casserole dish. Fry the pork in the avocado oil for ten minutes, stirring often. Transfer to the casserole dish. Top with the olives, cottage cheese, and garlic. Combine the marinara sauce with the heavy cream, and pour over the meat. Bake for 20 to 25 minutes.

Per serving: Cal 451; Fat 30g; Net Carbs 1.5g; Protein 40g

Buttery Pork with Lemon Asparagus

Ingredients for four servings
- 4 pork chops
- 7tbsp. butter
- Salt and pepper, to taste
- 2 garlic cloves, minced
- 4tbsp. butter, softened
- 1lb. asparagus, trimmed
- 1 small lemon, juice
- 1tbsp. dried cilantro

Method and total time: approx. 30 minutes

Season the pork well, then fry in three tablespoons butter for ten minutes. Reserve. In the same skillet, melt the rest of the butter and cook the garlic until aromatic. Add the asparagus, and cook until just softened. Add the cilantro and lemon juice, then toss and serve with the pork.

Per serving: Cal 538; Fat 38g; Net Carbs 1.2g; Protein 42g

Cheesy Pork Chops and Cauliflower

Ingredients for four servings
- 2 heads cauliflower, cut into 4 steaks
- 1tbsp. mesquite seasoning
- 4 pork chops
- 2tbsp. butter
- ½ cup parmesan cheese
- 2tbsp. olive oil

Method and total time: approx. 30 minutes

Season the pork with the mesquite flavoring, salt, and pepper, then fry in the butter for ten minutes. Reserve. In the oil, fry the cauliflower steaks for four minutes. Top with parmesan and cook until melted. Serve with the chops.

Per serving: Cal 429; Fat 23g; Net Carbs 3.9g; Protein 45g

Pork and Zucchini Omelet

Ingredients for four servings
- 3 zucchinis, halved lengthwise
- 1 garlic clove, crushed
- 4tbsp. olive oil
- 1 small plum tomato, diced
- 1tsp. dried basil
- 2tbsp. chopped scallions
- 1tsp. cumin powder
- 1lb. ground pork
- 1tsp. smoked paprika
- 3 large eggs, beaten
- ⅓ cup chopped cilantro
- 3tsp. crushed pork rinds

Method and total time: approx. 50 minutes

Preheat your grill to medium, then cook the zucchinis drizzled with a tablespoon olive oil for five minutes. Reserve. In a tablespoon oil, cook the tomato, garlic, and scallions for eight minutes. Add the basil, paprika, cumin, and salt. Add the pork, and cook for ten minutes. Reserve. Top the zucchini with the pork. In the same skillet, heat the remaining, and add the loaded zucchinis. Divide the eggs between the zucchinis, cover, and cook for three minutes. Top with pork rinds and cilantro.

Per serving: Cal 332; Fat 22g; Net Carbs 1.1g; Protein 30g

Lemon Pork and Capers

Ingredients for four servings
- ½ lemon, juiced + 1 lemon, sliced
- 1½lb. thin cut pork chops, boneless
- Salt and pepper, to taste
- 3tbsp. butter
- 1tbsp. avocado oil
- 2tbsp. capers
- 2tbsp. chopped parsley
- 1 cup beef broth

Method and total time: approx. 30 minutes

Cook the chops in the avocado oil for around fourteen minutes. Reserve. Fry the capers in the butter, stirring often, for three minutes.

Add the broth and lemon juice and deglaze the pan. Reduce by half, then return the pork to the pan, top with lemon slices and parsley. Simmer for three minutes.

Per serving: Cal 341; Fat 18g; Net Carbs 0.8g; Protein 40g

Sautéed Pork with Green Beans and Avocado

Ingredients for four servings
- 4 pork shoulder chops
- 4tbsp. avocado oil
- 2tbsp. avocado oil
- 2 large avocados, chopped
- 1½ cups green beans
- Salt and pepper, to taste
- 1tbsp. chopped parsley
- 6 green onions, chopped

Method and total time: approx. 30 minutes

Season the pork well, then fry in the oil for twelve minutes. Reserve. To the same skillet, fry the green beans until just softened, around ten minutes. Stir in the avocados and half the green onions, and cook for another two minutes. Plate up, garnished with the rest of the onions and parsley.

Per serving: Cal 557; Fat 36g; Net Carbs 1.9g; Protein 43g

Taco Pulled Pork

Ingredients for four servings
- ½ cup sliced yellow onion
- 4tbsp. ras el hanout seasoning
- 2lb. pork shoulder
- Salt, to taste
- 5tbsp. psyllium husk powder
- 2tbsp. olive oil
- 3½ cups beef broth
- 1¼ cups almond flour
- 2tbsp. butter, for frying
- 2 eggs

Method and total time: approx. 7 hours

In the olive oil, fry the onion for three minutes. Season the pork with the ras el hanout, and salt, and add to the onion. Sear for three minutes per side, then add the broth. Cover, and cook for four to five hours on a low heat Shred the pork with two forks, stir back into the sauce, and cook for another hour. Reserve. Mix together the psyllium husk powder, almond flour, and a teaspoon salt. Add the eggs and mix until a dough forms, then add a cup of water.

Divide into eight pieces and roll flat between two sheets of parchment paper. Fry each in the melted butter until browned on both sides. Top with the meat, wrap, and serve.

Per serving: Cal 520; Fat 30g; Net Carbs 3.8g; Protein 50g

Béarnaise Spareribs

Ingredients for four servings
- 4 egg yolks, beaten
- 3tbsp. butter, melted
- 2tbsp. chopped tarragon
- ½tsp. onion powder
- 2tsp. white wine vinegar
- Salt and pepper, to taste
- 2lb. spareribs, divided into 16
- 4tbsp. butter

Method and total time: approx. 30 minutes

Beat the butter slowly into the egg yolks, until well mixed. Mix together the white wine vinegar, tarragon, and onion powder. Stir this into the egg mixture, and season with salt and pepper. Reserve. Season the ribs well, then cook in the butter until browned and crisp, around twelve minutes. Top the ribs with the béarnaise sauce, then serve.

Per serving: Cal 878; Fat 78g; Net Carbs 1g; Protein 41g

Pork, Pecan, and Camembert Bake

Ingredients for four servings
- 9oz. whole Camembert cheese
- 3tbsp. olive oil
- ½lb. boneless pork chops, cut into small cubes
- 2oz. pecans
- 1tbsp. chopped parsley
- 1 garlic clove, minced

Method and total time: approx. 30 minutes

Preheat your oven to 400°F. Leaving the cheese in its box, Score around the top and take the top layer of skin off. Melt in the oven for ten minutes. Season the pork, and fry in the oil for twelve minutes. In a bowl, combine the pork with the garlic, pecans, and parsley. Spoon onto the cheese, and bake for ten minutes.

Per serving: Cal 452; Fat 38g; Net Carbs 0.2g; Protein 27g

Cheesy Burrito Bowl

Ingredients for four servings
- 1tbsp. butter
- ½ cup beef broth
- 1lb. ground pork
- 4tbsp. taco seasoning
- ½ cup sharp cheddar, shredded
- Salt and pepper, to taste
- ½ cup sour cream
- 1 avocado, cubed
- ¼ cup sliced black olives
- ¼ cup tomatoes, diced
- 1tbsp. fresh cilantro, chopped
- 1 green onion, sliced

Method and total time: approx. 30 minutes

Cook the pork in the butter for ten minutes, stirring frequently. Stir in the taco seasoning, broth, salt, and pepper, then cook until most of the liquid evaporates. Add half the cheddar cheese and cook to melt. Divide between serving bowls, and top with olives, tomatoes, avocado, green onion, and cilantro.

Per serving: Cal 386; Fat 23g; Net Carbs 8.8g; Protein 30g

Stuffed Mushrooms

Ingredients for four servings
- 2tbsp. butter
- 1tsp. paprika
- ½lb. ground pork
- 12 medium portabella mushrooms, stalks removed
- 3tbsp. chives, finely chopped
- ¼ cup shredded parmesan
- 7oz. cream cheese

Method and total time: approx. 30 minutes
Preheat your oven to 400°F, and grease a baking sheet. In a skillet, fry the pork in the butter along with the salt, pepper, and paprika. Cook for ten minutes. Add two-thirds of the chives and cream cheese. Divide between your mushrooms, then top with parmesan and bake for ten minutes. Garnish with chives.
Per serving: Cal 299; Fat 23g; Net Carbs 2.2g; Protein 19g

Kale and Bacon Pizza

Ingredients for two servings
- 1 cup shredded provolone cheese
- 10 eggs
- 7oz. can sliced mushrooms, drained
- 1tsp. Italian seasoning
- ⅔ cup tomato sauce
- 6 bacon slices
- 2 cups chopped kale, wilted
- 4 eggs
- ½ cup grated mozzarella
- Olive oil, for drizzling

Method and total time: approx. 45 minutes
Preheat your oven to 400°F, and line a pizza-baking pan. Beat six eggs with the provolone cheese and Italian seasoning. Spread on a pizza-baking, then bake for fifteen minutes. Leave to cool for two minutes. Increase the temperature to 450°F. Fry the bacon until crisp, then reserve. Spread the crust with the tomato sauce, then add the kale, mozzarella, and mushrooms. Bake for eight minutes. Crack the last four eggs on top, cover with bacon, and bake for another two to three minutes.
Per serving: Cal 1093; Fat 77g; Net Carbs 6.1g; Protein 69g

Bacon and Mushroom Lettuce Wraps

Ingredients for four servings
- ½ cup sliced cremini mushrooms
- 8 bacon slices, chopped
- 1 iceberg lettuce, leaves separated
- 2tbsp. olive oil
- 1 cup shredded cheddar
- 1½lb. ground pork

Method and total time: approx. 30 minutes
Fry the bacon until crisp, then reserve. In half the olive oil, season and sauté the mushrooms for five minutes. Brown the pork for ten minutes in the last of the oil. Share between the lettuce leaves, then top with cheddar, bacon, and mushrooms. Wrap, and serve.
Per serving: Cal 630; Fat 45g; Net Carbs 0.5g; Protein 52g

Thai Red Curry Pork

Ingredients for four servings
- 6tbsp. butter
- Salt and pepper, to taste
- 1 canon cabbage, shredded
- 1 celery, chopped
- 1½ pork tenderloin, sliced into ½-inch medallions
- 1¼ cups coconut cream
- 1tbsp. red curry powder

Method and total time: approx. 45 minutes
Melt two tablespoons butter in a skillet, and sauté cabbage until soft. Reserve. In another two tablespoons butter, fry the seasoned pork for ten minutes. Reserve. In the rest of the butter, sauté the celery until softened. Mix in the curry powder, cook for 30 seconds, and add the coconut cream. Simmer for ten minutes, then return the meat to the pot. Serve with the buttered cabbage.
Per serving: Cal 626; Fat 48g; Net Carbs 3.9g; Protein 43g

Barbecue Pork

Ingredients for four servings
- ½ cup grated flaxseed meal
- 1tsp. paprika
- 1tsp. dried thyme
- Salt and pepper, to taste
- 1½tsp. garlic powder
- ¼tsp. chili powder
- 1tbsp. dried parsley
- ⅛tsp. basil
- ½tsp. onion powder
- 4 pork chops
- ½ cup BBQ sauce
- 1tbsp. melted butter

Method and total time: approx. 70 minutes
Preheat your oven to 400°F. Combine the flaxseed meal, paprika, thyme, salt, pepper, garlic powder, chili, parsley, onion powder, and basil. Rub this all over the pork chops. Fry in the butter for eight minutes, the put into a greased baking sheet. Cover with BBQ sauce, and bake for fifty minutes. Allow to rest for ten minutes.
Per serving: Cal 385; Fat 19g; Net Carbs 1.6g; Protein 44g

Mustard and Garlic Pork Loin

Ingredients for six servings
- 3lb. boneless pork loin roast
- Salt and pepper, to taste
- 5 cloves garlic, minced
- 1tbsp. Dijon mustard
- 2tsp. garlic powder
- 1tsp. dried basil

Method and total time: approx. 30 minutes
Preheat your oven to 400°F, and put the pork in a baking dish. Combine the minced garlic, basil, pepper, salt, mustard, and garlic powder. Rub this all over the pork, then drizzle with olive oil. Cook for fifteen minutes. Leave to cool for five minutes before serving.

Per serving: Cal 311; Fat 9g; Net Carbs 2g; Protein 51g

Basil and Balsamic Pork Chops

Ingredients for four servings
- 2tbsp. balsamic vinegar
- 2 cups chopped beetroot greens
- 2tsp. freshly pureed garlic
- 4 thyme sprigs
- 2tbsp. freshly chopped basil
- 1tbsp. olive oil
- 2tbsp. butter
- 4 pork chops

Method and total time: approx. 30 minutes
Preheat your oven to 400°F. Mix together the vinegar, pepper, salt, garlic, and basil, then cook until syrupy. In the oil, fry the pork for four minutes per side. Brush with the glaze, sprinkle with thyme, and bake for eight minutes. Meanwhile, sauté the beetroot greens in the butter for five minutes.

Per serving: Cal 391; Fat 16g; Net Carbs 0.8g; Protein 40g

Scrambled Eggs and Pork

Ingredients for four servings
- 2tbsp. sesame oil
- 2tbsp. minced garlic
- 2 large eggs
- ½tsp. ginger puree
- 1lb. ground pork
- 1 medium white onion, diced
- 1 habanero pepper, chopped
- 5 scallions, chopped
- 1 green cabbage, shredded
- 3tbsp. coconut aminos
- 2tbsp. sesame seeds
- 1tbsp. white vinegar

Method and total time: approx. 30 minutes
Scramble the eggs in a tablespoon sesame oil for around one minutes. In another tablespoon sesame oil, sauté the ginger, garlic, and onion until tender and aromatic, around four minutes. Stir in the ground pork and habanero pepper, season well, and cook for ten minutes. Add the cabbage, aminos, scallions, and vinegar, and cook until the cabbage is tender. Add the eggs, then garnish with sesame seeds.

Per serving: Cal 295; Fat 16g; Net Carbs 3.6g; Protein 29g

Balsamic Pork and Brie

Ingredients for four servings
- 2 large red onions, sliced
- 3tbsp. olive oil
- 2tbsp. balsamic vinegar
- Salt and pepper, to taste
- 1tsp. maple syrup
- 4 pork chops
- 2tbsp. chopped mint leaves
- 4 slices brie cheese

Method and total time: approx. 45 minutes
Heat a tablespoon olive oil, then sauté the onions until brown. Add the maple syrup, vinegar, and salt. Stir often, and cook for around fifteen minutes. Reserve. In the rest of the olive oil, cook the seasoned pork for twelve minutes. Top each chop with a slice of brie, then a dollop of caramelized onions. Cook until the cheese melts, then serve garnished with mint.

Per serving: Cal 457; Fat 25g; Net Carbs 3.1g; Protein 46g

Chinese Meatballs

Ingredients for four servings
- 1lb. ground pork
- 1 zucchini, grated
- 2 scallions, chopped
- 4 garlic cloves, minced
- 1tsp. red chili flakes
- 1tsp. freshly pureed ginger
- 2tbsp. tamari sauce
- 3tbsp. coconut oil, for frying
- 2tbsp. sesame oil

Method and total time: approx. 30 minutes
Mix together the pork, zucchini, scallions, garlic, chili flakes, ginger, tamari sauce, and sesame oil. Shape into meatballs, then fry in the coconut oil for twelve minutes. Drain, and serve.

Per serving: Cal 296; Fat 22g; Net Carbs 1.5g; Protein 24g

<h1 style="text-align:center">Spicy Pork and Walnut Stir-Fry</h1>

Ingredients for four servings

- 2tbsp. coconut oil
- 1½lb. pork tenderloin, cut into strips
- Salt and pepper, to taste
- 1 small red onion, diced
- 1 green bell pepper, diced
- ⅓ cup walnuts

- 3 garlic cloves, minced
- 1tbsp. freshly grated ginger
- 1tsp. sesame oil
- 2tbsp. tamari sauce
- 1 habanero pepper, minced

Method and total time: approx. 30 minutes

Season the pork. In a wok, fry the pork in the coconut oil for around ten minutes. Push to one side of the wok, then add the bell pepper, walnuts, onion, ginger, sesame oil, garlic, and habanero pepper. Sauté until aromatic and tender. Stir in the tamari sauce. Stir-fry for another minute.

Per serving: Cal 325; Fat 16g; Net Carbs 2.8g; Protein 38g

<h1 style="text-align:center">Greek Pork</h1>

Ingredients for four servings

- ¼ cup olive oil
- 2tbsp. Greek seasoning
- 2 lemon, juiced

- 2tbsp. red wine vinegar
- 2tbsp. lard
- 1½lb. pork tenderloin

Method and total time: approx. 2 hours

Preheat your oven to 425°F. Mix together the olive oil, Greek seasoning, lemon juice, salt, vinegar, and pepper. Score the pork, then rub the marinade all over. Cover, and pop in the fridge for an hour. Cook the pork in the lard until browned all over, then put in a greased baking dish. Top with any leftover marinade, and bake for 45 minutes.

Per serving: Cal 383; Fat 24g; Net Carbs 2.5g; Protein 36g

<h1 style="text-align:center">Coffe and Chipotle Pork</h1>

Ingredients for four servings

- ½tsp. chipotle powder
- 1tbsp. finely ground coffee
- ½tsp. garlic powder
- ½tsp. cumin powder

- ½tsp. cinnamon powder
- 1½tsp. swerve brown sugar
- 2tbsp. lard
- 4 bone-in pork chops

Method and total time: approx. 20 minutes

Combine the coffee, garlic, chipotle, cinnamon, salt, cumin, pepper, and swerve. Rub all over the pork, then cover and pop in the fridge overnight. Preheat your oven to 350°F. Fry the pork in the lard for three minutes. Put in a bake dish, and cook for ten minutes.

Per serving: Cal 291; Fat 13g; Net Carbs 0.5g; Protein 39g

<h1 style="text-align:center">Pork Belly and Creamy Kale</h1>

Ingredients for four servings

- Salt and pepper, to taste
- 1 white onion, chopped
- 1tbsp. coconut oil
- 6 cloves garlic, minced
- 4 long red chilies, halved

- 2lb. pork belly, chopped
- ¼ cup ginger thinly sliced
- 1 cup coconut milk
- 2 cups chopped kale
- 1 cup coconut cream

Method and total time: approx. 40 minutes

Season the pork belly, then refrigerate for thirty minutes. In two cups water, boil the pork for fifteen minutes. Drain, and put in a skillet. Fry for fifteen minutes until the skin browns and crackles. Drain the fat, and reserve. In the same skillet, sauté the onion in the coconut oil, along with the ginger, garlic, and chilies for five minutes. Stir in the coconut milk and coconut cream, and cook for another minute. Add the kale, and cook until wilted. Add the pork, and cook for a final two minutes.

Per serving: Cal 608; Fat 36g; Net Carbs 6.7g; Protein 57g

<h1 style="text-align:center">Pork Medallions and Mushrooms</h1>

Ingredients for four servings

- 2tbsp. olive oil
- 4 large green onions, chopped
- 16 fresh morels, rinsed
- 1½lb. pork tenderloin, cut into 8 medallions

- ½ cup red wine
- 2tbsp. unsalted butter
- ¾ cup beef broth

Method and total time: approx. 25 minutes

Season the pork medallions, then sook in the oil for around five minutes. Reserve. In the same skillet, cook the morels and green onions for two minutes. Stir in the red wine and broth, then return the pork to the pan, and simmer for five minutes. Add the butter, season, and serve.

Per serving: Cal 328; Fat 15g; Net Carbs 1.2g; Protein 39g

Pork and Mozzarella

Ingredients for four servings
- 4 boneless pork chops
- 1 cup golden flaxseed meal
- Salt and pepper, to taste
- 1 large egg, beaten
- 1 cup shredded mozzarella
- 1 cup tomato sauce

Method and total time: approx. 30 minutes

Preheat your oven to 400°F, and grease a baking sheet. Season the pork well. Coat the meat in the egg, then in the flaxseed, and place on the baking sheet. Top with the tomato sauce and mozzarella. Cook for fifteen minutes.

Per serving: Cal 592; Fat 25g; Net Carbs 2.7g; Protein 62g

Parmesan and Raspberry Pork

Ingredients for four servings
- 2 cups fresh raspberries
- 1lb. pork tenderloin, cut into ½-inch medallions
- ¼ cup water
- ½ cup almond flour
- 1tsp. chicken bouillon granules
- 2 large eggs, lightly beaten
- Salt and pepper, to taste
- ⅔ cup grated parmesan
- 6tbsp. butter, divided
- Sliced fresh raspberries
- 1tsp. minced garlic

Method and total time: approx. 30 minutes

In your food processor, blitz the raspberries with the water and chicken granules. Reserve. Season the meat well. Coat in the flour first, then in the eggs, and then in the cheese. In two tablespoons butter, fry the pork for three minutes per side. Reserve. In the same skillet, melt the rest of the butter and sauté the garlic for a minute. Add the raspberry mixture and cook for another three minutes. Serve over the pork.

Per serving: Cal 488; Fat 23g; Net Carbs 6.1g; Protein 34g

Mushroom Meatballs and Mashed Parsnips

Ingredients for four servings
- 1 cup cremini mushrooms, chopped
- 2 garlic cloves, minced
- 1½lb. ground pork
- 2 small red onions, chopped
- Salt and pepper, to taste
- 1tsp. dried basil
- 1 cup grated parmesan
- 2tbsp. olive oil
- ½ almond milk
- 2 cups tomato sauce
- 1lb. parsnips, chopped
- 6 fresh basil leaves, to garnish
- 1 cup water
- ½ cup coconut cream
- 2tbsp. butter

Method and total time: approx. 60 minutes

Preheat your oven to 350°F, and line a baking tray. Combine the pork, half the garlic, half the onion, the mushrooms, salt, basil, and pepper. Shape into meatballs. Dip each meatball in the milk, then coat in cheese, and bake for twenty minutes.

In the olive oil, sauté the rest of the onion and garlic until aromatic and tender. Stir in the tomato sauce, and cook for twenty minutes. Stir in the meatballs, and simmer for seven minutes. Cook the parsnips in one cup salted water, for ten minutes or until softened. Drain, then add the butter, salt, and pepper. Mash well, then add the coconut cream and the rest of the parmesan until combined. Serve with the meatballs and sauce, and garnished with basil.

Per serving: Cal 642; Fat 32g; Net Carbs 21.1g; Protein 50g

Coconut and Paprika Pork

Ingredients for four servings
- 1lb. pork tenderloin, cubed
- Salt and pepper, to taste
- 4tsp. smoked paprika
- 1tsp. almond flour
- ¾ cup coconut cream
- 1tbsp. butter

Method and total time: approx. 30 minutes

Season the pork with salt and pepper and paprika, then sprinkle with almond flour. In the butter, sauté for five minutes. Stir in the cream and bring to a boil. Cook until thickened.

Per serving: Cal 310; Fat 21g; Net Carbs 2.5g; Protein 26g

Cheesy Pork and Mushroom Casserole

Ingredients for four servings

- 1 cup ricotta, crumbled
- 4 carrots, thinly sliced
- 1 cup Italian cheese blend
- Salt and pepper, to taste
- 1¼lbs. ground pork
- 1 clove garlic, minced
- 1 cup portobello mushrooms, chopped
- 4 green onions, chopped
- 4tbsp. pork rinds, crushed
- 15oz. canned tomatoes
- ¼ cup chopped parsley
- ⅓ cup water
- 3tbsp. olive oil

Method and total time: approx. 38 minutes

Preheat your oven to 370°F. Combine the ricotta cheese, parsley, and Italian cheese blend. In the olive oil, fry the pork for three minutes. Stir in the garlic, mushrooms, half the green onions, and two tablespoons pork rinds. Cook for another three minutes. Add the tomatoes and water, and cook for another three minutes. In a baking dish, spread two tablespoons pork rinds, followed by half the carrots. Season, then add two-thirds of the pork mix, then topped with the cheese mix. Repeat until you're out of ingredients. Cover with foil and bake for twenty minutes. To brown the top, broil for two minutes.

Per serving: Cal 672; Fat 56g; Net Carbs 7.9g; Protein 34.8g

Lemon and Mushroom Pork Steaks

Ingredients for four servings

- 8oz. white button mushrooms, chopped
- 2tsp. lemon pepper seasoning
- 4 large, bone-in pork steaks
- 3tbsp. olive oil
- 1 cup beef stock
- 3tbsp. butter
- 6 garlic cloves, minced
- 1 lemon, thinly sliced
- 2tbsp. chopped parsley

Method and total time: approx. 30 minutes

Season the pork, then fry in two tablespoons each of the oil and butter. Cook for ten minutes, then reserve. In the rest of the butter and oil, deglaze the pan with half the stock, then stir in the garlic and mushrooms. Cook until softened. Return the pork to the pan, add lemon slices, and cook until the liquid reduces by two-thirds. Garnish with parsley to serve.

Per serving: Cal 505; Fat 32g; Net Carbs 3.2g; Protein 46g

Red Wine Pork Shanks

Ingredients for four servings

- 3lb. pork shanks
- 3tbsp. olive oil
- 3 celery stalks, chopped
- 1½ cups crushed tomatoes
- 5 garlic cloves, minced
- ½ cup red wine
- ¼ cup chopped parsley
- ¼tsp. red chili flakes

Method and total time: approx. 2 hours 30 minutes

Preheat your oven to 300°F. In a Dutch oven, brown the pork in the oil for around four minutes, then reserve. Cook the celery and garlic for three minutes, then put the pork back in the oven and add the red wine, tomatoes, and chili flakes. Cover, and put in the oven for two hours, turning regularly. For the last fifteen minutes, remove the lid and increase the temperature to 450°F. Stir in the parsley to serve.

Per serving: Cal 520; Fat 20g; Net Carbs 1.4g; Protein 75g

Tuscan Pork and Cauliflower Rice

Ingredients for four servings

- 1 cup loosely packed fresh baby spinach
- 1½lb. pork tenderloin, cubed
- 2tbsp. olive oil
- Salt and pepper, to taste
- 2 cups cauliflower rice
- ½tsp. cumin powder
- ½ cup water
- ¾ cup crumbled feta cheese
- 1 cup grape tomatoes, halved

Method and total time: approx. 30 minutes

Season the pork in salt, pepper, and cumin, then cook for five minutes in the olive oil. Add the cauliflower rice and the in water. Cook for five minutes, or until the cauliflower softens. Stir in the spinach and cook until wilted. Add the tomatoes. Serve with feta cheese and hot sauce.

Per serving: Cal 377; Fat 17g; Net Carbs 1.9g; Protein 43g

Indian Pork Masala

Ingredients for four servings

- 2tbsp. ghee
- 1½lb. pork shoulder, cut into bite-size pieces
- 1tbsp. freshly grated ginger
- 6 medium red onions, sliced
- 2tbsp. freshly pureed garlic
- 1 cup crushed tomatoes
- ½tsp. chili powder
- 2tbsp. Greek yogurt
- 2tbsp. garam masala
- 2 green chilies, sliced
- 1 bunch cilantro, chopped

Method and total time: approx. 30 minutes

Blanch the meat in boiling water for three minutes, then drain and reserve. In the ghee, sauté the garlic, ginger, and onions for five minutes. Stir in the yogurt, tomatoes, and pork. Add the chili, salt, garam masala, and pepper. Cook for another ten minutes, then add the cilantro and green chilies.

Per serving: Cal 302; Fat 16g; Net Carbs 2.2g; Protein 33g

Sausages in a Cheese and Onion Sauce

Ingredients for four servings

- 16oz. pork sausages
- 1 egg, beaten
- 6tbsp. golden flaxseed meal
- 1tbsp. olive oil
- 2tsp. almond flour
- 3tbsp. freshly chopped chives
- 8oz. cream cheese, softened
- 3tsp. freshly pureed onion
- 2tbsp. almond milk
- 3tbsp. chicken broth

Method and total time: approx. 30 minutes

Season the flour with salt and pepper. Prick your sausages all over, then roll in the flour, followed by the egg, and then in the flaxseed meal. Fry in the olive oil for fifteen minutes. Reserve. Combine the cream cheese, onion, chives, broth, and milk in a saucepan, and cook until smooth, or around five minutes. Serve with the sausages.

Per serving: Cal 461; Fat 32g; Net Carbs 0.5g; Protein 34g

Hot Jalapeño Pork Meatballs

Ingredients for four servings

- 3 green onions, chopped
- 1tbsp. garlic powder
- 1 jalapeño pepper, chopped
- 1lb. ground pork
- 1tsp. dried oregano
- ½tsp. Italian seasoning
- 2tsp. parsley
- 2tsp. cumin
- 3tbsp. butter melted + 2 tbsp
- Salt and pepper, to taste
- 4oz. cream cheese
- ¼tsp. xylitol
- 1tsp. turmeric
- ½tsp. baking powder
- ½ cup almond flour
- 1½ cups flax meal

Method and total time: approx. 45 minutes

Preheat your oven to 350°F. In a blender, combine the green onions, jalapeño pepper, garlic powder, and a half-cup water. In two tablespoons butter, fry the ground pork for three minutes. Add the onion mixture, and cook for two minutes. Mix in the parsley, salt, cloves, cumin, a half-teaspoon turmeric, Italian seasoning, oregano, and pepper, and cook for three minutes. In a bowl, combine the rest of the turmeric with the almond flour, flax meal, xylitol, and baking powder. In yet another bowl, mix three tablespoons melted butter with the cream cheese. Combine the two mixtures to form a dough. Shape into balls, then press onto a sheet of parchment paper. On half of each circle, place the pork mixture. Cover with the unfilled half and seal with your fingers. Bake for 25 minutes.

Per serving: Cal 598; Fat 45.8g; Net Carbs 5.3g; Protein 35g

Greek-Style Pork

Ingredients for four servings

- ½ cup salsa verde
- 1lb. turnips, cubed
- 2tsp. chili powder
- 4 boneless pork chops
- 1tsp. cumin powder
- Salt and pepper, to taste
- 4 slices halloumi cheese, cubed
- 3tbsp. olive oil

Method and total time: approx. 30 minutes

Preheat the grill to 400°F. Cut out four 18x12-inch sheets of aluminum foil, and grease. Mix together the turnips, chili, salsa verde, and cumin, then season well. On each foil sheet, add a pork chop, then spoon on the turnip mixture and drizzle with olive oil. Add the halloumi cheese. Wrap in the foil, and grill for ten minutes. Turn, and cook for another eight minutes.

Per serving: Cal 501; Fat 27g; Net Carbs 2.1g; Protein 52g

Bacon-Wrapped Cheesy Pork

Ingredients for four servings
- 4 bacon strips
- 4 pork loin chops, boneless
- 2tbsp. fresh parsley, chopped
- ⅓ cup cottage cheese
- 1 onion, chopped
- 1tbsp. olive oil
- 1tbsp. garlic powder
- ⅓ cup chicken stock
- 2 tomatoes, chopped
- Salt and pepper, to taste

Method and total time: approx. 40 minutes

Spread the cottage cheese and parsley on the pork chops, then wrap in the bacon and secure with a toothpick. Heat the oil, then fry the pork parcels until browned. Reserve. Stir in the onion, and cook for another five minutes. Add the chicken stock and garlic powder, and cook for three minutes. Remove the toothpicks, then return the meat to the pan. Mix in the pepper, parsley, salt, and tomatoes, bring to a boil, and simmer for 25 minutes.

Per serving: Cal 433; Fat 23g; Net Carbs 6.8g; Protein 44.6g

Spicy Satay Pork

Ingredients for four servings
- Salt and pepper, to taste
- 2lbs. boneless pork loin chops, cut into 2-inch pieces
- 1 medium white onion, sliced
- ¼ cup tamari sauce
- ⅓ cup peanut butter
- ½tsp. garlic powder
- ½tsp. hot sauce
- ½tsp. onion powder
- 1 cup chicken broth, divided
- 1tbsp. chopped peanuts
- 3tbsp. xanthan gum

Method and total time: approx. 80 minutes

Season the pork, then put into a pot and add the onion. Mix together the peanut butter, garlic and onion powders, tamari sauce, hot sauce, and two-thirds of the chicken broth, then pour this over the meat. Bring to a boil, then simmer for an hour. Mix together the rest of the broth and xanthan gum, then add this to the meat and simmer until thickened. Garnish with peanuts.

Per serving: Cal 455; Fat 17g; Net Carbs 6.7g; Protein 61g

Pork and Turnip Pie

Ingredients for eight servings
- 1 cup turnip mash
- ½ cup water
- 2lbs. ground pork

Crust:
- 2oz. butter
- 2oz. cheddar, shredded
- 1 egg
- 1 onion, chopped
- 2tbsp. butter
- 1tbsp. sage

- 2 cups almond flour
- A pinch of salt
- ¼tsp. xanthan gum

Method and total time: approx. 50 minutes

Preheat your oven to 350°F, and grease a pie pan. Combine the crust ingredients, and divide the dough in two. Refrigerate for ten minutes. Sauté the onion in two tablespoons butter, then add the ground pork and cook for eight minutes. Let to cool, then stir in the turnip mash and sage. Roll out the pie crusts, and lay one over the bottom of your pan. Add the filling, then top with the other crust. Brush with beaten egg, and cut a small slice in the top. Bake for thirty minutes.

Per serving: Cal 477; Fat 36.1g; Net Carbs 1.7g; Protein 33g

Hoisin Pork

Ingredients for four servings
- 4oz. hoisin sauce
- Salt and pepper, to taste
- 1¼lbs. pork chops
- 1tbsp. xylitol
- 2tsp. smoked paprika
- ½tsp. ginger powder

Method and total time: approx. 2 hours 20 minutes

Combine the xylitol, pepper, ginger, and paprika, then rub this all over the pork chops. Cover and put in the fridge for two hours. Grill the meat for two minutes per side, then reduce the heat and brush with the hoisin sauce. Cover, and grill for another five minutes. Turn the meat, brush again, and cook for a final five minutes.

Per serving: Cal 352; Fat 22.9g; Net Carbs 2.5g; Protein 37g

Meatballs in Tomato Sauce

Ingredients for six servings
- 2 green onions, chopped
- 1lb. ground pork
- 1tbsp. olive oil
- 3 cloves garlic, minced
- 1 cup pork rinds, crushed
- ½ cup buttermilk
- 1 cup asiago cheese, shredded
- 2 eggs, beaten
- Salt and pepper, to taste
- 1 cup pecorino cheese, grated
- 29oz. tomato sauce
- Chopped basil, to garnish

Method and total time: approx. 45 minutes
Preheat your oven to 370°F. Combine the buttermilk, garlic, ground pork, asiago cheese, salt, eggs, pepper, and pork rinds. Shape into meatballs, and place into a greased baking pan. Bake for twenty minutes. Pour over the tomato sauce, and sprinkle with pecorino cheese. Cover with foil, and bake for another ten minutes. Remove the foil, and cook for five more minutes. Top with basil.

Per serving: Cal 623; Fat 51.8g; Net Carbs 4.6g; Protein 53g

Pork and Cauliflower Pie

Ingredients for eight servings
- 1 cup cooked and mashed cauliflower
- ¼ cup butter
- 1 egg
- ¼tsp. xanthan gum
- 2 cups almond flour
- ¼ cup shredded mozzarella
- ⅓ cup pureed onion
- 2lbs. ground pork
- ¾tsp. allspice
- 2tbsp. butter
- 1tbsp. ground sage

Method and total time: approx. 1 hour 40 minutes
Preheat your oven to 350°F, and grease a pie pan. Beat the egg with the butter, mozzarella, almond flour, and salt. Divide into two balls and refrigerate for ten minutes. In the butter, fry the ground pork, onion, salt, and allspice for five to six minutes. Transfer to a bowl and combine the cauliflower and sage. Roll one pie crust into the pie pan, then fill with the mixture and top with the other crust. Brush with egg and make a slit. Bake for fifty minutes.

Per serving: Cal 485; Fat 41g; Net Carbs 4g; Protein 29g

Pork Lo Mein

Ingredients for four servings
- 4 boneless pork chops, cut into ¼-inch strips
- 1 cup shredded mozzarella
- 1 cup green beans, halved
- 1 egg yolk
- 3tbsp. sesame oil
- 1-inch ginger knob, grated
- Salt and pepper, to taste
- 1 yellow bell pepper, sliced
- 1 red bell pepper, sliced
- 1 garlic clove, minced
- 1tsp. toasted sesame seeds
- 4 green onions, chopped
- 3tbsp. coconut aminos
- 1tsp. fresh ginger paste
- 2tsp. maple syrup

Method and total time: approx. 25 min + chilling time
Microwave the mozzarella for two minutes, then leave to cool for a minute. Add the egg yolk and mix until well-combined. Roll out between two sheets of parchment, then cut into thin spaghetti strands. Refrigerate overnight. Cook the pasta in two cups of water for one minute, then drain and reserve. In the sesame oil, fry the seasoned pork for five minutes. Reserve. In the same skillet, cook the bell peppers and green beans for three minutes. Add the ginger, garlic, and green onions, and cook for a further minute. Stir in the pork and pasta, and toss well. In a bowl, combine the rest of the sesame oil, the coconut aminos, maple syrup, and ginger paste. Pour over the pork, cook for a minute, then serve garnished with sesame seeds.

Per serving: Cal 338; Net Carbs 4.6g; Fats 12g; Protein 43g

Sambal Pork Noodles

Ingredients for four servings
- 1tbsp. olive oil
- 4 garlic cloves, minced
- 1lb. ground pork
- 1-inch ginger, grated
- 1tbsp. tomato paste
- 1tsp. liquid stevia
- 2 fresh basil leaves, chopped
- 2tbsp. plain vinegar
- 2 x 8oz. packs Miracle noodles, garlic, and herb
- 2tbsp. sambal oelek
- 2tbsp. coconut aminos
- 1tbsp. unsalted butter
- Salt, to taste

Method and total time: approx. 60 minutes

Strain and rinse the noodles, then boil in two cups water for around three minutes. Strain. Stir fry until dried, for a minute or two. Season well, and reserve. In the olive oil, cook the pork for five minutes. Next, add the garlic, ginger, and stevia for a few minutes, then stir in the tomato paste, vinegar, sambal oelek, one cup water, aminos, and salt. Allow to simmer for thirty minutes. Stir in the shirataki and butter, then serve garnished with basil.

Per serving: Cal 505; Net Carbs 8.2g; Fats 30g; Protein 34g

Pulled Pork Pasta Bake

Ingredients for four servings

- 1lb. pork shoulders, divided into 3 pieces
- 2tbsp. olive oil
- 1 egg yolk
- Salt and pepper, to taste
- 1 cup chicken broth
- 1tsp. dried thyme
- 2tbsp. butter
- 2 garlic cloves, minced
- 2 medium shallots, minced
- 1 cup shredded mozzarella cheese1
- 1 cup grated Monterey Jack
- 1 cup heavy cream
- 4oz. cream cheese, softened
- ½tsp. white pepper
- 2tbsp. chopped parsley
- ½tsp. nutmeg powder

Method and total time: approx. 100 min + chilling time

Microwave the mozzarella for two minutes, then leave to cool for one minute. Stir in the egg yolk until well-combined. Roll out between two sheets of parchment paper, then cut into macaroni-sized cubes. Refrigerate overnight. Boil in 2 cups water for one minute, then drain and reserve. Season the pork with salt, pepper, and thyme, then sear in the olive oil until browned. Add the broth, cover, and cook for an hour. Remove the meat and shred. Reserve. Preheat your oven to 380°F. In a skillet, sauté shallots and garlic in the butter for three minutes. Add a cup of water to deglaze the pan, then stir in half the Monterey Jack and cream cheese. Cook for four minutes. Stir in the heavy cream and season with salt, pepper, and nutmeg powder. Add the pasta and the shredded pork, then pour into a baking dish. Top with the rest of the Monterey Jack cheese. Bake for twenty minutes, then garnish with parsley.

Per serving: Cal 603; Net Carbs 4.5g; Fats 43g; Protein 46g

Lime Chimichurri Tenderloin

Ingredients for four servings

- ¼ cup chopped mint leaves
- 1 lime, juiced
- ¼ cup rosemary, chopped
- ¼ cup olive oil
- 2 cloves garlic, minced
- 4lb. pork tenderloin
- Olive oil, for rubbing
- Salt and pepper, to taste

Method and total time: approx. 1 hour 10 minutes

Combine the mint, garlic, olive oil, rosemary, lime juice, and salt, then reserve. Preheat the charcoal grill to 450°F, creating a direct heat area and indirect heat area. Rub the pork all over with the olive oil, and season with salt and pepper. Cook under direct heat for three minutes per side, then move to the indirect heat area. Close the lid, and cook for 25 minutes. Flip the meat, then leave for another twenty minutes. Leave to rest for five minutes, then serve with the lime chimichurri.

Per serving: Cal 388, Fat 18g, Net Carbs 2.1g, Protein 28g

Green Bean Pork Fettuccine

Ingredients for four servings

- 1 cup shredded mozzarella
- 4 pork loin medallions, cut into thin strips
- 1 cup shaved parmesan cheese
- 1tbsp. olive oil
- 1 egg yolk
- Salt and pepper, to taste
- 1 lemon, zested and juiced
- ½ cup green beans, chopped
- ¼ cup chicken broth
- 6 basil leaves, chopped
- 1 cup crème fraiche

Method and total time: approx. 40 min + chilling time

Microwave the mozzarella for two minutes, then leave to cool for a minute. Stir in the egg yolk until well-combined. Roll out between two sheets of parchment, then slice into thick fettuccine strands. Refrigerate overnight. Boil in two cups water for one minute, then drain and reserve. Season the pork well, then fry in the oil for ten minutes. Add the green beans and cook for another five minutes. Add the lemon zest, lemon juice, and chicken broth. Cook for another five minutes. Stir in the crème fraiche, fettuccine, and basil, and cook for another minute. Serve with parmesan cheese.

Per serving: Cal 586; Net Carbs 9g; Fats 32.3g; Protein 59g

Pork and Cauliflower Goulash

Ingredients for four servings
- 2tbsp. butter
- 1½lbs. ground pork
- 1 cup mushrooms, sliced
- Salt and pepper, to taste
- 1 onion, chopped
- 2 cups cauliflower florets

- 14oz. canned tomatoes
- 1tbsp. smoked paprika
- 1 garlic clove, minced
- 2tbsp. parsley, chopped
- 1½ cups water
- 1tbsp. tomato puree

Method and total time: approx. 30 minutes
Fry the pork in the butter for five minutes. Add the garlic, mushrooms, and onion, and cook for four minutes. Stir in the paprika, tomatoes, water, tomato paste, and cauliflower, then simmer for twenty minutes. Season, and garnish with parsley.

Per serving: Cal 533; Fat 41.8g; Net Carbs 7g; Protein 35.5g

Prosciutto and Basil Pizza

Ingredients for four servings
- 2 cups grated mozzarella cheese
- 4 prosciutto slices, cut into thirds
- 2tbsp. cream cheese, softened
- 1 egg, beaten

- ½ cup almond flour
- ⅓ cup tomato sauce
- 6 fresh basil leaves, to serve
- ⅓ cup sliced mozzarella

Method and total time: approx. 45 minutes
Preheat your oven to 390°F, and line a pizza pan. Microwave the mozzarella and two tablespoons cream cheese for one minute. Stir in the almond meal and egg.
Spread on the pizza pan, and bake for fifteen minutes. Once cooked, spread the tomato sauce on the crust, then add the mozzarella slices and the prosciutto. Bake for another fifteen minutes. Garnish with the basil.

Per serving: Cal 160; Fats 6.2g; Net Carbs 0.5g; Protein 22g

Bell Pepper Noodles and Avocado Pork

Ingredients for four servings
- 2tbsp. butter
- Salt and pepper, to taste
- 1lb. ground pork
- 1tsp. garlic powder

- 2lb. red and yellow bell peppers, spiralized
- 2tbsp. chopped pecans
- 2 avocados, pitted, mashed

Method and total time: approx. 15 minutes
Brown the pork in the butter for five minutes, then season well. Add the garlic powder and bell peppers, and cook until the peppers are tender. Add the mashed avocados, and cook for one minute. Garnish with the pecans.

Per serving: Cal 704; Net Carbs 9.3g; Fats 49g; Protein 35g

Caribbean Jerk

Ingredients for four servings
- 1tbsp. olive oil
- 1½lbs. pork roast
- ¼ cup jerk seasoning

- ½ cup vegetable stock
- 2tbsp. soy sauce, sugar-free

Method and total time: approx. 4 hours 20 minutes
Preheat your oven to 350°F. Rub the pork all over with oil and jerk seasoning. Sear on all sides in the olive oil, for around four to five minutes. Put the pork in a baking dish, the stir in the vegetable stock and soy sauce. Cover with aluminum foil and bake for 45 minutes, turning occasionally. Remove the foil, then continue cooking until done.

Per serving: Cal 407; Fat 20g; Net Carbs 5.6g; Protein 46g

Pork and Pesto Pasta

Ingredients for four servings
- 4 boneless pork chops
- ½ cup basil pesto
- Salt and pepper, to taste

- 1 cup grated parmesan cheese
- 4 large turnips, spiralized
- 1tbsp. butter

Method and total time: approx. 1 hour 30 minutes
Preheat your oven to 350°F. Season your pork well, and put on a greased baking sheet. Spread with the pesto, then bake for 45 minutes. Top with half the parmesan, then cook for another five minutes. Reserve. In a skillet, melt the butter and sauté the turnips for seven minutes. Stir in the last of the parmesan, and serve topped with the pork.

Per serving: Cal 532; Net Carbs 4.9g; Fats 28g; Protein 54g

Barbecue Pork

Ingredients for four servings
- 4 pork loin chops, boneless
- 1tbsp. erythritol
- ½ cup BBQ sauce
- ½tsp. ginger powder
- 2tsp. smoked paprika
- ½tsp. garlic powder

Method and total time: approx. 1 hour 50 minutes
Combine the pepper, ginger powder, erythritol, a half-teaspoon garlic powder, and smoked paprika. Rub this all over the pork, then leave in the fridge to marinate for one to two hours. Preheat your grill. Grill the pork for two minutes per side, then reduce the heat and brush all over with barbecue sauce. Grill for another five minutes, flip, brush some more, and cook for a final five minutes.
Per serving: Cal 363, Fat 26.6g, Net Carbs 0g, Protein 34.1g

Spiralized Kohlrabi and Sausage

Ingredients for four servings
- 1 cup grated Pecorino Romano cheese
- 1 cup sliced pork sausage
- 2tbsp. olive oil
- 4 bacon slices, chopped
- 6 garlic cloves, minced
- 4 large kohlrabi, spiralized
- 1 cup cherry tomatoes, halved
- 1tbsp. pine nuts for topping
- 7 fresh basil leaves

Method and total time: approx. 15 minutes
Brown the sausage and bacon in the olive oil for five minutes, then reserve. Stir in the kohlrabi and garlic, then cook until tender, around six minutes. Mix in the cherry tomatoes, salt, and pepper, and cook for another two minutes. Return the sausage and bacon to the pan, then add the basil, and Pecorino Romano cheese. Garnish with pine nuts.
Per serving: Cal 229; Net Carbs 2.4g; Fats 20.2g; Protein 8g

Chorizo Pizza

Ingredients for four servings
- 1 cup sliced smoked mozzarella
- ¾ cup almond flour
- 2tbsp. cream cheese, softened
- 2tbsp. almond meal
- 2 cups shredded mozzarella
- 1 cups sliced chorizo
- 1tbsp. olive oil
- ¼ cup marinara sauce
- ¼ red onion, thinly sliced
- 1 jalapeño pepper, sliced

Method and total time: approx. 45 minutes
Preheat your oven to 390°F, and line a pizza pan. Microwave the mozzarella and cream cheeses for thirty seconds. Stir in the almond flour and almond meal, then spread over the pan. Bake for ten minutes. Fry the chorizo in the olive oil for five minutes. Spread the marinara sauce on the crust, then top with smoked mozzarella, jalapeño pepper, chorizo, and onion. Bake for fifteen minutes.
Per serving: Cal 302; Fats 17g; Net Carbs 1.4g; Protein 31g

Chessy Sausage Pizza with Bell Peppers

Ingredients for four servings
- ½ cup grated Monterey Jack cheese
- 1½lb. Italian pork sausages, crumbled
- 1 cup chopped bell peppers
- ¼ cup grated Parmesan
- 4 cups grated mozzarella
- 2tbsp. cream cheese, softened
- 1 cup almond flour
- ¼ cup coconut flour
- 2 eggs
- 1 onion, thinly sliced
- 1tbsp. olive oil
- 2 garlic cloves, minced
- ½ cup pizza sauce
- 1 cup baby spinach

Method and total time: approx. 45 minutes
Preheat your oven to 390°F, and line a pizza pan. Microwave two cups of mozzarella with two tablespoons cream cheese for one minute. Combine with the sausages, almond flour, coconut flour, parmesan cheese, and eggs. Spread on the pizza pan and bake for fifteen minutes.
In the oil, sauté the onion, garlic, and bell peppers for five minutes. Add the spinach and cook to wilting. Spread the sauce on the crust, then top with the bell pepper mixture. Add the rest of the cheeses, and bake for five minutes.
Per serving: Cal 460; Fats 25.6g; Net Carbs 3g; Protein 47g

Sweet Pork and Spaghetti Squash

Ingredients for four servings
- 2tbsp. minced lemongrass
- 2tbsp. maple syrup
- 3tbsp. fresh ginger paste
- 2tbsp. coconut aminos
- 4 boneless pork chops
- 1tbsp. fish sauce
- 3lb. spaghetti squashes, halved and deseeded
- 3tbsp. peanut oil
- Salt and pepper, to taste
- 1tbsp. olive oil
- 1lb. baby spinach
- ¼ cup peanut butter
- ½ cup coconut milk

Method and total time: approx. 1 hour + marinating
Combine the lemongrass with two tablespoons ginger paste, aminos, maple syrup, and fish sauce. Submerge the pork in this, and leave to marinate for 45 minutes.
Sear the pork in two tablespoons peanut oil for ten to fifteen minutes. Reserve. Preheat your oven to 380°F. Place the spaghetti squashes on a baking sheet, drizzle with olive oil, and season well. Bake for 45 minutes, then shred with two forks. Reserve. In the rest of the peanut oil, sauté the last of the ginger paste. Add the spinach and cook for two minutes. Reserve. Beat the coconut milk with the peanut butter until well combined. Serve the pork with the squash, spinach, and peanut sauce.

Per serving: Cal 694; Net Carbs 7.6g; Fats 34g; Protein 53g

Spicy Spareribs

Ingredients for four servings
- 4tbsp. BBQ sauce + extra for serving
- 1tbsp. olive oil
- 2tbsp. erythritol
- 3tsp. cayenne powder
- 1lb. pork spareribs
- 1tsp. garlic powder

Method and total time: approx. 2 hours
Combine the erythritol, cayenne, pepper, salt, oil, and garlic. Brush this on the meaty sides of the ribs, then wrap in foil. Leave to marinate for a half-hour. Preheat our oven to 400°F. Bake your ribs on a baking sheet for forty minutes. Remove the foil, brush all over with barbecue said, and broil for ten minutes.

Per serving: Cal 395, Fat 33g, Net Carbs 3g, Protein 21g

Asian Pork and Celeriac Noodles

Ingredients for four servings
- 3tbsp. maple syrup
- 1tbsp. fresh ginger paste
- 3tbsp. coconut aminos
- ¼tsp. Chinese five spice
- 1lb. pork tenderloin, cubed
- Salt and pepper, to taste
- 2tbsp. butter
- 1tbsp. sesame oil
- 4 large celeriac, spiralized
- 24oz. bok choy, chopped
- 2tbsp. sesame seeds
- 2 green onions, chopped

Method and total time: approx. 1 hour 20 minutes
Preheat your oven to 400°F, and line a baking sheet with foil. Combine the maple syrup, ginger paste, coconut aminos, Chinese five-spice powder, salt, and pepper. Put three tablespoons of the mixture into a bowl and reserve. In the larger portion, coat the pork and leave to marinate for 25 minutes. In the butter, sauté the celeriac for seven minutes. Reserve. Remove the pork, then bake for forty minutes. In the sesame oil, sauté the bok choy and celeriac pasta for three minutes. To serve, top the bok choy and pasta with the pork, then garnish with green onions and sesame seeds. Drizzle with the reserved marinade.

Per serving: Cal 409; Net Carbs 3g; Fats 17.8g; Protein 44g

CPSIA information can be obtained
at www.ICGtesting.com
Printed in the USA
LVHW062038180720
661023LV00027B/387